*With the British Army
in Philadelphia*

GENERAL HOWE.

Sir William Howe, Commander in Chief of the British Army in Philadelphia. *Kean Archives, Philadelphia*

With the British Army in Philadelphia 1777–1778

John W. Jackson

PRESIDIO PRESS
San Rafael, California & London, England

Copyright © 1979 by Presidio Press

Published by Presidio Press of San Rafael, California,
and London, England, with editorial offices at
1114 Irwin Street, San Rafael, California

Library of Congress Cataloging in Publication Data

Jackson, John W.
  With the British Army in Philadelphia, 1777-1778.

  Bibliography: p.
  Includes index.
  1. Philadelphia Campaign, 1777-1778. 2. German-
town, Battle of, 1777. I. Title.
E233.J3   973.3'3   78-10657
ISBN 0-89141-057-0

Book design by Hal Lockwood

Jacket art by Karl O. Lichtenstein

Printed in the United States of America

To
Our Parents
and
Betsy

Contents

Preface

The occupation of Philadelphia by the British army in 1777-1778 represents the denouement of Sir William Howe's tenure as commander in chief of the royal forces in America. At first Howe was enthusiastically welcomed by Loyalist and neutral citizens. However, his personal behavior and the military regulations he was forced to impose on the garrison city soon appalled many residents.

Howe's activities that winter made him the most controversial British general of the war and, in historical perspective, a somewhat misunderstood figure. He was the target of malevolent attacks by Joseph Galloway and other Loyalists, and by a number of contemporary figures in the British government as well. Such cavil, and Howe's equally bitter rebuttals make it difficult to sift fact from fiction. The acrimonious pamphlet war that ensued merely reflected the vehemence on each side. The charges against Howe ranged from flagrant misconduct as commander in chief to over-fondness for the "rebels," and over-indulgence in a convivial table as well as in the arms of his paramour, Mrs. Elizabeth Loring. On the other hand, Americans have accused him of condoning the inhuman treatment of prisoners of war. As will be seen from his correspondence, orders, and proclamations, much of this criticism is unjust and bears the stamp of spite.

Unquestionably, Howe was not a great strategist. In fact, his failure to support Burgoyne's Canadian expedition may be considered the most disastrous decision of the war. Nevertheless, for some of his detractors to raise this point is specious as they were among the first to encourage Howe to march on the American capital. He was a capable field commander and tactician as his several victories in 1776 and 1777 attest. Unfortunately, his failure to follow up these victories and crush Washington's army raised the cry of indolence and lack of decision. Howe asserted, as did other British officers, that to engage the Americans on terrain that could entail heavy losses would be catastrophic for the British army. Even if victorious, heavy British casualties would gradually herald a decline in the army's effectiveness. The British losses could not easily be replaced, whereas the Americans could recruit from surrounding states. Terrain in America was rugged and heavily forested and a number of British officers bemoaned their inability to maneuver as they could on the open fields of Europe. Furthermore, every fifty to one hundred yards offered opportunities for an ambuscade. However, Howe's caution and indecision did not inhibit his determination somehow to teach the "rebels" a lesson since no one had a right to defy the British sovereign.

Most of the American charges of mistreatment of prisoners of war occurred in the first two months when quarters and provisions were scarce in the city. Over 2,000 British and Hessian soldiers were sick or wounded and every available public building was occupied as a hospital. In addition, the army was placed on half rations. Howe expected Washington to provide for the American prisoners, although no agreement had been reached to send provisions into Philadelphia. Eventually, through negotiation the plight of prisoners was relieved, albeit problems of supply continued to beset both commanders. All areas of understanding and communications were handicapped by distrust and the everpresent spies and double agents.

The winter of 1777-1778 in Philadelphia was the most gala of the British army in America during the war. There was a constant round of balls and parties; an officers' theatre presented a series of plays; gambling casinos were in operation — all were held concomitant with a steady parade of visitations, cards, and dinner parties. It cannot be denied that Howe's love of these companionable affairs found him in the center of most of the winter's festivities. The season reached a climax with the much criticized extravaganza, the "Meschianza," given in Howe's honor before he departed for England in May 1778.

Returning to England, Howe requested and received a court of inquiry before the House of Commons. Inconclusive, the inquiry resolved nothing and left Howe open to the continued vitriolic attacks of his enemies.

In his defense, it might be said that as a typical eighteenth century officer he loved his good times, but he did not permit his pleasures to interfere with efforts to provide for the comfort of his soldiers and the needs of the city's inhabitants. Acknowledging Howe's limitations as a commanding officer, his greatest weakness seems to have been excessive caution. However, his guilt was probably typical of most eighteenth century Englishmen. Eric Robson, English historian, notes that the self-confidence of most Englishmen resulted in grave miscalculations of the intentions and determination of Americans.

Life in Philadelphia and the actions of Sir William Howe and the British army have heretofore not received definitive treatment. With the able assistance of my colleague in England, Dr. Isabel Kenrick, a diligent search has been made of the archives in Great Britain and the United States for materials on the occupation period. I believe this narrative will clarify many of the misunderstandings and misconceptions of the winter of 1777-1778 in the American capital.

I have avoided the use of the terms ''Tory'' and ''Rebel,'' except in quotations, as they were odious to both antagonists. In their stead I have designated all who remained faithful to the existing government in America before the Declaration of Independence as ''Loyalists'' and their adversaries as ''Americans'' — as the citizens of the emerging United States proudly referred to themselves.

Many individuals have contributed valuable services and materials, both manuscript and printed, to make possible a better understanding of the British army's occupation of Philadelphia during the winter of 1777-1778.

It is always difficult to single out those to whom an author is indebted. First I must acknowledge the invaluable assistance of my colleague and friend Dr. John D. R. Platt of the National Park Service. He read the entire manuscript and, as a specialist on the Revolution, made many vital suggestions which were incorporated in the manuscript.

My friend Dr. William D. Timmins delved into the fact and lore of Salem County, New Jersey, and furnished much indispensable data.

Mrs. Kurt (Edith) Hoelle, librarian of the Gloucester County Historical Society and a friend with a corresponding interest in Revolutionary New Jersey furnished important information on the Loyalist activities in Old Gloucester County and on Fort Mercer.

The records of the Independence Historical National Park archives were graciously opened for my research by Martin Yoelson and Sandra Gutkind.

One of the largest collections of manuscript and printed materials on revolutionary Philadelphia are at the Historical Society of Pennsylvania. I am grateful to Dr. James Mooney for permission to use these collections. To Peter Parker of the manuscript section, and John Platt of the reading room and their staffs — Linda Stanley, Lucy Hrivnak, Anthony Roth, and Richard Baldwin — my deep appreciation for the many weeks of checking and rechecking the voluminous collections at the society.

The often overlooked but indispensable collection of Quaker material at Haverford College was made available through the gracious assistance of Elizabeth Tritle.

Willman Spawn cheerfully opened the records of the Meetings of the Society of Friends for my perusal and use.

Murphy Smith and Carl Miller of the American Philosophical Society graciously assisted in my examination of their manuscript collections. Roy Goodman was equally helpful on my visits to the society's library.

To prepare any work on the American Revolution it is necessary to take a lengthy journey through the Clinton Papers and other British military papers at the Clements Library, University of Michigan. My task was considerably facilitated by the outstanding cooperation of John C. Dann and Arlene Kleeb.

My thanks are extended to another friend and colleague, Dr. Edward M. Riley, director emeritus of the Colonial Williamsburg Research Department for the use of their splendid materials. To his staff, especially Nancy M. Merz, Barbara Dean, and Mrs. Blaine Franklin, I am very grateful.

The staff of the University of Virginia Library was extremely helpful on my visit in arranging for an inter-library loan of the microfilm copies of the Hamond Papers. My sincere thanks to Edmund Berkeley, Jr., Michael Plunkett, Gregory Johnson, and Elizabeth Fake.

To Edwin Wolf and Lillian Tonkin of the Library Company of Philadelphia my sincere thanks for the use of the library's outstanding collection of printed materials.

Many individuals provided valuable data and materials in

specialized areas, all of which have contributed to a better under-
standing of this study. To each one my sincere thanks: In
Philadelphia — Mildred Mathers, Christ Church; Walter L. Smith
and Anne M. Rourke, Philadelphia Contributionship; Frank Bobb,
Boris S. Kudravetz, and William Forrest, Masonic Temple; Neda M.
Westlake, University of Pennsylvania, Charles Patterson Van Pelt Li-
brary; Peter Chile, Athenaeum of Philadelphia; Howard T. Maag,
Mary Spratt, and Julia Riter, Old St. George's Methodist Church;
David J. Wartluft, Krauth Memorial Library, Lutheran Theological
Seminary; Larry Taylor and Ann Winkler, Catholic Historical
Society; Barbara Pinkerton, Third Presbyterian Church (Old Pine),
and to Gerald Gillette, Norotha Robinson, Anne Schulz, Judith
Coxe, and Sheila Hallowell of the Presbyterian Historical Society for
their assistance in researching the voluminous records in their li-
brary.

Others, the mere mention of whose names cannot indicate the
value of their assistance, are: Jean McNiece and John D. Stinson,
New York Public Library, and Thomas J. Dunning, Jr. and Reynold
Yuska, New York Historical Society. The manuscript collections of
these institutions are indispensable to a study of the Revolution as are
those at the Library of Congress. At the latter institution I was graciously helped by Carolyn H. Sung, Marilyn K. Parr, Ruth S.
Nicholson and Charles F. Cooney. At the National Archives Dr.
George C. Chalou offered several valuable suggestions and made
available their valuable microfilm collection. I am also grateful to
Robert Mann, Mardel Pacheo, and Agnes Sherman, Princeton
University Library; Dale Fields and James Lacey, Delaware Historical Society; and Elizabeth Moore, Bucks County Historical Society.

To the staff of the Springfield Township Library I am indebted
for the arranging of inter-library microfilm loans. My thanks to Dr.
David Lawrence, Virginia H. Gable, and Helen C. Kircher.

Although unknown, I wish to extend my gratitude to those who
assisted Dr. Isabel Kenrick in her visits to the many repositories in
England and Scotland.

To those whose names I may have inadvertently omitted, please
accept my apologies and my sincere gratitude for your valued assistance.

Last but not least, credit for the successful completion of the
book is due in large part to the dedication and patience of my wife

Kathryn. In addition to typing the manuscript, her many useful suggestions have immeasurably contributed to the clarity of the narrative.

John W. Jackson

Flourtown, Pennsylvania
August 1977

CHAPTER I

ON TO PHILADELPHIA

DURING THE SPRING of 1775 three British generals sailed into Boston harbor. They were General Sir William Howe, General Sir Henry Clinton, and General John Burgoyne. Their orders were to report to General Thomas Gage, commander of the British army in Boston. George III and his ministers hoped that with the assistance of these generals Gage would soon suppress the "Yankee Rebels."

Having tasted victory on the road from Concord to Boston, the Americans were gathering in large numbers around the latter city. At first the British generals were optimistic that the "rebels" would offer little resistance to British regulars; however, it soon became evident that a military victory was the only way to end the hostilities.

The Americans had fortified Bunker Hill (Breed's Hill), an eminence that dominated part of the port city. Realizing that the Americans must be driven from this position, Howe volunteered to lead an assault against their lines. Underestimating the firepower and courage of the untrained militia, Howe directed a frontal assault. The first attack was thrown back with staggering losses. Although the British regulars eventually overran the American line, it was achieved at a horrible cost. The battlefield was strewn with 226 dead and 828 wounded British soldiers, including 92 irreplaceable veteran officers. The effects of this "victory" and the losses sustained made a lasting impression on Howe. He later wrote that such triumphs were not worth the sacrifice of British blood.

Soon after the battle on Bunker Hill, Gage was recalled to England and was succeeded by Howe. It was at this time that the American Continental Congress made its first step to organize a Continental army. Selecting George Washington as commander in chief, the Congress ordered him to take command of the tatterdemalion force surrounding Boston. While the armies engaged in a few desultory firefights, the next eight months were relatively inactive.

During the late winter of 1776, Washington's soldiers dragged heavy cannon, taken by Colonel Henry Knox from the British at Fort Ticonderoga, to the summit of Dorchester Heights. These hills overlooked Boston, and American artillery on the heights could have destroyed the city. Howe planned to attack the American batteries, but the attempt was thwarted by a severe storm. Frustrated, Howe decided to evacuate the city rather than see it destroyed by American artillery fire.

On 17 March 1776, the British army, accompanied by about one thousand dejected Loyalists, sailed from Boston for Halifax. Awaiting reinforcements, Howe utilized his time in Halifax to devise his strategy for 1776. He planned to attack the port of New York. When preparations were complete, he sailed from Halifax, landing on Staten Island during the last week of June. He decided to assault the American position on Long Island. After an interminable delay, on 26 August he landed the British army and attacked Washington's troops the next day. The result was a complete rout of the Americans. A few days later he occupied New York.

As the year 1776 came to a close, Howe was at the peak of his popularity. He had soundly defeated Washington on Long Island and at White Plains and had seized Forts Washington and Lee on the banks of the Hudson River. The only interruption was a minor defeat at Harlem Heights. Notwithstanding these successes, a few critics surfaced to decry his failure to crush the American army.

Some detractors of Howe and his brother Lord Richard Howe, British naval commander in American waters, claimed they sought a peaceful reconciliation rather than a military conquest because of their overfondness for Americans. Others declared the brothers were too cautious. It was also contended that Sir William was self-indulgent, preferring a convivial table and the arms of his paramour, Elizabeth Loring, to the field of battle. Most of these and other charges, biased or valid, were based on Howe's conduct in Philadelphia during the winter of 1777-78.

On 30 November 1776, Howe wrote to Lord George Germain, the colonial secretary, and outlined his plans for the ensuing spring. Howe's strategy for 1777 did not initially include the occupation of Philadelphia. Instead he intended to dispatch Sir Henry Clinton with a column to overrun Rhode Island and, hopefully, to occupy Boston. In addition, a large detachment would move up the Hudson River to form a junction with the British expedition coming down from Canada. Another force, of 8,000, would invade New Jersey. This column was to divert Washington's attention and prevent his sending Continental troops to reinforce the American army facing the British troops along the Hudson.

If these objectives were met, Howe would then make a diversionary movement to give a "jealousy" to Philadelphia, the rebel capital. A garrison of 5,000 rank and file would remain in New York to ensure its defense against any surprise attack. In this, as in all Howe's plans, substantial reinforcements were needed to ensure success. He anticipated that the king, who had always bitterly resented the role of Massachusetts in starting the rebellion, would approve of this strategy.[1]

Shortly after Howe penned this proposal, a group of Pennsylvania Loyalists arrived in New York. Among the refugees were Joseph Galloway and members of the prominent Allen family who, fearing for their personal safety, had fled from Philadelphia. Once ensconced in quarters provided for them, they began extolling the advantages which the occupation of Philadelphia would bring to the crown. Galloway became the intimate of Ambrose Serle, Lord Howe's secretary, and through this friendship gained audience with the Howe brothers. He prepared several papers for them delineating the physical, economic, and psychological benefits to be gained by controlling Philadelphia. With the Allens, Galloway contended that seventy-five to ninety percent of Pennsylvania's citizens were loyal and, upon the appearance of a British army, would reaffirm their allegiance to the king. They believed an equal number of able-bodied men would form Loyalist regiments and would provide garrisons in Philadelphia and other Delaware Valley towns. This would relieve the regulars for further field service.[2]

Howe's correspondence gave no indication that the importunings of Galloway and his colleagues influenced a sudden change in his plans for 1777. Nevertheless, on 20 December, less than three weeks after submitting his first proposal, Howe again wrote to Germain. This time he disclosed that Philadelphia would be his objective for the following spring. If sufficient reinforcements arrived, he would also make a diversionary movement to open communications with the Canadian expedition along the line of the Hudson.[3]

British commanders in America unquestionably were cognizant of the delay in transmitting plans and receiving instructions from the home government. In the day of sailing ships, the full communications cycle consumed from ten to twelve weeks or longer. Before this time had elapsed, a commander in chief could implement his plan and claim that expediency made the move necessary. In this instance, Howe waited for and received somewhat reluctant approval of his revised plan, with a reminder that the king still hoped he would be able to send a column to chastise the hated Bostonians.[4]

At this time, the correspondence between Howe and Germain was filled with veiled sarcasm and gave evidence of mutual distrust. In fact, the king admitted to Lord North that Germain's uncompromising rudeness to Howe made cooperation between them impossible.[5]

Meanwhile, Washington had been in full retreat across northern New Jersey. His army was dwindling daily through desertion. The enlistments of many of his troops would expire on 31 December. Washington knew that a miracle was necessary to revive the morale of the people and to encourage enlistments and reenlistments in the Continental regiments. Desperate, the American commander conceived his brilliant exploit which completely surprised the Hessian garrison at Trenton on Christmas night. Later, on 3 January 1777, after an almost bloodless confrontation with Lord Cornwallis across Assunpink Creek south of Trenton, he circled the British left flank and defeated another column at Princeton. With his men exhausted and the roads marked by the blood of over 1,000 barefooted Continentals, Washington made his way to the New Jersey hills and established winter quarters at Morristown.

The victory at Trenton had netted over nine hundred Hessian prisoners, who were marched through the streets of Philadelphia. The effect of that march electrified the inhabitants and inspired many Continentals to reenlist.

Although dismayed by these events, Howe was determined to lure Washington out of the hills and force him to give battle on ground of British choosing. Washington responded to the invitation by sending out detachments to probe the British positions and determine their intentions, but under no circumstances to bring on a general engagement. The result was several indecisive skirmishes with casualties suffered by each side.

This particular section of New Jersey included a succession of

rugged defiles and impenetrable forests. Knowing this, Howe feared
that any attempt to march the army overland to Philadelphia would
afford Washington opportunities to set up ambuscades and harass the
strung-out column. He therefore decided that the sea route would be
the best way to move his army.

Except for Howe's personal military family, few British officers
had any knowledge about the change in plans. The correspondence
and diaries of several officers reflected the concern and confusion
they felt over where they were going and how. Washington was
equally perplexed. His sound military judgment told him that Howe
should sail up the Hudson to form a junction with the Canadian invasion force. In this way Howe could sever New England from the
rest of the new nation. Washington therefore found it necessary to
keep his army in a position to cooperate with the American force
north of Albany or to defend Philadelphia should the metropolis be
attacked.

Doubt disappeared in early July when Howe embarked an army
of about twenty thousand rank and file and noncombatant units
aboard the fleet and sailed south along the New Jersey coast. Accompanying the fleet were nearly six hundred camp followers and sixty
Pennsylvania Loyalists returning home in triumph.

In the meantime, Lord Howe had given instructions to Captain
Andrew S. Hamond, of the frigate *Roebuck,* stationed at the Delaware
capes, to reconnoiter the bay and river and select a landing place for
the British army. Hamond was well acquainted with the area, having
been on station in the bay for over a year. The fleet arrived in the
roadstead at the end of July. Hamond was ordered on board Lord
Howe's flagship, *Eagle,* to report to the commander in chief. He
detailed the river defenses, stating that several rows of river obstructions, called chevaux-de-frise, and a small nondescript fleet of boats
and ships, of which the most dangerous was a flotilla of thirteen
galleys, had been placed in the river below the city. Hamond warned
that if the pesky galleys were permitted to get close, they could wreak
havoc on the British ships. As the British men-of-war could not
depress their cannon at close range, the galleys would only suffer
minor damage. Hamond's opinion of the galleys was undoubtedly
influenced by the rough handling given the *Roebuck* in May 1776. He
also mentioned that the Americans had several forts and land fortifications and that Washington was at Wilmington with the Continental army.

Hamond appears to have been the victim of bad intelligence. Washington was actually encamped along the Neshaminy Creek north of Philadelphia. Unknown to the *Roebuck's* captain, the land fortifications were, except for a few laborers, without garrisons — a condition that existed until late in September. He was aware that the galleys rarely moved below the river obstructions. Furthermore, their effectiveness in the bay and lower river was limited, as they could easily be swamped by any rough water or swell. Hamond may not have known that the galleys were operating with only half their complement of men.

Despite his misgivings about the river north of Wilmington, Hamond strongly urged Howe to land his army at Newcastle in Delaware. This would place the British army only thirty miles from Philadelphia. Howe, reacting to the negative part of Hamond's report, did not agree with the recommendation. Instead, over the captain's protest, he ordered the fleet to sail south along the Delaware and Maryland coast. According to Hamond, Lord Howe mildly remonstrated with his brother on this decision. Howe later stated that the Chesapeake offered a better opportunity to destroy American supply depots located in the interior towns of Pennsylvania, and this might be done before proceeding to Philadelphia. It is questionable whether Howe ever intended to carry out this side expedition; at any rate, no column was ever organized to invade frontier Pennsylvania. It is likely that Howe, with his usual caution, may have considered it dangerous to split his force deep in enemy territory.[6]

Washington remained puzzled: Would Howe sail north to cooperate with the Canadian invasion? Again, this appeared to be sound military judgment. A courier soon arrived in camp, dispelling any doubts. The British fleet was sighted off the Maryland shore. Washington, still uncertain of Howe's destination, immediately ordered his army south and established headquarters at Wilmington. In mid-August he was informed that the British fleet was headed up Chesapeake Bay. A short time later he learned that advance elements of British and Hessian troops had landed at Head of Elk on 23 August.

For ten days following the initial landing the British army was busy disembarking the balance of the troops, provisions, ordnance, and other materiel of war. Howe directed Major General Lord Charles Cornwallis and Lieutenant General Wilhelm von Knyphausen to march their respective columns over separate roads through northern Maryland and rendezvous at Aiken's Tavern in

Delaware. Before these columns got under way, Hamond was ordered to escort several victuallers and supply ships down the Chesapeake and up the Atlantic to enter Delaware Bay and establish a base at Newcastle. Howe wanted to provide a refuge for the British army in the event of a disastrous encounter with the Americans. This was a rather strange development, as almost a month earlier Hamond had recommended landing the entire army at Newcastle. Now, with much valuable time already lost, Howe ordered one frigate to establish a supply depot at the Delaware town. Ironically, the British army was now twice the distance from Philadelphia than it would have been in July.[7]

Soon after Cornwallis and Knyphausen began their march from Head of Elk, Howe ordered General James Grant to protect the embarkation of the sick and wounded on the transports riding at anchor in the river. Grant was also to supervise the loading of all provisions, supplies, and ordnance that could not be carried by the troops. After everything was stowed on the ships, Lord Howe was directed to escort the ships down the bay and around to the Delaware to rendezvous with the army. The fleet departed and Grant set his column in motion to join the other troops in Delaware.

Howe may have been overconfident: he assumed that Washington would only offer token resistance to his occupation of the rebel capital. He may have also expected that the populace would rally to the king's standard once the royal army appeared, an idea fostered by Galloway and other Loyalists. Regardless, Howe had now severed all connections with his naval and logistical support.

Soon after arriving in Delaware, the Hessian jägers and British light troops engaged in a lively skirmish with Brigadier General William Maxwell and the American light infantry at Cooch's Bridge. Maxwell's men were forced to relinquish the field and withdraw to the main Continental lines.

In the meantime, Washington was in Wilmington and was concerned about the position of his army. He feared that Howe, by a series of rapid marches, would turn his right flank and thereby pin the Americans against the river. In that event, Washington did not have enough boats available to transport his army across the river to New Jersey. A withdrawal down the peninsula (modern Delmarva) would be equally disastrous and would merely postpone the destruction of the Continental army.

Fortunately for Washington, the unpredictable Howe had decided to march north to the main roads entering the city from the interior of Pennsylvania. Two such roads existed: the Nottingham Road (present Baltimore Pike) and the Lancaster Road, which was somewhat further north. Howe had decided that he would be able to reach Nottingham Road before Washington could challenge his entry into Philadelphia. He ignored the fact that Washington, operating on interior lines, would be able to take position astride his line of march.

Unknown to Howe, Washington was determined to contest any further advance by the British. Congress and the people of Philadelphia had demanded that Washington not surrender the city without a fight. While Howe advanced to Kennett Square on the Nottingham Road, Washington had reached Brandywine Creek near John Chad's house and established a defensive position.

At daybreak on 11 September 1777, Howe set two columns in motion to drive the Americans out of their position on the Brandywine. Knyphausen was directed to march east along the Nottingham Road and amuse Washington, while a second and larger British column under Cornwallis would take a circuitous route and come up in the American rear.

Maxwell's light infantry contested every foot of the ground between Kennett Square and the creek at Chad's. This slowed the Hessian general's progress, and Knyphausen thus did not reach the west bank of the Brandywine until mid-morning. His orders were to occupy the heights overlooking the Brandywine valley from the west, but not to bring on a general engagement unless attacked. When musket and cannon fire were heard in the American rear, it would herald the attack by Cornwallis's column. Knyphausen was then to cross the Brandywine and assault the enemy's front. Knyphausen and Washington spent the morning and early afternoon in a desultory exchange of cannon fire, punctuated by an occasional sortie across the creek by American light troops.

Some time before two o'clock, Washington conceived a rather reckless plan. Based on his mistaken belief that he outnumbered Knyphausen's force, Washington intended to assault and destroy the Hessian forces before Cornwallis's column could come up to join in the battle. Confusing rumors and bad intelligence had placed Cornwallis crossing the Brandywine far upstream and unable to reach the Continentals' rear for several hours. It was fortunate for Washington that before he could execute this maneuver he was informed that Cornwallis, accompanied by Howe, was moving down Birmingham Road and threatening the American right. This intelligence forced Washington to revise his plan. He immediately ordered Major

General John Sullivan, Major General William Alexander "Earl" Stirling, and Major General Adam Stephen, with their divisions, to form a defensive position near the Birmingham meetinghouse.

A hot engagement ensued, and after throwing back several savage attacks, Sullivan was forced to withdraw. The remnants of his command streamed down Birmingham Road toward Dilworthtown. His men were physically exhausted and most of their ammunition had been expended. Washington, advised that the conflict was going against Sullivan, immediately ordered Major General Nathanael Greene to leave his position on the Brandywine and rush to Sullivan's assistance. Always impetuous and eager to be in the center of action, Washington decided to accompany the relief column. Marching at double-quick, he and Greene reached Birmingham Road in time to set up a defensive line that permitted Sullivan's men to pass through to safety. Greene then closed ranks and hotly contested any further advance by Cornwallis. Late in the afternoon both armies were exhausted and the battle was broken off. Greene retired toward Concordville and Chester, where Washington planned to regroup his army. Cornwallis's troops, having marched about seventeen miles since daybreak and having fought a bitterly contested battle, were in no condition to pursue the Americans.

At this time, Brigadier General Anthony Wayne, back at the Brandywine with a token force, tried to contain Knyphausen until the main part of the American army could safely leave the Birmingham Road battlefield area. Knyphausen, who had heard heavy firing in the American rear, ordered his men to cannonade Wayne's position. After a heavy exchange which lasted about half an hour, the Hessian general directed an attack across the creek. A brief engagement resulted, and outnumbered and outgunned Wayne was forced to pull back. Wayne's troops contested the British and Hessian advance at every fence and rise of ground. Suddenly a large British detachment emerged from the woods on his right. These troops had strayed from action near the Birmingham meetinghouse and became lost in the woods. Their unexpected appearance threw Wayne's men into total confusion. Panic-stricken, they fled down Nottingham Road towards the rest of the American army.

For the next several days both armies spent time caring for the wounded and re-forming their regiments. Washington realized that at best he could check, but not prevent, Howe's occupation of Philadelphia. In the eighteenth century, the river usually froze over in November and, even in periods of thaw, was dangerous for wooden ships. Even with the provisions and supplies Howe had on board the victuallers and supply ships, he would be hard pressed to provide for a population of sixty thousand soldiers and civilians. The American army was forming a cordon around the city, and the countryside could not be depended on for any significant amount of provisions. Washington hoped the distress of the British army would force Howe to evacuate the city in the dead of winter and fight his way across New Jersey toward New York.

In the two weeks which followed the battle at the Brandywine, Howe and Washington carried on a cat-and-mouse game of engagements and minor skirmishes. Finally, on 25 September, Howe entered Germantown and made plans to send Cornwallis with a large detachment into Philadelphia the next day.

CHAPTER II

CORNWALLIS ENTERS THE CITY

BEFORE AND AFTER the Battle of Brandywine, there was considerable excitement in Philadelphia. Only the most optimistic expected Washington to prevent Howe from taking over the city; realizing this, the Americans were crestfallen and the Loyalists were elated. The Continental Congress prodded the Pennsylvania Supreme Executive Council to take measures to remove from the city any supplies or materiel useful to the enemy.

Between 9 September and 17 September, Philadelphia was a scene of feverish activity. Frantic efforts were made to remove all books and papers from the State Library, money and papers from the Public Loan Office, and all court records to a place of safety. All bells, including the Liberty Bell, were ordered to be taken down from public buildings. At first little thought was given to where these records and bells should be stored, but eventually they were secured in the Lehigh Valley towns of Allentown, Bethlehem, and Easton.

Panic was evident in many of the decisions the American authorities made. In fact, a number of citizens were to become the victims of a tragic miscarriage of justice. On 25 August, a congressional resolution recommended that in Pennsylvania and Delaware, all "notoriously disaffected" persons be secured and confined until such time as they could no longer offer injury to the "common cause." It was feared that citizens not in sympathy with the Americans would let Howe know about the inadequate city and river defenses and the glaring weakness in materiel and manpower.[1]

The situation was exacerbated by the discovery of a spurious communication originating from the nonexistent Quaker Yearly Meeting in Spanktown (Rahway), New Jersey. This paper had been conveniently placed in baggage and was found, as intended, by General Sullivan during a raid on Staten Island. Neither Congress nor Sullivan tried to verify the accuracy of the statements made in the document or the existence of a Spanktown meeting.

With Galloway and other prominent Loyalists out of reach, however, a group of forty-one Quakers and Anglicans was singled out for questioning. A committee of liberal Americans was chosen to screen the suspects. The Quakers and Anglicans were offered limited freedom provided they would refrain from speaking, writing, or otherwise giving intelligence to Howe and provided they remained in their homes — a polite form of house arrest.[2]

After some minor difficulties, nineteen citizens gave acceptable written or verbal compliance, and twenty-two were taken into custody. Incarcerated in the Free Mason's lodge hall, the prisoners petitioned Congress for an audience to learn the specific charges against them. Their demands were ignored. Neither Congress nor the Pennsylvania Supreme Executive Council would accept responsibility for the imprisonment of these men who were respected Philadelphia residents. Suspicion ran rampant through Congress. The cynicism of its members appeared in the letter that John Adams wrote to his wife, Abigail: ''We have been obliged to attempt to humble the pride of some Jesuits, who call themselves Quakers, but who love money and land better than liberty or religion. The hypocrites are endeavoring to raise the cry of persecution, and to give this matter a religious turn, but they can't succeed.''[3]

To save face, Congress passed the buck to council and suggested it determine the guilt or innocence of the prisoners. Apparently Congress had second thoughts; had they overreacted? These so-called seditious citizens were respected members of Philadelphia's society. The council was in a quandary. To appease the clamor of witch-hunters, it ordered the prisoners transferred to Virginia. However, before their departure two recanted and were permitted to remain in the city.

During the winter of 1777-78, Congress was petitioned repeatedly to restore the exiles to their families. Finally, in April the authorities realized the prisoners were of little danger to the American cause and authorized their return from Winchester, Virginia, to Philadelphia. Unfortunately, everyone did not rejoice at their liberation; two families had been saddened by the death of their menfolk at

Winchester. Upon reaching Pennsylvania, the prisoners futilely sought to determine the exact reason for their confinement.

In September, as the British army neared Philadelphia, Alexander Hamilton advised the Continental Congress and the Pennsylvania Supreme Executive Council that Howe was momentarily expected to cross the Schuylkill River. Washington's aide added that with the weakened condition of the American army, there was little hope that the British could be prevented from entering the city. In fear for their personal safety, authorities and civilians made frantic preparations to leave Philadelphia. Ironically, it was subsequently discovered that Hamilton's letter had merely said Howe was approaching the Schuylkill. It was rumored that the appearance of two or three British dragoons at the river created the impression the enemy was about to cross. About 1:00 A.M., panic gripped the city as men went from door to door awakening everyone. Almost instantly the streets were filled with every conceivable type of conveyance piled high with personal possessions. Soon the ferries to New Jersey and the roads leading north to Allentown, Easton, and Bethlehem were crowded with refugees. To avoid capture by British patrols, they did not take roads heading west or northwest. Sarah Logan Fisher graphically described the frenetic activity in the early morning hours of 19 September. She remembered "wagons rattling, horses galloping, women running, children crying, delegates flying, & altogether the greatest consternation, fright & terror that can be imagined. Some of our neighbors took their flight before day, & I believe all the Congress moved off before 5 o'clock [A.M.]."[4]

Congressional letters revealed the fright that gripped members of that body. Thomas Burke said the decision to leave the city "was made not by a Vote but by universal Consent, for every Member Consulted his own particular Safety." On the other hand, Charles Carroll, with more equanimity, considered the responsibilities of Congress. He wrote Washington, requesting that reliable persons be sent to Bristol and Trenton to impress wagons to transport the valuable Continental stores from Philadelphia.[5]

Most congressmen had fled their posts before 3:00 A.M. When it was revealed that Hamilton's letter had been misunderstood, however, a few returned to the city. Curiosity brought the crabbed James Lovell back from Bristol. He was unaware of the whereabouts of other members of Congress, saying, "I know not which Way Coll. Dyer and Co. steered after they crossed into the Jersies." Eliphalet Dyer offered a possible explanation to Lovell's dilemma. He

the State House

The East Prospect of the City of PH.

East prospect of the City as drawn by N. Scull and G. Heap. *Philadelphia Maritime Museum*

remarked that when they had discovered that Howe was not knocking at Philadelphia's door, they nevertheless "were soon on the wing and made our flight with all speed to Trenton where we arrived early that day [19 September]." Just before receiving Hamilton's letter, the ever acrimonious Adams confided to his diary his consistently low opinion of the city and its people. "We are yet in Philadelphia, that mass of cowardice and Toryism," he wrote. It is possible Henry Laurens best summed up the frenzied state of Congress: "Fright sometimes works Lunacy. This does not imply that Congress is frighted or Lunatic but there may be some men between this and Schuylkill who may be much one and a little of the other."[6]

When word was received that Howe had successfully crossed to the east side of the Schuylkill, final plans were implemented to ensure

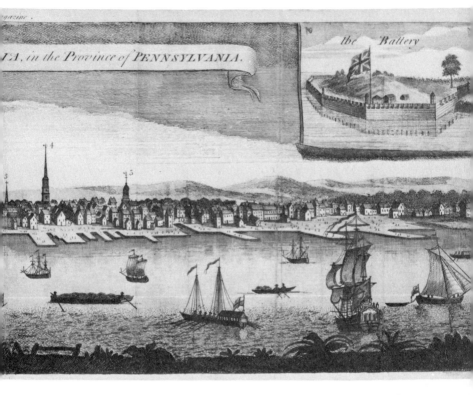

the *Battery*

IA, in the Province of PENNSYLVANIA.

that nothing remained in the city which would aid the British. On 23 September, all decked vessels above the Market Street wharf were ordered to Burlington, and those below were directed to Fort Mifflin to report to the American Commodore John Hazelwood. All shallops, sloops, and flats were to remove what public or private goods remained in the city. All small craft not employed in the removal of supplies were to be secreted in the New Jersey creeks. Only the Delaware River ferries and those shallops supplying the inhabitants were exempted. Otherwise, any boats found at the city's wharves twenty-four hours after the posting of instructions for their removal were to be destroyed.[7]

On 24 September, with the British momentarily expected at the gates of the city, Hazelwood ordered several galleys to patrol the river opposite the main streets leading to the wharves. After planting two fieldpieces on the Market Street wharf, they suddenly removed them and withdrew down river. This was probably a reconnoitering movement to determine if any British troops were in the city.

The next day word reached Philadelphia that the British army was in Germantown. A large concourse of Loyalists, some reported several hundred, immediately repaired to greet their liberators. Others less desirable were attracted by the approach of the British army. Elizabeth Drinker observed, "A great number of ye lower sort of ye People are gone out to them." Later in the day, a messenger arrived from Howe with a letter for Thomas Willing requesting that all residents remain quietly in their homes. Willing, Robert Morris's business partner, was respected by both sides, and Howe evidently thought he could calm the people.[8]

In spite of all assurances that the Philadelphians would be safe, rumors were rife that arsonists planned to burn the city. A report was circulated that tarred faggots were stored in several strategically located outhouses, to be ignited at an appointed time. Concerned citizens, both American and Loyalist, met at the State House and organized watches to patrol the streets each night. Two men who were apprehended admitted that it was their intention to set the city on fire. It appears there was no official sanction for this nefarious rumor — it was just the product of sick minds. With or without foundation, Elizabeth Drinker hoped the threatening skies on the twenty-fifth would produce sufficient rains to dampen the ardor of any arsonist. Her wishes were answered, as it rained hard for several hours.[9]

About 8:30 A.M. on 26 September, Cornwallis's column moved out of Germantown and headed toward Philadelphia. They marched along in a gay mood. One British officer observed that it was like a procession, with bands playing martial music. Leaving the Germantown Road at Second Street, the British and Hessian troops proceeded through Northern Liberties and entered the city about ten o'clock[10] through "Streets crowded with Inhabitants who seem to rejoice on the occasion, tho' by all accounts many of them were publickly on the other side before our arrival." Captain John Montresor noted the troops received the "acclamation of some thousands of inhabitants mostly women and children."[11]

In the van of the column were the light dragoons, escorted by at least two Philadelphia Loyalists — some accounts mention Phineas Bond, Jr., and Enoch Story.[12] They were followed by a band playing "God Save the King." Loyalists acclaiming the conquering army and hearing this tribute to their king acknowledged that it added solemnity to an otherwise joyous occasion. In contrast to the ragged Continentals, the British and Hessian grenadiers made a fine martial appearance with strict discipline, solemn countenance, and methodical behavior. The British grenadiers made a lasting impression on a ten-year-old boy, as he recalled their tranquil and exalted deportment and their friendly attitude and hearty handclasp. By contrast, the Hessians frightened him with their satanic mustaches and somber demeanor. Their band was playing a mournful tune which sounded like "Plunder! Plunder! Plunder!" to the youth. One observer declared that the antithesis of the orderly grenadiers was the heterogeneous collection of camp followers, animals, and wagons bringing up the rear: "baggage wagons, Hessian women [also, British women], horses, cows, goats and asses."[13]

A few Quaker residents confided their pro-British sentiments to their diaries and journals. There is little reason to believe such injudicious remarks were confined to the privacy of their personal memorabilia. These innocent jottings were easily misunderstood and converted into a hate campaign, causing some bitterness towards the Quakers. Robert Morton, with considerable vehemence, declared the arrival of the British army was a "great relief of the inhabitants who have too long suffered the yoke of Arbitrary Power; and who testified their approbation of the arrival of the troops by the loudest acclamations of joy." On the other hand, Sarah Logan Fisher was grateful that the city had surrendered without a gun being fired; she thought it "called for great humility and deep gratitude on our part."[14]

On the eve of the British entry into the city, Loyalists roamed the streets in quest of all known American sympathizers who were still in the city. Several hundred were apprehended, subjected to a "Loyalist citizen's arrest," and confined in the Walnut Street gaol. This malicious harassment continued for several days, and other American sympathizers were also confined. It appears that the majority were released after being interrogated by British authorities. This was not necessarily a sign of justice, but simply an expedient, as Howe had great need of the gaol to incarcerate the hundreds of prisoners taken at Brandywine and Germantown. At this time an abbreviated drama was unfolding, unknown to the Loyalists or British. A real prize, Thomas Wharton, president of the Assembly, had delayed his departure from the city and was in grave danger of being detected. He was disguised and eluded the incoming British army. Making his way to Point-No-Point, just south of Frankford Creek, he was hidden by the Conrad Baker family until they were able to arrange his passage over the Delaware to New Jersey.[15]

Before occupying the city, Howe and Cornwallis had coordinated plans for its defense and security. The British and Hessian grenadiers were to be stationed in a semicircle fronting out from center city, thereby providing a defense ring on all land approaches to Philadelphia. The Hessians were assigned the northern perimeter, with headquarters at the old barracks on Second Street; the British Second Grenadiers were stationed to the west and quartered in the Bettering House on Spruce between Tenth and Eleventh streets; the British First Grenadiers were positioned to the south at the shipyard. Because of limited space in the assigned quarters, many soldiers, especially the First Battalion, encamped in tents. For internal security, a main guard post was established at the State House with patrols assigned to key locations throughout the city. As hundreds of houses and stores were vacant, the threat of fire and looting was a major concern to Cornwallis and most residents. Several Englishmen who were comparatively recent arrivals in Philadelphia attempted to quiet the fears of those who had heard of the rapine of the British army in New Jersey. Deborah Logan remembered an amiable gentleman and former British officer named Gurney who attempted to assure her family they would not be ill-treated. However, he did caution them to keep off the street and to keep their house closed until the army had established the necessary security measures. Captain John Peebles said he had dinner with Gurney on the night of the twenty-sixth and noted the main topic of their conversation was Gurney's irritation at the "great Tyranny exercised by Congress . . . against those who would not join them."[16]

To guard against surprise attacks by the Pennsylvania navy, batteries were constructed on the riverbank in Southwark. One was located near present Reed and Swanson streets, another in the vicinity of Christian and Swanson streets. The old Association Battery was scheduled to be reactivated; however, there is some question whether the work was completed. Further north, near the mouth of Cohocksink Creek, another battery was started as protection against any waterborne assault from above the city. The batteries were in various stages of completion when attacked by elements of the State navy on 27 September.[17]

Some mystery surrounds the intelligence American naval officers received on the movements of Cornwallis. At a conference of the State and Continental naval officers on 26 September, it was decided to send a small flotilla to reconnoiter the city's waterfront, and, if the British were in the city, to observe their activities. Hazelwood immediately drafted instructions to Captain Charles Alexander of the frigate *Delaware*. In addition to his frigate, Alexander was ordered to assemble the State guard ship *Montgomery,* the sloop *Fly,* and four galleys, move upstream, and take position opposite the main streets and wharves. Hazelwood continued, ''Do Every Thing in your Power . . . to annoy the Enemy should they attempt to Come in to our City . . . see them preparing any works for Cannon or Hauling Cannon near the river . . . send a flag . . . warn them if they do not desist . . . you will fire on the City.''[18]

The British started construction of the waterfront batteries on the evening of 26 September. According to Howe, the batteries were unfinished when the American flotilla began the action; however, Montresor declared that the two lower gun emplacements were completed early on the twenty-seventh. Nevertheless, at about ten o'clock that morning, Alexander approached the lower battery (Reed Street), which consisted of two medium twelve-pounders and two howitzers. An ineffectual but heavy cannon fire ensued, with many balls falling in the Southwark district. Howe and Major John Andre believed the cannonade of the city was deliberate. Alexander had come up with the tide and, carelessly, paid little attention to the falling tide; as a result, the *Delaware* ran aground, and an excited Alexander obviously concentrated more on refloating the frigate than directing its cannon fire.[19]

General Samuel Cleaveland of the Royal Artillery rushed to the waterfront to assume personal command. Upon arriving at the lower battery, he continued to fire its guns on the helpless *Delaware* and ordered the battery at Christian Street to bring their two medium twelve-pounders into action. To deal the coup de grace to the hapless frigate, he brought up the grenadiers' four light six-pounders. The *Delaware* was soon on fire, and the sloop *Fly* had her mast shot away. Alexander realized that his situation was hopeless and surrendered to the British, who quickly sent Captain James Moncrieff, with carpenters, to extinguish the fire. By cutting away the burning wood sides, they soon accomplished their mission. The balance of the American fleet had withdrawn downstream, except for the *Fly,* which ran ashore on the New Jersey side of the river where the Americans were able to refloat her during the night.

The action lasted slightly under one hour, and the casualties were insignificant. Montresor claimed one killed and six wounded on the *Delaware* and four killed and six wounded on the *Fly*. Elizabeth Drinker stated that the cook on the *Delaware* had been decapitated. No British losses were reported. The British lost little time in bringing up Lieutenant Watt, two midshipmen, and fifty sailors, shortly followed by fourteen additional seamen from the *Roebuck*, to man the *Delaware*. Until after the fall of Fort Mifflin and the breaching of the rather formidable obstacle of the sunken chevaux-de-frise, the former American frigate was to be the principal water defense of the city.[20]

Cornwallis had taken the necessary precautions to prevent a surprise attack on the garrison. With the grenadiers and the gun emplacements on the waterfront forming a defense ring around the city, he turned to other pressing business. Quarters had to be secured to accommodate an army and its followers numbering almost twenty thousand. In addition, several thousand Loyalists from four states were expected to seek refuge with the British army. Permanent fortifications had to be constructed, as Philadelphia was expected to be the British headquarters for an indefinite period.

Galloway was requested to recruit his staunchest supporters and assume responsibility for taking a census of the city. He was instructed to tally all houses and stores and determine if they were occupied, apprehend any residents suspected of being dangerous to the security of the city, and confiscate any weapons in their possession.[21] He selected personal henchmen in every ward to conduct the survey and take the necessary action against the disaffected rebels.

Cornwallis was perplexed: Where was he to locate sufficient quarters to accommodate the various brigades, battalions, and regiments? He recognized that at that time the problem was academic, as the men could live in their tents or build temporary huts; but in less than two months such habitations would become unbearable, and better accommodations had to be provided. The hundreds of vacant houses and stores were adequate for barracks. To ensure proper discipline, brigades and regiments were assigned specific districts. The privates and noncommissioned officers were billeted in the empty buildings in their districts, with the officers obtaining lodgings in the homes of residents.

Adjutants to the barrack master, with other officers, were to supervise the selection of quarters and their conversion to barracks. One interesting document survives that reports the results of the investigation of an officer into the availability of nineteen stores, Carpenters' Hall, the Academy (later the University of Pennsylvania),

British barracks which extended from Second to Third streets and from Tammany to Green streets. *Free Library of Philadelphia*

other large schools, and the Fish House. It suggests that little coercion was employed at this time. Marginal comments indicated what stores ''may be had,'' ''cannot be had,'' ''expect to be insured,'' and ''expect payment,'' and other notations stated where stores were already rented or owned by a lady. A footnote suggested these structures could by a ''moderate computation'' accommodate 3,000 men. The private stores were not restricted to prominent Americans, but included those owned by Loyalists. Robert Morris was the proprietor of one marked ''uncertain,'' while Samuel Shoemaker's store was unavailable. Officers were observed numbering or marking houses with chalk, an assignment intended to identify houses available for officers' quarters and possibly barracks for soldiers.[22]

Of course, the old barracks on north Second Street were to be utilized, but they would accommodate only a limited number of troops. In addition, bivouacs had to be provided for regiments near their assigned positions on the defense lines. This permitted their turning out quickly in the event of an American attack. Churches were viewed with a jaundiced eye, especially the Presbyterian and Lutheran churches whose congregations were known to be active in the American cause. Saint Paul's Episcopal Church was also considered because its parishioners, according to their rector, were "rebels." However, the churches were reserved for later use as hospitals and riding academies for British officers.

Other space requirements included quarters for the commissary and quartermaster generals, yards for the storage of forage, ordnance stores, and other auxiliary units. A few days after the city was occupied a complete army bakery was in full operation. More important was the need for buildings to be utilized as general, naval, and regimental hospitals. After the battles of Brandywine and Germantown, the British army had over two thousand sick and wounded. In addition, while the gaol had to be used for the American privates and noncommissioned officers, accommodations had to be made for their officers and wounded.

Cornwallis next turned his attention to building fortifications on the northern perimeter of the city. Montresor, as chief engineer, was directed to select the terrain suitable for a chain of redoubts, demilunes, and ravelins with a connecting curtain of earth forming a solid defense line from the Delaware to the Schuylkill. Early on the morning of 28 September, Montresor surveyed an area in Northern Liberties on the same line selected by General Israel Putnam when the Americans believed Howe threatened Philadelphia in December 1776. Montresor quickly drafted proposals for Cornwallis's approval, and later that afternoon escorted the general over the chosen ground.

Preliminary plans called for ten redoubts, with a demilune between redoubts seven and eight and a ravelin between five and six. The curtain was fronted with an abatis and ditched, and the escarpment of the redoubts, demilune, and ravelin was fraised. One redoubt was to be constructed at each road leading into the city. Not included in Montresor's original plan were two advanced redoubts about two hundred fifty yards north of the main defense line. One was on Wissahickon Road (further north it became Manatawny Road, now Ridge Pike) and the other was on Fourth Street just below Germantown Road.[23]

Soldiers could not be spared to work on the proposed fortifications; therefore, it was decided to recruit laborers from the city's residents. Montresor engaged John Palmer, a master mason, and Samuel Griscomb and Elias Smith, master carpenters, to supervise the construction of the defenses. He determined that 340 laborers would be needed. However, citizens were slow to volunteer, and only a few had reported by 2 October. Disappointed, Cornwallis directed that the required number of civilians offer their services or be conscripted. The next morning 200 laborers reported, although Montresor had hoped for a full complement of 340.[24] While civilians were being recruited to build the redoubts, headquarters ordered Montresor to give his attention to the gun emplacements being constructed on Carpenters' and Province islands. Opening the river had to take precedence over the land defenses north of the city. Work on the redoubts proceeded slowly, and it was several weeks before they were ready to receive garrisons.[25]

Stenton, the home of James Logan, was Sir William Howe's headquarters before the Battle of Germantown. *Free Library of Philadelphia*

Meanwhile Howe had established his headquarters at Stenton (residence of the Logan family), about one mile south of the village of Germantown. With Cornwallis's detachment in Philadelphia and the 71st Regiment and Colonel Werner von Mirbach's Hessians garrisoned in Wilmington, the British army remaining in Germantown numbered about twelve thousand.

Howe advised Germain that the British line of encampment crossed the main street at right angles. To the left and fronting to the north were "Lieutenant General Knyphausen, Major Generals Stirn and Grey, Brigadier General Agnew, with seven British and three Hessian battalions, the mounted and dismounted chausseurs . . . extending to the Schuylkill, the chausseurs being in front." His right extending to the vicinity of Old York Road included "Major General Grant and Brigadier General Matthew, with the corps of guards, six battalions of British, and two squadrons of dragoons." The Queen's American Rangers and the 1st Battalion of light infantry were advanced to the front of this wing. Patrols were sent as far east as Frankford. Lieutenant Colonel Thomas Musgrave, with the 40th Regiment, was stationed about one mile above the main encampment along Germantown Road, with the 2nd Battalion of light infantry a half mile further north (Mt. Airy).[26]

On 26 September all sick and wounded were ordered transferred to the hospitals that were being set up in the city. They were attended by a surgeon and the necessary complement of mates, with each corps sending one woman to act as a nurse. As an escort, each corps and regiment furnished one corporal and six men, and each brigade one subaltern and a sergeant. All American prisoners except officers were directed to accompany the train of sick.

Howe's official correspondence describing the position of the army units in Germantown is at some variance with this order. It is apparent that a number of corps were stationed along Germantown Road leading into the city; certainly some were posted in close proximity to headquarters. This suggests that the assigned areas on the east-west defense line were not at full strength. Howe ordered the escort of the train of sick, wounded, and prisoners "to be relieved by the first Corps encamped on the road, and so on from Corps to Corps to Philadelphia, and back again to Camp."[27]

Cornwallis and Howe continued to be haunted by the acts of rapine and vandalism committed by British and Hessian soldiers. Courts-martial were held almost daily with the death penalty or from 400 to 1,000 lashes meted out to the guilty. At least one Loyalist soldier of the Queen's Rangers was executed in Germantown. Howe offered rewards of up to $200 for information and identification of those who had robbed or plundered the inhabitants.

Cornwallis was having problems in the section called the Neck and along the Schuylkill (part of modern South Philadelphia). Many beautiful cottages and residences dotted this section, and virtually every one was pillaged. It became necessary to place sentries at these properties to prevent further depredations. In the first twenty-four hours of occupation, almost every wooden fence disappeared in the southern and western sections of the metropolitan area. Morton complained of the rudeness of certain officers, and Cornwallis dealt out summary punishment when a marauder was apprehended. If the death penalty resulted, most Quakers, even though their properties had been plundered, pleaded for mercy for those condemned. In Philadelphia, Mary Pemberton wrote to Howe pleading for the life of a British soldier convicted of breaking into her Germantown house. She appealed to Howe, emphasizing "thy goodness and humanity may induce thee to Pardon the Person who has been guilty of the Mischief as at least so far as not to permit his life to be taken."[28]

On the lighter, but slightly uncomfortable, side was the efforts of British officers to obtain personal quarters with the inhabitants. Many officers expressed their discomfort at living with families of the same ethnic background and posing as enemies. A single incident involving Cornwallis illustrated the embarrassment of both British officers and householders. Deborah Logan (then Deborah Norris) related how horror-stricken her mother was when she heard Cornwallis had selected her home as his headquarters. Her house was on the south side of Chestnut, near Fifth Street. In Deborah's words:

Early in the afternoon Lord Cornwallis' suite arrived, and took possession of my mother's house. But my mother was appalled by the numerous train which took possession of dwelling, and shrank from having such inmates; for a guard was mounted at the door, and the yard filled with soldiers and baggage of every description; and I well remember what we thought of the haughty looks of Lord Rawdon and the other aid-de-camp, as they traversed the apartments. — My mother desired to speak with Lord Cornwallis, and he attended her in the front parlour. She told him of her situation, and how impossible it would be for her to stay in her own house with such a numerous train as composed his Lordship's establishment. He behaved with great politeness to her, said he should be sorry to give trouble, and would have other quarters looked out for him — they withdrew that very afternoon.

Such politeness could not last long as the city became crowded with officers, refugees, and soldiers. Almost every householder was obliged to accept lodgers. Mrs. Norris was later required to accommodate two British artillery officers.[29]

American detachments were constantly annoying British outposts, causing little damage, but gathering valuable information on the strength and distribution of the British army. According to two British officers, the Americans attempted to destroy some of the British ships in the Chester roadstead. Their version states that on 30 September a chain of fire rafts was sent down the river, but was foiled by the tide and the severe cannonade of British men-of-war. American accounts make no reference to this action. It is very unlikely that Hazelwood would have sent the fire raft chain that far below the chevaux-de-frise. It was maneuvered by small guard boats, which could not have survived in the open water of the Delaware, as claimed by Montresor. Montresor also said there were three rafts in the chain, another officer declared there were four, whereas all Pennsylvania chains had six fire rafts.[30]

In the meantime, Hamond, with the *Roebuck* and several other frigates, lay off Chester. He persuaded Howe to send a detachment to reduce the fort at Billingsport. It was his opinion that if the anchor of the lower chevaux-de-frise was in British hands, he could easily breach the obstructions, thus permitting their men-of-war to pass through and bombard Forts Mifflin and Mercer.

On 29 September, Howe ordered Colonel Thomas Stirling, with the 42nd and 10th Regiments, to march at 4:00 P.M. to Middle Ferry on the Schuylkill (opposite the western extension of Market Street). The next day he was to proceed to Chester.[31] He was instructed to take two six-pounders from the 3rd Brigade.

American authorities never anticipated that a land attack would be made on Billingsport; as a result, the land side had been left indefensible against artillery or a determined assault. In any event, the fort was too large for the available garrison, so the Americans converted the northwest salient into a redoubt and evacuated the remainder of the fort. In fact, the State Navy Board had questioned the advisability of retaining a fortification there, but was overruled by Congress. Colonel William Bradford was dispatched to take command of the garrison and the redoubt. When he arrived, he discovered that General Silas Newcomb had withdrawn the New Jersey militia, leaving a garrison of about one hundred men to defend the fortification.

Aided by Hamond, Stirling's regiments were ferried across the Delaware from Chester on 1 October and landed near Raccoon Creek. Proceeding overland, they approached the overambitious outer works without encountering opposition. Bradford saw the futility of resistance and ordered the immediate evacuation of the fort.

All guns that could not be carried off were spiked, and most of the buildings, including the barracks, were burned. Bradford pulled out for Fort Mifflin after loading cannon, ammunition, supplies, and men in the galley *Franklin*, a guard boat, and a few nondescript craft. The Americans reported that brief, but sporadic, gunfire was exchanged, and one man was wounded.

It has remained a mystery why Stirling neglected to complete the conquest of river forts. Had he marched a few miles north, he could have taken Fort Mercer at Red Bank. Fort Mercer was without a garrison and would have been easy prey; it was also the lifeline for the supplies and ammunition needed by Fort Mifflin. If Mercer fell, Mifflin would have surrendered in a few days. However, Stirling was ordered to take and dismantle Billingsport, which he accomplished the first five days in October. Recrossing the Delaware, Stirling's command was joined by another regiment and directed to provide an escort for a provision convoy to be taken to the army at Germantown. Chester had become the post where all supplies were unloaded and carried overland to the army. To protect this depot, two battalions of the 71st Regiment were sent from Wilmington.[32]

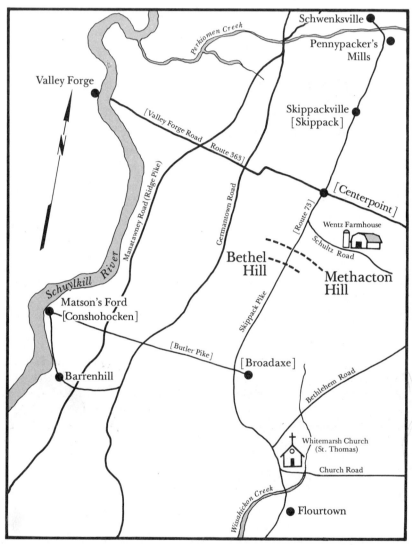

American positions before Germantown

CHAPTER III

GERMANTOWN

THE DEFEAT AT Brandywine and the surprise of Wayne's command at Paoli would have daunted a less resolute general than Washington who was often referred to as the American Fabius. His aggressive strategy frequently astonished both compatriots and enemies. Shifting his encampments between Pottsgrove (Pottstown) and Pennypacker's Mills[1] (Schwenksville), he impatiently awaited Continental troop reinforcements from New York State and militia from Maryland, New Jersey, and Virginia. With their arrival (and given a propitious opportunity), he was determined to attack the British army at Germantown, regardless of the opinions of his general officers.

By 28 September, most of the expected reinforcements had reached camp, and as was his habit, Washington called a Council of War to consider the feasibility of attacking Howe. He advised his generals that their army numbered 8,000 Continentals and 3,000 militia. His best intelligence reports indicated that Howe's army in Germantown did not exceed 8,000. Did they consider it prudent to attack the British position, or should they wait for additional reinforcements? By a vote of ten to five, they cautioned that it would be inexpedient to attack, and they suggested that the army move within twelve miles of the British and await favorable developments or reinforcements.[2]

On the twenty-ninth, in accordance with the council's decision, Washington marched the army five miles down to Skippack Creek, near the hamlet of Skippackville (Skippack). Two days later he moved an additional four miles to Methacton Hill in Worcester Township. Methacton Hill towers above the surrounding countryside and bisects the Skippack Road one and a half miles south of the modern village of Center Point. At this encampment Greene and Stephen's Continentals and Brigadier Generals William Smallwood and David Foreman's [Forman] militia were quartered on Bethel Hill, a slight shelf on the south side of Methacton Hill a half mile from the crest. Sullivan, with Wayne and Stirling's divisions plus Major General John Armstrong's Pennsylvania militia, were camped on the top of Methacton Hill. Washington set up his headquarters in the Peter Wentz farmhouse, below the northern base of the hill.

While headquartered here, Washington's patrols intercepted two letters which indicated that Colonel Stirling, with the 10th and 42nd British regiments, had been detached to reduce the fort at Billingsport in New Jersey. At the same time Washington learned that the 23rd, or Royal Welsh Fusileers, had marched to Chester to join Stirling. With this intelligence, and believing that Howe had seriously weakened his position, Washington decided to attack the British at Germantown. Again Washington underestimated the size of the British army. He communicated his decision to attack to the general officers — without calling a Council of War. By neglecting to do so, Washington affirmed a single-purpose determination to carry out his plan, regardless of the consensus of the generals. However, he added that the generals unanimously agreed with his proposed strategy. The colonial commander expressed amazement at Howe's rash tactics of dividing his army at Brandywine. But now he was about to unleash a four-pronged attack which for audaciousness and intricacy would not be duplicated during the Revolution.

The site of the impending attack, Germantown, was principally a one-street village which extended for nearly two miles along Germantown Road.[3] There were no important cross streets; those that did intersect the main street were little better than narrow country lanes. School House Lane, which stretched west from Market Square, and Church Lane (or Luken's Mill Street), which extended for over a mile east of the village, were the two most important. In addition to Germantown Road, three additional roads entered Germantown from the northwest and northeast and were important to Washington's plan. On the west, near the Schuylkill, was Manatawny Road, or Ridge Pike, while Limekiln Pike and Old York Road approached from the northeast, entering the town by way of Church Lane.

Washington's orders called for:

The Divisions of Sullivan and Wayne,[4] flanked by Conway's Brigade, were to enter the Town by way of Chestunt [sic] Hill, while Genl Armstrong, with the Pennsylvania Militia should fall down the Manatawny Road by Vandeerings Mill and get upon the Enemy's left and Rear. The Divisions of Greene and Stephen, flanked by McDougal's Brigade, were to enter by taking a circuit by way of the Lime Kiln Road at the Market House and to attack their Right wing, and the Militia of Maryland and Jersey under Generals Smallwood and Foreman were to march by the old York road and fall upon the rear of their Right. Lord Stirling with Nash and Maxwell's Brigades was to form a Corps de Reserve.

The entire army was to be under arms at 6:00 P.M. on 3 October, taking with them nothing but their arms, accoutrements, ammunition, and provisions. Each man had been ordered to cook three days' provisions and to carry forty rounds of cartridges, with all arms being in the best order.[5]

Greene's headquarters were at the Cassel farm on Bethel Road. According to Hance Supplee, who lived nearby with his grandmother, on 2 October Washington visited Greene and they had a long talk. Greene was Washington's most dependable general and the man with whom he usually discussed the strategy of a campaign. Washington probably called the conference at the Cassel farm to work out the final details of the projected march to Germantown. Young Supplee recalled that Washington and other officers, both on foot and mounted, were joined by Greene and went into a neighboring meadow. "Forming a semi-circle they faced General Washington holding their swords in front of their faces. They stayed in this position for quite a long time, after which each officer went to his command, General Greene coming into the house and going to his room."[6]

At 7:00 P.M. on 3 October, Greene's and Stephen's divisions, accompanied by McDougall's brigade, moved down the Skippack Road. Smallwood and Foreman were to follow. Meanwhile, Sullivan, Wayne, Stirling, and Armstrong were still forming their commands, preparing to abandon the encampment as soon as the vanguard had cleared the area. With Sullivan in command, these divisions moved forward about nine o'clock and were closely followed by Armstrong. Unfortunately, Washington and his column commanders were only vaguely familiar with the precise distance each column had to cover, the condition of the roads, or the exact location and size of the British advance posts.[7]

Each column was to march over its designated route and, hopefully, at 2:00 A.M. on 4 October, halt within two miles of the British pickets. Washington had received intelligence reports that indicated that Howe had established posts of at least regimental strength somewhere on Germantown Road and Limekiln Pike. Mounted patrols were sent to locate these outposts. For several nights patrols harassed the British outposts so that their sudden appearance on the night of 3 October would not create undue alarm.

After resting two hours, each column was to move out and simultaneously attack the British positions at 5:00 A.M. Mounted couriers would be the only contact between the widespread columns. On a straight line, the front would extend from Armstrong's division on the Manatawny Road to Smallwood and Foreman on Old York Road — a distance in excess of six miles. The intervening terrain was badly broken up by numerous ravines, especially the deep upper gorge of Wissahickon Creek. Heavy woods dotted the landscape. Wherever clearings existed, as they did along stretches of Germantown Road, successive rows of fences hindered progress. This made an orderly advance in line difficult, particularly for inexperienced troops.[8]

Between eleven o'clock and midnight, Greene's column arrived at the junction of Skippack Road and the road to Bethlehem. Swinging south on the Bethlehem Road a few hundred yards, he turned left on Church Road, past the Whitemarsh (Saint Thomas) Church.[9] With Church Road the only artery for several miles capable of accommodating his column, Greene followed this road four miles to Limekiln Pike. At this intersection he filed to the right, and unexpectedly his advance scouts discovered a sizeable British force to his front. The British 1st Light Infantry, backed up by the 4th Regiment, were actually about two miles from Church Road in the vicinity of Limekiln Pike and Abington Road — modern Washington Lane.

Smallwood and Foreman continued two miles beyond Limekiln Pike and wheeled right on Old York Road. Their circuitous route consumed so much time that they arrived too late to be a deciding factor in the forthcoming battle.

Sullivan, accompanied by Washington, and Armstrong proceeded south on Bethlehem Road, passed through Flourtown, and ar-

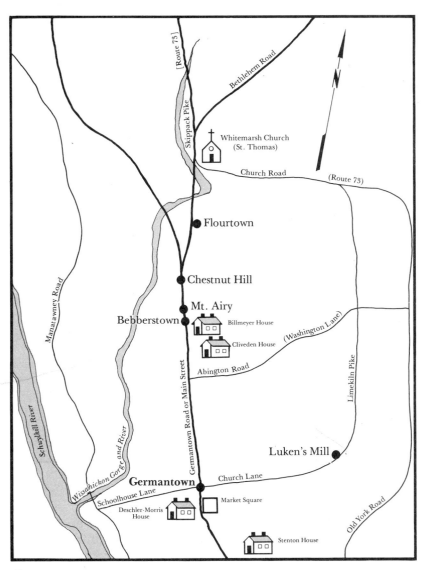

[Route 73]

Bethlehem Road

Skippack Pike

Whitemarsh Church
(St. Thomas)

Church Road

(Route 73)

Flourtown

Chestnut Hill

Mt. Airy

Bebberstown

Billmeyer House

Cliveden House

(Washington Lane)

Manatawney Road

Abington Road

Limekiln Pike

Schuylkill River

Wissahickon Gorge and River

Germantown Road or Main Street

Luken's Mill

Germantown

Church Lane

Schoolhouse Lane

Deschler-Morris
House

Market Square

Stenton House

Old York Road

Germantown

rived at Chestnut Hill near daybreak. Sullivan was to deploy along Germantown Road and fall upon the center of the British line. Washington decided to accompany this column because it offered him a better position to observe the heaviest action and to exercise overall direction of the battle. Armstrong, with the greatest distance to cover, engaged two guides to direct him to the nearest ford across the upper gorge of the Wissahickon. He then moved down the Manatawny Road to the mouth of the creek.[10]

According to Sullivan, while he was rolling back the British center, Greene was to turn their right and pin Howe against the Schuylkill. In a similar situation in early September, Washington, then in Wilmington, had expected Howe to turn his right and pin the Continental army against the Delaware. Now, to carry out the present maneuver, Greene had been assigned more than two-thirds of the army. Yet the exact size of Greene's command is difficult to establish, as after the losses at Brandywine, Paoli, and other engagements in September, the brigades and divisions were significantly below their authorized strength. In addition to battlefield casualties and sick, many Continentals had been taken prisoner. Furthermore, the plight of those in camp — without shoes, adequate clothing, and blankets — caused many to desert. Regardless, Greene had suffered fewer casualties at Brandywine and received a temporary reassignment of some units and reinforcements from the north.[11]

The Continentals and militia were clad in assorted nondescript garments. With the attack scheduled to start at dawn, Washington was anxious to ensure that his men could identify each other in the early morning shadows. Every officer and soldier was instructed to put a piece of white paper in his hat. Several British officers observed these pieces of paper. Andre commented that they believed it indicated the Americans had intended a surprise night attack. Another British officer offered the singular statement that the Americans were so certain of victory that billets in their hats listed the quarters which they would occupy in the city. Echoing this observation, Captain James Parker claimed that the Americans had paper in their hats to distinguish them from others, and which listed "houses in Philadelphia so sure were they of Victory."[12]

Sir William Howe and the British army were also making plans. Howe's main defensive position stretched from the Schuylkill on the west to Luken's Mill on the east, paralleling School House and

Church lanes. Except for a few small redoubts on the bluff overlooking the Schuylkill and at Luken's Mill, no fortifications had been erected.

Knyphausen, commanding the left wing, was posted along a line marked by School House Lane. Two-thirds of his line faced the deep gorge of the Wissahickon, a sector considered impregnable. Starting at the Schuylkill were the Hessian battalions Minnigerode, Du Corps, and Donop with the chasseurs, or jägers, on their front. Next to the Hessians on the east was Agnew's 4th British Brigade, the 33rd, 37th, 46th, and 64th regiments. On Agnew's right, near Germantown Road, was Major General Charles Grey with the 15th, 17th, and 44th regiments of the 3rd Brigade. Knyphausen's command, excluding artillerymen, consisted of about four thousand seven hundred rank and file.

The right wing, commanded by Grant, was east of the main street. His troops were in a line extending for slightly over one mile along Church Lane to Luken's Mill. The 55th and 5th regiments of the 2nd Brigade were just across Germantown Road. Next in line was the 49th Regiment of the 1st Brigade, although refused slightly to the right. Further east were Brigadier General Edward Matthew's [Mathew] two battalions of foot guards. Near Luken's Mill, about one mile from the center of the line, were the 27th and 28th regiments of the 2nd and 1st brigades respectively, and two squadrons of light dragoons. Grant's force numbered about three thousand rank and file.

To forestall a surprise attack by the Americans and provide time for the defense line to be brought under arms, Howe established strong outposts along the main roads leading into the village. About one and a half miles north, at Bebberstown, he stationed the 2nd Light Infantry with pickets advanced a few hundred yards to Mt. Airy. A short distance south of the light infantry's main bivouac, the 40th Regiment of the 2nd Brigade was encamped as a reserve.

A detachment of equal strength was placed along Limekiln Pike. Near the intersection of Limekiln Pike and Abington Road was the 1st Light Infantry and, as their reserve, the 4th Regiment of the 1st Brigade. Further east on Old York Road were the Queen's Rangers. No advance detachment was assigned to Manatawny Road as the Hessian jäger post, at the gorge of the Wissahickon, was considered secure against surprise. As an added precaution, Howe had placed a sizeable force of approximately one thousand men at each of the advance posts on Germantown Road and Limekiln Pike. The Queen's Rangers on Old York Road numbered nearly three hundred.

Howe had committed his entire force (of ten thousand rank and file and several hundred artillerymen) to a defensive action! If the Americans broke through the British defenses, he was without a reserve to buttress any part of the line.[13]

British officers disagreed on whether Howe had been warned of the impending American attack or if adequate preparations had been taken to prevent a surprise. Howe maintained that patrols had discovered the American army's approach about three o'clock on the morning of 4 October. Upon receipt of this intelligence, the army was immediately ordered under arms.[14]

Andre noted that some intimation of an American attack was received on 3 October, but was discredited. Charles Cochrane claimed that the Americans were upon the British advance posts before being detected. He blamed the "uncommon thick Fog" for covering their approach. Major Carl Leopold Baurmeister reported a Hessian jäger patrol had encountered an enemy detachment of 300 men one mile in advance of their position along the Manatawny Road. However, Captain Johann Ewald denied that the jägers would have penetrated beyond the Wissahickon gorge unless they were supported by larger detachments.[15]

Baurmeister's statement may have been simply a secondhand version of Ewald's unusual report that the Americans proposed to attack the British position in Germantown. According to Ewald, he was approached on the evening of the third by a Professor Schmidt who owned a country home near the jäger post. (This was probably Dr. William Smith, first provost of the Academy in Philadelphia, who was frequently suspected of having Loyalist sympathies.) Smith owned a house on the bluff overlooking the Schuylkill. Ewald had protected this property from the Hessian soldiers in the vicinity. Asking Ewald to take a walk with him, Smith thanked him for his humanitarianism. To clarify his position, the educator explained that he was a devoted follower and friend of the States and affirmed his wish for the success of American arms. He added, however, that he was positive that an attack was planned on Germantown. Because of Ewald's kindness, he had come to warn the Hessian that his post would be the first objective of the American army.

Ewald considered their conversation for a short time and then hurried to Colonel von Wurmb, who immediately reported it to Knyphausen. The Hessian general then conveyed the information to Howe. Ewald was chagrined to hear that Howe's only comment was "That cannot be." As incredible as the conversation between Smith and Ewald may seem, the Hessian repeated it in later life, but carefully avoided mentioning Smith's name — merely claiming that his informant was an American, but not a Tory. Though Washington's plan to attack the British was an open secret around the American camp, it is not known how Smith came by this intelligence — especially when the British command was in the dark.[16]

Sullivan arrived at Chestnut Hill near daybreak, the prearranged hour for the attack, and hastily formed his command. Temporarily, he proceeded in column, even though it was proposed to engage the British in line, with Wayne on Sullivan's left, or east of Germantown Road, and Sullivan's own division parallel to him, west of the road. Major General Thomas Conway's brigade would act as the vanguard until contact was established with the British and would then deploy to Sullivan's right. Conway's assignment was difficult, as he was to protect the right flank and maintain a liaison with Armstrong. Washington feared that British detachments might pass up the Wissahickon gorge and get in the rear of Sullivan or Armstrong. As the militia had frequently been untrustworthy, Conway's brigade was insurance against a debacle on the extreme right.[17]

With visibility limited to forty or fifty paces, Sullivan was forced to alter his tactics. Patrols had reported a British picket post at the Allen house in Mt. Airy. Conway was ordered to take one regiment from his brigade and one from the Second Maryland Brigade and, with Allen McLane's troop of light horse as outriders, to move down Germantown Road. After his advance had moved out, Conway formed the rest of his brigade in column and quickly followed. Sullivan's division swung in at the rear of Conway, closely followed by Wayne. Stirling's division, acting as a reserve, temporarily remained at Chestnut Hill.

The Americans hoped to overwhelm the British picket without alarming the main British army in Germantown. Lieutenant Forbes, who commanded the picket, was unable to see the oncoming Americans, but was aware that there was unusual activity at Chestnut Hill. McLane quickly overran the advance sentries, killing two and losing one man. Nevertheless, Forbes was not completely surprised as he discharged one round from his two six-pounders before falling back. The withdrawing troops found the 2nd Light Infantry drawn up and ready to give battle to the advancing Americans. While the British may not have been aware of the magnitude of the American attack, the readiness of the light infantry substantiates Howe's statement that the British army was under arms shortly after 3:00 A.M.[18]

When Conway found his advance regiments confronted by a superior force, he quickly formed his brigade in line to repulse an anticipated attack. The fog made Conway's estimate of the size of the British detachment a mere conjecture, but he immediately dispatched a courier to Sullivan for assistance. Sullivan sent one regiment to bolster Conway's left and formed the remainder of his division on the right. The combined force then advanced to engage the British light infantry. While the British stubbornly resisted, the weight of numbers soon forced their withdrawal. Initially they doggedly fought for each fence and hedge, but at last they became demoralized and fled in disorder, abandoning their camp at Bebberstown. In an effort to trap the retreating British, Sullivan ordered Wayne to bring his Pennsylvania Continentals forward and attempt to get in the enemy rear by passing to the east of Germantown Road. Before Wayne could accomplish this maneuver, the British were safely below his position. But he soon again encountered the 2nd Light Infantry.[19]

The fleeing 2nd Light Infantry, suddenly reinforced by Colonel Musgrave and the 40th Regiment, soon reencountered Wayne's Continentals. For a short time the British offered stiff resistance, contesting every foot of ground. It was so dark, Sullivan said, that the British were indistinguishable in the thick haze. Confused and concerned, Sullivan thought he was facing the entire left wing of the British army. He hastily redeployed his command, sending two regiments with Colonel Stephen Moylan's dragoons to his right. Unexpectedly his fears were dissipated when, about one mile from the center of the village, the British suddenly broke and rushed pell-mell to the rear.

During this disorderly withdrawal an unfortunate incident occurred. The 2nd Light Infantry had spearheaded the night surprise on Wayne's encampment at Paoli. Many of Wayne's soldiers recognized their adversaries and went berserk. Both Wayne and British Lieutenant Hunter described the savagery of the Pennsylvanians. To his wife, Wayne wrote that his men took ample revenge for the cruel actions of the British on 20 September. He added, "Our officers exerted themselves to save many of the poor wretches, but to little purpose; the rage and fury of the soldiers were not to be restrained for

Lieutenant General Thomas Musgrave with a view of Cliveden in the background. *National Trust for Historic Preservation*

some time, at least not until great numbers of the enemy fell by their bayonets." The Americans did not exhibit any compassion for the wounded nor, as far as can be determined, were any prisoners taken.[20]

As the retreating soldiers passed the Chew mansion (Cliveden),

Cliveden, the home of Benjamin Chew, became a fortress for Musgrave's 40th Regiment during the Battle of Germantown. *Free Library of Philadelphia*

Musgrave, with six companies of the 40th Regiment, occupied the house. To make the house as impregnable as possible, all wooden shutters were closed and secured. Furniture and every suitable article were erected into barricades near the windows and at the base of the staircase.

Lieutenant Hunter asserted that at the first sound of battle Howe mounted his horse and rode in the direction of the musket fire. Riding up to the fleeing soldiers, he chided them and called out they should be ashamed, as the light infantry never retreated. At that moment, grape shot burst in the branches over his head, scattering leaves above the general's head. Hunter was amused at Howe's discomfort. Captain Frederick Ernest von Munchhausen claimed that Howe was forward at the time and ordered the 40th Regiment to advance to reinforce the 2nd Light Infantry.[21]

Back at Cliveden, part of the American advance had come to a grinding halt. Wayne and Sullivan had passed the mansion in pursuit of the retreating British. The presence of a British force, however, was considered serious enough to hold up the American reserve until it was decided if the fortified house posed a threat to the victorious American army. Washington and Knox were the only general officers present, although several aides were nearby. Colonel Timothy Pickering presented a graphic portrayal of the decision-making conference. Knox was adamant that it would be unmilitary to leave a castle in the army's rear. Junior officers, especially Pickering, argued that this premise was true in theory, but not applicable to the present situation. Their protests were to no avail. Knox was an avid student of military tactics and strategy; but, unfortunately his reading had failed to help him recognize the practical application of theory.

Oblivious to the passage of time, the officers wasted over a half hour before they agreed on a suggestion to call on Musgrave to surrender. An effort was made, but the flag bearer, Lieutenant Colonel William Smith, was shot down, and later died of his wound. Someone else suggested burning the house; this effort was equally futile. Washington, who frequently deferred to Knox's theoretical knowledge, finally agreed to detach Maxwell's brigade from the reserve and placed a cordon of artillery around the mansion. Knox's biographer relates that the artillery commander was chagrined when the cannon balls bounced off the stone walls like rubber balls. Although Knox then turned the artillery on the shuttered windows and soon blasted them away, the British used everything at their disposal and rebuilt the barricades inside the windows. Embarrassed, Knox refused to acknowledge his error and maintained an ineffectual bombardment.[22]

Discounting the military significance of Knox's "citadel," Washington's decision was a very costly mistake. The delay prevented the reserve from supporting the advancing troops of Wayne and Sullivan and took its toll in American lives. Maxwell's brigade was one of the more efficient in the army and had been in the forefront of all engagements since Howe landed at the Head of Elk in August. The brigade, typical of its aggressive conduct, made several unsuccessful attempts to storm the mansion. While the losses are difficult to document, several British officers commented that numerous bodies were found on the grounds of Cliveden. British estimates varied between seventy and one hundred dead Americans. Two New Jersey regiments in Maxwell's brigade disclosed losses of forty-six officers and men, making the British claims for the entire brigade plausible.[23]

As Sullivan drove deeper into Germantown, he became more concerned. Visibility was practically nonexistent. In addition, he was uncertain of the British strength on his front. The retreating light infantry and remnants of the 40th Regiment were like shadowy wraiths in the haze. Also distressing was the depleted supply of cartridges. Unaware that Wayne was advancing on the east side of Germantown Road under equally adverse conditions, Sullivan dispatched an aide to Washington to order the Pennsylvanian to advance and attack the British in that sector. He also requested the support of Nash's and Maxwell's brigades. He obviously did not know about Maxwell's engagement with Musgrave at Cliveden. Nash did advance, but was not powerful enough to stem the storm that was about to break. The moment of decision had passed, the Americans had reached their pinnacle of success, and victory had been in sight; but the combination of weather, shortage of ammunition, and a too ambitious and elaborate plan soon reversed the fortunes of battle.

Washington established a temporary command post at the Billmeyer house, a few hundred yards north of Cliveden.[24] Beset by the same problems of uncertainty as his commanders in the forward action, he judged from the sound of firing — that ammunition was being expended on targets the men could not see. Pickering was ordered to ride forward and caution Sullivan to conserve that scarce commodity. The aide found the division commander a few hundred yards south of Cliveden, near the main road.

Sullivan recalled that he had begged Washington not to recklessly expose himself to British musket fire. Washington had a penchant for seeking out the heat of battle, but the problems which beset him in Germantown deterred any display of personal exuberance. So much had gone wrong, and now the entire advance seemed to be losing the cohesion that had been expected. Pickering, who only left Washington's side for the short time required to carry the admonishment to Sullivan, was unyielding in his opinion that Washington never left the post at the Billmeyer house until the retreat became general.[25]

During this period Howe was not waiting for the Americans to enter the heart of the village. Instead, he quickly formed plans for a counteroffensive. Knyphausen was to order the 15th and 37th regiments (from the 3rd and 4th brigades, respectively) to swing out of line, wheel right, cross Germantown Road and, there, file to the left of the 55th and 5th regiments. The four regiments were to form in line, inclined slightly to their right, and advance to form a junction with the 49th and 4th regiments, which were stationed on Limekiln Pike as a reserve for the 1st Light Infantry. Knyphausen ordered the remaining regiments of the 4th Brigade (33rd, 46th, and 64th regiments) to file obliquely to the right and clear out any Americans west of the main road. The 3rd Brigade was reduced to two regiments, the 17th and 44th. The former was ordered to march to the center of the road and drive straight north, while the latter, with Grey in personal command, formed to its right. The two Hessian battalions of Du Corps and Donop moved into position on the left of the 4th Brigade, leaving Minnigerode to support the chasseurs near the Schuylkill. As the 4th Brigade prepared to take its position in line, the men unaccountably halted and engaged in a hot firefight with an imaginary foe in their front. After having battled another apparition caused by the fog, they soon swung into line. On the far right, the foot guards and the 27th and 28th regiments moved out between Limekiln Pike and Old York Road and prepared to form on the right of the 4th Regiment.

The British, with their plan to advance in line, were subject to the same frustrations the Americans had faced. Heavy fog hung over the center of the village, preventing any cohesion between the various elements of the British army. Howe had intended for the thirteen British infantry regiments, two battalions of foot guards, and two Hessian battalions, or about six thousand eight hundred rank and file, to advance in line and sweep everything before them. Instead, gaps appeared in the line as brigades and regiments advanced independent of those on their flanks. Fortuitous circumstances saved the British from suffering severe reverses.[26]

While the battle along Germantown Road was developing, Greene was encountering unforeseen obstacles along Limekiln Pike. Expecting to sweep down the pike to Luken's Mill before meeting opposition, he discovered British vedettes soon after turning off Church Road — four miles short of his target at the mill.

Greene had been marching in column. Upon seeing the vedettes, he quickly formed his command in line, according to the prearranged battle plan. Yet he did not recognize that it was a mistake to form his command at that distance from the British position. In fact, it is doubtful if at that moment Greene had any idea of the British location. Unfamiliar with the topographical hazards of the area and handicapped by the fog, his soldiers stumbled through woods and marshes. Stopping occasionally to tear down or scale fences, they soon became disorganized. Any possibility of victory Greene might have had was lost in the first two miles of his march down Limekiln Pike.

On Greene's right, Stephen's division floundered helplessly in the fog-shrouded woods until his men became hopelessly lost. Stephen heard firing to the west and faltered momentarily to further endanger the American cause. Then Stephen headed southwest with his own brigade, while his other brigade (Woodford's) filed off in a more westerly direction. Stephen's division was thus separated for the remainder of the battle.

Woodford's brigade wandered through the woods toward the sound of the firing. The brigade emerged from the woods at the rear of Cliveden and joined Maxwell's attack on Musgrave's "fort." Finding that their small arms fire was ineffective against the stone house, they brought light cannon into play. This proved equally futile and considerable time was lost. Unsure of the location of Stephen or Greene, Woodford's brigade became immobilized for the remainder of the day.[27]

Meanwhile, Stephen was lost and entangled in underbrush and deep woods, uncertain whether he was near friend or foe. After a sudden movement in the mist, a sporadic gunfight developed with the unknown apparition. This chance meeting was with part of Wayne's division. Startled, Stephen's and Wayne's men began to withdraw, believing they had accidentally stumbled upon a part of the main British army. As a result of this unfortunate confrontation, other units of Washington's army were removed from the battle. Except for a few small detachments lost in the fog, their withdrawal left the area between Germantown Road and Limekiln Pike cleared of American troops.

Stephen was later charged with drunkenness and misconduct in the field and was subsequently cashiered. He, like all the American officers and men, was fatigued and utterly confused. The men were exhausted after a march averaging about fourteen miles and being engaged in a running fight. After the battle, most of them had to walk an additional twenty miles back to Pennypacker's Mills. Added to their physical discomfort was the tension of fighting under bad weather conditions. Many officers fell asleep on their horses. Washington issued rum as a stimulant to the men, and officers were also seen occasionally imbibing.

Towards the end of the battle, Greene, without Stephen, continued to drive ahead. McDougall kept pace on his left. Near Abington Road, Greene espied a British force drawn up across the road and extending into the adjacent woods. Pushing ahead, he quickly overwhelmed the British position.[28] Hastily withdrawing, the 1st Light Infantry passed through the advancing line of foot guards, the 49th, 4th, 27th, and 28th regiments. Greene's drive had gained such momentum that part of his division thus carried through the main British line. One regiment, the 9th Virginia, dashed all the way to the market house in the center of Germantown. Suddenly a series of incidents occurred in quick succession which forced Greene to make a precipitate withdrawal. Greene realized that he was outnumbered; that Smallwood had failed to come up on the British right; that his own right, without Stephen, was up in the air; and that with the appearance of Grant's artillery, he had no choice but to leave the field before disaster struck.[29]

With no choice but to retreat, Greene still saw virtually no possibility of bringing off the impetuous Virginians. Colonel George Matthews's 9th Virginia Regiment was busy plundering the huts in the British camp.[30] The soldiers, hungry and tired, were gorging themselves on the foodstuffs found in the huts when the British discovered them. A British officer in the detachment that captured the Virginians gave an eyewitness account:

My Company and the 42nd Light Company . . . separated in the Fog from the rest of the Battalion, were seeking for it when we observed a considerable Body twas it turned out to be the 9th Virginia Reg:t in our Rear and between us and our own Hutts. At first they were supposed to be our own people But on further examination proved to be Rebels who had contrived to get around us. It occured to me that their intention was to come in from the appearance of some of them coming forwards [to surrender]. I therefore called to them to throw down their arms but was soon undeceived by their beginning to fire. We made the best haste we could to them, drove them through and into our own Hutts & killed Col Sayer, Potter and most of them with our bayonets: It afterwards appeared that they had been [to the huts] before we fell in with them, in my Companys Wigwams & the 42d had taken out *our Bread* and divided it among themselves so certain they then were of carrying the Day.[31]

Few, if any, of Matthews's Virginians escaped, as they were surrounded and forced to surrender.

Sergeant Sullivan, of the 49th British Regiment, related an incident which may have involved elements of Wayne's division, and which contributed to their panic. In preparing the British right wing's counterattack, Grant sent the 49th, with four six-pounders, forward and to the left of the 4th Regiment. With the 4th slightly refused to the left of the 1st Light Infantry's original position at Limekiln Pike and Abington Road, the 49th was positioned near the modern streets of Haines and Washington Lane near Chew. Wayne's division had passed a short distance east of Cliveden and was thus on a direct collision course with the 49th, 55th, and 5th regiments advancing on the British right.

Sullivan said "they fell in with" a party of Americans who had surrounded three companies of the light infantry and made them prisoners. Observing the infantrymen's plight, the 49th immediately opened fire and drove the Americans back, freeing the prisoners, who picked up their arms and reentered the battle. Confronted by the 49th, with Stephen, coming through the impenetrable fog on their rear and left flank, some of Wayne's regiments panicked. Stephen made no mention of any engagement other than unexpectedly blundering into the path of Wayne's division with the resulting negligible gunfire. Surprise and fright were Stephen's most serious adversaries. [32]

Greene's withdrawal was orderly, retracing his route back over Church Road. Grant followed, apparently at a respectful distance, with two battalions of foot guards plus the 27th and 28th regiments. On his retreat, Greene rallied at several natural obstacles, and after several short firefights, he continued toward Whitemarsh Church (Saint Thomas) at Bethlehem Road. Pursued by the circumspect and overcautious Grant, he was able to bring off his command in relatively good order. [33]

Back along Germantown Road, Sullivan was suddenly conscious of increased activity on his front and left. Unknown to him, a force of over three thousand British was about to open a counteroffensive. Agnew, covered on his left by Du Corps and Donop's Hessians, advanced his 4th Brigade in line to drive the Americans out of the village west of the main road. Grey, with three regiments of the 3rd Brigade, covered Agnew's right. East of Grey were the 5th and 55th regiments of the 2nd Brigade driving north and clearing out any pockets of resistance. The impetus of the British drive carried all American positions and relieved Musgrave's beleaguered garrison at Cliveden. By this time the remnants of Sullivan's, Wayne's, and Stirling's divisions were in full flight north on the Germantown and Bethlehem roads.

Sullivan described the American dilemma during the waning minutes of the battle:

> My division, with a regiment of North Carolinians commanded by Colonel Armstrong, and assisted by part of Conway's brigade, having driven the enemy a mile and a half below Chew's house [Sullivan had a tendency to exaggerate distance — he was probably slightly over half a mile below Cliveden], and finding themselves unsupported by any other troops, their cartridges all expended, the force of the enemy on the right collecting to the left to oppose them [the British 3rd Brigade and the 5th and 55th regiments], being alarmed by the firing at Chew's house so far in their rear, and by the cry of a light-horseman on the right, that the enemy had got round us, and at the same time discovering some troops flying on our right, retired with as much precipitation as they had before advanced, against every effort of their officers to rally them.[34]

Early on the morning of 4 October, Captain von Munchhausen was riding toward Philadelphia, when, at about five-thirty, he heard cannonading to his rear. He hastened into the city and gave himself the credit for having alerted Cornwallis to the news of cannon fire at Germantown. Regardless of the source of Cornwallis's intelligence, the British commander reacted promptly, ordering two battalions of British grenadiers, one of Hessian grenadiers, and a squadron of light dragoons to move for Germantown. Cornwallis rode ahead and reached Germantown just as Grey was routing Sullivan. Assuming command of the advance, Cornwallis followed the Americans as far as Whitemarsh Church, where Grant's column joined him. As Howe expressed it, the grenadiers were "full of ardor . . . could not arrive in time to join in the action."[35]

To prevent Cornwallis from reinforcing Howe at Germantown, Washington sent General James Potter, with a thousand Pennsylvania militia, down the west side of the Schuylkill. Potter's men were to create a diversion at Middle Ferry, opposite the west end of Market Street (Philadelphia). While small arms fire and a cannon shot or two were exchanged between the militia and the British dragoons on the opposite bank, Cornwallis obviously was not deceived by this feint. Instead, he immediately sent three grenadier battalions to help Howe at Germantown.[36]

What happened to Smallwood and Armstrong, who had been

assigned the task of turning the British flanks? Had they succeeded, Howe would have been forced to divert several regiments to support his jägers on the left and the Queen's Rangers on the right. This would have weakened the British center and the counteroffensive against Greene and Sullivan. However, time, terrain, and their normal lack of resourcefulness defeated any chance Smallwood and Armstrong had of carrying out their objective. If this aspect of the strategy was important, why was it entrusted to the militia? Or did Washington contemplate little more than a holding action to divert a part of the British army, and thus to prevent any wide flanking movement by Howe? He rarely had sufficient confidence in the militia to commit them to important independent assignments.

Covering Greene's left flank, Smallwood, with his Maryland militia, accompanied by Foreman's New Jersey militia, accomplished nothing on Old York Road. After a minor skirmish with the Queen's Rangers, they beat a hasty retreat and joined other elements of the American army on the Skippack Road.

As Armstrong approached the defile near where the Wissahickon empties into the Schuylkill, he was spotted by one of the jäger patrols. Ewald, quickly withdrawing his men, reported to Wurmb, who immediately occupied the heights overlooking the Wissahickon gorge. Armstrong took position above the creek, and a brisk cannonade developed with the Hessians. The dismounted jägers and the militia descended to the bottom of the gorge, where a lively, but inconclusive, firefight developed.

Armstrong reportedly received a message about nine o'clock ordering him to report to Washington. Instantly he marched with the majority of his command, leaving a detachment with one field piece to conduct a holding action at the Wissahickon. No verification can be found of Armstrong's arrival at headquarters or of his forming a junction with Sullivan or Wayne. Although Armstrong later claimed that he sent reinforcements to the detachment left at the gorge, they never arrived.

Some evidence indicates that Washington may have ordered Armstrong to cover the vacuum created between Sullivan and the upper gorge of the creek. This unguarded area included extremely dense forests, sharp defiles, and the gorge with a steep escarpment exceeding two hundred feet in some places. Armstrong indicated that the terrain forced him to circle back so that, then filing to the left, he came out some three miles above Germantown.[37] Confronted by a superior force, he quickly broke contact and retreated in the direction of Washington's main army.

The focal point for all retreating elements of the American army was the junction of Skippack and Bethlehem roads. Without a pause except to leave some seriously wounded men at "the Episcopalian Church [Saint Thomas] as their hospital, at Flourtown" they streamed out of the Skippack Road.[38] It was believed that this church was a safe distance from the British pursuit.

Cornwallis, upon reaching Chestnut Hill, exchanged a few shots with the American rear guard and then proceeded out Bethlehem Road to Whitemarsh Church. Hale wrote that they pursued the Americans for eight miles, but only got close enough to fire a few shots. Parker remembered seeing a few Americans on the hill at "Sandy Run Church" [Saint Thomas] as the British were marching through Flourtown. Cornwallis's decision to call off the pursuit may have been based on his inability to bring the Americans to action.[39]

Accounts agree that battle fatigue and fear showed on the faces of the fleeing Americans. These observations agreed with the known panic and fatigue of Wayne's and Sullivan's divisions. Washington and Sullivan mentioned that their soldiers retreated with such precipitation that it was impossible to rally them. On Bethel Hill, young Supplee gathered with family and neighbors to watch the American army's return from Germantown: "In the afternoon the soldiers were seen coming up the Skippack Road in full retreat and were in a demoralized condition. At times they would travel slowly, seeming ready to give out; then a report would come that they were being pursued by the British, and they would again go on a full run." A different viewpoint was expressed by Thomas Paine, who said nobody hurried, everyone marched at his own pace, with the British keeping a respectful distance.[40]

By the evening of 4 October, Washington, again encamped at Pennypacker's Mills, was perplexed at what he had considered "the most promising appearances." He recalled the events of the day with an optimistic note: "Upon the whole it may be said the day was rather unfortunate than injurious. . . . The Enemy are nothing the better by the event; and our Troops, who are not in the least dispirited by it, have gained what all young Troops gain by being in Actions."[41]

Much has been written about the rashness of Washington's

strategy, the elaborate plan, and the impossibility of coordinating attacks by the various columns. Washington's plan undoubtedly would have taxed the abilities of the most veteran soldiers; in spite of the reverses, it did not depress the average American soldier. Throughout the battle, both commanders in chief consistently misjudged their opponent's strength. Washington understated the size of Howe's army, and Howe overestimated the American army. In retrospect, it appears unlikely Washington could have gained a victory with the force at his command. Washington, with only 8,000 Continentals, thought he was facing an equal number of British and Hessians. Rather, Howe had in excess of 10,000 rank and file in Germantown, and another 1,800 men coming from Philadelphia. The fog has been offered as a major factor in the American defeat, and undoubtedly it added to the uncertainty, confusion, and, later, panic. In spite of Washington's declaration that the men fled from victory, it is probable the fog was a mixed blessing, contributing to the surprise of the British outposts and, conversely, completing the disaster that befell Wayne's division.

American officers were unanimous in their belief that victory had been imminent. Thomas Rodney wrote his brother, "Had not Genl. Sulivans Division which began the attack in the centre pushed on with too much rapidity, Howe would have got a total overthrow he having Regulated his retreat & given notice to the friends of Government [Loyalists]as they call them to be ready to move [such an order by Howe is subject to doubt]." Then there was the optimism of Armstrong, who wrote, "Seldome was victory more nearly won, nor strangely lost."[42]

British casualties reported were 4 officers and 66 men killed, 30 officers and 396 men wounded, one officer and 13 men missing. Whereas the official report of Hessian casualties listed 24 wounded, Ewald claimed the jäger picket alone lost "three killed and eleven wounded, most of whom died from their severe wounds after several days." (The official British return lists 10 jägers wounded.) Among the slain British were General Agnew and Lieutenant Colonel John Bird.[43]

American casualties, reported by the Board of War, numbered 30 officers and 122 men killed, 117 officers and 404 men wounded, and about 400 prisoners. Included among the slain was General Nash of Stirling's division.

The day after the battle, Howe sent patrols throughout the

woods in front of the British positions to search for American arms. The men were to deliver any such equipment to the artillery park, where they were to be paid for it, agreeable to army regulations.

Montresor recorded an epilogue to the battle: ''During the action of this day, the countenances and actions of many of the Inhabitants of Philadelphia were rather rebellious and seem to indicate their wish for the rebels to regain the city.''[44]

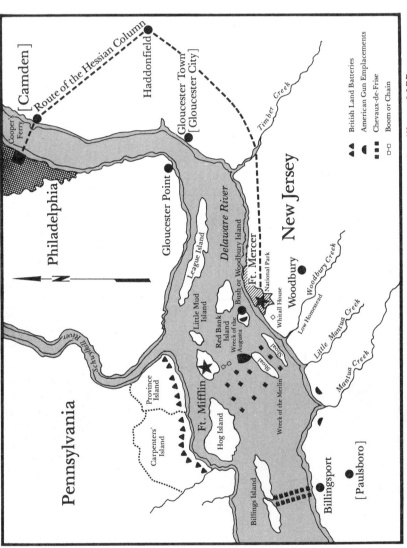

Operations on the Delaware (October and November 1777), John B. Squillace, 1977

CHAPTER IV

HOWE SEVERS
THE GORDIAN KNOT

WHILE CORNWALLIS WAS absorbed with the problems of a garrison city, Howe, in Germantown, directed his attention to reducing American defenses on the Delaware.

With the Schuylkill and Delaware on all sides of Philadelphia, except the northern perimeter, a new defense line, when completed, would make the city a veritable island. It was Howe's self-imposed prison for himself and for nearly fifty thousand civilian and military personnel. To insure adequate provisions and supplies for so many people, Howe recognized the need for the Delaware River to be opened to British shipping before the river froze over, as usually happened.[1]

Colonel Stirling had occupied and razed the redoubt at Billingsport, but by neglecting to march north and take Fort Mercer, he had missed an excellent opportunity in early October to bring about the fall of all river defenses. Unfortunately, his orders had been to leave Billingsport, return to Chester, and escort a provision train to the main army at Germantown. Montresor questioned the need to retain a garrison at Wilmington; he thought those troops could have joined Stirling and easily conquered the east bank of the river, including Fort Mercer. After the disastrous repulse of the Hessians on 22 October, another British officer commented, ''The detachment that destroyed Billins fort (if they had the orders for it) might have taken red bank, without loosing one man.''[2]

At his inquiry in 1779, Howe made certain puzzling statements in rebuttal to those who questioned his delaying tactics in capturing

the river forts. On the defensive, he made the specious observation
that if he had taken Fort Mifflin before the Americans had readied it
for defense, it would have been difficult to supply the garrison. He
added that his men would have been exposed to the galleys and floating batteries, with the army helpless to support them. Then, apparently confused in his dates, he said the heavy rains which flooded
the trenches and sapped the foundation of the gun emplacements
prevented an early capture of the fort.[3]

Adding yet another dimension to the question of why the forts
were not attacked earlier was a development that occurred in mid-
October. Howe was subject to criticism within his military family
because he had retained headquarters in Germantown, and had not
moved to Philadelphia and assumed direct command of reducing the
American defenses. Either aware of this stricture or impatient for
results, on 16 October, he summoned Cornwallis, General Samuel
Cleaveland, and Montresor to his Germantown headquarters. He admonished his officers, stating that three weeks had elapsed with no
progress. This remark rankled Montresor, who recorded rather
petulantly that perhaps this was because the commander in chief was
in Germantown instead of directing the campaign from Philadelphia.[4]

The American defenses along the Delaware could hope to accomplish little more than delay the overpowering might of the British
army and navy. Fort Mifflin, on Mud or Fort Island, was situated between 500 and 600 yards off the Pennsylvania shore. It was designed
primarily for river defense. East and south ramparts were constructed
of stone; the west and north walls were wooden palisades. Wooden
blockhouses stood at all corners except the southeastern salient,
which faced the river. Although the fort was well designed for river
defense, the land approaches were particularly vulnerable to heavy
artillery. Fort Mercer, across the river on the New Jersey shore, was a
large earthen fortification with eight- and nine-foot parapets. It had
been the ambitious undertaking of Colonel John Bull of the Pennsylvania militia. Too large for any force available to garrison, the fort
was later reduced to accommodate two regiments of Continentals.

To protect the approaches to the land fortifications, the
Americans sank chevaux-de-frise, large hopperlike frames, into the
river. These frames were customarily thirty feet square and thirteen to
twenty-four feet high — the height depending on the depth of the
river where they were to be placed. Sunk at designated spots, usually

sixty feet from center to center, they were temporarily weighted down with iron anchors. They were constructed of huge timbers with the bottom, or seat, floored with two-inch pine plank, and the sides framed with sturdy logs and lined with rough pine planks. A perfect receptacle for twenty or more tons of stone, the frames were floated down the Schuylkill in barges. Two or three heavy, wooden, iron-

Deshler-Morris House. Sir William Howe's headquarters for two weeks after the Battle of Germantown. Official residence of President George Washington during the yellow fever epidemic of 1793. *Independence National Historical Park Collection*

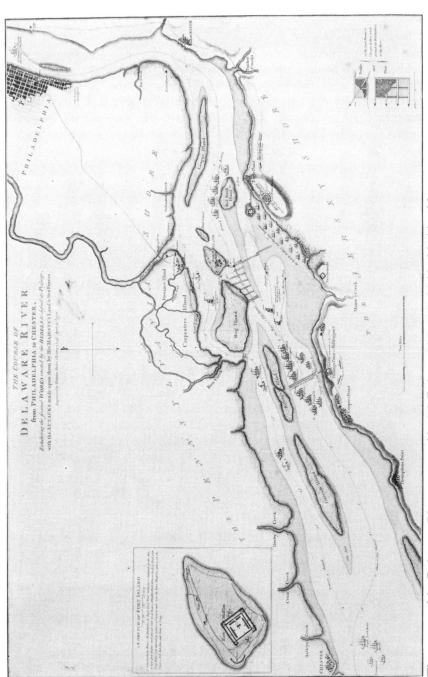

The course of the Delaware River, engraved by W. Faden, 1778. *Philadelphia Maritime Museum*

tipped spears pointing downstream were affixed obliquely on the frames; at low tide each spearpoint was about six feet below the water. The frames were interlocked with heavy iron chains to impede their removal. By September, two rows of chevaux-de-frise had been sunk opposite Billingsport, and three or four irregular rows were installed below Fort Mifflin at different locations in the river.

Several small and indefensible land batteries, or redoubts, had been erected at Billingsport, the mouth of Darby Creek, Bush (or Woodbury) Island, and near the mouth of Mantua Creek, but all were abandoned by early October except that at Billingsport.

The need to maintain adequate garrisons in the river forts, especially at Fort Mifflin, was self-evident to Washington and the Pennsylvania authorities. In the past, Washington had been unwilling to weaken the main army by sending troops to defend the river passes. In mid-September he had asserted that if the Continental army was destroyed, there would be no need to retain control of the Delaware. However, upon realizing the river's importance to the British, he importuned the Assembly and Hazelwood to furnish men for Fort Mifflin, with an added request that the commodore station a cordon of galleys around the island.

In spite of his protestations, Washington decided to place the defense of the river in Continental hands. His confidence in the militia had not been enhanced by Pennsylvania's delaying tactics. During the third week of September, he dispatched a detachment of Continental troops under Colonel "Baron" Heinrich d'Arendt to Fort Mifflin. Because of the temporary indisposition of d'Arendt, Lieutenant Colonel Samuel Smith assumed command at the fort.

Inexplicably, Washington had not sent troops to Fort Mercer, the left anchor of the defense chain. Mercer was the supply point for Fort Mifflin, and without this base the latter fort would have to be evacuated or would capitulate within one week. After the battle at Germantown, Washington finally rectified this situation. He welcomed news that General James Varnum's brigade had reached Coryell's Ferry. Orders were sent to Varnum instructing Colonels Christopher Greene and Israel Angell, with their Rhode Island regiments, to march to Fort Mercer. Later, Varnum, with the balance of his brigade, was sent to Woodbury to establish headquarters for the river defense and to cooperate with the naval command.

Near the Pennsylvania shore were two low marshy islands, Province and Carpenters'. These islands were intersected by narrow creeks. Levees, or dikes on the river side protected the rich meadows during periods of high water. Farmers used the meadows to graze their livestock. As the British army neared Philadelphia, Washington ordered the dikes cut in order to flood the area. Farmers had built several small dams further back along the waterways, and contrary to orders, they were not opened at this time. Through some misunderstanding, the American commander was not advised that several elevations would remain above water, making them suitable for the erection of redoubts and batteries.

Belatedly, the Americans arrived at a reasonable defensive posture, closing the river to British ships for nearly seven weeks. From the British viewpoint, it was almost disastrous, aggravating the need of provisions and supplies for the city.

Two British officers were designated as the principal architects to devise methods to destroy the American defenses. Hamond, on the frigate *Roebuck,* with his knowledge of the river volunteered to breach the chevaux-de-frise once Billingsport had been conquered. If successful, this breach would permit the larger men-of-war to move upstream and join the attack on the forts and against the small Pennsylvania navy. Captain John Montresor, chief engineer, was ordered to construct the land fortifications and batteries needed for the city's defense and the reduction of Fort Mifflin.

At the beginning of October, Cornwallis, accompanied by General Archibald Robertson, personally reconnoitered the area around the mouth of the Schuylkill and its adjacent islands. Upon returning to his headquarters in the city, Cornwallis, as instructed by Howe, directed Montresor to devote his full attention to the construction of batteries to operate against Fort Mifflin and to protect the mouth of the Schuylkill from incursions by the Pennsylvania galleys.

Montresor knew that the pest house (quarantine station) on Province Island had been converted by the Americans into a hospital and that it was guarded by a small detachment of militia. To make a preliminary survey of the islands and to determine the distance from the east bank of the Schuylkill to the British fleet and the American forts, he decided on a night excursion. On the evening of 3 October, two skiffs were brought to the Schuylkill Ferry to convey Montresor, Captain James Moncrieff, two additional officers, and a detachment of twenty grenadiers to Province Island. To his embarrassment, Montresor found that the skiffs could only accommodate Moncrieff, nine grenadiers, and himself. Upon crossing the river, they discovered that the Americans had already removed their wounded and evacuated the island. Unseen by the Americans at Fort Mifflin, the British party sloshed through the marshy islands and located sites where batteries and redoubts should be constructed.[5]

Hamond, with the *Roebuck, Pearl, Camilla,* and *Liverpool,* was lying in the roadstead off Chester, patiently awaiting the arrival of Lord Howe and the British fleet. With the fall of Billingsport, Hamond took soundings of the river and made plans to remove or cant the frames of the lower chevaux-de-frise. He consistently overrated the effectiveness of the American galleys and other boats of the little navy. In a somewhat subtle attempt to eliminate the wasplike harassment of these boats, he sent a flag with a message to Hazelwood offering amnesty to the officers and sailors of the fleet. Hazelwood advised Washington that Hamond proposed the American surrender the fleet without permitting any damage to the boats and warned that it would soon be impossible to hold out against the overwhelming might of the British navy. As no avenue of retreat was open, he suggested that Hazelwood accept this offer of the king's pardon and freedom. With a spirit of bravado, Hazelwood said he recognized the "valour and bravery" of the British navy and army, but he intended to fight and offer a glorious defense. In addition, Hazelwood explained that he did not wish to receive any more such proposals. Hamond made no mention of this incident; however, his autobiographical writings are strangely silent on his efforts to remove the river obstructions.[6]

In early October, the main elements of the British fleet arrived in the Delaware and anchored between Newcastle and Reedy Island. On the sixth, Lord Howe boarded the tender of his flagship, *Eagle,* and sailed up river to Chester to consult with Hamond.

After Hazelwood's rebuff, Hamond moved the *Roebuck* into position near the first row of chevaux-de-frise and, with auxiliary raft, began the arduous task of removing the first frame. Hazelwood, equally determined to prevent a breakthrough, returned daily to cannonade the British ships and create any annoyance that would frustrate Hamond. On at least two occasions, he was joined by chains of fire rafts, which were taken by British tenders, towed ashore, and destroyed.

Hamond removed one frame on 12 October and breached the second row five or six days later. On 20 October, the first ships, the *Liverpool* and the *Pearl,* warped through the lower obstructions. Hamond undoubtedly would have led the way with the *Roebuck,* but he ran aground on the twentieth, as did the *Augusta* and the *Isis.*[7]

Hazelwood faced a dilemma. Beset by desertions and short of

ammunition, he was suddenly confronted with the necessity of splitting his little flotilla of thirteen galleys. The British had made progress in building their batteries on Carpenters' Island. At Fort Mifflin, Lieutenant Colonel Smith demanded that Hazelwood give assistance in that quarter.

Although his night survey of Province and Carpenters' islands had not been completely satisfactory, Montresor realized that the erection of gun emplacements and redoubts would be fraught with hardship. At night, to escape detection, his men would have to work in waist-deep water and be subject to steady cannon fire from American galleys and Fort Mifflin. As work progressed, conditions became increasingly unhealthy, and men had to be relieved daily. A few civilians were employed, but deteriorating conditions soon made it necessary to use only soldiers. By 18 October, water on the island was so high that it flowed over the completed gun platforms. Small boats passed over the flooded meadows between the dikes and elevated areas. In addition, as a result of the American bombardment, the dikes were porous, and Montresor notified Howe that no significant progress could be made until they were repaired. Still, nothing was done until the problem was brought to the attention of Cornwallis, who immediately made arrangements for the necessary repairs. However, almost a month of valuable time had been lost, and the cuts in the dikes were found to be twice their original size.[8]

The first battery of two medium twelve-pounders was constructed on the Philadelphia side of the Schuylkill. Work on a battery of two iron eighteen-pounders began near the pest house on Province Island. Two small batteries, each with one eight-inch howitzer and one eight-inch mortar, were built on the Carpenters' Island dike opposite Fort Mifflin. On 10 October, the first battery on the dike was finished. At 9:30 A.M. on the eleventh, Hazelwood ordered three galleys and a floating battery to attack the British battery. After a two-hour bombardment, Captain Vatass (or Vatap) of the British 10th Regiment, surrendered his detachment of 100 grenadiers. In landing men to secure the prisoners, the Americans discovered fifty Hessians, commanded by Captain Moncrieff, advancing across the meadow. Smith, in an effort to intercept the Hessians, opened fire from the northwest blockhouse at Fort Mifflin. Shooting over the heads of the landing party, Smith threw the Americans into confusion and some of the prisoners escaped. However, one lieutenant, one ensign, and fifty-six privates were taken off in the galleys.[9]

Hazelwood returned the next morning to renew the attack on the dike battery. After a heavy cannonade, he landed a party to storm the battery. Taking cover in back of trees and bushes beneath the dike, they exchanged a brisk musket fire for three-quarters of an hour. Espying another British detachment marching across the marsh to outflank them, the Americans hastily withdrew to the boats. Losses were light on both sides, but the Continentals impressed the British with their tenacity and determination to carry the fight.

By mid-October, the British had made progress in removing the chevaux-de-frise and erecting batteries on Province and Carpenters' islands. Even so, Howe expressed dissatisfaction with the headway; others believed the responsibility could be directly tracted to Howe's remaining in Germantown instead of personally directing the river campaign. Regardless of whether Howe was aware of the criticism, he decided to move the army to Philadelphia, and on 18 October issued marching instructions to all brigades and battalions to move the next day. More than likely he was acting in accordance with his plan to make the city his winter headquarters and realized the army must be safely ensconced in their quarters before cold weather set in. On the other hand, unhappy with the progress of his subordinates, he may have finally realized that he should personally direct operations.

Concurrent with his move to the city, Howe's ultraconservative nature emerged. Still believing that he needed a larger force to defeat Washington, he ordered Clinton to immediately forward 4,500 reinforcements.[10] On 30 October, Clinton reluctantly embarked the 17th Dragoons, 7th, 26th, and 63rd regiments, with all the convalescents of the battalions and brigades then with Howe as well as the recently arrived recruits from Europe, about four thousand rank and file. Major General Sir Thomas Wilson with Brigadier Generals Alexander Leslie and James Pattison commanded the contingent, and arrived in the upper Delaware Bay between 3 and 5 November.[11]

Another problem besetting Howe was an apparent scarcity of money. Montresor rather petulantly recorded that he had to advance "thirty guineas out of my own pocket" to civilians working on the city's defenses and that he "lent out of my private purse to Elias Smith, Master Carpenter Fifty 1/2 Johannes on account of the work now carrying on at Philadelphia." Over fifteen years after the war Montresor was still embroiled in a dispute with the Auditor's Office in London over his expenditures at Philadelphia. They were inclined to disallow a claim for £26,459 11s. 5-1/2d., all, with the exception of

L645 spent in New York, for the fortifications at Philadelphia. Included in the claim was the amount he had advanced to Smith.

Howe was always punctilious in his orders that all inhabitants, regardless of their political sympathies, were to be paid for every item taken by the army. Two days before the army left Germantown, John Miller said the British appropriated and appraised all horses in the village and its environs, but only Loyalists were paid. He admitted that Sir William Erskine permitted him to keep his horse. Refusing payment to those suspected of American sympathies was either in violation of Howe's orders or a further indication of a cash shortage. On 26 October, Howe wrote to Gordon and Crowder, Agents for Supplying Money to His Majesty's Forces in North America, stating that the current and anticipated expenses of his command would be "Three Hundred Thousand Pounds Sterling." This figure included expenses for the garrisons at New York and at Newport, Rhode Island.[12]

Cornwallis and Montresor were fearful that winter might arrive before the river could be opened. In searching for an alternate route to bring provisions to the city, Montresor decided on a combination of small Bow Creek and a connecting road to be built — passing near the Blakely house — to the Schuylkill. There a floating bridge would be constructed. Flatboats coming up from the fleet entered Bow Creek and then transferred their contents to wagons. The wagons proceeded up the road, crossed the bridge, and entered the city. Their cargoes comprised only a dribble of the provisions and supplies needed for the army and thousands of civilians. On dark nights a few flatboats passed up the back channel between the islands and the fort. Flatboat crews were afraid to run the channel gauntlet. Ewald said that on one provision flotilla he saw arrive the sailors had been plied with so much rum, to stimulate their courage in case of attack, that they were "completely drunk."[13]

At this same time, rumors filtered through crowded, smoke-filled rooms of taverns and clubs that Burgoyne had suffered a disastrous defeat at Saratoga. Officers and Loyalists bore a look of stunned disbelief. They were incredulous at a defeat of such magnitude being dealt to a royal army. The rumors were soon confirmed. However, the immediate crisis confronting the army in Philadelphia left little time to dwell on the tragedy that had befallen their comrades to the north. Unless American river defenses were breached so that supply ships could reach the city's wharves before winter set in, Howe's men would face a catastrophe of their own.

After establishing his headquarters in Philadelphia, Howe began immediate preparations to step up the British offensive. He had been advised that the first men-of-war would warp through the lower chevaux-de-frise on 20 or 21 October and would then approach the upper obstructions below the forts. Howe's plan called for an assault on Fort Mercer while the fleet bombarded both forts. In addition, British grenadiers would cross the back channel from Province Island and storm the palisaded parapets of Fort Mifflin. They would be supported by the *Vigilant,* mounting sixteen twenty-four-pounders and capable, under favorable circumstances, of coming up the back channel.[14]

Colonel Donop requested, and was granted, command of the force to attack Fort Mercer. He was given three Hessian grenadier battalions under Minnigerode, Linsing and Lengerke, Mirbach's Hessian infantry regiment, jägers under Wurmb — except for a small mounted patrol left in Philadelphia, the battalion guns, and two Royal English howitzers commanded by Captain Downman. He was assigned Major Charles Stuart as aide and interpreter.[15]

Crossing the river on 21 October, Donop marched to Haddonfield and camped for the night. Ewald, with a jäger detachment, acted as rearguard and skirmished with New Jersey militia. Donop believed that by taking a circuitous route he could conceal his objective. On 22 October he left the village at 4:00 A.M., and, accompanied by two local guides, arrived within a mile of the fort near noon. Then, dividing his column, Donop sent the Linsing and Mirbach commands over a country road to the left (closely parallel to modern Hessian Avenue in National Park, New Jersey). Captain Stamford and Lieutenant Schieck were in command of Linsing's battalion and Mirbach's regiment, respectively. Although indisposed, Linsing was with the expedition, apparently attached to Donop's staff, as he later commanded the retreat. Donop, with the balance of the column, filed to the right and established a position on the fringe of the woods northeast of the fort.

Minigerode was to assault the northern perimeter of the fort, while Lengerke and the jägers would act as a reserve and guard the gun emplacement from a foray by the crews of the American galleys.

Fort Mercer was commanded by Colonel Christopher Greene, who was assisted by Colonel Israel Angell and a French engineer officer, the Chevalier Plessis du Mauduit. The garrison included the Rhode Island regiments of Greene and Angell and a company of artillery — about five hundred rank and file. New Jersey militia were in the vicinity, but as the fort could not accommodate them, they were ordered to move and hover on the flanks of the invader. When the fort was first occupied, it became obvious to Greene and du Mauduit that it was too large for the available men and ordnance to defend. Du Mauduit was instructed to contract the works to a defensible size. Working night and day, he converted the southern section into a redoubt with nine-foot parapets, ditched and fraised. A thick abatis was placed around the fort except on the river side, where a steep escarpment and the galleys protected the garrison.

Donop took over four hours in preparing for the attack. With a number of officers, he reconnoitered the area to determine the strength of the fort. Some of the officers considered the affair little more than a dress parade while other Hessian officers were apprehensive at what they saw, believing the fort impregnable if resolutely defended. They had misgivings that the nine-foot walls could be scaled without scaling ladders, and they believed their cannon were incapable of breaching the walls. They also had no saws or axes to cut their way through the abatis. Disaster seemed inevitable. Donop, a brave soldier, permitted his emotions to dominate his judgment and ordered an attack on the fort. Conscious of the opprobrium placed on his command after the debacle at Trenton the previous Christmas, he was determined to vindicate his honor and the bravery of the Hessian soldier.[16]

Each battalion was instructed to make 100 fascines (bundles of small tree branches tied together). They were to be piled in the ditch around the fort by soldiers preceding the advancing troops. If properly placed, they could be useful in an attempt to scale the walls. An emplacement for the artillery, consisting of the eight battalion guns (small three-pounders), two six-pounders, and two howitzers, was started on the edge of the woods. To the right of the artillery and near the landing, Donop stationed Lengerke's grenadiers. The jäger corps, except for Ewald and sixteen marksmen, were further to the rear as a reserve.[17]

Apparently moderately satisfied with his arrangements, Donop decided to send a flag to Greene demanding his surrender. Stuart was asked to carry the flag. Greene summarily rejected the demands, defying the Hessians by stating he would defend to the ''last extremity.'' Stuart told General Archibald Robertson that Donop recognized the impropriety of attacking the fort without heavier cannon. According to Robertson, Donop agreed to delay the attack if the young Englishman considered it advisable. Stuart answered that he was too young and did not have the authority. Donop recalled Howe's admonishment that the attack was to be made unless a good reason existed for not doing so.[18] Another Hessian report stated Donop made another summons upon his arrival before the fort.

After an ineffectual cannonade by his light artillery and with little daylight remaining, Donop ordered a general attack. But, unfortunately for his hope of success, the attack was not coordinated. Ewald's marksmen were advanced and instructed to shoot at any object that appeared above the parapet. Stamford, with Linsing's grenadiers, was ordered to open the attack from the south and southeast. Minnigerode's grenadiers advanced and began to scale the wall of the abandoned northern section of the fort. The latter, surprised at no opposition, used the fascines and each others' shoulders to climb over to the open parade, where they mistook the absence of resistance for an easy victory. Huzzahing and streaming across the ground, they quickly arrived at the abatis and found themselves unable to advance. Tearing at the pointed peach tree limbs with their bare hands, they finally opened several holes in the abatis. Puzzled by the lack of any opposition, the Hessians poured through the abatis and neared the new parapet of the fort. Suddenly the entire fort was ablaze with grapeshot, musket, and cannon fire. Without warning, the Hessians found their left flank enfiladed by musket fire. A part of the wall of the abandoned section had been converted into a screened salient, or curtain, which permitted the Americans to trap anyone who penetrated the abatis in a deadly cross fire. Panic-stricken, the Hessians fell in rows; a few attempted, unsuccessfully, to scale the parapet. In the meantime, Schieck, with Mirbach's infantrymen, entered the old section from the east, merged with the frightened grenadiers, and met a similar fate. As enthusiastically as they had stormed the abatis, the grenadiers and infantrymen now fled in terror back over the wall to the cover of their reserve.

Hessians attacking from the north were unaware that Linsing's grenadiers had been repulsed and, having suffered heavy losses, were in full retreat. When Stamford attacked on the southwest, Americans on the banquette[19] of the north parapet stood and fired across their kneeling comrades on the south wall. With Linsing's grenadiers in headlong flight, the Americans reversed the operation against Minnigerode's grenadiers and Mirbach's infantrymen. By not attacking all faces of the fort simultaneously, Donop exposed each separate attack to the devastating fire of almost the entire garrison and was defeated in detail.

The action lasted slightly less than three-quarters of an hour. As scattered remnants of the shattered Hessian battalions fled toward the protection of Lengerke and the jägers, Linsing assumed command. He ordered the grenadiers and jägers not previously engaged to form and protect the retreat. As no one had considered defeat, no wagons were available to transport the wounded. Ewald recorded that the seriously wounded officers were carried on the guns, gun carriages, or horses. [20]

Citizens of the area, who had marvelled at the Hessians' self-assurance and poise on the previous day, were shocked by their wild appearance on the retreat. [21] After resting in Haddonfield overnight, the Hessians recrossed the river the next morning.

As darkness had descended, the Americans made no effort to pursue the fleeing Hessians. Fearing a trap if the Hessians merely retired to regroup and then renew the attack, nobody left the fort. Du Mauduit and Major Simeon Thayer finally ventured out to review the damage to the fort and found the Hessians gone. They also found the Hessian commander, Donop, who had been seriously wounded. Although given every possible care by American surgeons and a visiting Hessian doctor, the luckless officer succumbed to his wounds three days after the attack. In addition to the wounded officers, they also found twenty Hessian soldiers in the ditch under the berm of the fort.

The Hessian casualties were tremendous. Knyphausen's official report stated 377 killed and wounded. Losses among officers were extremely high. In addition to Donop, Schieck, commanding Mirbach's infantry regiment was killed, and Stamford of Linsing's grenadiers was severely wounded. American losses were relatively light; Samuel Ward of Greene's staff notified Washington that 14 were killed, 23 were wounded and one was missing. [22]

In Philadelphia, a frustrated and disillusioned Howe, after prolonged consideration, arrived at a traumatic decision. Writing to Germain on 22 October, he requested leave to return to England:

From the little attention, my Lord, given to my recommendations since the commencement of my command, I am led to hope that I may be relieved from this very painful service, wherein I have not the good fortune to enjoy the necessary confidence and support of my superiors. . . . I humbly request I may receive his Majesty's permission to resign the command. [23]

On the Delaware, Lord Howe could only bring a part of his fleet into the engagement. The chevaux-de-frise and the river's natural

Lord Richard Howe, Commander of the British fleet on the American station. Painting by P. Mequignon, engraved by Robert Laurie, 1794. *Philadelphia Maritime Museum*

obstructions made it hazardous to maneuver more than a small flotilla in the limited available open waters. Lord Howe, Hamond, and Senior Captain Francis Reynolds, of the sixty-four-gun ship *Augusta,* were in constant fear of running the men-of-war aground on the sandbars or the chevaux-de-frise. Since the removal of the lower obstructions, this had been a daily occurrence.

Lord Howe's command on the American station was divided. Three or four men-of-war originally assigned to Howe were with Admiral John Byron in English waters, and a few frigates were on detached service.[24] To cooperate with the army, his plan included stationing the frigate *Camilla* and the sloop *Zebra* in the back channel to prevent surprise night raids by the Pennsylvania galleys on the defenseless transports and to protect the flatboats carrying supplies to the city. In the eventual attack against Fort Mifflin's weak side, he intended to use the *Vigilant* and *Fury.*

The main channel of the river would be the principal theatre of naval operations, with Reynolds of the *Augusta* in command of the squadron. At dusk on 22 October, Reynolds maneuvered the *Augusta,* the *Roebuck,* the *Pearl,* the *Liverpool,* the *Merlin,* and the *Cornwallis* into position above the lower obstructions. The first men-of-war through engaged in sporadic gunfire with the galleys. By 6:00 P.M., Reynolds was in position to bring his entire flotilla into action and immediately opened up with a crescendo of broadsides. The cannonade with the galleys and floating batteries continued for nearly two hours.

Between the flotilla and the New Jersey shore were two sandbanks, or shoals, separated by a narrow and shallow channel. Reynolds sent the *Merlin* and the *Cornwallis* up this channel to prevent the galleys from dropping down and coming in on the flank of the larger men-of-war in the main channel.

Fresh winds coming out of the northeast made it difficult for Reynolds to warp into position. The logbooks of the British frigates and British journals, especially Hamond's, commented on the heavy and effective fire of the American galleys and floating batteries. No reference is made to any involvement of the British fleet with Fort Mifflin on the twenty-second. Lord Howe wrote that Reynolds's participation in the action was intended to forestall Hazelwood's going to the assistance of Fort Mercer. ''The diversion was endeavoured to be continued by the frigates, at which the fire from the enemy's gallies were chiefly pointed for some time. But as the night advanced, the Hessian detachment having been repulsed, the firing ceased.''[25]

As darkness settled over the river and the firing ceased at Fort

Mercer, Reynolds ordered the ships to withdraw below the lower chevaux-de-frise. The night hindered the endeavor to slip downstream, and the *Augusta* and the *Merlin* went aground. During the night an unsuccessful attempt was made to refloat the ships. Hazelwood, who had been forced to withdraw his galleys and floating batteries in order to replenish their exhausted ammunition racks, therefore did not know of the *Augusta's* and *Merlin's* plight.

At about 6:00 A.M. on the twenty-third, the *Roebuck*, the *Liverpool*, the *Pearl*, and the *Cornwallis* passed through the lower obstructions and moved upstream in a last and futile attempt to refloat the stranded ships. The *Roebuck* threw a stream cable to the *Augusta*, but to no avail.

Hazelwood, soon alerted to the British dilemma, brought his galleys and floating batteries into action. He directed an unmerciful cannon fire on the *Augusta*, in which he was joined by the cannon at Fort Mifflin, and also inflicted severe damage on the ships that had come to aid the sixty-four gun ship. The British sent empty transports to lighten the *Augusta*, hoping this would permit the *Roebuck* to pull her off the sandbar. As this action was unsuccessful, all efforts were soon directed to saving the ship's company. Hamond declared that they were making headway in ''getting her afloat, when she took fire, and in ten minutes the Flames had reached the Mast Head.'' The men-of-war engaged with the galleys immediately broke off their firing, concentrating instead on rescuing the crew. More than half the ship's crew had been rescued from the water when Hamond observed the fire had spread so fast that it became impossible to help those who were unable to leap into the water. All of the seriously ill and wounded died on board ship. Men on the *Roebuck's* barge succeeded in pulling Reynolds out of the water. Hamond admitted the heavy fire of the galleys hampered all rescue efforts. [26]

Hazelwood called four fire ships into action, but, as usual, they were of little use. On the other hand, eyewitness accounts attest to the destructive fire of the galleys. Although Lord Howe contended that the Americans remained at such a distance as only to score a random hit, this statement is manifestly inconsistent with Hazelwood's normal use of the galleys, inasmuch as their most effective range was within half a mile of their target. Another rebuttal of Howe's assertion was the extensive damage suffered by some British ships. The *Roebuck* engaged the galleys all morning and, after being hulled several times, reported six killed and ten wounded.

About noon the *Augusta* suddenly blew up, taking, according to

Blowing up of the frigate *Augusta*. Artist unknown. *Historical Society of Pennsylvania*

Montresor, more than sixty men to a watery grave. Shortly after noon the *Isis* warped the lower chevaux-de-frise and joined the engagement which continued, with a sporadic exchange of cannon fire, for nearly three hours. On Lord Howe's orders, the *Merlin* was set on fire soon after the destruction of the *Augusta* to prevent her falling into American hands. At 3:00 P.M. the *Merlin* was consumed by an explosion. Shortly thereafter, the engagement was broken off by both sides.

The destruction of the *Augusta* and the *Merlin* reverberated across the countryside like a series of earthquakes. John Miller, in Germantown, had listened to the heavy cannonading on the river when "10 Minutes past 12 a Violent Shock that shook the Earth & about 20 Minutes after Another Shock not quite so Violent." Hugh Smyth, the Continental postmaster, wrote, "The shock was felt at camp; several windows were exploded . . . Headquarters are 16 miles from Philadelphia on the old York Road." J. P. Norris described the "Shock similar to that of an Earthquake." Thomas Paine wrote Benjamin Franklin that while traveling between Germantown and Whitemarsh, "we were stunned with a report as loud as a peal of a hundred cannon at once . . . saw a thick smoke rising like a pillar and spreading from the top like a tree."[27]

While jubilation naturally reigned in the American camp, Washington exhibited caution. With tongue in cheek, he advised Congress that he hoped the defeat would act as a deterrent to any future attempts to breach the river fortifications. While disappointment was evident among the British, they were more resolute than ever to open the river passages. Sir William Howe best expressed the British attitude: "These disappointments however will not prevent the most vigorous measures being pursued for the reduction of the fort, which will give us the passage up the river."[28] The need to open the river to British shipping before winter set in was obvious to both Washington and Howe.

There was much hustle and bustle at British headquarters. With time at a premium, preparations were being made quickly to reduce the American defenses. Although Fort Mifflin was the first objective, Fort Mercer and the opening of the river passage were of equal importance. Montresor hurried to complete all batteries and redoubts on Carpenters' and Province islands. As each battery was completed, it immediately played its cannon on the fort. Unfortunately for the British cannoneers, their ammunition supply was limited, and instead of a steady bombardment, they were forced to concentrate on a well-directed, but sporadic, cannon fire. The British hoped that constant pressure would weaken the morale of the American garrison, as well as destroy the wooden blockhouses and the weak west wall of the palisades.

Developing a multipronged offensive, Howe directed his brother to widen the breach in the chevaux-de-frise and be ready to move his fleet into position to support a land assault on Fort Mifflin. Cornwallis was commanded to prepare an expeditionary force to cross the river to Billingsport. There he would be joined by General Wilson and the reinforcements momentarily expected in Delaware Bay. Their combined command was to march overland to invest Fort Mercer. This time Cornwallis and Wilson, unlike Donop, would be furnished all the necessary tools of war and heavy artillery needed to breach the walls of the fort.

In the meantime, at Fort Mifflin Smith had received the assistance of Major Francois Louis de Fleury, a French engineer officer who was recognized for his expertise on military fortifications. De Fleury worked under extremely adverse conditions during the ensuing daily cannonade. The western bastions of the fort were either destroyed or leveled, the American cannon were rendered useless, and, during daylight hours the garrison was forced to seek shelter under the southern rampart, where they were safe from everything except a lucky or random shot. The fort was reduced to shambles. De Fleury, working almost exclusively at night to repair the damage, found his task increasingly disheartening and dangerous to accomplish. The physical and psychological effect these conditions wrought on the garrison forced Smith, and later Varnum, to relieve the men every night. On a rare occasion they were compelled to serve for forty-eight hours.

Varnum, with the balance of his brigade, was ordered to the area in early November to assume command of the land defenses. Accompanying Varnum were over a hundred Continental soldiers who possessed maritime experience; they were to join Hazelwood and serve on the galleys. Arriving at Fort Mercer on 2 November, Varnum set up headquarters at Woodbury. The men with him who were destined for the galleys reported to the commodore. Thus the small brigade of New England Continentals and the Pennsylvania navy galleymen were ready for a British attack — at least as prepared as their deficiencies would permit.

In the meantime, across the river on Carpenters' and Province islands, Montresor was proceeding apace to complete his gun emplacements. Unfortunately, storms set in on 24 October and continued with little abatement until the thirty-first. Beset by gale-force winds and heavy rains, all works were soon inundated. Struggling knee-deep in water, soldiers worked to close the cuts in the dike while others toiled to complete the batteries. Exhausted, like the garrison at Fort Mifflin, men had to be relieved daily.

Day and night were replete with danger and frustration for British engineers. While the soldier-workmen and artillerymen were relieved at regular intervals, engineers and artificers never left the islands. The latter were exhausted, and many were very sick. Frustrated, Montresor noted, "At night a severe Tempest. No working parties this day and indeed from the nature of this overflowed land and the heavy rains . . . retards our progress beyond description." At another time he wearily noted "not being scarce a night in Bed."[29]

The day of the *Augusta* debacle Montresor pushed the completion of a floating bridge across the Schuylkill. The following day he completed three "Lodgments," each capable of accommodating forty men, to serve as a bridgehead on the island side of the Schuylkill. Starting on 25 October, Montresor battled the elements for three days and accomplished little. His men were only able to mend the causeway between the dikes and the redoubt at the Blakely house. Construction was started on two floating batteries, each capable of carrying two thirty-two-pounders. It was soon discovered that their construction was too light to support the heavy cannon.

On the twenty-eighth, the velocity of the wind and rain increased, destroying the floating bridge over the Schuylkill River at the Middle Ferry (opposite Market Street). The river was so rough that work parties could not cross to relieve exhausted soldiers on the islands. In spite of the bad weather, flat-bottomed boats continued to pass up the channel with provisions for the city. The crews believed they could not be detected on the dark stormy nights.[30]

Depressed, Montresor became critical of Howe, asserting he was being bypassed by the commander in chief. Howe ordered various type and size ordnance without consulting the engineer as to their adaptability to the batteries. In addition, the gun platforms which Howe ordered were unsatisfactory. Montresor said Howe had no knowledge of the terrain, never personally surveyed the area, and did not consult the chief engineer.[31]

31 October dawned with fine weather, and it continued to be reasonably fair for the next ten days. Feverish activity swirled about the gun emplacements on the dikes and the batteries on elevated areas. Flatboats were reported sneaking through on dark nights. Fort Mifflin and the galleys kept up an almost incessant cannonade of the

British positions in an effort to destroy the partially completed works.

The British navy in the meantime was licking its wounds and repairing damages. Lord Howe and his captains were planning their strategy in conjunction with the army's attack on the forts. Their chief priority was to prevent the Americans from establishing new river defenses or strengthening existing ones. In early November Americans were observed building a one-gun battery near the mouth of Mantua Creek in New Jersey. At 9:00 A.M. on 5 November, the battery opened fire on the *Isis.* She returned the fire and was soon joined by the *Pearl* and the *Cornwallis.* Soon after the engagement started, the galleys dropped down in support of the battery and maintained a firefight with the British men-of-war until 11:30 A.M., when they were forced to retire because their ammunition was exhausted. The action resumed around noon and lasted until late afternoon, when it seemed to be called off by mutual consent. The next day action continued, but proved inconclusive.

Howe was determined that the next attack would be more carefully prepared and would not fail. With customary caution, he ordered that the assault was not to be launched until Montresor completed the batteries on the islands and weather would permit the *Vigilant* to come up the back channel and anchor close to the fort. Montresor assured the commander in chief that all installations would be finished by 10 November and the attack could be launched on the appointed date.[32]

As promised, Montresor was ready on the tenth. On Carpenters' Island dike, he had constructed three batteries; the largest consisted of one eight-inch howitzer, an eight-inch mortar, and six twenty-four-pounders brought up from the *Eagle.* Montresor had trouble with the gun platform at this battery. Under the weight of the twenty-four-pounders, the platform sank in the soft mud. However, it was soon raised and strengthened. A short distance south was a small battery of one eight-inch howitzer and an eight-inch mortar. Below this emplacement was a battery for one thirteen-inch mortar used to throw pound shot and carcase. Epaulements were erected on the flank of each battery to protect the artillerymen and grenadiers. On the bench of land containing the Blakely house, two redoubts had been constructed. These were principally to cover the traffic on Bow Creek and the road to the Schuylkill. Near the former pest house on Province Island a battery of two thirty-two-pounders was ready, as well as one eighteen-pounder installed on the old ferry wharf. Other gun emplacements were situated across the Schuylkill, but would have little effect on the forthcoming battle.[33]

On the morning of the tenth, a thunderous cannonade commenced from the British batteries. Each cannon was directed to fire eighty rounds. The already damaged buildings and blockhouses of the fort were almost demolished. With the hundreds of projectiles crashing into the gun positions, all the fort's cannon except one were silenced by noon. Outgunned, the valiant defenders nevertheless inflicted considerable damage to the British positions.

Rain began during the afternoon and continued throughout the night. At daybreak it cleared, but it was extremely cold. A heavy frost blanketed the meadows and a half inch of ice covered the still water. Montresor, like de Fleury, worked all night to repair the damage. Soldiers of both armies and the galleymen were suffering untold hardships, with no cover or heat. Although each army attempted to relieve the troops, the men served their tours of duty standing in water without adequate provisions.

At daylight on the eleventh, British ordnance resumed the bombardment. Casualties were again severe, especially at Fort Mifflin. Repairs made to the fort during the night had to be repeated as the cannonade continued to raze the works along the western ramparts.

November 12, 13, and 14 were carbon copies of the preceding two days: a constant cannonade each day, with feverish activity to repair the damages at night. The western and northern ramparts were a shambles, breached in at least twenty places. Few buildings or fortifications remained standing. The stone wall on the east and south survived, but after five days the garrison, albeit relieved every night, was almost defenseless. Few cannon were serviceable and little ammunition was available to fit those capable of being fired. Command of the post had shifted from the wounded Smith to the valiant Major Simeon Thayer.

During this interval, Montresor built another small battery for a medium twelve-pounder on a wharf on Province Island. The bitter resistance offered by the fort slightly modified the British timetable. With only a few serviceable cannon, they had inflicted extensive damage to the British positions. Montresor was having other problems; his men, after working all night, were battling fatigue. However, he had one significant advantage over de Fleury; his work parties did not have to double as soldiers during the day. To add to Montresor's woes, the bad weather had ruined the pasturage in the meadows and, combined with the cold, had destroyed a number of horses, which handicapped his work.

During this three-day period, one of the British floating batteries came out of the Schuylkill and opened fire on the fort, but received such a hot reception that the crew, after suffering a few casualties, jumped overboard and waded ashore. Montresor nonetheless insisted she put up a good fight for two hours.

Lord Howe was advised that the Americans had erected another small battery a short distance north of Mantua Creek. As he believed this emplacement might be an annoyance when the attack commenced, on 12 November he sent the *Isis,* the *Liverpool,* and the *Cornwallis,* with some tenders, to silence it. Unsuccessful in their first attempt, the ships returned the next day and engaged in another indecisive firefight.

At a briefing session on 14 November, Lord Howe designated the men-of-war which were to assist in the forthcoming attack. He then ordered the assigned ship captains to survey the river and determine stations they should take during the assault. Hamond maintained that the admiral named the *Somerset,* the *Isis,* and the *Roebuck* to participate, although the *Camilla,* the *Liverpool,* and the *Cornwallis* were later also assigned to the attack. Captain William Cornwallis of the *Isis* and Hamond proceeded upstream to take soundings and to locate any openings in the chevaux-de-frise. Working under adverse conditions and subjected to frequent cannon fire from the fort and galleys, they nevertheless accomplished their mission. They were suddenly aware that Captain George Curry of the *Somerset* had neglected to follow them. In his absence, the captains placed a buoy where they thought it would be safe to station the *Somerset.*

Returning to the fleet anchored off Chester, Hamond boarded the *Somerset* to get instructions for his part in the planned attack. Curry, since the loss of the *Augusta,* was senior captain in the fleet and would command the flotilla. Hamond informed Curry that they had placed buoys for the three ships and asked for orders. The *Somerset's* captain refused to give directions. Curry asserted that his ship was ready for the attack at the hour mentioned, but that he wanted a pilot to take his ship to the assigned buoy. Hamond immediately repaired to the flagship to see the admiral and found him aware of Curry's insistence on his prerogative. With the attack scheduled for the next day, Lord Howe flew into a rage and asked Hamond for a suggestion. Hamond offered to approach Curry and volunteer to pilot the *Somerset* personally, or send the *Roebuck's* master. Back on the *Somerset,* the petulant Curry accepted the master, not Hamond. The admiral later censured Curry, but treated the incident diplomatically, stating merely that "greater caution being necessary in placing the *Somerset.*"[34]

Thayer realized the fort could not hold for more than one or two days. While Americans had so far been free of an attack from the river side, as soon as the weather moderated he realized the fort would be confronted by the British fleet. November 15 dawned clear and cold. British men-of-war were seen warping through the chevaux-de-frise and heading upriver. The *Isis* and the *Roebuck* took position abreast of the fort, about six hundred yards off the southeast battery; the *Somerset* assumed her station near the upper end of a sandbar. Near the New Jersey shore above Mantua Creek, the *Pearl* and the *Liverpool* took position, joined later by the *Cornwallis.* Lord Howe praised the discipline and general conduct of Cornwallis, Hamond, and other captains in safely bringing their ships into position for the attack.

Once in position, the men-of-war opened with broadsides, causing great damage to the east wall. The Pennsylvania galleys and floating batteries, unable to operate during the gale-force winds of the previous five days, now dropped down to oppose the British fleet. Their presence forced the British ships to direct a major part of their fire on the little boats. Whatever respite the galleys gave the brave defenders of the fort was soon offset by the appearance of the *Vigilant* and the *Fury* off the southwest battery of the fort. Like the galleys, the weather change had permitted the *Vigilant* to enter the conflict. She was able to anchor so close to the fort's ramparts that the marines in her crow's nest could throw grenades into the works. By 11:00 A.M. the fort's ammunition was almost exhausted, but the men pleaded with Thayer to continue the uneven defense. Thayer was fully aware that the galleys must direct their attention to the fleet — a contest as hopeless as his own. However, the presence of the *Vigilant* had rendered the garrison helpless, and faced with a dilemma, he was compelled to ask Hazelwood to drive the floating battery downstream. Six galleys warped around the northern perimeter of Fort Island and entered the back channel. The galley captains soon found they were fighting the *Vigilant* on their front while being enfiladed by the British batteries on their starboard. They could not return the fire of the batteries, as their only heavy ordnance was a cannon in the bow. Suffering heavy casualties and damage to the galleys, they were forced to withdraw.

As dusk approached, Thayer decided to give up the hopeless struggle. Sending off most of the surviving garrison, he retained forty men as a forlorn hope. He destroyed all materiel not capable of being carried off and finally, near midnight, after setting fire to what remained, stepped into a boat and rowed to Fort Mercer. Leaving the American flag flying in the midst of the flaming fort, it climaxed one of the gallant defenses in American annals. The men of the Continental regiments and the galleymen fought heroically and suffered heavy casualties in defending Fort Mifflin.

Captain John Peebles, a British officer, expressed the admiration shared by other Englishmen when, on 22 November, he "took a ride to see Mud Island, which is prodigiously Shatter'd & torn to pieces & leaves a Spectacle very much to the honor of those that defended it."

Montresor reported that a boatload of sailors landed at the fort at 7:30 A.M. on the sixteenth and raised the flag of Great Britain. At 9:00 A.M., Sir George Osborne and a detachment of 280 soldiers, accompanied by engineers and carpenters with fascines, scaling ladders, flying bridge, and other equipment, landed at the fort; they were equipped for their original assignment of storming the fort. Immediate steps were taken to place the fort in a defensible posture and to provide protection to the ships engaged in removing the chevaux-de-frise. Thus, the passage for supply ships carrying the desperately needed provisions was opened to Philadelphia.[35]

General Cleaveland entered the fort later in the day to catalogue the American ordnance left by Thayer. A substantial number of cannon and a large quantity of shot or ball were found, but no powder or cartridges. Someone in the American command had neglected to coordinate the fort's ordnance and ammunition requirements. To further emphasize this apparent oversight, Cleaveland found 1,475 twenty-four-pounder round shot, but only one cannon of that caliber.

British strategy called for a detachment of British and Hessian troops to cross over to Billingsport concurrent with the fall of Fort Mifflin. Lord Cornwallis departed from Philadelphia on the seventeenth with about two thousand rank and file and bivouacked at Chester.

On the same day, Wilson landed at Billingsport with his reinforcements from New York. Early the next morning, Cornwallis crossed the river and joined Wilson. Cornwallis assumed command of the combined force of 6,000 rank and file and made immediate plans for the reduction of Fort Mercer. Although Cornwallis was certainly familiar with the number and disposition of the forces at Woodbury and Fort Mercer, scouting parties were ordered out to reconnoiter the American position. He proceeded cautiously, with intermittent skirmishing, covering only five or six miles in two days.[36]

Confusion was evident in the American command — resistance was useless. Varnum and Greene decided to abandon the fort and move out toward Haddonfield and later to Mount Holly. Hazelwood and Captain Isaiah Robinson, the senior Continental captain, quickly decided the little fleet could not hold the river pass without land-based assistance. They agreed to attempt to take the fleet upriver to Bristol, attempting to complete the journey on two successive nights between midnight and dawn. The first flotilla was to move up in the early hours of 20 November, and the second twenty-four hours later. Preparations were made to destroy various boats and ships rather than permit them to fall into British hands. Hugging closely to the New Jersey shore, the Americans were under constant fire from the waterfront batteries in Philadelphia and the former American frigate *Delaware*. All galleys and a number of guard boats and service ships reached Bristol in safety. Unfortunately for the Americans, the larger Pennsylvania ships and the Continental vessels were burned.

Cornwallis, after destroying the works at the fort, abandoned his position at Woodbury and marched toward the hamlet of Gloucester. His objective, to destroy the American fortification, was accomplished. As soon as the American naval units were out of the area, he planned to cross the river at Gloucester.

Uncertain of Cornwallis's intentions, Washington dispatched Brigadier General Jedidiah Huntington's brigade to support Varnum. Reconsidering, he thought additional troops would be required to prevent the British general from overrunning southern New Jersey. Nathanael Greene, with his division, and Brigadier General John Glover's brigade were sent to reinforce Huntington and Varnum. Greene was in command of the combined force.

On 24 November, Cornwallis began to embark his troops, and the first contingent passed over the river on the twenty-fifth. Before embarkation was completed, a detachment of American troops commanded by Lafayette roughly handled a Hessian outpost near Gloucester. Although the British lost this engagement, they had nevertheless succeeded in opening the river passes to their ships.

Back of Independence Hall, called State House in Colonial times. It became a prison for many American officers during the winter of 1777-78. From a 1799 engraving by William Birch. *Independence National Historical Park Collection*

CHAPTER V

A BELEAGUERED CITY

WHILE HOWE WAS busily involved in coordinating the British strategy to destroy the American defenses on the Delaware, Washington's surprise attack at Germantown had left the British camp nervous. Jittery pickets fired at shadows. Early on the morning of 6 October, part of the camp turned out under arms only to discover it was a false alarm. Again on the eleventh an officer alarmed the camp and called out a portion of the army. Exasperated at the shadowboxing pickets and officers, Howe ordered that no troops were to be turned out without his approval or that of another general officer. Twenty-four hours later he followed this directive with a threat to punish severely anyone giving a false alarm or any sentry firing at ghosts and frightening the camp. Concerned with morale, Howe moved his headquarters from Stenton to the Morris mansion at Market Square.[1]

Constant patrols were sent out on all roads leading into Germantown. Almost daily, contacts were made with American militia detachments. Captain Johann Ewald reported that the jägers were roughly handled and that their officers had neglected to take necessary precautions against surprise. Washington ordered a detachment of 100 militia from Armstrong's division to move down the Manatawny (Ridge) Road, conceal themselves near the British lines until dawn, and then open fire. Similarly, General William Smallwood was to lead an equal number on the British right flank by marching down Old York Road. These detachments were to be relieved with fresh troops each night. Although strictly a harassing tactic, Washington hoped to keep the British camp in a constant state of alarm.[2]

Before the battle, Howe had established outposts of battalion strength. Now he contracted his lines slightly and placed his reliance on frequent patrols to prevent a surprise by the Americans.

In addition to securing all approaches to the main encampment at Germantown, Howe was aware of the discomfort suffered by civilians in a garrison city. Criticism has been leveled at him for being insensitive to the atrocities committed by his soldiers. It was believed that he had been preoccupied with his paramour, Mrs. Loring. However, Howe's constant orders and directives against plundering or ravishing and the severity of the punishments meted out belie this judgment. Most of the charges of brutality were blamed on the Hessians, but scrutiny of the courts-martial records reveals that many British soldiers and camp followers were equally guilty of rapine.

An almost daily fare of camp life and a diversion for the officers was service on courts-martial. During the encampment at Germantown, the common crime was plundering. Soldiers were also tried for murder, desertion, and bearing arms in the American army. While there were a few acquittals, most plundering convictions carried from six hundred to one thousand lashes, and in at least two cases conviction resulted in execution. Desertion and serving with the American army were always punished with death.

The absence of rapprochement between Hessian and British officers occasionally led to recriminations. While at Germantown, a British officer accused Donop of seizing private property. In an effort to strengthen his claim, the officer invited two other British officers, Abercrombie and Maitland, to join him in making a joint claim for the booty. A drinking bout ensued, but the two Scotchmen left the Hessian under the table; and thus ended the proposed cabal.[3]

Numerous British and Hessian soldiers had come from the ghettos of English and German cities. Service in the armed forces was not considered an enviable profession for sons of middle-class merchants and artisans. However, the British soldier, although ill-qualified for civilian life, did develop an esprit de corps. Hundreds of wives and children were always in camp. Howe usually permitted only one woman to accompany each company on the march. Hundreds of others had a rather doubtful status, having been picked up along the route. All women served as laundresses, cooked, and mended for their men; and, on occasion, they served as nurses at general and field hospitals.

Given this quota system, desertion often resulted whenever the wives were prohibited from joining their husbands. Yet some control was necessary as the majority of women were footloose. Many wives, indifferent to discipline, disrupted the line of march and often were more vicious than the soldiers. The women rarely distinguished between Loyalists and Americans in their pillaging excursions. On the voyage from New York to Head of Elk, 626 women and 26 children were on board the transports. A number of others accompanied Wilson's reinforcements, sailing from New York in October; others joined the troops in Philadelphia. A ration report of 13 December showed a sizeable increase in the number of women from 626 to 1,648 and of children from 26 to 539. As many as 500 Philadelphia girls and women left with the British army in June 1778. Although the majority of the women who joined the army in Philadelphia were Germans, all ethnic groups were represented. One Hessian chaplain in Southwark was said to have married 100 German girls to Hessian soldiers. Nameless, guilty of many atrocities, and some just loyal soldiers' wives, these women formed an important auxiliary to the army — some have called them the lost souls of the Revolution.[4]

Howe was aware that any effort to enforce discipline was impossible while the soldiers remained idle in the camp. He ordered each battalion and regiment to make fascines. Daily quotas were set, from ten to forty, for each battalion. The fascines were transported to the old playhouse on South Street and were then taken to Carpenters' and Province islands to be used in the construction of fortifications.

Even before the battle, Howe recognized that the tedium of camp life would create problems among the officers. The village of Germantown offered little entertainment, and with Philadelphia only a little over five miles away, the temptation to visit the city was great. The absence of officers from their commands only increased insubordination among the rank and file. As early as 25 September, Howe had ordered that no officer, soldier, woman, or follower could go to the city without his personal approval. Three days later, corps commanders were granted permission to allow two or three officers to enter the city if they had specific business to transact, and provided that sufficient officers were always on duty. Soldiers were not to be sent into Philadelphia, unless on the king's business. During these weeks in the village British officers supposedly played cricket for the first time in America.[5]

Finally, on 18 October orders were given for the army to march at daybreak for Philadelphia. The straw, thatch, rails, and boards

1. *La Vache, à lait, représente le Commerce de la Grande Bretagne*
2. *Le Congrès est représenté par l'Américain, qui est occupé à enlever à la vache sa force naturelle, et aux cornes défensives, en lui ôtant ses cornes, dont l'une est déja par terre, et l'autre prête à tomber.*
3. *Ils sont chacun de bonne humeur, profitant des circonstances, se coque à tirer la pauvre vache.*
4. *Les hommes à la vache sont un François et un Espagnol, le premier, d'un air très-content, emporte son pot plein de lait, et le second, levant tout prête une modeste part, semble en attendre sa part.*
Le maison de guerre Anglais nommé l'Aigle, à quelque distance de Philadelphie, paroît dormant sans voiles.

et sans artillerie, le reste de la flotte hors de vue, personne ne sachant où elle est.
7. *Les deux Frères, deux Philadelphes, commandant, et éloigné de la flotte et de l'armée.*
8. *Le Lion Britannique profondément endormi, ne sent par plus petit déput, fort éveillé, marche sur son dos, et semble se s'apperçevoir de rien.*
9. *A côté du lion, on voit un Anglois en deuil, dans une attitude de désespoir... hors d'état, d'étudier le lion, pour punir tous ses usurpateurs et ses prolongateurs équivalent de proposition de ces légères.*

Caricature called "A Picturesque View of the State of the Nation for February, 1778." The lackadaisical efforts of the Howes represented by an American cutting the cow's horns while a happy Dutchman profits by milking the animal and a self-satisfied Frenchman carries a bowl of milk as a Spaniard waits his turn. The British lion is in a deep sleep and the Howe brothers slumber far from their commands. *J. Welles Henderson Collection, Philadelphia Maritime Museum*

used in the Germantown camp were to be transported on spare wagons to the rear of the redoubts in the city. Huts, or wigwams, constructed with these materials would be quarters for the majority of the army until December.

On 28 September, Howe reissued his proclamation of 27 August granting amnesty to all Americans. Three days later he revised this offer and warned those who had aligned themselves with the king's enemies that they had until 25 October to take the oath of allegiance to His Majesty, or be placed outside the pale of royal favor.[6]

The day after the battle at Germantown, the wounded and prisoners were brought into the city. Facilities were already taxed to the utmost. The Pennsylvania Hospital and Bettering House were filled

Morris and Galloway houses, on the south side of Market between Fifth and Sixth streets. *Free Library of Philadelphia*

with the sick and wounded from the battle at Brandywine. On 27 September, the British moved their wounded into the hospital, crowding the wards and inconveniencing the patients. Several mental patients and one slave "eloped" in the confusion. This disruption of hospital services continued until 26 November, when Dr. Michael Morris, inspector of the British military hospitals, was escorted through the facilities by the managers and staff. An agreement was reached whereby civilian patients were assured of hospital care. They were transferred to a small house that had been recently built; the insane and emotionally disturbed were incarcerated in their usual cells. The steward and matron retained their apartments and the managers their office. The remainder of the hospital was appropriated for military use, including whatever furniture and supplies could be spared.

The hospital operated under serious handicaps during the occupation. At a great loss for funds, the managers were compelled to borrow money. Finally, in April 1778, they appointed a committee to draft a memorial to Howe asking for his assistance. In May they were still considering a rough outline when Clinton supplanted Howe and rumors that the British would soon leave the city became more prevalent. With these changes, it did not appear propitious to submit a memorial to British authorities. Desperate, the hospital managers appealed to Dr. Morris for compensation for the blankets, medicines, instruments, and hay appropriated by British surgeons. Nearly two weeks after the evacuation, the buildings and wards were still being cleaned of debris and filth. It was three months before the managers could report the hospital in good enough order to assume full operation.[7]

A somewhat similar situation was evident at Bettering House, usually referred to by the managers as the House of Employment, and by others as the Alms House. This charitable institution provided shelter and employment to the city's neediest citizens. With British wounded occupying the east wing, the destitute were forced into the west wing. Afraid that they would soon be deprived of that sanctuary, they appealed to Joseph Galloway (a Pennsylvanian and Howe's civilian administrator) to intercede for "the most helpless kind of paupers that can reasonably be thought of." Galloway referred them to Dr. John Stewart, army surgeon, who promised to avoid taking possession of the west wing if he could possibly do so. In mid-November it became evident that Stewart's promise could not be honored. The managers were given twenty-four hours to vacate the premises, as the surgeons needed both wings.

Added to many other problems was the fact that money was scarce. It was becoming impossible to provide funds to permit the poor to be even partly self-supporting. The board decided to present a memorial[8] to Howe requesting financial or material assistance. On 30 November 1777, two managers delivered the petition to one of Howe's aides, who informed them the commander in chief was too busy to see them. After several days they were referred to Commissary Wier, who apologetically refused their application, asserting the army was in short supply and would be until the supply ships reached the city.

Searching their larder, the frustrated managers found a few vegetables, but nothing else to feed over two hundred men, women, and children. Concurrent with this depressing discovery was the desperate need to find lodgings for their homeless charges. Appeals for an extension of time proved fruitless. The British barrack master suggested they transfer the city poor to the Masonic lodge hall. This hall was small and completely inadequate for so many people. Application was made to the Society of Friends for the use of their meetinghouse on Fourth Street south of Chestnut and to the Carpenters' Company for the use of their hall. Both requests were granted. At least two looms were installed in the cellar of Carpenters' Hall and raw yarn was worked into linen for the poor. The lot of these unfortunate indigents did not improve, and the future looked even more bleak than the present. All paupers who had the remotest possibility of making it on their own were discharged and told to shift for themselves. For the balance of the occupation period, there were rarely more than 100 on the rolls of the almshouse.[9]

Galloway and the magistrates of police noted the lamentable condition of the poor, and on 19 February 1778, they suggested a public subscription be taken to raise needed funds. Accordingly, Howe issued a proclamation authorizing a collection for the "Relief and Employment of the Poor." Money was collected in each ward and eventually totalled £904 1s. 11-1/2d.[10]

Every available building or house capable of housing the sick and wounded was utilized. A majority of the officers were treated in private homes; some vacant houses were converted to regimental hospitals.[11] American wounded were placed in the State House and in two houses on Fourth Street south of Market according to John Morton, a Quaker youth. Most of the prisoners except the officers were taken to the new Walnut Street gaol; the officers were confined to the State House.

Regrettably, the British medical staff could not adequately serve their own wounded and also tend to the Americans. Howe's return for 13 October disclosed 2,612 sick and 850 wounded British and Hessian rank and file. Undoubtedly some of the more seriously wounded could not be moved from Germantown.[12]

Deborah Logan said the wounded started arriving in the city toward evening on 4 October. American wounded were literally dumped in the State House, spread on the floor, staircase, or any convenient location. This was not an act of inhumanity, as the British and Hessian patients were handled similarly. The Americans unfortunately had to wait while overworked and understaffed British surgeons attended to their own men. The trauma of the situation was the inability of the British surgeons to ease the sufferings of the Americans.

Ladies of Philadelphia could not endure such suffering. To relieve the distress of their countrymen, they flocked to the State House with lint, bandages, and refreshments. Although the number of British and Hessian soldiers who died in these makeshift hospitals is unknown, contemporary accounts described trenches dug near the church hospitals and bodies dumped in them and covered over, only to surface after a heavy rain. Hundreds of soldiers from both armies were buried in present Washington Square.[13]

In early October, one of those amenities occurred that occasionally characterized eighteenth-century warfare. A dog wandered into the Continental encampment, probably to the Peter Wentz farmhouse at the base of the Methacton Hills. On the dog's collar were the words "General Howe." Stephen Moylan and the Chevalier de Pontigaud said the dog came into camp on 3 October, although the latter remembered it happening at Valley Forge. On the sixth, Washington returned the dog under a flag, with his compliments.[14]

Another vignette of the war relates to the noted Episcopalian rector of Christ Church, the Reverend Jacob Duché. Duché had married Elizabeth Hopkinson, sister of Francis Hopkinson, signer of the Declaration of Independence. After the states declared their independence, Duché, as chaplain of the Continental Congress, had visibly moved the members with his impassioned prayer for the new nation. On the Sunday following the entry of Cornwallis, Duché offered prayers for the king. As he walked out of Christ Church, he was arrested and taken to the Walnut Street gaol, where he spent the night. Apparently recanting his previous allegiance to the United States, he was released the next day. Some observers claimed that friends convinced him of his earlier mistake in deserting the king; others said he was a Milquetoast and the fear of prison was overpowering. Still others have contended that his fidelity to the American cause had always been shallow and unconvincing.

Either ill-advised or stupid, on 8 October Duché addressed a letter to Washington condemning independence and appealing to what he considered the commander in chief's patrician characteristics. He described the current leaders as plebeian, not the social equals of members of the earlier Congresses. In fact, he noted that Washington would never consider inviting any of them to share the hospitality of his table. Duché urged Washington, as the only leader Americans had faith in, to forswear independence, that he "alone has the strength sufficient to remove this bar." If unsuccessful, Washington could still "negotiate for your country at the head of your army."

Duché had prevailed upon Elizabeth Graeme Ferguson (American wife of a British commissary of prisoners) to deliver the letter. Incensed by Duché's urgings, Washington transmitted the letter to Congress and warned Mrs. Ferguson to tell the rector if she should again meet up with him that if he had been aware of its contents he would have returned the letter unopened. Many people thought this act confirmed Mrs. Ferguson's Loyalist leanings; however, there is no evidence that she had any knowledge of the letter's contents. Later Washington advised Francis Hopkinson that he was willing to believe the cleric acted out of fear rather than conviction. However, he was certain that members of Congress and the army, on whom Duché had vented his abuse, would never forgive a man who had endeavored to have Washington sacrifice them for his own personal safety.[15]

With the British army in Philadelphia, it became a garrison city. For a number of weeks, however, until the river passes were opened, it was actually a beleaguered city. In spite of all the vicissitudes of hunger, lack of fuel, being forced to accept unwanted guests in their homes, and suffering indignities and rapine, citizens put on a good face. Loyalists and those opposing violence appeared contented that at last they were under the protection of His Majesty's troops.

Although certain diarists attempted to minimize the distress felt in the city, great suffering was evident, especially among the poor. The Americans had drawn a tight cordon around Philadelphia. Only a bare trickle of provisions reached the city from the supply ships, and these goods were distributed to the army. During the early days of the occupation, Washington had permitted the wives of American soldiers and others with relatives in the country to obtain provisions outside the cordon; but the obvious espionage activities of some visitors forced him to curtail this traffic. A large number of these women were the wives of British soldiers; others were camp followers posing as American sympathizers in order to carry provisions and intelligence back to the city. As a result, orders were sent to the various outposts, and mounted patrols were dispatched to intercept and detain anyone coming out of the city and to permit them to pass only if they declared their intention of remaining in the country. Otherwise they were to be forwarded to headquarters for interrogation, and their horses were to be appropriated for the Continental army.[16]

In an editorial, the *Pennsylvania Ledger* berated the Americans for callously cutting off intercourse between the city and country. Inadvertently, James Humphreys disclosed the serious situation of the inhabitants: ''How greatly are the wives, children, and other as near connexions of many of the militia, that are stationed around this city, for the avowed purpose of preventing provisions coming in, indebted to them?" He continued to excoriate the Americans for their "cruelty, distress and folly," asserting the British army had sufficient resources without depending on the countryside. He then embroidered his fanciful comments with ". . . rebels mouths [would] have watered at the waggon loads of provisions belonging to the army that passed through the streets within these few days past."[17]

British foraging parties were unable to obtain sufficient food unless they were strong enough to withstand attacks of battalion strength. Washington had large patrols of cavalry and infantry, mostly Pennsylvania militia, moving throughout the area beyond Germantown, Frankford, and across the Schuylkill. They were to intercept and frustrate any detachments seeking forage and provisions. Many minor engagements were fought. Captain John Simcoe's Queen's Rangers were the most active British contingent in many of these actions.

Numerous affluent Philadelphians owned summer estates in the Neck (lower South Philadelphia) and along the banks of the Schuylkill. Residents of the area watched with dismay the wanton pillaging of their properties by Hessians. Young Morton was near the Pemberton plantation and observed "about 100 Hessians coming down the road on a foraging expedition, or rather a plundering party." The Hessians swarmed over the area, digging up potatoes, turnips, and other vegetables. Ten or more soldiers would take over a garden, working alongside the owner as he harvested his crops; if he protested, they would threaten him, declaring there was enough for all. The next day wives of these soldiers were seen sitting in the market house selling the products of their thievery. At night Hessian soldiers slinked out to private property and stole cattle, slaughtered them, and the next day offered the meat for sale. The Hessian looting, however was petty thievery compared to the cupidity of certain British soldiers and civilians. Fleeing American families had deserted their homes, with a number left fully furnished. Furniture and other articles left behind were confiscated and sold at public vendue. One informant stated an occasional vacant house was sold by the British to incoming refugees or sutlers.[18]

Certain fresh provisions were in short supply throughout the winter. However, a shortage of all varieties of provisions existed until the river passes were opened to British supply ships. Everyone in the city suffered, but the anguish of the poor and the American prisoners was especially heartrending. Joseph Reed said Howe had regretfully advised the civilian population that the limited provisions available for his troops made it impossible to supply their food requirements.

All contemporary accounts mentioned the misery and distress of the city's residents. All Loyalist, Quaker, British officer, and American spy descriptions of life in the city agreed, in detail, on the exorbitant price of all commodities and, in addition, that they were of inferior quality. Dr. Hutchinson said the only foodstuffs found at the market were very small quantities of flour and extremely bad beef, with no other kind of meat or vegetable brought to the shambles. Elizabeth Drinker and some friends were not able to purchase butter for three or four weeks. On 17 November, an unknown intelligence agent of Washington reported, ''Everyday increases the price and scarcity of Provision, Heavens only knows what will become of us, if you do not soon relieve us by routing them.''

Desperate and dejected, many tried to reach the countryside and purchase provisions from the farmers, only to be turned back by American patrols. The few who succeeded in obtaining supplies kept within the protective screen of British detachments, especially on the road to Frankford. One woman walked miles to procure one egg.

Many young farmers and their wives braved the threat of being apprehended and dealt severe punishment, as decreed by Washington, for carrying meat, poultry, eggs, and a few vegetables into the city. There they traded their products for hard money or a very scarce item for the farmer — salt. They avoided the roads patrolled by American dragoons by crossing fields at night and stealthily entering the city. The provisions they could transport constituted a mere trickle compared to the quantities required by inhabitants and the army.

Small quantities of dairy products were surreptitiously ferried across the Delaware from New Jersey. This was probably done to avoid confiscation by the authorities and to charge black-market prices for the products. Sarah Logan Fisher mentioned that a pound of cheese could be purchased for one silver dollar. Merchants and farmers were deliberately inflating food prices and refusing to accept paper currency in payment. Residents in the Neck were killing their milch cows for food and to prevent their falling into the hands of marauding soldiers.[19]

The Society of Friends as well as individual Quakers were concerned by the plight of the city's poor, but were powerless to extend permanent relief. The Society's almshouse on Walnut between Third and Fourth streets and the Quaker needy boarded in private residences received subsistence from a committee appointed to distribute funds for their welfare. In November, subscriptions were solicited within the Society and £200 were raised; eight days later, the Quakers were £150 overexpended, and the committee estimated an additional £400 was needed to cover current needs. Mary Pemberton, whose husband was a prisoner at Winchester, wrote Howe requesting relief for the destitute and needy. She reminded him that many inhabitants had been stripped of everything by the licentious soldiers. Continuing, she bemoaned her inability to provide them the bounty previously furnished by her husband.[20]

British and Hessian soldiers were not well fed. Deserters arriving in Germantown said the troops had been placed on an allowance and were in extreme want of provisions. On 10 October, Wier informed John Robinson, secretary to the Lord Commissioners, that he had a six months' supply of beef, pork, bread, flour, butter, and oatmeal, and a seven months' supply of rice, peas, and rum for twenty thousand. Unfortunately, this supply was almost entirely in storage on board the transports and victuallers on the river below Chester. Wier was also concerned about fresh vegetables needed for the hospital. The present reserve for the wounded and sick would last about twenty-four or twenty-five days. His plight was desperate, and Wier was convinced there was no way to replenish the store of fresh produce. It was impossible to go a hundred yards beyond the redoubts without a sizeable escort.

To add to Wier's dilemma, the quality and quantity of provisions on the ships was sadly deficient; already, inferior flour and other items were musty, sour, and full of maggots. All barrels were running from fifteen to forty pounds short of invoice quantity, except pork, which ran five to ten pounds light. John Robinson had the added responsibility of being the watchdog on military expenditures in America. As a dedicated civil servant, he zealously watched the activities of army contractors. Concerned that the army receive the quantities of provisions contracted for, he was equally afraid an oversupply might be sent to America.[21]

Army officers were appalled by the austerity evident throughout the city. Serle visited the market and saw very few vegetables and not one piece of meat or fowl. He observed everything was very dear due "to the very small Extent of Country at this time under our Command." If Captain William Dansey's descriptions of an officer's table is typical, then the soldier's mess must have been woefully short of all provisions. He wrote to his mother, ''Your talking of Ribbs of Beef makes me wish to be at home now I shou'd so much enjoy a good joint of meat well dress'd clean set down and good Company. . . . Sometimes [we have] good meat ill dress'd nothing to eat or drink with it other times plenty to drink and nothing good to eat in short things are never all of a Piece with us except when we have nothing at all but Thank God that seldom happens.''[22]

While British patrols conducted forays for food, Howe concentrated on the problem of fuel. With defense lines sharply contracted, he ordered all wood necessary for the army and civilians to be cut down within the defense perimeter. Civilians were not to be harassed when they gathered wood near the Center House commons (present City Hall) and westward to the Schuylkill. A number of residents with estates in the Neck and along the Schuylkill had substantial stands of timber. The army offered to cut and cart away timber and pay the owner seventeen shillings a cord for oak and twenty-five a cord for hickory. On 1 November, a broadside was released encouraging workmen to engage as woodcutters for the ''Winter Season'' for the benefit of the army. Undoubtedly these fortunate property owners first filled their personal needs. When word reached Philadelphia that Howe was moving the main army into the city, some property owners removed their fences and stored the rails in their cellars. Others, less prescient, lost their fences to the soldiers, who used them to build huts and stables. Some churches sacrificed their fences and pews to the needs of the army. The German Society had purchased ground on the west side of Seventh Street between Walnut and Chestnut and had assembled a quantity of building materials. The British used these materials to build military stables. Wood became so scarce that British troops tore down a number of wooden houses near the lines. Sarah Logan Fisher said most inhabitants had less than half a cord of wood. She said, ''Such is the lamentable prospect of distress that the rich have not themselves, nor have they it in their power to relieve the cries of the poor, for money will not procure the necessaries of life.''[23]

Rum was an indispensable commodity for eighteenth-century armies. It was distributed on a regular basis, and irregularly only when the troops were operating under combat conditions. With the commissary's stock of rum being on board the supply ships, an immediate shortage developed. On 6 October, Wier ordered all persons having rum or any kind of spirituous liquors to deliver their supply to his office by noon the next day. Those who did not comply he threatened with severe penalties.

After the river was opened, sutlers and ship masters brought in large quantities of liquors, much of an inferior quality. Recognizing the danger that an unrestrained liquor traffic posed for a garrison city, Howe released a proclamation that all ship captains with a cargo of "Rum, Brandy and other spirituous Liquors" present a proper manifest at the office of his secretary. If any liquors were landed contrary to the instructions of the proclamation, or to whatever conditions Howe set down, the cargo would be seized and forfeited and the owner subject to imprisonment. [24]

Wier and the British command in America had been supplied by Mure, Son & Atkinson, army contractors, but on occasion had obtained small quantities of rum at a lower price from local merchants. Suggestions had been made that purchasing locally might be a less expensive method of supplying the army. When asked for a decision on this method, the Lords Commissioners of the Treasury refused to venture an opinion, claiming they were too far removed from the scene. Wier proposed that army contractors be retained, as they were more reliable and the local merchants' supply was always suspect. His recommendation proved accurate because, in addition to having only a limited supply, local merchants also raised their prices. Howe, without much hesitation, agreed to accept Wier's recommendation. [25]

Obtaining provisions remained a problem. Wier had provisions for six months on the supply ships below Chester. None of these provisions were intended for civilians; they had to rely on the merchant ships with the fleet and area farmers. Howe expected more victuallers from New York, supplies which he knew were desperately needed if the army was to survive until the summer of 1778. However, until it was certain that the river passes could be opened, he ordered Clinton to place an embargo on all ships destined for Philadelphia. Howe had no desire to add to the overcrowded condition on the Delaware. In addition, if the river froze over before the American defenses fell, ice would probably tear gaping holes in the wooden hulls, and their only sanctuary would then be tied up at the city wharves. Later, when the river was cleared of American opposition and the chevaux-de-frise removed to permit ships to come up to the city, an express was sent to New York to lift the embargo.

November had been an unusually cold month. Afternoon temperatures rarely reached forty degrees, and for several days dropped into the twenties. Officers and men, still in summer uniforms, suffered extreme discomfort. To add to their distress, blankets and other camp equipage were on board the ships down the river. On 31 October an appeal was made to the inhabitants to furnish the barrack master with 500 or 600 blankets. Only on 20 and 21 November were regimental commanders finally instructed to send to New York for winter uniforms and baggage for officers and men. It was another two or three weeks before their winter equipment arrived.[26]

The northern defense line started by Montresor in late September had received very little attention from the army engineers until after the batteries on Carpenters' and Province islands were completed. Work had, however, continued on the redoubts with civilian laborers being supervised by army officers and an occasional engineer. The redoubts and connecting entrenchments, shaped like a crescent, extended from the Delaware to the Schuylkill River. Starting in the vicinity of modern Spring Garden Street at the Delaware, the defenses turned slightly toward the northwest and passed above the British barracks.[27] Then, stretching westward along a low ridge between present Green Street and Poplar Street to redoubt nine near the Schuylkill, the line swung sharply to the southwest to redoubt ten on Lemon Hill.

To serve as outposts, two redoubts were constructed about two hundred fifty yards in advance of the main fortifications along Wissahickon and Germantown roads.

While Howe was still in Germantown, it was not considered necessary to man the fortifications under construction. The five miles between Philadelphia and Germantown were under constant patrol, and few American soldiers were to be found in the area. Rarely, an American patrol came down the Frankford Road, but always withdrew without challenging the makeshift British defenses.

When the British moved their main army from Germantown into the city on 19 October, immediate steps were taken to defend the unfinished redoubts. Various British and Hessian battalions and regiments were assigned positions in the rear of the redoubts. With the rails and straw transported from Germantown, huts were constructed to serve as temporary quarters. As materials were in short supply, every fence within reach was carted away, and most farmers in the Neck and near the lines lost their straw. Howe proposed to quarter the troops in the huts until winter made it unlikely that

Washington would attack and until he could ascertain where the American army would establish its winter encampment. Although Howe continued to abhor the thought of a winter campaign, he was not as certain of Washington's plans, especially after the surprise attack at Trenton the previous Christmas. Regardless, it was evident that the British soldiers could not live in their huts beyond mid-December — even though Washington's Continentals would live in similar huts at Valley Forge.

Galloway's civilian lieutenants and army officers were directed to canvass the city and locate private residences adaptable to winter quarters for officers and men. Regiments and battalions were to be quartered in designated enclaves, with their officers living with or near enough to their men to ensure strict discipline.

On the other hand, general officers and staff were scrambling to find quarters in the more fashionable homes in center city. Most residents demurred when asked to accept officers in their homes; however, the British command considered that the need for housing far outweighed personal objections. Early in the occupation period, when greeted with a strong protest, officers sometimes sought other quarters. This became impossible later, when adequate accommodations were at a premium. Apparently as a concession to good taste, officers having mistresses were assigned to the empty houses which fleeing Americans had left behind. In certain instances, wives of known patriots were ordered from their homes in order to provide lodgings for British officers or, in the case of larger buildings, to be used as a regimental hospital.

Howe was incensed by reports that certain officers, soldiers, and even camp followers were appropriating vacant houses for their own use without his personal approval. The Philadelphia Contributionship was concerned that irresponsible conduct in the care of these properties would lead to the danger of fire. Their board of directors therefore decided to have all chimneys swept and to pay for this service out of public stock until the cost could be recovered from the owners or tenants. On 2 December, Christian Apple was paid £10 7s. 6d. for sweeping 140 houses occupied by officers and soldiers.

Before the end of the occupation, most residents grew to like their British officer tenants. Veterans seemed to have been more acceptable, as some of the younger officers making the rounds of convivial activities, became particularly obnoxious.[28]

To Howe, the security of the city and the comfort of his army were of paramount importance. On 28 September, when he first visited Philadelphia, and again on 19 October, when he established his permanent headquarters in the city, he was warmly, and in certain instances enthusiastically, greeted. This warmth was soon expressed in generous terms. At the outset of the occupation, the British army exchequer was badly depleted. A number of zealous citizens, including some affluent Quakers, reportedly loaned Howe sums of L5,000 and L20,000.[29]

Unfortunately, the rapport between the army and citizens was gradually undermined. The inhabitants were reluctantly reappraising their attitude toward the army because of the many "shameful acts committed by the soldiers." Later the licentious conduct of some officers further diminished civilian respect for the British military command. Morton claimed looting was condoned by British and Hessian officers. Never sympathetic to the American cause, he was now disgusted with the British army's conduct, stating, "I presume the fatal effects of such conduct will shortly be very apparent by the discontent of the inhabitants, who are now almost satiated with British clemency, and numbers of whom, I believe, will shortly put themselves out of the British protection."[30]

Regrettably, many citizens, some desperate, others merely rapacious, condoned the acts of soldiers and army followers by purchasing their plunder. This became such a common incident that Howe issued a proclamation on 7 November 1777 threatening "the most exemplary Punishment" for any persons found guilty of rapine and for civilian purchasers of plunder. Howe was convinced that the residents' willingness to purchase plunder posed a serious threat to discipline in his army. Recognizing the economic background of most soldiers, he realized that the prospect of profit was irresistible. This problem continued throughout the occupation, and Howe reissued his proclamation threatening severe punishments at frequent intervals during the winter.[31]

Daily, "Shameful Irregularities" were reported to headquarters. Citizens found it dangerous to venture out on the streets at night. Finally, on 28 November, Howe found it necessary to admonish the commanding officers of corps for their lack of "Due Exertion of their Authority in Preserving Good order & Discipline," and to order "Frequent Patrols to be sent through the town during the Night from the 16th & 17th Dragoons & 17th Foot with orders to take up all Straglers or Disorderly persons." Courts-martial were held almost daily, but the avarice of many soldiers and followers could not be stopped by the horrendous prospect of the lash or even death.[32]

Throughout the occupation, there is evidence of venality among certain British officers, including one general officer, who bilked citizens and their own government. As an example, William Ball, owner of land above Kensington, lost a large quantity of hay to British foraging parties. Desiring compensation for the hay, he protested and demanded payment. He was advised it was too late, as the hay had already been charged to His Majesty's account. A British officer suggested that he put on a bold front, repeat his demand for payment to the quartermaster general's office, and, if it was not forthcoming, say that he would place his claim before the ministry. Ball adopted this stance and was told to submit a bill for straw used in roof-thatching soldiers' huts. Ball was promptly reimbursed, but the British government had thus paid twice for the same hay.[33]

While Howe had been in command in New York, he had encountered many vexatious situations centering on civil administration of the city. In Philadelphia, he was anxious to avoid similar pitfalls. He proposed assigning a number of civil posts to citizens of unquestioned loyalty. It was obvious to him that these posts only involved nominal administrative authority. He knew that with the presence of a large military force, it would be impossible to grant autonomy to civilian officials. There was no question that civil police or watchmen could detect fires or control minor civil disturbances; but, they would be absolutely ineffectual in dealing with any riotous conduct by military personnel.

After the American river forts fell, Howe virtually governed the city by proclamation. These manifestos regulated the daily economic life of every inhabitant, and directed the functions of merchants, sutlers, and ship captains. To soldiers, the manifestos were a constant admonishment against infringements on the life and property of the civilian population. They were issued by the commander in chief, or a civil or military functionary — but always with Howe's approval.

On 1 December, he appointed Galloway Superintendent General of Philadelphia, but the Loyalist leader soon realized he had little authority. He was in fact not much more than a figurehead, with his presence giving some dignity to a quasi-civil administration. To Galloway, these limitations in his office served to widen his developing rift with the British commander.

Though Howe rarely employed Loyalist regiments, he now

Return of money expended for repairing, fitting up the Barracks Births (sic) hospital, and guard house of the 1st Battalion of British Grenadiers.
Historical Society of Pennsylvania

decided they would be ideally suited for daily patrols around Philadelphia. Regular British troops would be used for the wood details, but Americans familiar with the countryside would be better equipped to cope with the irregular American militia. Acting on glowing reports of Loyalist sentiment in Pennsylvania, Howe appealed for men to serve in a Provincial corps. All men who served for two years or until the termination of the war were offered bounties of vacant land upon their discharge — 200 acres for every noncommissioned officer and 50 for each private. The response was disappointing. Howe ordered the proclamation repeated at regular intervals for nearly three months.[34]

Concurrent with Howe's appeal for volunteers, three Provincial regiments were proposed. Howe retained the colonelcy of each regiment, and three well-known area Loyalists were given the position of lieutenant colonel. Alfred Clifton was authorized to raise a regiment restricted to "Roman Catholics." He was also ordered to appoint a captain, a lieutenant, and an ensign for each fifty-seven rank and file who were recruited. This figure included noncommissioned officers. Rank and pay for officers would be determined by their success in recruiting. A quota system was established, and each captain had to enlist a minimum of thirty approved rank and file.; each lieutenant, fifteen; and each ensign, twelve. Clifton endeavored to obtain as many qualified Catholic officers as possible, believing the men would serve more efficiently under officers of their own faith.

William Allen set up a rendezvous to recruit men for the "First Battalion of Pennsylvania Loyalists," appealing to "All Intrepid Able-Bodied Heroes." Recruitment headquarters were at Patrick Tonry's on Second Street, three doors above Market. Allen was authorized to recruit four hundred privates, twenty-four sergeants, twenty-four corporals, and eight drummers, to be divided into eight companies of equal strength. The men were to receive the same pay as British regular troops.

James Chalmers, a Maryland Loyalist, requested permission to raise a regiment among Maryland refugees. Designated the Maryland Loyalists, Chalmers's recruits included many Pennsylvanians. None of these regiments enjoyed great success. Howe stated that when he left Philadelphia in May 1778, Chalmers had 336 rank and file, Clifton had 180, and Allen had 132. The total, 648 men, fell far short of Galloway's optimistic predictions.

In addition to these regiments, Richard Hovenden was authorized to raise the Second Troop of Philadelphia Light Dragoons. The troop was to consist of a captain (Hovenden), a lieutenant, a coronet, a quartermaster, two sergeants, two corporals, a trumpeter, a farrier, and forty privates. The captain was directed to recruit twenty-five men, the lieutenant twelve, and the coronet nine. If they were successful, in one month the designated officers would receive their rank and pay. In addition to their bounty, recruits would receive £16 sterling for every horse approved by General Sir William Erskine.[35]

Efforts to attract new recruits to the Provincial regiments and the regular army were not confined to those with Loyalist sympathies. Officers also tried to attract deserters from the Continental army. These men were considered good prospects, as most were of foreign birth and had developed little affection for America. To Howe's dismay, many Continental deserters were found enlisting with two recruiting officers, thereby collecting double bounty. To those discovered reaping double rewards, he promised punishment in the "most Exemplary manner." Howe knew that a number of British soldiers who had deserted were serving in the American army. He offered these men complete amnesty if they returned to their commands before 1 December.[36] James Humphreys's editorial in the *Pennsylvania Ledger* on 29 October suggested that Howe would soon be able to fight the American army with their own men, adding, "Surly they will not have less heart and courage, upon hard dollars, good cloaths, good provisions, a good cause and good officers . . . than they had with paper stuff, ragged cloaths, stinking provisions, and bad officers." As Howe was at this time unable to supply provisions to the civilian population or full rations to his troops, this type of propaganda must have had a hollow ring to its readers.

Philadelphia, with a large seafaring population, was considered a likely spot to obtain naval recruits. A number of men-of-war were shorthanded, and others had suffered significant losses during the river engagements. Newspapers carried an appeal for all able-bodied seamen and landsmen to enlist in the navy. The notice promised, "Any Seaman that wishes to serve in any particular ship in the Navy, will be entered for the ship he prefers, and entertained on board the frigate (at full pay) until he joins his respective ship." Several British sailors had jumped ship and entered the city. They, too, were urged to come aboard the frigate *Delaware,* where they would be given amnesty and "entertained" until they could be returned to their ship.[37]

Howe and Washington were concerned about the intercourse between city and countryside. Spies were constantly passing in and out of the city, and many were rightfully suspected of being double agents. Both commanders in chief decided to restrict travel into the city. Washington ordered American dragoons to intercept all farmers who attempted to enter the lines and to retain and send to headquarters all persons leaving the city.

Farmers were willing to risk running the American blockade to sell their produce for English specie (hard money), a preferable alternative to the almost worthless Continental currency. Other marauders, irregular militia, and deserting Continental soldiers harassed farmers, excusing their action as preventing the countrymen from carrying livestock and produce into Philadelphia. These highwaymen broke into springhouses and looted them of butter, cheese, bread, and other articles; likewise, they took cattle, sheep, and horses from barns and fields.[38]

The presence of American patrols near the lines caused much confusion among British sentries. Howe, upset by the sentries' repeated unnecessary firing, warned officers to discontinue the promiscuous firing as he was "determined to punish with Rigour the first Man that dares to disobey it."

Constant alerts brought the various regiments into a defensive posture, and on several occasions, the 1st and 2nd light infantry were ordered to scour the area in front of the redoubts. By mid-November the redoubts were completed, and each eventually received a garrison of a captain and fifty rank and file. Captain Johann Ewald and Captain John Peebles referred to many brushes between American and jäger patrols. Peebles gives an account of a typical skirmish, saying both patrols "pop'd at each other for a while, but little harm done."[39]

To assist the military patrols, it was decided to augment the civilian night watch. A plan was laid before Howe which proposed to raise the 17 watchmen to 120. A committee of nine prominent Philadelphians plus one each from Southwark and Northern Liberties was selected to manage the monies and regulate the duty of the additional watch. Howe expressed his "perfect satisfaction" with the plan and directed it be "carried into immediate execution."[40]

While Howe was busy reducing the pesky American river defenses and establishing military control of the city, many civilians looked to the future with misgivings. As the weeks passed, some inhabitants faced starvation. Cold houses were common as fuel became unobtainable. Despair was everywhere. Little hope of securing the necessities to sustain life remained. All prospects depended on Howe's success on the river.

A majority of the residents clutched at the hope that better times were coming and, in the interim, amused themselves with the few diversions available. Most fraternal organizations, fire companies, and philanthropic societies, such as the Society for the Relief of Poor and Distressed Masters of Ships, Their Widows and Children, functioned on abbreviated schedules or discontinued operations during the occupation. A few, like Bettering House, held regular meetings with reduced boards and still attempted to serve the needs of the community's poor. According to Loyalists and British authorities, many of these organizations were "hotbeds of sedition" and their members had naturally made a hasty exodus from the city.

One of these "seditious" fraternal organizations was Masonic Lodge No. 2. Its meeting room was broken into and all jewels, books, and paraphernalia were stolen. This lodge had sixteen colonels, ten majors, and twenty-eight captains in the American army. In addition, it had many members who served in less exciting roles. All the members were considered traitorous and had fled the city. Captain William Cunningham was instrumental in restoring twenty of the stolen items.[41] Cunningham and other British officers attended meetings of two lodges that met regularly while the army was in Philadelphia. Tradition relates that the close fraternal bond which developed between British and American officers did much to ease the austerity and rigors of imprisonment for the Americans.[42]

During the occupation, lodges 3 and 4 had their lodge room at the corner of Elfreth's Alley and Second Street. An advertisement in the *Pennsylvania Ledger* on 20 December announced that the anniversary of Saint John was to be celebrated by a festival and dinner on the twenty-seventh, to which were invited brethren in the army and navy or others as may be accommodated.[43]

Crowds of onlookers always watched the British drill or parade and on pleasant afternoons were entertained by the regimental bands on the State House grounds. The British army utilized every open area, or commons, for military purposes. Center House commons, in addition to being used as a parade ground, was also the scene of executions and lashings meted out to offenders convicted at the almost daily regimental and general courts-martial.

British officers and their ladies were frequently seen riding into the Neck, the only area safe from American patrols. This region was graced with several beautiful estates. Howe made an effort to protect these residences by assigning them as quarters for several officers.

Newspaper advertisements during the occupation included some personal insertions. An oft-quoted example read: "Wanted to live with two single gentlemen, a Young Woman to act in the capacity of housekeeper, and who can occasionally put her hand to anything. Extravagant wages will be given, and no character required. Any young woman who chooses to offer, may be further informed at the bar of the City Tavern."[44]

The Loyal Association Club, one of many dinner and social clubs to function during the occupation, held its first meeting during October at Michael Clark's opposite the State House.

For those interested in cultural and educational instruction, several private schools and tutors offered their services. Francis Johnson, professor of languages, offered a three-month course in "complete" French for a three-dollar entrance fee and six dollars a month. Instruction would be given at Johnson's lodgings or the student's apartment. John Heffernan conducted a day and night school for children, youth, and foreigners. He taught the principles of "a complete English education" and a "multiplicity of modern improvements in . . . practical mathematics." Patrick Wright advertised he "proposes" to teach English, writing, and arithmetic, and he also intended to open a night school. An anonymous instructor offered "Instruction on Violin, German Fute [flute], Claronet, Guitar." For those interested in art, Du Simitière offered engravings of William Penn for sale at his painting room on Fourth Street.[45]

Bibliophiles could browse to their hearts' content in Robert Bell's bookstore next door to Saint Paul's Church on south Third Street. Bell successfully weathered the political storms and remained in the city throughout the war. He carried books in the arts, sciences, languages, history, biography, divinity, law, voyages, travels, poetry, plays, novels, instruction, and entertainment by the most modern and ancient celebrated authors. James Humphreys, publisher of the *Pennsylvania Ledger,* carried an equally diversified selection of books and, on occasion, published titles like "Rural Economy or Essays on the Practical Parts of Husbandry — to which is added The Rural Socrates, Being Memoirs of a Country Philosopher." On Market Street opposite the butchers' shambles, Joseph Crukshank published and sold "Poor Will's Almanack for 1778," "containing besides the usual astronomical calculations, a variety of essays in prose and verse, and sundry useful receipts [sic], &c."[46]

November 22 was an eventful day in Philadelphia, starting with a phenomenon of nature, followed by an act that was the "Shame of the British Nation," and ending with the joyful news that ships were finally coming through the river obstructions.

At about 7:00 A.M. "a pretty shock of an earthquake was felt by several persons in the city."[47] Several diarists neglected to report the earthquake, probably because they were distracted by the wanton destruction of many estates north of the redoubts, between the city and Germantown. The exact number of homes which were needlessly burned is not known. Deborah Logan said she saw seventeen fires from the roof of her mother's house on Chestnut Street; other eyewitness accounts give varying numbers, but all deplored the action. Robert Morton's observations best epitomize the reaction of Loyalists and Americans alike.

The reason they assign for this destruction of their friends' property is on acco. [account] of the Americans firing from these houses and harassing their Picquets. The generality of mankind being governed by their interests, it is reasonable to conclude that men whose property is thus wantonly destroyed under a pretence of depriving their enemy of a means of annoying y'm [sic] on their march, will soon be converted and become their professed enemies. But what is most astonishing is their burning the furniture in some of those houses that belonged to friends of government, when it was in their power to burn them at their leisure. Here is an instance that Gen'l Washington's Army cannot be accused of. There is not one instance to be produced where they have wantonly destroyed and burned their friends property.

Joseph Reed wrote Thomas Wharton: "The enemy have made great destruction of the little villas in the neighborhood of their lines. The bare walls are left; the doors, windows, roofs and floors are all gone to make huts. Not the least trace of a fence or fruit tree is to be seen."[48]

A few small sloops reached the city wharves on the evening of 22 November, and others arrived in increasing numbers over the next eleven days. Morton counted sixty-three sails on the twenty-sixth. Inevitably, losses occurred in the mad dash through the chevaux-de-frise as each army supply ship and merchantman raced to unload its cargo. Sutlers and merchants commandeered every vacant store and hurriedly prepared to open for business. They knew the needs of the inhabitants and were ready to take full advantage of the scarcity in all classes of marketable goods. Prices for all commodities skyrocketed. A British officer reported that meat was a half dollar a pound; butter, over one dollar; sugar, ten and twelve shillings; wine, ten shillings a bottle; and rum, *L*3 or *L*4 a gallon, with other items similarly overpriced. Quartermaster General Sir William Erskine wanted specific scarce articles on board the merchantmen to be made available to the military. Also concerned about the condition and quantity of the commodities, he ordered all "Merchants, Adventurers and Masters of Vessels" to submit a detailed report of their cargoes. The penalty for not complying with this order was possible confiscation of the cargo, and anyone acting as an informer would receive a "sufficient reward." Fear that the poor or waterfront thugs would loot the supply and merchant ships anchored at the wharves was so great that the entire waterfront was fenced off, and 250 marines were assigned to night patrol.[49]

On 27 November, Erskine and his deputy, Lieutenant Colonel William Sherriffe, were ordered to find quarters in the city for the twelve thousand British currently living in huts near the redoubts. Two days later the men of the artillery train that had captured the American frigate *Delaware* received the good news that a £10,000 prize evaluation had been placed on the vessel and that they would soon receive their bounty.[50]

In the midst of his plans to lure Washington out of his strong position at Whitemarsh, Howe wrote to Germain and painted a gloomy picture of the military situation in America.

As a duty I owe to your Lordship, and in obedience to his Majesty's commands, I candidly declare my opinion, that in the apparent temper of the Americans a considerable addition to the present force will be requisite for effecting any essential change in their disposition, and the re-establishment of the King's authority, and that this army acting on the defensive will be fully employed to maintain its present possessions.[51]

Howe's letter to the colonial secretary reflects his constant fear that the British army in America was not adequate for the task assigned to it. His despair had increased after the loss of Burgoyne's army at Saratoga and the stubborn resistance of the Americans at Germantown, the Brandywine, and on the Delaware River. Howe was certain his request to the king for permission to return home to England would soon be honored. Nevertheless, he still hoped to induce Washington to move out and give battle on terrain advantageous to the British army.

CHAPTER VI

HOWE AT WHITEMARSH

THE SPIRITS OF the army and inhabitants were revived by the colorful spectacle of the supply ships, merchantmen, victuallers and transports that lined the city wharves. Supplies and provisions were arriving in quantities sufficient to ease any immediate distress, but contributed little to relieve the suffering of the American prisoners and the poor. Howe and Wier were fully cognizant that additional quantities of all types of provisions were needed for the army to survive until the British regained access to the countryside in the late spring of 1778. The inhabitants would be forced to pay the sutlers' inflated prices for all articles or to buy the small amounts brought in by farmers. Wier was also concerned with his inability to purchase fresh provisions for the hospitals.

Before the river became unsafe for navigation, Lord Howe made plans to sail to Rhode Island and spend the winter there. Hamond was assigned command of the squadron which would remain in the Delaware.

Sir William Howe feared that Washington would set up his winter quarters near enough to the city to harass the British lines. As it was, pickets and sentries were frequently sounding false alarms, thereby creating confusion in the army. Howe was convinced that the Americans must either be defeated or pushed back to where the danger of surprise would be minimized.

In the Germantown area, rumors circulated that Washington planned to station all or part of the American army there for the winter. Afraid their village would again become a battleground or would be burned by Howe to prevent American occupation, many residents began to move their possessions to Chestnut Hill and other more remote areas.

With Cornwallis's return from New Jersey, Howe thought he was strong enough to force the issue before the weather made campaigning impossible. In justification of his decision to move against Washington, Howe later wrote Germain, ''The enemy being joined by upwards of four thousand men, with cannon, from the Northern army, assembled their whole force in a strong camp at Whitemarsh. . . . Upon a presumption that a forward move might tempt the enemy, after receiving such a reinforcement, to give battle for the recovery of this place, or that a vulnerable part might be found to admit of an attack upon their camp. . . .''[1]

Washington's position was well chosen. His troops occupied a line of hills stretching from Militia Hill on the right to Limekiln Pike and Susquehanna Road on the left.[2] His center was protected by an escarpment that rose about two hundred feet. Below this bluff was Sandy Run and, further to the right, Wissahickon Creek, which provided additional obstacles to an advancing enemy. The weakness of his position was its exposed flanks, defended only by militia. (Characteristically, Washington placed militia on the flanks.) Another problem was terrain: No roads of consequence existed except on the flanks, making it somewhat difficult to maneuver, withdraw, or reinforce pressure points.

That a major movement of the British army was about to take place was apparent to most British and Hessian officers. Even a layman could observe the preparations being made. For example, in late November a local baker working with the military was ordered to bake forty thousand rations of bread — enough to feed ten thousand men for four days. Both commanders in chief, of course, realized that it was impossible to prevent spies from entering or leaving the city. Consequently, on 20 November, Howe permitted persons to pass in and out of the city between 8:00 A.M. and 5:00 P.M. This permitted civilians to go to Frankford or other areas and buy flour or provisions to add to their scanty larders. At all other hours no one was to leave, and anyone who attempted to enter Philadelphia was to be detained at the picket post until morning and then reported to the field officers.[3]

Like many other incidents of the Revolution, Howe's plan to attack Washington produced a heroine. The familiar story of Lydia

Darragh[4] has had its champions and scoffers, although few have actually researched British records. Her exploits reveal the patriotism of a petite and courageous Quaker lady, but not the sole savior of the Continental army.

Lydia Darragh and her husband William moved from Carter's Alley to the "corner of Dock Street, in Second at the Blue House," in February 1777.[5] According to Lydia's daughter, Ann,[6] her mother told her the upper back room in their house on Second Street was occasionally used by British staff officers as a council chamber. Howe's headquarters were across the street in the home of General John Cadwalader. On 2 December, an officer asked the family to retire early, as they desired to conduct a meeting free from interruption. Lydia's curiosity was aroused. Being sympathetic to the American cause, with a son in the American army, she decided to eavesdrop. She heard only snatches of the conversation, but enough to learn that the British intended to march against Washington.

Anxious to warn Washington, she resolved to go out through the lines the next day to give the American commander this information. Versions of the story differ. Some say she used an old pass or obtained one at Howe's headquarters; but Howe's order of 20 November stated that no pass was needed in the daytime between 8:00 A.M.and 5:00 P.M. Near Frankford she encountered Lieutenant Colonel Thomas Craig, who commanded the outpost at that village, and related her story. Craig agreed to forward her information to headquarters immediately.[7]

Washington's informants, or spies, were a combination of known and unknown, professionals and amateurs. Most American agents in Philadelphia, unlike Lydia Darragh, have remained anonymous. A number of unsigned letters sent to Washington with private intelligence on activities in the city still exist. Whether the writers of the communications were known to the commander in chief is not certain. In addition, Major John Clark, McLane, and Craig were constantly sending agents into the city to obtain information. Typical of their reports was Clark's from Newtown on 1 December, stating the British troops had been ordered to march at a moment's notice. At noon on 3 December, McLane wrote that the enemy was in motion. Craig sent intelligence to headquarters on 2 and 3 December (before he met Lydia Darragh) that the British were planning a major thrust to destroy the American army and burn Germantown and Frankford. Captain Robert Smith reported from Germantown on 2

December at 7:00 P.M., "Some Ladies who got out by special Favor say as the accts from British officers are to be attended to a movement [which] will take place early tomorrow Morning."[8]

A letter dated 4 December that Washington received from Frankford asserted that the British had on the previous night prepared four days' provisions and packed their baggage. Their preparations gave the appearance that they were marching on the fourth, when, inexplicably, the order was countermanded. Regrettably, the signature has been removed from this letter. The time and place of the letter coincide with Mrs. Darragh's meeting with Craig, but she did not have the knowledge of the countermanded orders.[9]

To add an element of mystery to the stream of information reaching Washington, Elias Boudinot mentioned meeting "a little, poor looking, insignificant old Woman" at the Rising Sun Tavern. He said the woman handed him a pocketbook. After examining several pockets, he discovered a small roll of paper on which was written that Howe "was coming out the next morning with 5,000 men — 13 Pieces of Cannon — Baggage Waggons, and 11 Boats on Waggon Wheels." Boudinot compared this information with other data at hand and discovered the reports were in substantial agreement. He hurried to headquarters and submitted his information to Washington. Again, the time factor is difficult to reconcile. If Boudinot received this information on 4 December, then the old woman's note would have the British army leaving the city on the fifth. But, Howe's initial order had been issued on 3 December and directed that two columns be ready to march at 6:00 A.M. on 4 December.[10]

Nonetheless, Howe's order was countermanded and the march was delayed until nearly 10:00 P.M. on the fourth. One British officer noted that a number of British and Hessian soldiers deserted during the night of 3 December. One deserter, an artillery corporal, carried off an orderly book which contained a transcript of Howe's orders, including the proposed line of march. Other officers did not know the cause of the delay, although all agreed that the columns were supposed to move out early on the fourth. Howe, fearing that the missing orderly book had fallen into Washington's hands, ordered the delay to make changes in the expedition. Additional brigades and battalions were ordered to join Cornwallis and Knyphausen. To protect the columns against ambuscade and snipers on the march, the flank companies were also strengthened. Anxious to have his columns proceed in light marching order, Howe ordered all baggage wagons to remain in the city. He did not expect to surprise Washington, but hoped to lure him from the Whitemarsh hills and then to engage the Americans on a battlefield of his own choice.[11]

Agents and other Philadelphians, like Lydia Darragh, kept Washington apprised of British activities in the city. Washington acknowledged that for several days before 4 December he had known that Howe was preparing to move a major part of his army. It would be absurd to believe that Washington did not take immediate steps to deploy his divisions into position and fortify the heights at Whitemarsh. He had no intention of leaving his strong position. Specific strategy could wait until he could confirm Howe's objective and establish his exact line of march.[12]

The British and Hessian huts in the rear of the redoubts had been abandoned except for those occupied by the troops still on duty. The remainder of the garrison had moved into winter quarters. About three thousand men were housed in the old barracks near present Third and Green streets. Other soldiers occupied specified city blocks with two or more soldiers quartered in most houses.

General Alexander Leslie was to command the garrison remaining in Philadelphia. Baurmeister maintained that Wolwarth's brigade, Mirbach's regiment, the British 63rd Regiment, and two battalions of Anspachers were ordered to man the trenches while Howe was on the march. In addition, fifty dragoons were to patrol the country west of the Schuylkill.[13]

Howe was concerned about the security of the homes and property in the city during the army's absence. To offer protection, he assigned the convalescents of each corps to police "their Respective Encampments or Quarters with Positive Orders to allow no Baggage, Stores or Hutts to be destroyed." One officer from each brigade and a "Carfull" noncommissioned officer from each regiment would command the convalescent details.[14]

Howe ordered all battalions and brigades to prepare to march at 10:00 P.M. on the fourth. The night was dark and cold, with temperature in the high twenties.[15] At midnight, the vanguard, under the command of Cornwallis, moved out of the lines heading up Germantown Road.[16] Close behind was Knyphausen with the main column.[17]

Advancing up Germantown Road, the British light infantry, acting as Cornwallis's van, encountered an American picket and engaged in a desultory firefight. The Americans appeared to be more anxious to observe the British movement than to risk an engagement. Accordingly, they retreated slowly, never losing contact until they reached the heights at Chestnut Hill.

As the army passed through Germantown and the hamlet of Bebberstown, soldiers from various regiments looted and burned houses and other property. In at least one instance, the destruction of private property was justified by claiming that American snipers in the house were firing on the British column.

The advance elements approached Chestnut Hill at about three o'clock, with their arrival announced by the alarm guns in the American camp. By six o'clock, most of the army was in position on the ridge which extended from the Wissahickon on the west to a post about one mile east of the village. The rear of the main column came up at about eight o'clock. British officers were somewhat awed by the fine view they had of the American camp three miles across the valley. American campfires lighted the sky. General Robertson commented, ''The fires Extended between 4 and 5 Miles which they purposedly illumin'd on hearing our Approach.''[18]

At dawn, Howe studied the American position and concluded that Washington's right was too strong to attack. It became obvious that the American commander could not be tempted to leave his fortifications. Therefore, Howe knew he had to look elsewhere for a weakness in the American line. He decided to rest the troops for two days while a provision train was brought out from the city. The 71st, 5th, and 27th regiments were dispatched to Philadelphia to escort the provision wagons back to the encampment. Howe then moved to his right along the ridge, hoping to find a vulnerable spot on the American left.[19]

The 5th and 27th regiments became exhausted by the long return march to Philadelphia. Their condition caused a delay as other regiments had to be assembled to escort the provision train. At 2:00 A.M. on 7 December, the 40th and 55th joined the 71st with the wagons and proceeded out Germantown Road. The delayed start and their subsequent slow progress narrowly averted a catastrophe for Howe. Many units in the army had consumed their supply of provisions, while others were suffering from exposure to the cold rain. Fortunately, a rendezvous was finally effected on York Road to the delight of the troops.[20]

Early on 5 December, Washington ordered detachments of the

Pennsylvania militia, under Brigadier Generals James Potter and James Irvine, to reconnoiter the British position and attack any advance pickets. A patrol of British dragoons had been sighted as far north as Flourtown observing the American artillery position at Whitemarsh Church. Potter, with part of his brigade, advanced to Barren Hill on Manatawny Road. After a brief skirmish with the British pickets, Potter withdrew his brigade to its former post on Militia Hill. Irvine, with about six hundred militiamen, moved down Bethlehem Road. About one mile below Chestnut Hill, he engaged two advance battalions of British under Colonel Abercrombie and Major Maitland. The militia behaved bravely for twenty minutes, but after Irvine fell wounded, they broke and fled. Losses were minor except for Irvine and about a score of militiamen who were taken prisoners.[21]

Throughout 6 December the British watched the American troops shift from their left to their right. Washington appeared to be concentrating his strength in front of the British position at Chestnut Hill. Howe was convinced that by a night march to the Jenkintown area on Old York Road, he would be able to turn Washington's weakened left flank. Orders were issued to the British army to be ready to march between midnight and 1:00 A.M. on 7 December. Unfortunately, there were no roads of consequence connecting Bethlehem Pike or Germantown Road with the principal roads to the east, Limekiln Pike and Old York Road. As in the Battle of Germantown, the main east and west thoroughfares were Church Road, about three miles north of Chestnut Hill, or at Germantown, equidistant to the south. Church Road, however, passed directly in front of the American post at Whitemarsh Church and the strengthened American right at Whitemarsh heights. Therefore, to reach his objective, Howe had to retrace his line of march to Germantown. Upon reaching Germantown, the army probably filed left at Abington Road and then proceeded east to "Jenkins Town." Major General Charles Grey, with the rear guard, turned left at Limekiln Pike and took post at Edge Hill.[22]

At first the Americans believed that the British were in retreat and headed towards Philadelphia. During the afternoon of the seventh, with the appearance of British troops on their left, they realized Howe had merely shifted his position. To deceive Washington, Howe had sent a detachment to harass the American right while he completed his withdrawal from Chestnut Hill. An American officer affirmed that Washington was not misled by this maneuver, but immediately sent troops back to the left in anticipation of an attack from that quarter.[23]

Cornwallis's advance arrived at Jenkintown at about 8:00 A.M. and moved to the vicinity of the Abington Presbyterian Church. Knyphausen's column, with Grant commanding the leading units, reached the area soon after and formed on Cornwallis's left. Grey had taken position near Edge Hill. This alignment placed Grey opposite the American center and the balance of the line on Washington's left.

Washington sent out two detachments numbering about one thousand to harass the British and determine if Howe intended a full-scale attack on the left. As Grey marched up Limekiln Pike, he encountered one of these detachments a short distance north of Church Road. He sent the jägers with their light cannon up the road and deployed the Queen's Rangers to the left and the guards on the right. The Rangers and guards quickly outflanked both wings of the American force, driving them back into their lines.

Further along the ridge at Edge Hill, the 1st Light Infantry was attacked by General Daniel Morgan's riflemen and other American units. After a heavy firefight, Morgan discovered he faced superior numbers and was forced to withdraw to his former position. This was the most severe engagement of the expedition. Robertson attested to the riflemen's accuracy by acknowledging one officer killed and two wounded and forty men killed and wounded.

Howe constantly shifted his position during the afternoon, probing for a weakness in the American defenses. Light skirmishing occurred along the front of both armies, but Washington steadfastly refused to leave his strong position. There was constant skirmishing on the left, which Washington considered just a prelude to an all-out attack.[24]

The British commander in chief and his general officers decided the denseness of the woods and the rough terrain made an assault foolhardy. Howe explained his decision to abandon the expedition: "the enemy's camp being as strong on their centre and left as upon the right," and Washington seeming determined to hold his position. Usually considerate of his soldiers, he was "unwilling to expose the troops longer to the weather in this inclement season . . . without tents or baggage of any kind for officers or men."[25]

In mid-afternoon, Knyphausen's column moved out of line and marched down Old York Road toward Philadelphia. He was closely followed by Cornwallis at 4:00 P.M., and at the same hour Grey retired down Limekiln Pike. With the exception of some sniper fire, their march was uninterrupted, and the army arrived back in the city about 9:00 P.M.

Unfortunately, the withdrawal was again characterized by the wanton destruction of private property. No distinction was made between friend or foe. One Loyalist expressed his dismay, stating, "The sole purpose of the expedition was to destroy and to spread desolation and ruin, to dispose the inhabitants to rebellion by despoiling their property."[26]

By his withdrawal, Howe had again revealed an unwillingness to assault a prepared position. As expressed by Robertson, "How far this move of the Army may be considered as good or bad I shall not take upon me to determine, as much may be said for as against it."[27]

Neither army suffered extensive losses, although both sides exaggerated their enemies' casualties. Howe reported that the different skirmishes resulted in nineteen killed, sixty wounded, and thirty-three missing — a total of 112 — during the expedition.[28]

CHAPTER VII

PRISONERS OF WAR

THE INHUMAN TREATMENT of American military prisoners in Philadelphia and New York remains a blemish on the honor of the British army. British and American official policy was consistent with the rules of eighteenth-century warfare. However, under the stress of a campaign and without adequate supplies or accommodations, military prisoners became the victims of negligence and occasionally brutal treatment.

William Cunningham, the British provost, and his aides were guilty of savage cruelty. Contemporary Americans and historians have vilified his character. He arrived in New York in 1774 and quickly ingratiated himself with the royal authorities, but soon became obnoxious to the Americans. His hatred for Americans intensified when he was mobbed and beaten by members of the Sons of Liberty. Cunningham apparently avenged this humiliation at every opportunity.

In 1776, he was appointed provost in New York and then vented his spleen on the hapless American prisoners entrusted to his care. Howe brought him to Philadelphia and entrusted him with the same position at the new gaol at Sixth and Walnut streets. Only two incidents are known concerning his personal life in the city. As previously mentioned, he attended a special meeting of Masonic Lodge No. 3 on 10 October, at which time he was instrumental in returning twenty jewels, books, and papers of Masonic Lodge No. 2. The minutes state they "fortunately fell into the hands of our worthy Brother Capt. William Cunningham." This is the only reference to Cunningham in the minutes — he may have fallen out of grace with lodge brothers.

The only other mention of Cunningham appeared in the newspapers in early April, announcing a robbery at his home at Second and Walnut streets. Among the articles stolen was a "Freemason's *Medal* with the name Campbell engraved thereon." It is possible that this and the other items taken were the spoils of his position as provost.

Another side of Cunningham was suggested by John Binns, a prominent Philadelphia journalist and politician. In the spring of 1799, Binns, as a political prisoner, was transferred to Gloucester prison in Great Britain. The governor of the prison greeted him at the gate, and Binns discovered his name was Cunningham, a retired half-pay British officer. Binns wrote, "He was well known in Philadelphia — in 1777, while it was in possession of the British Army. At that time, and in that service, Cunningham was Provost Marshall at Walnut Street prison." He said the governor had married an American lady, an intelligent and well-bred woman younger than her husband. Binns estimated that Cunningham was about fifty years of age and was "well made and well mannered — So long as I was in prison [about one and a half years] I never had an angry word with him, nor any reasonable cause of complaint against him." Cunningham was reportedly executed in 1791 for forgery, and his dying confession was published in 1792. There is some question, then, about who was Binns's Cunningham.[1]

During the war, British armies were concentrated in cities where accommodations for prisoners were limited. On the other hand, Washington was forced to quarter British and Hessian prisoners in many communities in the interior parts of Pennsylvania, Maryland, and Virginia. At least eight towns in Pennsylvania — Easton, Allentown, Reading, Lancaster, York, Hanover, Carlisle, and Middletown — were prisoner-of-war camps.

On 5 October, Captain William Dement was directed to act as commissary for the American prisoners until the Americans appointed an agent. From this date until early November, neither commander in chief devoted much time to the prisoner-of-war problem. Both were licking their wounds after Brandywine and Germantown and were preparing for an all-out struggle for control of the Delaware River. Headquartered at Germantown until 19 October, Howe permitted his provost virtual autonomy over the welfare of hundreds of prisoners. Cunningham availed himself of the opportunity to rob and abuse his charges.

The first prisoners to reach Philadelphia were those taken at

JOSEPH GALLOWAY.
Member of the Congress of 1774

Joseph Galloway, titular leader of the Loyalists and head of the civil
government during the occupation. Etching by Max Rosenthal. *Historical
Society of Pennsylvania*

Brandywine. They were soon followed by the Americans captured at Germantown. Officers and the wounded occupied every available space in the State House. The remaining privates were sent to the gaol at Sixth and Walnut streets. The condition of the wounded who had to endure without food or medical attention was pathetic. British medical authorities apologized, but all their attention had to be given to their wounded. Ladies of the city, horrified by the suffering of their countrymen, rushed to the State House with bandages and refreshments. Such relief was only temporary, and the men were compelled to wait until British surgeons could attend their wounds.

Howe had over two thousand eight hundred sick and wounded British and Hessian soldiers. Almost every public building and many houses were converted into hospitals. The overwhelming number of his sick and wounded made it necessary for Howe to transfer many American privates to the old gaol at Third and Market streets. Later in the winter, one of the regimental hospitals was turned over to American wounded.

Civilians as well as privates and noncommissioned officers were crowded into the new gaol at Sixth and Walnut streets. The main building, built in 1775, was 32 feet deep and had a 184-foot frontage on Walnut Street. Wings on the east and west extended 90 feet to the south. The compound included a number of small buildings and an exercise yard. Enclosing the entire prison area was a stone wall 20 feet high stretching 400 feet south and approximately 225 feet along Walnut Street.[2]

The prisoners did not sympathize with the problems of the military command. Starving and treated with sadistic cruelty, most did not know that many inhabitants were hungry and cold or that the British garrison had been placed on reduced rations. British soldiers echoed American complaints of moldy provisions crawling with maggots. One American acknowledged that the British soldier's lot was little better than his; however, this remark could offer little comfort as the British soldier at least had regular rations.

Prisoners, both officers and privates, received no rations during the first days of their confinement — ranging up to five or six days. The city was in chaos. Washington's audacity at Germantown and inclement weather had filled all hospitals with several thousand soldiers. With medical supplies and provisions stored on the ships down river, little succor was available to ease their suffering. Under these conditions, Howe cannot be overly censured for inattention to

Walnut Street Prison, for American privates and non-commissioned
officers. *Free Library of Philadelphia*

American prisoners. Likewise, Washington, with similar problems,
could devote little consideration to the widely scattered British and
Hessian prison camps.

Also incarcerated in the new gaol were a number of civilians

suspected of being inimical to the British cause. Many were sin
guilty of an incautious expression of sympathy for the rights of
Americans. Others were the target of personal animosity, and a few
were Loyalists. In the latter case, mistaken identity or per
vengeance was usually the cause of their imprisonment.[3]

Although Cunningham was responsible for the sadistic tr
ment prisoners received in the new gaol, he was usually not m
tioned in narratives or journals. Rather, they deplored the lack of pr
visions, fuel, and blankets. Prisoners were concerned about food an
fair treatment. Those accounts which mentioned the provost pictured
him as a brute, beating soldiers with the heavy key to the gaol's door
and, in one account, using the butt end of his whip. He reportedly indulged his ghoulish humor by bringing broth and other food to the
soldiers and then deliberately spilling it on the ground to watch the
starving men lap it up.

Surgeon Albigence Waldo at Valley Forge was one of the most
vitriolic critics of the treatment accorded the prisoners. He admitted
that the most devious form of harassment was to ''suffer them to
starve, to linger out their lives in extreme hunger.'' Waldo related that
the prisoners ate clay, lime, stones, wood, and bark and were found
dead with these articles in their mouths. Often quoted, this secondhand account is a curious mixture of fact, half-truth, and rumor.
The men's plight was so desperate that they preferred enlistment in
the new provincial units being raised. Some three hundred men
availed themselves of this opportunity to escape confinement.[4]

Various accounts differ on the quantity of bread and meat the
prisoners received. All agreed that their first rations were slow in
coming, but the amount varied from a quarter to a half pound of beef
or salt pork and four or five biscuits every three days. On occasion
this fractional meal allowance was decreased or spread over a longer
period of time. Without the charity of the inhabitants, regardless of
political sympathies, the death rate during October and November
would have been much higher. Pelatiah Webster, acting as a civilian
commissary, collected provisions and clothing throughout the city
and distributed them to Americans at the new gaol. He bemoaned
''their sufferings . . . many of them almost naked, with very little Bedding and blankets, their allowance of Provisions by no means
sufficient — with very little firing [wood].'' Still, the scarcity and high
prices of all the necessities of life made it improbable that the inhabitants could continue their humanitarian assistance. Webster, who

istered to the needs of the prisoners for three weeks, estimated
about four hundred privates were in the new gaol.[5]

Officers, more articulate than their men, petitioned Howe to
ress their grievances. Typical was a memorial presented by several
cers on 17 November. They admitted that while sometimes
nted exercise privileges in the enclosed State House yard, more
quently they were denied this right. Friends and families were for-
dden to see them. They categorically refuted the accusation that a
andestine correspondence had been carried on with American
ntelligence officers. Food quality was satisfactory, but not the quantity. In addition, adequate kettles, tools, and wood were not available.
Sick officers were forced to remain in the cold State House. Although
limited quantities of medicines had been furnished, the unhealthy
conditions in the gaol compounded their physical problems. Monies,
watches, and other items had been stolen by their guards. Finally,
they protested the mistreatment of officers from the frigate *Delaware*.

Their remonstrance soon produced results. Sick officers were
allowed to request parole and seek quarters in the city. They were
given permission to supplement their needs by purchasing provisions,
clothing, and other necessaries from the city's merchants. Granted
this perquisite, they bombarded fellow officers at Whitemarsh and
lias Boudinot, commissary of prisoners, for funds to ease the
ksome life at the State House. Many continued these requests
roughout the winter.[6]

Officers quartered in the State House received the same rations
is privates and noncommissioned officers. Howe later asserted that
all prisoners were given the same allowance that British officers and
soldiers received on board transports — or two-thirds of the regular
ation. This statement varied with the actual quantities distributed to
e prisoners. The reason for the discrepancy can only be conjec-
red, but provisions were scarce, and the British soldier was on
duced rations. Only when in a combat zone was a soldier given a
ll ration; therefore the commissary general may have made certain
at British soldiers received the bulk of the meager provisions at
nd. It is also possible that provost gaolers appropriated some provi-
ons intended for the privates. In any case, Howe considered that he
nly needed to feed American prisoners temporarily — until
Washington made plans to provide for his men in confinement at
Philadelphia. In the eighteenth century, armies customarily supplied
the requirements of their own soldiers in gaols.[7]

Availing themselves of a slight easing in restrictions, a number of officers effected their escape from the city. The attempted escapes were not without their humor or pathos. Thomas Hartley related, "Several of our officers have escaped from their confinement at Philadelphia. They have used great address, particularly Captain Plunket by impersonating a British officer in passing five sentries who guarded his room & afterwards by putting on the Cloathes of a Quaker girl he obtained a pass and passed the lines." Other prisoners apparently escaped by dressing as women. Finally, to frustrate further escapes of this nature, at least three camp followers, May Hanesy, Jane Jones, and Eleanor Reynolds were stationed at the gates leading out of the city and were ordered to search and secure all prisoners trying to escape in women's clothes.[8]

Some British soldiers were sympathetic to the suffering American prisoners. While on duty, Corporal Owens Grant of the 42d Regiment was court-martialed for aiding a Major Wright to escape. He was sentenced to receive 500 lashes on the bare back, but was pardoned because of his youth and inexperience.

From the beginning of the war, British and Hessian soldiers were encouraged to desert and, if prisoners, to enlist in American regiments. Samuel Cranston, an English soldier captured at Saint John's, Canada, had enlisted in the Continental line. He was retaken at Brandywine. Upon finding that his former regiment was in Philadelphia, he reaffirmed his allegiance to the king and reenlisted. This was simply a subterfuge, as he wanted to rejoin his American comrades, which he did at the first opportunity.[9]

Of all the escapees, Lieutenant Colonel Persifor Frazer has received greatest attention. He was captured on 16 September near his Chester County home by an advance British patrol. On the twenty-eighth, at Germantown, he signed his parole, "sacredly" promising to do or say nothing "directly or indirectly to the Prejudice of the King's Service or bear Arms against His Majesty, until exchanged." He was transferred to the State House in Philadelphia on 7 October.

Frazer experienced the same vicissitudes as other officers — insufficient provisions, crowded quarters, and a lack of attention. After going without food for six days, he received rations that "did not exceed from 4 to 6 ounces of salt Pork & ab/t half a pound very ordinary Biscuit p. day —." His other grievances were similar to those of all officers.

Near the end of December, Frazer and a number of officers were sent to the gaol on Walnut Street. During the third week of January 1778, because of lung illness, Frazer was paroled and allowed to secure lodgings at the Golden Swan on Third Street. He was asked to sign a ''sick'' parole, promising not to leave the tavern without permission. Although exercise was considered vital to his health, he was restricted to his quarters and sentries were posted at the front and back doors. With these limitations, he did not consider his parole binding and decided to try to escape. Succeeding, he rejoined Washington at Valley Forge.

The British, however, disagreed with Frazer's conclusion and declared that he had violated his parole. They stated that the posting of sentries had not limited his movements. Washington seemingly gave tacit support to Frazer's stand by reassigning him to his regiment.[10]

Regardless of the circumstances, the escape of American officers mitigated against the granting of future paroles. A number of officers were forced to post bond to guarantee their remaining in the city. Without funds, some officers beseeched civilians to put up their bond. John Roberts, for example, agreed to stand as bondsman for John V. Egolf. Much to his dismay, Egolf escaped, and the British demanded that Roberts pay the bond of £100. Thomas Franklin, who deplored Egolf's perfidy, asked Elias Boudinot to send him back to Philadelphia if he could be found. Three weeks later he appealed to Bradford, stating ''that many of ye prisoners have got Out on Security that must otherwise have Suffered in Jail, & if they was to observe their Ingagement, or be obliged to Return in Case of Escape it w^d be more easy for Others to obtain their Liberty to the City.'' As the British evacuated the city three days later, Roberts was probably forced to pay the £100 bond. Ironically, within a few months he was executed for treason by the radical element in Philadelphia.[11]

A few civilian prisoners voiced complaints that rations were insufficient and said they survived only because their families brought additional provisions. John McKinly, president of the State of Delaware, was taken captive at his Wilmington home. After a period of imprisonment on the *Solebay,* he was confined on another prison ship, and then transferred to the State House in Philadelphia. He had feared being treated as a military prisoner, but commented on the unexpectedly fair treatment he received.[12]

Prison camps for British and Hessian soldiers were in several towns in the interior of Pennsylvania. The common grievances Brit-

ish prisoners directed against their captors were bad quarters, food of
inadequate quantity and poor quality, and, occasionally, inhuman
treatment. After investigation, many of these complaints were verified
and were the result of conditions similar to those in Philadelphia —
lack of provisions and supplies, and personal hatred of the British,
especially of local militia. Protests continued until a mutual arrangement could be worked out for each army to supply the needs of their
own prisoners. To relieve the condition of the Hessian prisoners,
American authorities permitted their employment by local merchants
and farmers. There is no evidence that British soldiers were granted
the same privilege. The prospect of working for German-speaking
farmers appealed to the Hessians. On 8 October, at least 37 were employed around Lebanon. From 16 September to 20 November, 111
soldiers of the Lossberg Regiment worked in Lancaster County, and
two others in Maryland. Richard Lemon received permission to hire
10 Hessians to work at his saltworks. The usual remuneration was
one dollar a day. For a period in late December, Boudinot temporarily forbade any additional employment of Hessians. However,
in mid-May 1778, when all prisoners were being gathered in anticipation of a general exchange, many Hessians were still employed by
farmers.[13]

   There is no evidence that American prisoners were employed by
merchants or tradesmen in Philadelphia. Like Washington, Howe
was probably apprehensive about allowing English-speaking enemy
soldiers such freedom in the city. Congress had heard rumors that the
British were forcing Americans to work on the redoubts. Washington
was requested to ascertain the truth and retaliate if necessary; however, the report was apparently groundless.

   On 9 October, Frazer wrote Washington that Major Nisbet
Balfour, one of Howe's aides, said it would be injurious to the king's
cause to permit large numbers of American officers to have freedom
of the city. This attitude was to change in November. The real purpose of Balfour's communication was to ask Frazer to communicate
Howe's sentiments on a prisoner exchange to Washington. Howe
was anxious to negotiate a fair exchange or otherwise release all
officers on parole to their friends until exchanged. For some unac-
countable reason, Washington did not respond to Frazer's letter until
4 November. He then lamented the treatment accorded American
prisoners. If all officers could not be exchanged, he agreed a partial
exchange might be possible as circumstances of rank and numbers
permitted.[14]

That same day he wrote to Howe concurring with his desire for an exchange. In the meantime, Washington was beset by charges that British and Hessian prisoners were abused and deprived of needed provisions and supplies. Boudinot assured him that these charges were false. In fact, Washington's request to the British commissary for clothing, especially for the Hessians, had been ignored.[15]

Neither commander in chief seemed aware of conditions in their gaols until early November, probably because both generals were too deeply absorbed with the struggle for Philadelphia. Rumors of abuse filtered through to alert Washington and Congress, while a number of British officers, disgusted with the treatment of American prisoners, protested to Howe's aides. Boudinot was strangely inactive. Perhaps he was more concerned with what he termed his "intelligence" activities. Joshua Loring wrote Boudinot from New York that he was the only British commissary of prisoners and did not believe anyone had been appointed for Philadelphia.[16]

Conditions within Provost Cunningham's gaol and on prison ships at New York were well known to both Washington and Boudinot and unquestionably clouded the atmosphere for future negotiations. While some suspicion lingered as to the good faith of British negotiators, two other points were of greater importance to a successful cartel. First, Washington, prodded by Congress, insisted that civilian prisoners be included in any exchange. Howe rejected this, insisting on a military exchange. According to Howe, the exchange of civilians should be treated separately. The second problem was that Howe refused to discuss any exchange until Washington showed good faith by returning British and Hessian prisoners equivalent to the 1,821 Americans he had released at the end of 1776. While Howe realized that his insistence on this point would block all efforts for a successful cartel on the exchange of prisoners, he nevertheless encouraged the British and American commissaries to hold meetings. He also exchanged proposals with Washington on methods to provide food and clothing for their men held as prisoners.

In spite of their differences, the two commanders began a correspondence in mid-November that increased in volume until Howe sailed for England in May 1778. Both generals desired to ameliorate the suffering of the prisoners. While it was natural there would be charges and countercharges, followed by recriminations, it was obvious both were sincere. Washington concurred with Howe's statement that a general exchange was necessary "in Justice to the Officers and men immediately concerned." To show his good faith,

Howe voluntarily released several officers "on Account of some Peculiarity in their Situation." All points of mutual concern were not immediately corrected, but, as Washington wrote, he ultimately hoped that a general exchange would be concluded "without regard to the dispute subsisting between us."[17]

Howe, in a somewhat petulant mood, wrote on 24 November and reiterated that the only thing standing in the way of an exchange was a settlement for the prisoners released the previous year. Having unburdened himself on that point, he stated there were no grievances on either side, real or imaginary, to impede a general exchange. The question of the Americans released in 1776 was finally resolved after Howe relinquished command.

Both commanders agreed that all prisoners were entitled to good treatment, but Howe believed "that Indulgence can only be regulated by the Situation of the Place, in which prisoners happen to reside." He did not object to a commissary's coming into the city to visit the prisoners and bring them clothing, money, and other necessaries; but when Boudinot attempted to enter the lines, he was denied entrance. Howe had temporarily reversed his offer, apparently based on misinformation. However, the way was soon cleared to bring provisions for the prisoners into the city.[18]

Following the commanders' friendly exchange, Washington was informed that Congress had received reports of abuse of prisoners in Philadelphia. These may not have been new incidents, but ones already known to the commander in chief. Regardless, Congress ordered him to retaliate if the abuse was not discontinued. Howe replied with a countercharge declaring that British officers had been placed in irons (handcuffed together) at Princeton. Before Howe's complaint, Washington had investigated this situation and found it was typical of local animosity toward Loyalist officers. He wrote Howe, "This was without my Privity or consent," and that he had ordered immediate relief for the officers. As this had happened sometime before, Washington was hopeful that it would not interfere with negotiations or lead to retaliation.[19]

Howe took steps to keep himself apprised of conditions in the gaols and State House. On 17 November, all field officers of the British pickets were ordered "to visit the Rebel Prisoners once a Day and Enquire into their Complaints" and report to headquarters. With Loring in New York, he selected Hugh Ferguson to be commissary of prisoners at Philadelphia.[20]

After his appointment as commissary, Ferguson made arrangements to meet Boudinot to explore areas of cooperation. All points raised in the correspondence between Howe and Washington were reviewed. A tentative protocol was reached to deliver provisions to the prisoners of both armies. The deliveries were to be made by soldiers not above the rank of quartermaster, although Boudinot was somewhat skeptical about the scheme's implementation. It was agreed that Americans could purchase clothing for their privates by selling provisions at the market. This was a further indication that the city was in desperate need of fresh provisions. To superintend the distribution of food, clothing, and other needs of the American prisoners, Ferguson suggested that Boudinot nominate an agent residing in the city. Both agreed that Thomas Franklin, a man respected by all parties, would make a good agent.

Ferguson asserted that Howe wanted a list of all British and Hessian prisoners in order to provide for their maintenance. Boudinot submitted a figure of 4,650, but excluded those surrendered by Burgoyne at Saratoga, usually referred to as the Saratoga Convention troops, as they were covered under a separate agreement. Ferguson expressed amazement when he was informed the Americans had been supplying provisions to all but about 1,900 of the British prisoners. He advised Boudinot that it was customary for each army to maintain its own prisoners.

Another meeting was scheduled for the next day, but because Howe was dissatisfied with Boudinot's figures, the British representatives did not appear. Boudinot received a letter from Ferguson on 3 December demanding a more accurate accounting of British prisoners. Howe was certain that more prisoners were with the Americans than Boudinot had indicated. The American commissary apparently satisfied Ferguson's demand. On 10 January 1778, Ferguson reciprocated by furnishing a report on the numbers and locations of American prisoners. To confirm the number of American soldiers who were missing, Howe ordered all corps commanders to report the names of their prisoners, where they had been captured, and where they were imprisoned. This permitted proper arrangements to be made for Boudinot to furnish ''some subsistence'' to the prisoners.[21]

The suffering and mistreatment prisoners experienced during the first two months of the British occupation of Philadelphia cannot be excused. Some accounts are exaggerated, tending to portray a sadistic British attitude toward rebel prisoners. It was never Howe's intention to starve Americans in the city gaols. Still, no justification can be offered for the brutality of Cunningham or explain why he was placed in a position of responsibility. Nor can the inattention to the prisoner problem by the commanders in chief until it had deteriorated to the point where needless suffering and death occurred be excused. The fact that men starved cannot be justified by the short supply of rations in the city. Although full rations were not available for distribution to the gaols, the meager quantities delivered represented a graphic example of man's inhumanity to man. Howe may not have known of the conditions, but as commander in chief, he should have accepted responsibility for the actions of his subordinates.

Both leaders were compassionate men and would not knowingly have countenanced abuse of prisoners. As 1778 dawned, they took definite steps to ensure better conditions for the unfortunate captives. By appointing Thomas Franklin as the American agent and Ferguson as British commissary at Philadelphia, a liaison was provided which had previously been missing.

At last everyone, from commanders in chief to agents, was willing to negotiate on every complaint or misunderstanding rather than resort to threats and retaliation. With the agreement that each army would feed and see to the comforts of its own men, most bickering and charges of abuse and neglect ceased. Problems still remained, especially regarding a fair exchange, but now the prisoners could look to their own agent to supply their needs.

Although a rapport had emerged between the two commanders and was shared by their commissaries, obstacles continued to surface during the remaining months of occupation. Loring, now in Philadelphia, either on Howe's order or on his own initiative decided to clean the new gaol and make it more habitable. He purchased brooms, brushes, buckets, mops, and even one lamp. Wheelbarrows and axes were bought to clean up the exercise yard. Even a store was fitted out, although Loring did not indicate its exact purpose. Ironwork was repaired, and pumps were installed to provide water for the prisoners. As officers and privates had often complained that kettles were needed to cook their meager rations, Loring purchased two dozen additional ones for the gaol. William Terrett was appointed keeper of the officers' gaol at the State House, and Robert Knott keeper at the new gaol.

Anticipating a wholesale release of officers on parole, Loring directed James Humphreys to print 700 blank parole forms.

Ironically, at the same time Loring was also paying citizens for reporting any attempted escapes from the gaol. The going rate for turning in escaped prisoners was ten shillings. Apparently Howe authorized a bounty payment to any American officers who could be induced to desert. Major Madden, by order of Howe, paid two officers who came through the lines *L*6 15s. 3d.[22]

With the appointment of Franklin, Ferguson turned his attention to catering to the needs of the British and Hessian prisoners. Ferguson and Boudinot had tentatively agreed to allow the purchase of provisions locally. This procedure obviated the expense of long hauls and ensured regular deliveries to the men. There was some confusion during the transition period, and a few American civilian authorities, who should have been better informed, continued to carp about British negligence. On 22 December, Joseph Nourse commented on the cruelty endured by Americans in the gaol and contrasted this to the good care afforded the British prisoners. British negligence, he continued, "has rendered it necessary for Congress to send in Provisions for their support lest a greater number shou'd fall a sacrifice to their inhumanity."[23] His statement might be attributed to ignorance, but as an employee of the Board of War, he should have known that Boudinot was temporarily supplementing the prisoners' fare.

Unfortunately, a controversy soon developed over the right of the American agent to purchase clothing in the city. Ferguson had granted this privilege to Franklin, only to have it countermanded by Howe. In retaliation, Washington ordered Boudinot to advise Ferguson that effective 1 February, all British prisoners were to be supplied from Philadelphia. Under no circumstances was Ferguson or his agents permitted to purchase provisions in the country. Proper passports were to be issued to British agents, enabling them to distribute provisions to any town where their men were confined. Boudinot was to be responsible for supplying all needs of Americans in the city. He agreed to send firewood or to supply the British prisoners with as much for ten men as Ferguson allowed for every ten Americans. This change in policy applied only to prisoners west of New Jersey.

Boudinot immediately advised Ferguson of the changes. He regretted the British decision that had precipitated this crisis, adding, "If any Inconvenience should arise to the unfortunate Prisoners on this account, it cannot be chargeable on us."[24]

Howe expostulated with Washington for denying British agents the privilege of purchasing provisions in the country. He argued that there was little difficulty in supplying prisoners in one location — Philadelphia. However, British prisoners were scattered, many as far as three or four hundred miles in the interior. Adding to Howe's annoyance was Boudinot's statement that the commander's refusal to permit the purchase of clothing had prompted the change in provisioning prisoners. Howe asked, "How subtile & disingenous is this argument, Provisions, or the means of Existence, can only from the nature of Things, be supplied by Agents or Commissaries on the Spot: Clothing can be provided at a Distance, & sent in to our respective Prisoners. The one is a Demand of daily Necessity, indispensible & immediate. The other but occasionally requisite."

The contents of this curious letter to Washington reflect Howe's anger. He previously had ordered the Americans to feed their own prisoners; but he had obviously forgotten this agreement. He added a little invective to his communication by inferring that the Americans may have reacted vindictively:

Mr. Boudinot does not mention by whom this Measure is threatened to be adopted. But it is so repugnant to the Rules of War in all civilized Nations, & so marked with Inhumanity, that I cannot persuade myself it has been derived from your Advise; and I am unwilling to suspect that even the present Rulers of this Country, are so entirely lost to all Sense of Honor, & to all Feelings of Humanity, as to pass an Edict for the deliberate Destruction of those whom the Chance of War has thrown into their Hands.

Washington apparently took a cooling off period, as he did not respond to Howe until 30 January. Even then, his anger surfaced at the preceding remarks:

There is one passage of your Letter, to which I cannot forbear taking particular notice of. No expressions of personal politeness to me can be acceptable, accompanied by reflections on the Representatives of a free People, under whose Authority I have the Honor to act. The delicacy I have observed in refraining from every thing offensive in this way, entitled me to expect a similar Treatment from you. I have not indulged myself in invective against the present Rulers of Great Britain, in the course of our Correspondence, nor will I even now avail myself of so fruitful a Theme.[25]

Except for this one acrimonious exchange, the official correspondence of the generals was marked by respectful cordiality. Both men let the point of contention drop and directed their attention to the prisoner of war situation, although Howe did remark he would not apologize for what he considered only observations. On 5 February, Howe repeated his allegation that all Americans had received the same provision allowance as his troops not on active service. He asserted that he had granted American prisoners the right to purchase additional provisions at the market. Upon hearing that Americans were cold; he had immediately authorized the procurement of extra blankets. Most important, he was anxious to relieve the distress of "Prisoners on both Sides" and proposed a cartel to arrange for an exchange.[26]

Howe, visibly upset on 21 February, wrote a long letter to Washington reviewing most of the points previously covered in their correspondence. His irritation was evident, especially at the repeated charges of abuse and ill-treatment of prisoners. Confronted by public opinion and the official protests of Washington, he took umbrage at what he considered false statements. It mattered little to him that many of the rumors were exaggerated. Howe asked Thomas Franklin to prepare a declaration on conditions in the gaols and prisoner hospital. To refute the attempts at calumny, he forwarded a copy of this declaration to Washington on 21 February. He requested that Washington obtain a similar statement on favorable treatment of British prisoners so that all charges of abuse would be put to rest.[27]

Franklin's declaration said:

I the Subscriber declare that ever since I have attended to the Prisoners I've seen nothing like Cruelty exercised towards them, nor heard of any insult offered to them on the Contrary I have observed a Care and Attention has been paid to their wants, and that the Jail keepers have behaved to them Civilly and with humanity, I also have the greatest Reason to believe that the allowance given them by the King has been faithfully served out both to Officers & Privates Viz^t to the Privates Eight ounces of Pork and two thirds of a Pound of Bread to Officers twelve ounces of Pork and one pound of Bread each day. that Surgeons are appointed to attend the Sick, that Fresh Meat, Oatmeal, Barley, Sugar, Rum, Medicines &^{c} are administered to them — That the Sick officers have their parole and those in Confinement are allowed the Priviledge of walking out every day for an hour or two in their turns for the advantage of Exercise and Air — and I am informed that it is on account of the Publick Safety and the necessity of Guarding prisoners in a Garrisoned Town, which prevents greater Indulgence being granted to them.

NB Women Nurses are appointed by Genl Howe to tend the Sick, and I have by permission furnished Blankets and other Clothing that the prisoners are Comfortable on that Account.[28]

The tenor of Joseph Simon's deposition was equally benevolent regarding the care of British prisoners:

I the Subscriber do hereby declare that I have had the Care of the Prisoners in the British service in Pennsylvania except Easton for above two years last past, as agent to Mr. David Franks of the City of Philadelphia, that during this whole Time I have seen nothing like Cruelty exercised towards them, nor heard of any Insult offered to them: on the Contrary, I have observed a Case of attention has been paid to their wants and that the Gaol Keeper has behaved to them Civilly & with humanity — That the greatest Part of them have had the liberty of several Miles limits and know that they have faithfully rec^d One Pound of Meat & One Pound of Bread per Man per Day until within two months past — That Surgeons are appointed to attend the Sick, who have necessaries provided for their comfort — That all the Officers are & have been on their Parole & none ever confined to my Knowledge except Seven or Eight at Carlisle, (who I have been informed have been kept confined on Acc^t of some American Officers who it is said are confined in like manner in New York) and a Chaplain of the 10th Regt who did not choose to give his Parole.

That such Prisoners who have wanted necessaries as shoes, Shirts &c have had liberty to purchase them in the Town when they had money.[29]

David Franks, the British agent in Philadelphia, made a payment of *L*33,118 15s. 4-1/4d. to Joseph Simon for expenditures made on behalf of British and Hessian prisoners in Pennsylvania and Maryland. This payment is a further testimony to Simon's concern for the prisoners entrusted to his care.[30]

Notwithstanding the scarcity of provisions, high prices, and bickerings, Boudinot and Thomas Bradford were soon forwarding substantial numbers of cattle, plus large quantities of flour, and other foodstuffs to Franklin. By early January, Boudinot was writing enthusiastically to American agents for British prisoners throughout Pennsylvania. He advised William Atlee that he had 200 barrels of flour in the city and expected to have an additional thousand in a fortnight. He also noted that he had a supply of very good fresh beef. His enthusiasm was obvious when he advised Richard Peters that he had ordered one thousand barrels of flour, thirty cords of wood, and a quantity of Indian meal to be shipped up from Port Penn (Delaware) — only to have his spirits dashed by Howe's prohibition of water traffic. Most of the vegetables and flour that reached the city came by boat from Delaware and areas of New Jersey. Howe was angered that boats had arrived without his previous knowledge or permission. He expressed his displeasure to Washington: ''A sloop with Flour has been received yesterday Evening for the Use of the Prisoners here: but I am to desire no more Flags of Truce may be sent by Water either up or down the River without Leave being previously obtained.''

Both commanders considered essential to internal security that the movements of enemy representatives be closely controlled. Washington allowed only one quartermaster or soldier of a lower rank to accompany a convoy of provision wagons passing through the lines. Before proceeding into the country, they were joined by an American officer who was to make certain no one communicated with the inhabitants. Similar orders were issued by Howe, although many land convoys were stopped at the redoubts and their cargoes were turned over to British officers on command. The cargoes were then delivered to Ferguson, who faithfully forwarded them to Franklin.[31]

Many letters and receipts verify the acceptance by Franklin of cattle, flour, and other provisions. A typical shipment was one received on 11 February of fifty barrels of pork and two tons of hay for the cattle. Ten cords of wood, 150 barrels of flour, and a quantity of turnips, cabbage, potatoes, parsnips, and carrots came in on 12 March. Nevertheless, fresh vegetables were often scarce, and this scarcity became the direct cause of a dreaded illness at the gaol. In February Peebles declared, ''There is a vary bad putrid fever, of [which] they are dying very fast.'' Two months later Franklin wrote Bradford that doctors feared a reoccurrence of the fever unless the desperately needed vegetables were received soon. In fact, ''a plenty of them without Meat w^d be more Use full than the flesh without ye Vegetables.''[32]

Another problem Franklin faced was a shortage of funds needed to provide for the comfort of the officers. He did not consider these men to be his responsibility. Reluctantly, he furnished them provisions and other articles which he thought should have come from ''ye Kings allowance.''[33]

Howe refused to permit American agents to make purchases with Continental money; only gold and silver were acceptable. Congress resolved that all commodities purchased by the British in the countryside must be paid for in hard money. The exchange rate was set at four shillings, six pence in gold or silver for every dollar of American currency.

It was natural that many prisoners availed themselves of every opportunity to flee the gaols. In February a number escaped. Orders were issued to the guards to shoot to kill in any future escape attempts. All privates and noncommissioned officers were forbidden to communicate with families or friends without first obtaining written permission from headquarters.[34]

Following the numerous protests of Cunningham's abuse of his office, Howe ordered him back to New York. Much to the amazement of most Americans, Cunningham was restored to his position as provost of that city. However, with his departure reports of indignities and mistreatment of Americans ceased. Now their major fear was the devastating fever which sporadically raged through the gaol. Many men died. Howe ordered proper medical attention be given to all prisoners at the new gaol. A British army hospital was cleaned and then turned over to the Americans. Two surgeon mates were in constant attendance. Dr. Morris was ordered to have one surgeon attend the sick and wounded rebels once a week and ''to be answerable that all proper care is taken of them''[35]

A small crisis arose in March, when the Americans inadvertently violated the agreement forbidding commissioned officers to command a boat bringing provisions to the city. Captain Isaiah Robinson volunteered to act as master of a shallop with its cargo to be delivered to Franklin. Robinson was the senior Continental naval captain on the Delaware. As his wife wanted to visit her mother in the city, the worthy captain thought this was an excellent opportunity to satisfy her wish. Unfortunately, his identity was soon revealed, and he was imprisoned. Compounding his problem was the fact that he had permitted Captain Galt of the Pennsylvania navy to accompany him and assist in sailing the shallop. Although both officers were released after a short confinement, it naturally placed a strain on the issuance of passes to the masters of the shallops.

During March, April, and May, cattle, flour, and other provisions arrived in good quantities. Nevertheless, there was never a surplus, and when shortages did occur, the men looked to the inhabitants for assistance. Elizabeth Graeme Ferguson, wife of the British commissary, was constantly solicitous of the needs of the prisoners and attended to their wants as far as her resources permitted. She lived at Graeme Park and, pathetically, was never to see her fortune-hunting husband again. After the war, radicals accused her of treasonable acts, but her property was partially saved by the intercession of a number of moderate Americans. Boudinot thanked her, saying, "Your great attention to our unfortunate Country & fellow-citizens [prisoners in Philadelphia] demands the Thanks of every friend of humanity."[36]

On April 22, the *Pennsylvania Packet* carried a story that showed the compassion for those less fortunate was not limited to any social class:

A free Negro woman (who is in the service of a gentleman of the city of Philadelphia now in the country) having received two hard dollars for washing, and hearing of the distress of our prisoners in the gaol, went to market and bought some neck-beef and two heads, with some green, and made a pot of as good broth as she could; but having no more money to buy bread, she got credit of a baker for six loaves, all which she carried to our unfortunate prisoners, who were much in want of such supply. She has since paid the baker, and says, she never laid out money with so much satisfaction —. Humanity is the same thing in rich or poor, white or black.

Like their American counterparts, British and Hessian prisoners were frequently exposed to unpleasant circumstances. Although militia guards were not as abusive as Cunningham, many were cruel and often were detected stealing the possessions of their captives. In small towns, space to house the prisoners was limited, and at the beginning foodstuffs and fuel were scarce. Conditions in the gaols aroused the sympathy of American deputy commissaries and agents. R. L. Hooper, at Easton, deplored his inability to relieve the prisoners' sufferings: "The poor wretches under my care are almost all sick & dead I stretch your orders to me in their favour to the utmost and have saved some of them from perishing." At another time he lamented the death of a number of prisoners.[37]

British officers were little different from their opposite numbers; they complained about their quarters and persecution, and many tried to escape. Some officers were released on parole pending their exchange, after which they were allowed to return to Philadelphia. Most honored their paroles; as one deputy remarked, they were "men of honour, have behaved well." In any case, the road to the city was fraught with citizen protests and harassment. Some officers had purchased articles for their comfort on credit. Others had borrowed money from residents and left without liquidating their obligations. Several were arrested on the road to Philadelphia and others were followed into the city. Whenever possible, the officers were forced to give a promissory note guaranteeing payment. A few American officers suggested that a German-speaking officer should escort the

Hessian officers. It was anticipated that he could ingratiate himself with the Hessians and gain entrance to the city to obtain intelligence. It appears Washington frowned upon this deception.[38]

The narrative of Thomas Sandford of the guards illustrated some delivery problems experienced by the quartermasters and the harassment of the drovers and escort. On 16 January, Sandford, with one other British quartermaster, two Hessians, and a few surgeons and sergeants with their escort, left Philadelphia. Thomas Bradford met them at the Spread Eagle Tavern on the road to Lancaster and forwarded their passports and identification to Washington. Early on the eighteenth Lieutenant Colonel John Fitzgerald, one of Washington's aides, arrived and said the commander in chief objected to having more than one British and one Hessian quartermaster accompany the convoy. He also objected to the surgeons, but in the interest of humanity and relief of the sick and wounded, they were allowed to proceed with the column.

An American officer was delegated to accompany each quartermaster. The officers' instructions were not to allow the British to talk to any inhabitants except in their presence. They were also to protect the prisoners from insult and to make certain any purchases they made, such as lodging, food, or forage, be paid in gold and silver at the current rates.

From the tavern on, they were subject to many minor delays and harassments. As the innkeeper at Lancaster was anxious to receive gold and silver, he reduced their bill after hearing that they paid in hard money. This brought about a local *cause célèbre* which involved members of Congress and the State Assembly. A recent state law made all payments in gold or silver on a parity with Continental currency. The scared innkeeper was, therefore, compelled to recalculate his bill, which raised the charges from £2 0s. 9d. to £4 14s.

Further mishaps occurred. Before leaving Lancaster, three members of the party were arrested for passing counterfeit money. After examination, the sergeant was judged innocent. He had purchased the counterfeit currency for hard money from the other two prisoners, a carpenter and the conductor of the convoy. They were remanded to jail for possessing and passing counterfeit money.

Sandford and the British wagons left for Reading on the twenty-fourth. They were soon followed by the Hessian party which was on its way to Virginia. After proceeding nine miles, Sandford's party was stopped and ordered back to Lancaster. They learned that a letter from Boudinot had cited abusive treatment of American prisoners in Philadelphia, which was a violation of the agreement. Upon their return to Lancaster, Sandford, Dr. Hamond Beaumont, and two surgeon mates were well treated and were housed in a local tavern. The British soldiers, however, were placed in gaol and treated as common criminals. Soon after Sandford's return, the Hessian wagons were also brought back.

Dr. Beaumont dispatched a letter to Fitzgerald protesting the interruption of their humane mission. The Board of War had ordered Boudinot to write the letter without consulting Washington. Boudinot neglected to investigate the charges, thereby compounding the mistake. It was another example of an attempt to embarrass Washington.

Within twenty-four hours, a letter arrived from Fitzgerald declaring that Boudinot's letter was a misrepresentation. The convoy was at liberty to proceed. Before departing, Beaumont again wrote to Fitzgerald. This time he stated that six sergeants, a corporal, and one civilian employee of the party had their blankets, shirts, shoes, hose, gaiters, soap, and razors stolen at the gaol. The greatest loss was suffered by Sergeant McMahon of the 16th Dragoons, whose horse, arms, accoutrements, and £40 19s. sterling were stolen. The money was intended for the prisoners at Reading.

When Sandford's party prepared to leave, it was discovered that their wagons were being used by people of the town and that the horses were badly jaded. Regardless, as arrangements were being made to leave, Lafayette arrived in town and apologized for their mistreatment. Seeing the British about to depart, many civilians — Sandford thought they were people of authority — raised objections because of the reported abuse of Americans in Philadelphia. The cry was raised that the wagons must not be allowed to proceed — some going so far as to question Washington's authority. Chagrined at being unable to comfort the British prisoners, Sandford and his men crawled back to the city with their exhausted teams.

On 2 February, Fitzgerald met them at the Admiral Warren Tavern, where he expressed Washington's regrets that obstacles had been thrown in their way. He explained that it was the desire of the commander in chief to provide for all the victims of the war imprisoned in the various gaols. This mishap was another example of the interference of the Board of War. Washington wrote the Board and tactfully explained that Sandford and his party ''came out by my permission and in consequence of a Stipulation between myself and General Howe." It was obvious he was annoyed and did not appreciate the meddling with his authority.[39]

The carping criticism and interference of the Board of War was another factor which prompted Washington to request Simon's deposition on the Americans' treatment of British and Hessian prisoners. There is no doubt that the scathing remarks by the board on the handling of prisoners had aroused the ire of Boudinot. Writing to General Horatio Gates on 10 March, Boudinot stated, "The Board of War have themselves only to blame, for every inconvenience we now labour under." He tried to soften his condemnation by saying he was not referring to present members. He added that it was impossible to maintain proper surveillance over thousands of prisoners, especially when they were scattered in private homes and were without the benefit of a guard or "overseer." The manifold problems of supply and delivery to American prisoners occupied all his efforts and those of his deputies and agents. Irritated, he stated that it would be impossible to appear before the board, as his responsibility to the prisoners demanded he remain at camp. Washington was undoubtedly aware of the contents of Boudinot's letter, as the commissary was at headquarters.[40]

In May, after the cartel negotiations were completed, Boudinot resigned as commissary of prisoners. In his stead, Congress appointed F. Johnston, who declined because he did not want to lose his rank in the army. Congress then elected Major John Beatty on 28 May as the new commissary.

On 2 March, Howe moved to consummate the cartel by the appointment of Colonels Charles O'Hara and Humphrey Stephens. As a precondition of the cartel, Howe was to release General Charles Lee in exchange for Major General Richard Prescott. Unbeknownst to Howe, Prescott had been released a few weeks earlier. Then a misunderstanding developed over whether Lee was to travel by land or by sea to Philadelphia. Regardless, Washington refused to hold the cartel until Lee reached his camp. Like most Americans, the commander in chief was obsessed with Lee's presumed military ability. Almost a month passed before the machinery of the cartel could be implemented. Meanwhile, Howe, tired of ambiguities, reminded Washington that his delay was causing unnecessary suffering for the prisoners of both sides. At last, it was agreed to meet in Germantown on 31 March.[41]

Washington wrote Congress and promised to work for the exemption of civilians as prisoners; but he reminded them that by a previous resolve they had implied the right of considering civilians as prisoners of war.[42]

The two commanders in chief agreed on the details of protocol for the cartel. In addition to O'Hara and Stephens, Howe appointed Captain Richard Fitzpatrick as a commissioner. Joshua Loring was also expected to make an occasional appearance at the meetings. Washington selected Colonel William Grayson, Lieutenant Colonel Robert H. Harrison, and Lieutenant Colonel Alexander Hamilton as commissioners, and Loring's counterpart, Elias Boudinot, as civilian representative. Each delegation was to be escorted by a captain and twelve dragoons. Germantown was considered neutral ground for the duration of the meetings.

Boudinot, in his reminiscences, made a curious statement about some behind-the-scene maneuvers of a congressional committeee. A meeting of the committee and commissioners, presided over by Washington, was held at Valley Forge. After discussing the cartel, the committee "soon discovered their Sentiments, agt [against] an Exchange, and urged it as the Opinion of Congress — That the settling of this Cartel should be merely ostensible for the purpose of satisfying the Army and throwing the blame on the British, but true policy required us to avoid an Exchange of Prisoners just at the opening of the Campaign."

Washington was aghast to hear that members of Congress would approach the British commissioners with such a shabby private objective. The American commissioners, with Washington's approval, refused to engage in a cartel that did not provide an honorable basis for the immediate liberation of all prisoners. Boudinot revealed that the committee, upon returning to Congress, passed an offensive resolution "couched in the most insulting Terms." The resolution contended that Washington had selected commissioners who agreed with his determination to establish a successful cartel. Angered, but not deterred from his objective, Washington told his representatives that he would sign and take full responsibility for any agreement they made to free all prisoners. Boudinot, who became a delegate to Congress in June, conducted a fruitless search for the resolution. He concluded it had been "expunged from the Minutes."[43]

The conference opened on 31 March. It was the consensus that the first business on the agenda would be a presentation of arguments on a general exchange. Then representatives could direct their attention to secondary matters, such as individual exchanges, methods, and places for the return of prisoners.

After a few days of discussion, several differences, some trivial, were apparent, and the commissioners returned to their respective headquarters for further instructions. Before returning to the conference table, Howe wrote to Washington and requested that future meetings be transferred to Newtown. He considered Germantown too close to the city and a possible base for espionage activities.

The sessions were renewed at Newtown on 6 April. American commissioners proposed a permanent cartel to cover all soldiers presently incarcerated and any prisoners taken in future actions. An immediate protest was raised by the British commissioners. They objected to any agreement that extended beyond the duration of Howe's command in America. Two British representatives considered themselves without authority to proceed further and returned to the city for direction. Howe recognized that his authority was limited to the present negotiations; he knew that he would soon be relinquishing his command to return to England. The commissioners were ordered back to Newtown after being admonished not to deviate from their original orders.

Another point of contention was the British refusal to consider the plight of civilian prisoners. They were adamant, declaring the two issues were not debatable.

Much time was wasted on protocol and petty personal and political machinations. However, an agreement was finally reached. The commissioners were to return to their headquarters and recommend that an exchange of current prisoners be made as far as rank and numbers made it possible.[44]

The cartel encountered several obstacles that made it impossible to effect a complete exchange for several years. Howe's anticipated recall was finally announced, and Sir Henry Clinton was selected as supreme commander in America. This change was not conducive to a harmonious solution. Howe always seemed willing to cut through most of the objectionable facets of the cartel, but the querulous Clinton demurred.

Congress, in an effort to be conciliatory, approved the cartel in principle. On 21 May, Congress passed a resolution embodying most of the proposals. It agreed to exchange all officers and privates as far as rank and number applied. This exchange could also be extended to the Saratoga Convention troops. Under no condition would it agree to release officers in exchange for a designated number of privates. The transfer could be made in Rhode Island, New York, and Pennsylvania at such times and places as were mutually acceptable. On 23 May, Washington, unaware of the change in command, sent Howe a copy of the congressional resolve.[45]

Clinton replied to Washington on 3 June, protesting that some features of the resolution were unacceptable. However, he believed Loring and a designated American representative could work out an equitable arrangement.[46]

Washington advised Clinton that Hamilton would meet with Loring at Germantown on 6 June and would be accompanied by John Beatty, the new commissary. As Hamilton had prepared a status report on British and Hessian prisoners in late May, he was well qualified to discuss the various issues with Loring. Loring had disclosed that there were 120 commissioned officers and 670 noncommissioned officers and privates in Philadelphia. Of the latter, 80 were hospitalized. Hamilton expected the long-standing dispute over the prisoners released by Howe in the winter of 1776 could be resolved. In early June, Washington finally consented to return 900 privates, which Clinton agreed to receive "in full discharge & release of all Claim and demands whatsoever relative to the s^d Eighteen Hundred & Twenty one Prisoners of war on the Part of the Army of Great Britain."[47]

An agreement was approved, and Boudinot was ordered to send in without delay British and Hessian prisoners sufficient to "redeem" all Americans in the city gaols. This simple order did not recognize the hurdles confronting the American agents: British and Hessian prisoners were scattered throughout three states, with many Hessians working on isolated farms. There was no conceivable way this order could be complied with before the British evacuated Philadelphia. Some prisoners were exchanged, but they represented a mere fraction of the number of those imprisoned.[48]

An illustration of the agent's dilemma was that of Hooper at Easton, where thirty prisoners had died and more were sick. However, on 13 June, he forwarded the prisoners he had collected from the surrounding farms. He cautioned Boudinot that the Hessians had developed a fondness for America and would probably desert at the first opportunity.[49]

Impatient and unwilling to release Americans before the British prisoners had reached the city, Clinton ordered all American prisoners placed on shipboard and taken to New York. On the evening of 16 June, he directed "a detachment of one Captain, three Subalterns, nine Sergeants, nine Corporals — and one hundred privates from the 10th regiment" to proceed at 7:30 the next morning to the new gaol and escort the prisoners on board nine vessels lying at Penrose wharf. The captain was to use his discretion in dividing the prisoners, and his command, among the various ships.[50]

Loring was astounded by Clinton's order. An hour before the prisoners were taken to the ships, he notified Boudinot to approach the lines and summon General Robinson [Robertson], adding, "I have reasons why I would wish you to be as expeditious as possible." Boudinot responded, "The embarking of the Privates, Prisoners of War, is a direct breach of the Faith pledged to me in our agreement." The former commissary wrote to Robertson, with whom he had been on good terms in New York, deploring Clinton's decision: "I transacted the Business relative to Prisoners with Mr. Loring as a Person having full authority for the Purpose."[51]

With the reoccupation of Philadelphia, Benedict Arnold became the military governor. Three hundred Hessian prisoners reached the city on 20 June, and Arnold was hopeful that they could be exchanged for Americans on board the British fleet. He ordered Bradford to sail down the river under a flag of truce and try to overtake part of the British fleet. Unfortunately, he was unsuccessful. Hundreds of additional prisoners arrived in Philadelphia and were transferred to the new gaol. Meanwhile, Thomas Franklin had given Loring a receipt for the prisoners in the hospital. In late May Loring had reported eighty sick in the prison hospital.[52]

An interesting footnote revolves around a group of eighty-one American officers, including General Irvine of the Pennsylvania militia and Colonel Matthews of the 9th Virginia Continental Regiment, who were carried to New York. The list naming these officers is the only existing record of those imprisoned in Philadelphia during the winter of 1777-78. Included on this list were Continental and militia officers taken at Brandywine, Germantown, and in minor actions near the city. A few men were taken in New Jersey, while others were captured in their homes. Although the majority were Pennsylvanians, twenty-eight were Virginia Continentals, most of whom were captured at Germantown.

Upon arriving in New York their paroles were accepted, and all except possibly three were eventually quartered on Long Island. About half of them were given some funds; however, there is no evidence the remaining officers received anything. Regardless, the money received would not have paid their lodgings or sustenance. In fact, when they were released in 1780, a number of the officers were forced to remain on Long Island until they could settle their obligations.

In 1780, General William Phillips and Loring met with several American officers, including Matthews and Abraham Skinner, the American commissary, to attempt to resolve the prisoner-of-war problem. Most controversial issues were settled, and the officers were exchanged at the end of the year and in the first quarter of 1781.[53]

CHAPTER VIII

BUSINESS DURING THE OCCUPATION

BEFORE THE BRITISH army occupied Philadelphia, few merchants advertised in local newspapers. Residents of the city were familiar with the lines of merchandise offered by the various merchants and shopkeepers. Occasionally a merchant would announce the arrival of a special shipment. The newspapers were popular media for schools, booksellers, manufacturers, vendues, and a few tradesmen. However, a dramatic shift in the use of the newspapers by the merchants occurred during the winter of 1777-78.

A combination of circumstances made the winter of 1777-78 the heyday of commercial newspaper advertising for the Revolutionary period. The incoming merchants who dominated the mercantile scene were unknown to the inhabitants and the hundreds of refugees who sought the protection of the British army. British officers and, to a lesser degree, enlisted men frequented the shops of these merchants, especially shops selling liquors and books. It was, therefore, necessary for newcomers to identify themselves and their newly acquired quarters. To survive, many local merchants replenished their stocks by purchase from the newly arrived wholesalers and inserted advertisements in the local newspapers.[1]

At least 307 merchants, sutlers, artisans, craftsmen, schoolmasters, and other professional people were operating in Philadelphia during this period. A large number of businessmen, mostly Loyalists and Quakers who had remained in the city, were now joined by refugees from New Jersey, Maryland, Delaware, and the Pennsylvania countryside. About 200 merchants and sutlers arrived from New York. These merchants and sutlers transported large stocks of merchandise on the merchantmen that had accompanied the fleet. Included in this number were about twenty-five one-shot operators such as ship captains, speculators, and adventurers.[2]

Business conditions in New York were sluggish, and merchants were worried because of overstocked shelves and depressed prices. Many businessmen considered Philadelphia the leading commercial center of British America and a panacea for their economic ills. A number of arriving merchants represented partners still in New York or acted as consignees for wholesalers. Others were speculative sutlers and adventurers who had followed the fortunes of Howe from Halifax to New York and now to Philadelphia.

It was well known that Philadelphia suffered from a shortage of all merchandise and staples except fresh vegetables and meat, and now, with Washington throwing a tight cordon around the city, these were also in short supply. Drygoods, hardware, and other commodities had trickled into port on merchantmen or privateers. Philadelphia merchants had found it a highly profitable gamble even if only one privateer or merchantman in four eluded the British blockade.

The newcomers were soon comfortably ensconced in the stores vacated by the fleeing American merchants. Others rented stores, front rooms, or even cellars in the homes of residents. Some formed temporary partnerships or rented floor space from other merchants. Most of the new arrivals took advantage of the shortage by extorting the top prices for every item. In certain instances, local shopkeepers joined the inflation parade as soon as they could restock their shelves. Officers and civilians deplored the exorbitant costs, especially of groceries and staples. Mrs. Fisher's observations were typical: "Potatoes are 15 [shillings] a bushel, butter a dollar & 10 a pound, common Irish butter 3/9 a pound, cheese the same price, mutton 4, turkey 20, geese 12, very small fowls 7/6. Flour £5 a hundred, & what is to be bought of that very ordinary. Such is the distressed situation we are in."[3]

Profiteering was not confined to the merchants. It also whetted the avarice of a local Quaker historian. Robert Proud, writing to his brother in London, commented on high prices and the scarcity of articles such as flour, beef, pork, beer, cheese, and other groceries and then referred "the same to thy Consideration, whether it might be worth while to ship some such Articles, if proper Permission was obtained, the Trade not yet being free to this Place; but that these Articles are very profiting. . . ." He cautioned his brother on the dangers of oversupply and the financial weakness of the people, as their legal paper currency was being refused by almost every merchant.[4]

The newcomers were concentrated on Water, Front, and Second streets between Race and Spruce streets, with a number located on the intersecting streets and alleys. At least twenty-one shipmasters, speculators, and merchants opened stores on the wharves or sold direct from shipboard. A few reserved tables at the London Coffee House and, infrequently, other taverns where, in a convivial atmosphere, they sold merchandise in case lots and occasionally a ship's manifest. To make it easier for customers to find them, most newcomers identified their location by stating they occupied the premises of former American merchants and storekeepers.

Some occupations were noticeably more prevalent than they had been in formers years. In these categories were sixteen vendue masters, fifteen printers and booksellers, and eight private schools. The products most widely sought after were liquors, wines, and beer. Many merchants with general stocks advertised spirituous liquors for sale, while nineteen shopkeepers dealt exclusively in these items.

The public vendue or auction became a thriving business from the outset of the British entry into Philadelphia. With no merchandise entering the city, a number of merchants suddenly directed their interests to this vocation. Americans who were still anxious to leave the city disposed of their personal property at vendue sales. They were the lucky ones, because in the first weeks of confusion British officers, soldiers, followers, and civilians looted the homes and stores of departed Americans. In most cases these articles found their way to the auction market. Many city residents who returned after the evacuation found the property and furniture of other Philadelphians in their homes and stores.

Public and private sales were conducted at stated intervals; George Haughton held auctions of household furniture and drygoods every Tuesday and of livestock on Wednesday and Saturday. Robert Footman, Jonas Philips, and Haughton held horse auctions at the London Coffee House on market days. Later in the occupation period, many ships, sometimes with cargoes, were sold at public sale. Usually purchases were paid for in gold or silver, as paper currency was not accepted. If the seller demanded money, some vendue masters advanced part of the anticipated proceeds.

Protests of misconduct and dishonest practices by vendue masters reached the office of the superintendent general. Galloway decreed that the "multiplicity of public vendues greatly tend to the prejudice of the fair trader and are even introductive of fraud and imposition on the inhabitants, which renders it necessary that numbers should be limited, and that such as are permitted should be under just and reasonable regulations." He instructed magistrates to supervise all vendues and to permit only one vendue each in Philadelphia, one in Southwark, and one in Northern Liberties. Galloway named David Sproat vendue master for the city, Richard Footman for Northern Liberties, and John Hart for Southwark.[5]

Abuses eventually developed, particularly in the sale of articles which had been prohibited by Howe. Shipmasters and merchants were discovered bringing in items that were in short supply, but in great demand, throughout the city. Rum, molasses, and salt were brought in without any effort to control their sale or cost. Some hoarding was evident, and the needy residents were unable to obtain these needed items. Abuses were called to the attention of Howe and Galloway, who took immediate steps to place restrictions on the importation of certain proscribed articles. An attempt to control the possession of liquor had been undertaken as early as 6 October. All residents were ordered to report any quantities of liquor in their possession to the commissary general. As previously noted, seven weeks later Howe commanded every shipmaster to report any quantities of rum, brandy, or spirituous liquors to his secretary, who issued the permits to land. Those neglecting to obey the proclamation were subject to confiscation of cargo and liable to imprisonment. Galloway placed further restrictions on enumerated articles, limiting the sale of rum, molasses, and salt to everyone except importers. He also prohibited the sale of medicines without a special permit from his office.[6]

In mid-December the problems of intoxication and riotous conduct brought forth another proclamation from Howe. He was determined to see the "suppression of vice and immorality, and prevent the disorders and mischiefs, which may happen in the army, and among the inhabitants . . . from the multiplicity of public houses, dram shops, and retailers of strong liquors." All keepers of establishments that sold liquors were to obtain a license from the superintendent general. The magistrates of police would help enforce this regulation. The usual punishment, confiscation and imprisonment, was threatened for those who did not comply.[7]

To further control the admission of certain commodities, Howe directed all ship captains to present the proper manifest of their cargo to Galloway's office. Conversely, all goods or merchandise loaded on outgoing ships had to be approved for shipment by the superintendent's office.

A short time before this proclamation, Francis Gilbert and John Henderson were appointed wardens of the Port of Philadelphia. All masters of vessels and all individuals having business with the port were to report to them for instructions.

Government by proclamation continued as Galloway received many protests about the excessive charges made by draymen and porters. They added to the inflationary spiral by asking ''exorbitant prices'' and irritated businessmen by refusing to work. Galloway ordered all draymen and porters to register; he then established porterage rates ''of goods, wares and merchandise . . . for unloading, hauling, unloading and storing'' all commodities.[8]

Butchers and others who sold at the markets were discovered intercepting farmers who attempted to enter the city by boat at the wharves and purchased their products. Most of these farmers came from Delaware and New Jersey and usually brought beef, pork, mutton, veal, lamb, poultry, butter, and vegetables to the markets. Others met Pennsylvania farmers who had eluded American patrols at the gates of the city and made similar purchases. The farmers were happy to dispose of their wares without haggling over prices at the market. Foodstuffs were then resold at the markets at inflated prices. The poor, who had little money — and that usually was unacceptable paper currency, were thus unable to buy needed foods.

To correct these gouging tactics, another edict came from the pen of Galloway on 22 January, forbidding the purchase for resale of any produce, meat, or vegetables at the wharves or any place other than the market. If apprehended in this practice, the transgressor had to forfeit his purchases. Persons reporting the malefactor would receive half of the proceeds, with the remainder given to the poor.[9]

In the business district, some shops sold only one product, such as cakes or tobacco, while emporiums of large merchants carried a limitless assortment of hardware, drygoods, groceries, liquors, staples, and miscellaneous items such as hairpins, combs, watch chains, and razors. Barnabas Higgins on the Chestnut Street wharf and James Robertson on Front between Chestnut and Walnut streets were typical of the latter class of merchants. They offered the discriminating buyer rum, molasses, wines, sugar, teas, cheese, salt, soap, butter, raisins, currants, drygoods, silk stockings, thread, paper, combs, linens, thimbles, watch chains, stationery, buckles, buttons, money scales, scissors, razors, and many other commodities. Higgins also sold all items at wholesale. A few merchants advertised that they had well in excess of a hundred different items for sale.[10]

Many less pretentious shopkeepers offered specialized products or services. William Gardner on Second between Market and Chestnut was in this category with "Ruffled shirts of different sorts, remarkably well made; Shilala [sic] Stockings and Gloves; camp capes and some sadlery." James Clark had remained in the city and continued "Dying in General" at his house on Second Street, five doors above Chestnut, or at his shop on Carpenters' wharf. He also cleaned "mens clothes, and removed stains; likewise scarlet cloth damaged at sea, with the color recovered as it was originally."[11]

Elizabeth Hubbard lived on Third Street near Saint Paul's Episcopal Church. She described herself as a "Clear Starcher from London" working in all its branches, with thread and blown laces done to the greatest perfection. As a footnote, she added silk stockings would be whitened in the best manner. William Harrison, on Chestnut Street, noted that he "makes ladies toupees, pads, braids, and cushions; likewise, Gentlemens wigs and scalps, scarcely perceivable from the natural hair. Likewise perfumes, hard and soft pomatum best English powder, powder bags, down and silk puffs, the genuine London court plaister [plaster], hair pins, from No. 1 to No. 20, hair ribbands, shaving and powder boxes, and combs, wash balls and wash boxes."[12]

Many widows had little recourse but to remain in the city, protect their properties, and pursue their livelihoods. An advertisement in the *Pennsylvania Evening Post* on 24 February 1778 reported that Margaret Trotter had moved from Second Street to Norris Alley opposite Mary Newport, a pastry cook. At the new address, among the wares she offered for sale were pickled walnuts, cucumbers, spirits of lavender, and peppers.

Robert Bell's bookstore, next door to Saint Paul's Church, was a very popular establishment. Bell did business throughout the war without giving umbrage to either side. He conducted frequent book auctions, for which he issued catalogues available for one dollar. His circulating library was well patronized by officers and civilians. A large selection of titles for sale appeared regularly in all newspapers.[13]

Many merchants had little faith in the army's retaining permanent possession of the new nation's capital. They were virtual prisoners of Washington's inferior fighting machine and had little confidence that Howe would throw off the intertia which gripped him. Regardless, most were realists and were determined to sell their stocks as quickly as possible. Tench Coxe expressed the merchants' hope for profit in the Philadelphia market: "If we must suffer misfortunes, we ought to drain all the good from them possible." Unfortunately, most merchants had overestimated the area's potential sales capacity.[14]

Initial sales on all products in the exhausted market at Philadelphia inspired consignors and partners in New York to clear their overstocked shelves and ship everything to the new Utopia. Eventually, in such commodities as drygoods, apothecary items, and hardware, this merely meant transferring the oversupply from New York to Philadelphia. Howe was aware of the serious glut on the market and to stop it ordered a temporary embargo on all products coming from New York. Simultaneously, he prohibited ships from the West Indies to come into either port. He did this as the loss of merchantmen to American privateers had increased the prices of goods coming from the Caribbean. Both Howe and Clinton were concerned that the greed of the merchants had created a serious food problem for the civilian population of New York. As Edward Goold noted, the embargo was imposed "to prevent our provisions being all sent off Which are going fast." On the other hand, Hamond reported that the embargo had been placed on 24 December and was to remain in force until the end of February 1778. This precaution was necessary because the frozen river normally made shipping dangerous, if not impossible, between those dates.[15]

Coxe described the high prices and slow movement of certain commodities: "Wet goods by which I would be understood to mean all groceries and things not usually termed dry Goods are the most likely to do well because they are to be eat and Drank and Townsfolks together with the navy make a great body of people to consume them."[16]

The civil authorities and even Galloway were unhappy with the many restrictions that Howe had placed on trade. Merchants chose to ignore the fact that Galloway's actions were a direct result of the dishonest business practices by certain of their fraternity.

The spirit of friendship that had existed between Howe and many merchants, such as Coxe, was gradually becoming strained. An example of Coxe's rapport with the commander in chief was evident during the early days of the occupation. In October, while other merchants were impatiently waiting for their stocks of merchandise, Coxe was offering a diversified assortment of products for sale. Only small sloops and flatboats were permitted to sneak up the back channel on dark nights, and Howe was adamant that they carry only provisions for the army. Through some dispensation, however, Coxe received a part of his inventory from the fleet. As restraints were gradually imposed on all merchants, Coxe became disillusioned with Howe. He had probably expected that the preferential consideration he had previously enjoyed would be continued.

Another circumstance which was widening the schism between merchants, townspeople, and the military and civil government was the continuing dilemma over currency acceptance. Merchants refused to accept the paper money formerly issued by the Proprietary government with the king's approval. Further, the merchants believed the Pennsylvania currency would not be acceptable in transactions with the army. And, if they were compelled to leave Philadelphia, such currency could only be exchanged in New York at a discount. As spring approached, the question became academic. By then, civilian resistance had disappeared, and only hard money was offered and accepted.

Rapport between merchants and the military deteriorated further as the belief became general that British officers and government officials were engaged in speculation of prohibited goods. Edward E. Curtis, in his study of the British quartermaster's department, came to the conclusion that many British officers "came home with more gold in their pockets than they had when they went out or than their slender salaries in America could warrant." Coxe wrote, "I really believe [they] shipt cargoes on their own acct under the appearance of Government business."[17]

With competition keen, merchants and craftsmen used various devices to lure potential customers. To impress the "colonials," many advertised that they were lately from London, England, or Europe, little realizing that Philadelphians had few peers in the various crafts among their counterparts in the British Isles. Others made temporary partnership arrangements to move special shipments. Two merchants or speculators would band together to market a specific product and as soon as the sale was consummated would dissolve their association.

Merchant losses continued to mount as a number of ships were sunk by sailing on the chevaux-de-frise. Salvaged cargoes and recoverable parts of the merchantmen were sold at public vendue. As winter progressed, conditions worsened throughout the city. Business became stagnant and prices skyrocketed until even the affluent had difficulty in purchasing necessities. In spite of minor successes by British detachments, American patrols had tightened the blockade around the city. Coxe lamented the total lack of beef, pork, butter, or tongue in his stock. Fresh provisions were in such short supply that almost any price was paid — by those who could afford them. The situation became more acute as "Philadelphia is every hour filling up with refugees from the adjacent Provinces — Nothing scarcely, which [is] used by people of every Rank can be long very cheap here."[18]

The hopelessness of the British position in Philadelphia gradually became apparent to all civilians. Many Loyalist merchants refused to believe that the splendid British army in Philadelphia would not march out in the spring and destroy the tatterdemalion force at Valley Forge. However, those who shared the opinion that the army would eventually evacuate Philadelphia made preparations to leave the city. As early as February, a few merchants requested customers indebted to them to settle their accounts, as they were planning to sail to New York or England. James Greenhow asked for payment in seven days from the date of his announcement "to avoid further trouble; as he intends for England by the first fleet."[19]

In April, two decisions by the king had the effect of elevating and then depressing the spirits of merchants and civilians. The announcement that a Peace Commission was coming to America and would grant almost every demand of the rebels except independence raised hopes "for a speedy & happy peace, in which America will have a fixt constitution, not to be infringed by either side." On the other hand, the news that there would be a change in commanders in chief created confusion. Merchants realized that it lowered the likelihood of the merchants obtaining additional indulgences from the army. Fortunately for inhabitants and the commissioners, the news that George III had ordered the evacuation of Philadelphia had not yet reached them. When this command was known, it negated the effectiveness of the commissioners and gave Clinton little more than a temporary caretaker government in the city.[20]

Enoch Story was responsible for overseeing that the ban on the importation of certain proscribed items was enforced. Bond was re-

quired of anyone desiring to sell such products as rum, molasses, salt,
and medicines. It was also obligatory for them to make a strict accounting of their marketing practice. On 27 May, Story prepared a
detailed statement of the importation, sale, and inventory on hand of
these products. It was compiled in anticipation of the evacuation of
the city and revealed substantial stocks of all items. These were either
shipped to New York or sold at public auction.[21]

	Imported	Sold	Remains
Gallons Rum	293,120	165,190	127,930
Gallons Brandy	3,716	950	2,766
Gallons Geneva	6,120	292	5,828
Gallons Molasses	39,520	32,140	7,380
Gallons Arrack	104	36	68
Packages Medicines	40	2	38
Bushels Salt	42,147	12,787	29,360

Notwithstanding Story's vigilance, prohibited cargoes were still
smuggled into the city. Barnard Solomon sold several small quantities
of rum without obtaining permission. Story offered a reward of five
guineas to any person who could offer sufficient evidence as to
Solomon's whereabouts so that he could be brought before the
magistrates of police. One guinea of the reward was offered to anyone
who knew the location of any rum belonging to Solomon. There is no
record that he was ever apprehended.[22]

As these commodities were much in demand, they offered lucrative potential, albeit there were severe penalties if the offender was
caught. Coxe advised his associates of the problems connected with
this type speculation:

In The Severity of the new regulation here, Together with the Vigilance of
the officers, & Great number of King's Ship's & Tenders render the landing
of any prohibited Articles extremely difficult. . . . I think . . . it would be imprudent to hazard a Cargo of this Nature. The Odium on the importer & the
Vessel would at the present period be so great, that it would Cut of[f] all
hope of softening the offense or of mitigating the rigour of the penalty.

He added that any effort to sell proscribed items would lead to their
seizure.[23]

After 1 June, all commercial advertisements except for a few
scattered announcements suddenly disappeared. Merchants had
started packing their stock for reshipment to New York. Unfortunately, many found that available space on the merchantmen was

limited, and they were compelled to leave large quantities of merchandise in their abandoned stores. A number of Quaker and American merchants, along with twelve or more who had entered the city with Howe, remained and carried on their mercantile operations. In June and July, many of the merchants who had returned to New York were noticed advertising in the *Royal American Gazette.*

Manufacturing was almost nonexistent during the occupation. In an effort to have Philadelphia become more self-sufficient, a number of small manufactories came into existence during the early days of the dispute with Great Britain. The largest of these, The United Company of Philadelphia for Promoting American Manufactures, discontinued its operations in 1777 as Howe neared the city. Over four hundred women were thereby deprived of a livelihood. The manufactory and all appurtenances were sold at auction in January 1778. These businesses had all been operated by American sympathizers who had fled the city. During the occupation no manufacturing was evident, although a few breweries appear to have been in service for a time.

CHAPTER IX

PLANS FOR A GARRISON WINTER

FOLLOWING THE DEPARTURE of Lord Howe for Rhode Island, Hamond became commander of the flotilla in the Delaware. He was soon confronted by many perplexing problems. Hamond had to assure a good rapport between the army and navy, organize the river defenses, provide protection for commercial and private shipping, insure that the fleet was capable of action in the spring, and see to the comfort and health of naval personnel.

To establish good relations with the army, Hamond's office required that he maintain a fraternal board. He arranged for Sir William Howe and his staff to attend the table one day each week. After a sumptuous dinner, they were to spend a festive evening at Hamond's house. These gatherings proved very expensive, but Hamond was convinced that until Lord Howe returned in early April, they contributed to harmony between the services.

Provisions for the navy were stored on navy victuallers and were dispensed to various ships by victualler agents. Unfortunately, foodstuffs for the navy were discovered to be in just as deplorable a condition as those of the army. Captain John Bourmaster investigated the cargo on the transport *Providence* and found "a quantity of Bread, Flour, Oatmeal, Rice, Raisins and Cheese rotten, Mouldy, stinking, and unfit for Men to eat." John Mason, victualler agent, received word from the master of the victualler *Blessing* that the casks of rum on his ship were deficient in quantity. Hamond demanded an immediate investigation of these reports and, if they were true, to affix the responsibility. Investigations and guilty contractors still did not feed the sailors. Therefore, individual ship captains were authorized to purchase an assortment of navy slops at as reasonable a rate as possible. However, the men who received this largesse would be charged.[1]

To compound Hamond's problems, a report was received on the *Roebuck* that the *Juliana* had run aground on the chevaux-de-frise (a not uncommon accident). A check of the damaged cargo revealed that 360 puncheons containing 80,640 pounds of bread, 63 hogsheads filled with 505 bushels and seven gallons of "pease," and one barrel of raisins were destroyed.[2]

Equally distressing was the scarcity of clothing. With the advent of an extremely cold winter, sickness among the crews increased. Hamond reported a serious outbreak of "Fever and Flux." Another problem was the high price of fresh provisions. Hamond instructed James Mason, the *Roebuck's* purser, to purchase fresh beef to replace salt beef one day a week. A hospital to accommodate 150 patients was readied, and for each ship a small house near the wharf was allotted to lodge the overflow.[3]

Snugly ensconced in his headquarters, Hamond turned his attention to a great fear of eighteenth-century naval commanders — the danger of fire on wooden ships tied up at wharves. All captains, the masters of transports, and traders were issued warnings to pay strict attention to fire prevention regulations. The city's waterfront was divided into three districts. Lieutenant Parry was put in command from the upper wharf to Market Street; Lieutenant Chads' station extended from the Market Street wharf to Hamilton's wharf; and Lieutenant Barker was responsible for the area between Hamilton's and the lower wharf.

Night patrols made up of a master, a mate, and four men were to visit each ship and ascertain that all galley fires and lights except the shipmaster's were out. Any irregularities were to be reported instantly in writing. Also, each ship was to have a regular night watch of two men, except for the smaller vessels which only needed one man. And, except the patrols, no one was to be allowed to pass between the ships and wharves after gunfire.

To further alleviate the threat of fire, ships were to have one or two casks of water near the galley or cooking place with their heads out and with buckets nearby. When the river was frozen, concern mounted over a possible water shortage. During the night ship bells were to be rung only when a ship or house fire was discovered. Crews were to turn out to assist in the firefighting, leaving two men on board for security.

Hamond organized a river and bay patrol with designated stations for the various men-of-war. Initially, the *Experiment* was posted off Billingsport with instructions to help ships through the chevaux-de-frise. The passage through these obstructions was "very narrow and confined," and Sir James Wallace was ordered to remove "or pull them to pieces." Captain John Linzee of the *Pearl* was assigned to patrol the area between Chester and Reedy Island. Captain Charles Phipps, with the *Camilla*, was sent to the bay below Reedy Island. Men-of-war were occasionally reassigned or relieved, but one was always on station. The one exception was during the embargo period from 24 December to 8 March, when the men-of-war were tied up at the city wharves. At that time, the *Experiment* dropped down to take position at the capes.[4]

An important aspect of the ship assignments was the destruction of the American guard boats that infested the mouths of many creeks. Most of these small boats had been a part of the Pennsylvania navy. In February, the Americans took the boats overland from Burlington to Salem and launched them in the river. The majority were officered and manned by men of the State navy. The most celebrated commander was Captain John Barry of the Continental navy.[5]

Hamond also wanted to protect the boats supplying provisions to the city. The majority came from Salem County in southern New Jersey and Delaware. Passes to unload cargo were obtained from the magistrates of police and were limited to a prescribed time. The thirty-ton schooner *Adventure*, for example, had eight carriage guns, a crew of nine, and a license for one month.

When Lord Howe sailed for Rhode Island in late November he took sixty transports, or half of the fleet in the Delaware. Other transports and hay ships sailed later, when the river ice had broken up. In early March, as the first convoy was about to sail, midshipmen from each man-of-war searched every ship for naval deserters. While most ships had escorts, at least one flotilla of armed victuallers sailed without one.

Hamond was aghast at the extravagant prices of materials in the city. He ordered that no repairs should be performed on the ships and rigging until a survey found them absolutely unfit for use.[6]

In late December small vessels braved the dangers of the ice and were constantly employed in gathering badly needed forage for the

army. One expedition of thirty vessels had been anchored off
Tinicum Island for three days when it began to snow, forcing a recall
of the boats. Three vessels failed to reach the city and were driven up
and down the river by the ice. After a day or two, they grounded on
the New Jersey shore near Gloucester, where American militia
burned them.[7]

During the early spring, news of the arrival of hay ships from
Rhode Island was anxiously awaited. Howe, recognizing the dire
need for forage, had written to Brigadier General Sir Robert Pigot requesting all of that commodity that could be spared. Buffeted by high
seas, snow, and ice, the ships carrying this sorely needed commodity
were often separated and frequently captured by Americans. In
mid-March, nine ships of an original fleet of eleven arrived at
Philadelphia. By then the army was reduced to a one week's supply of
forage. Always welcome were other hay ships which arrived at various
intervals.[8]

Howe was anxious to receive official dispatches from London.
This provided Hamond with a serious challenge until the ice broke
up in the river. He ordered the *Liverpool* to New York, but it was
several weeks before a temporary thaw gave Captain Henry Bellew an
opportunity to make a quick exit from the port. On her return to
Philadelphia, the *Liverpool* was damaged and unable to return to active duty.[9]

Anticipating Lord Howe's return, Hamond had been busily engaged in making the river and bay safe for the expected heavy
maritime traffic in the spring. Men-of-war were dispatched to
assigned positions along the shore. Buoys were set out to warn ships
of the position of shoals and other obstructions. This made the river
practical for all navigation except for the narrow channel through the
chevaux-de-frise.

Upon Howe's return to the city from the abortive expedition to
Whitemarsh, many pressing problems confronted his command.
Under the most favorable circumstances, the army and civilians were
faced with a winter of uncertainties. Howe's well-known love of the
festive board and convivial evenings have overshadowed his concern
and attention to the needs of the garrison city. A quasi-civil government had to be established and assigned responsibilities to relieve the
headquarters staff of many vexatious tasks.

Howe envisioned the eventual sufferings of his troops unless immediate steps were taken to stockpile fuel, forage, and provisions.
Wood for fuel had to be obtained locally. While forage was abundant

around Philadelphia, it would have to be supplemented by hay shipments from other areas, particularly Rhode Island. Before the river
froze over, provisions would have to be accumulated in sufficient
quantities to supply the army for the winter. Although ration provisions would be plentiful, they seldom were of the quality desired.
Ewald said every man received one pound of the best wheat flour (for
bread) and three-quarters of a pound of salted beef or pork daily. In
addition, rice, peas, and vinegar were issued at various times each
week. Unfortunately, most civilians enjoyed neither plenty nor ex-
cellence in their diet.

Fresh provisions were rarely found in abundance. Farmers and
speculators reached the city's markets by skirting main roads and
sneaking through fields at night. However, there was usually a shortage in some commodities and never enough in any item for the overcrowded city. Larger amounts were carried by river boats from New
Jersey and Delaware. The greatest reliance, especially for livestock,
was placed on large detachments of soldiers who roamed both sides of
the Delaware.

Neither commander in chief could control the nefarious exploits
of their soldiers. Brigadier General John Lacey advised the Council
he had more difficulty restraining the villainous actions of his men
and certain civilian marauders than he had with British parties that
penetrated his area. Farmers lived in constant fear of strolling bands
of civilians, soldiers on furlough from Valley Forge, and deserters
who skulked about the British lines. These hooligans posed as
American militiamen and confiscated farmers' produce and livestock
in the name of Washington. Joseph Hart wrote, ''Violence, Rapine
and Robbery, are odious to all; but more especially in the Soldier,
who is armed to oppose the Common Enemy and not to distress his
Countrymen.''[10]

Occasionally, a farmer carrying produce toward the city was
murdered by American pickets. These acts of violence temporarily
made some men reluctant to go to market. Nevertheless, farmers attempted to pass the American pickets despite harassment as long as
the British offered gold or silver. It is unlikely that the quantities carried in eased the shortage of fresh provisions. Emas Thomas said he
carried 12 pounds of butter to market on six different occasions;
Joseph Long brought 107 pounds of butter to the city, and on a second visit 15 pounds of butter and two fowl. Others testified to similar
trips. Richard Lewes recalled being paid twenty shillings hard money
to help drive an ox, a cow, and a calf to the British outpost near the

ruins of the Rising Sun Tavern. Years after the war, a former American officer recalled what he termed the fun of brother officers who killed a "milk fed British *horse*" and then permitted an American spy to carry it into the city and "sell it as Bullock beef for gold."[11]

On the other hand, Washington was amazed to hear that large quantities of produce daily entered Philadelphia from Bucks County. The prohibition of all intercourse with the city was impossible to enforce. He considered it especially pernicious for city women to visit friends at Valley Forge. Initially he had condoned women passing through the lines. As a British officer remarked, "Here we have almost a plentiful country, the little provision that is smugled in through the Rebel Lines & Spies, is sold very dear, and indeed many in the town would starve were it not for the help from the Army Rations & from the flour which Mr Washington allows the wives & families of his Adherents to have through his lines." American officers acknowledged that women expected and received less careful examination because of their sex and conceded it was difficult "to counteract their seductive Wiles." On at least one occasion, camp followers were sent out ahead of a British detachment in order to lure American pickets from their posts. Efforts were sometimes made to reverse the procedure by carrying scarce commodities into the country. On 8 February a suspicious noncommissioned officer stopped two seemingly pregnant women at the picket on Germantown Road. Upon examination, one pregnancy was discovered to be a quantity of salt and the other to be twenty-five calfskins the woman had wrapped around her waist.[12]

In New Jersey conditions were equally bad, as undisciplined British soldiers and Loyalist militiamen ravaged the countryside. In retaliation, American militia vandalized the houses and farms of those who clandestinely met British boats along the banks of the Delaware.

Loyalists in significant numbers were evident throughout southern New Jersey. Gloucester County alone tried, in person or in absentia, over one hundred of the most active British partisans. The majority of Loyalists eventually returned and were brought before the commissioners of inquisitions for offenses ranging from service with the British Provincial units to joining roving gangs of Loyalist sympathizers. A number had held unlawful and seditious meetings. Others had attempted to induce militiamen to desert. In one instance, Deborah Lippincott had "seduced" Joseph Humphreys to seize and capture American militia officers. Most trials in absentia involved those serving in the British army. Of those who returned and were adjudged guilty, the commissioners imposed fines ranging from *L*20 to *L*200, mild sentences compared to other states. Frank H. Stewart stated that in Salem County similar fines were imposed for seditious remarks and misdemeanors. He also stated that four men were ordered hanged for high treason, but does not indicate whether the sentences were carried out. Most Loyalists guilty of treason had fled and their estates were confiscated.[13]

Soon after the appointment of Galloway as superintendent general and superintendent of imports and exports, Howe advised John Robinson that he "found it necessary to make an arrangement as similar as circumstances will admit to those at New York, for regulating the landing and sale of goods imported, and for establishing a police, under the direction of . . . citizens who have distinguished themselves by their sufferings and attachment to Government."[14]

With his appointment Galloway received detailed instructions on the administration of the port. Howe was uncertain of the responsibilities of Galloway's position, as it did not have a parallel in America, except in minor details at New York. Regardless, he specified basic procedures to be followed in the seizure of vessels attempting to enter the port with prohibited merchandise, payments to informers, and military assistance, if needed: Smith and Story were to inspect all such goods. Howe believed that the inspectors' pay should be sufficient to ensure that no fees or gratuities were accepted. Any changes in procedure required his approval. He asserted that Galloway was appointed to ensure that there was no "misapplication of Cargoes" intended for the British army or the inhabitants and to make certain that no merchandise or other necessaries reached "Rebel America." Last, Galloway was to send Howe monthly reports on port activity.[15]

For a period of time Galloway faithfully advised Howe of conditions and requested orders on what distinction he should make between His Majesty's ships and commercial vessels. He recommended that the oversupply of tobacco and indigo in Philadelphia should be shipped to New York, where they were in great demand. Despite surface indications of harmony, undercurrents of discord existed between the two men. As time passed, Howe apparently ordered his secretary, Robert Mackenzie, to relay various instructions to Galloway. This condition was probably demeaning to the egotistical superintendent. Late in March Howe ordered Mackenzie to award Galloway and the magistrates of police twenty-five pounds sterling

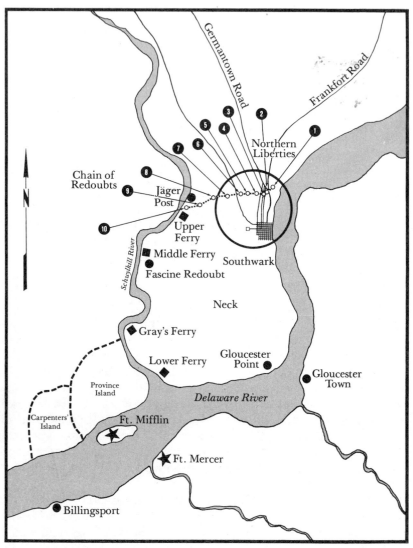

Germantown Road

Frankfort Road

3
5 **4** **2**
6 **1**

Northern
Liberties

7

Chain of
Redoubts **8**

9 Jäger
Post

10

Upper
Ferry

■ Middle Ferry

● Fascine Redoubt

Southwark

Neck

Schuylkill River

◆ Gray's Ferry

Lower Ferry
◆

Gloucester
Point ●

Gloucester
Town ●

Province
Island

Delaware River

Carpenters'
Island

★ Ft. Mifflin

★ Ft. Mercer

● Billingsport

Philadelphia and environs 1777–1778

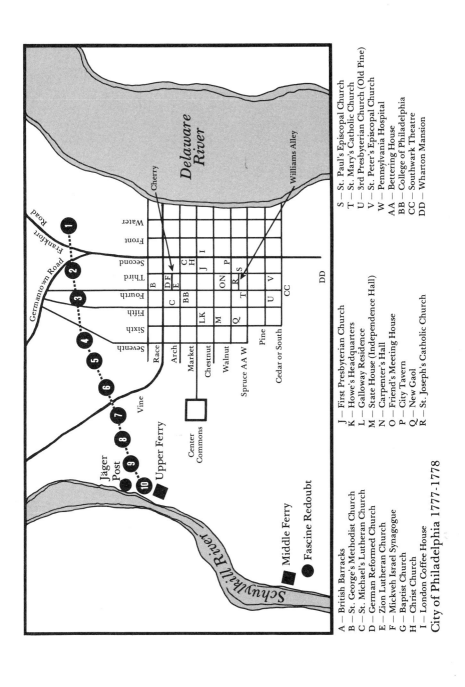

City of Philadelphia 1777-1778

A — British Barracks
B — St. George's Methodist Church
C — St. Michael's Lutheran Church
D — German Reformed Church
E — Zion Lutheran Church
F — Mickveh Israel Synagogue
G — Baptist Church
H — Christ Church
I — London Coffee House
J — First Presbyterian Church
K — Howe's Headquarters
L — Galloway Residence
M — State House (Independence Hall)
N — Carpenter's Hall
O — Friend's Meeting House
P — City Tavern
Q — New Gaol
R — St. Joseph's Catholic Church
S — St. Paul's Episcopal Church
T — St. Mary's Catholic Church
U — 3rd Presbyterian Church (Old Pine)
V — St. Peter's Episcopal Church
W — Pennsylvania Hospital
AA — Bettering House
BB — College of Philadelphia
CC — Southwark Theatre
DD — Wharton Mansion

Middle Ferry

Fascine Redoubt

each quarter, in addition to their regular salary, for extraordinary services in preserving order in the city.[16]

Galloway entered upon his dual duties with enthusiasm. With Howe's sanction he issued a series of proclamations designed to improve the cleanliness and safety of the city. On 9 January a curfew was declared forbidding anyone to appear on the streets without carrying lanterns between evening tattoo and reveille the next morning. A few days later, annoyed by the filth and other trash in the streets and alleys, he ordered householders, sextons of churches, and keepers of public buildings to sweep their fronts and pile such rubbish along their cartways. This was to be done on the last day of each month, and failure to comply was subject to a fine not exceeding twenty shillings. As a fire prevention measure, all chimneys were to be swept. Unfortunately, with virtually every house occupied at least in part by the military, few acknowledged their responsibility. Conditions did not improve, and Galloway was compelled to reissue this proclamation sixty days later.[17]

Fire was the most feared catastrophe that could befall a colonial city, and chimneys represented the greatest danger. Christian Apple, who was employed by the military to sweep barrack chimneys, was recommended to all householders. In November, with many owners and tenants out of the city, the Philadelphia Contributionship for Loss by Fire ordered all chimneys in houses they insured be swept. This was to be paid out of public stock. The insurance company expected to be reimbursed by the absent owners. This provision was cancelled when it was learned these owners possessed nothing but paper money. Short of cash, the Contributionship was forced to sell Continental currency at a discount.

Fortunately, few fires occurred during the winter. The most serious blaze took place in Kensington, where three houses were consumed despite the valiant efforts of the military and citizens. A curious claim for fire damage was filed by Thomas Hemberger in Elm Street. His loss was disallowed because he had stowed hay in the cellar. Many residents, fearing confiscation, had stored combustibles in their basements. The insurers made a public announcement that they would not honor any policy on a dwelling where inflammable materials, including hay, were kept unless this was specifically mentioned in their policy.[18]

Other decrees followed, covering the regulation of ferries on the Delaware, appointment of police, and naming of solicitors for funds to aid the House of Employment. In addition, he warned that exemplary punishment would be imposed on persons who, masquerading as Loyalists, roamed up and down the river taking the property of His Majesty's subjects.[19]

With winter less than two weeks away, forage expeditions and woodcutter detachments penetrated the surrounding countryside almost daily. Near midnight on 10 December, Cornwallis crossed the Schuylkill with 5,000 men, including light infantry and British and Hessian grenadiers. His front and flanks were covered by the jägers and light dragoons. Darby became the expedition's headquarters, with foragers spreading over the region. Each party of foragers was accompanied by a strong detachment of troops. As usual, occasional acts of vandalism were reported, and several fires were seen as far away as Germantown.

Until Sullivan's Continentals joined them, Potter's militia skirmished with Cornwallis's advance parties. A spirited engagement developed in which the Americans put up a stubborn resistance. However, as the main elements of British and Hessians moved into position, they were forced to withdraw. Casualties were apparently light except among the American militia, where between 50 and 160 men were taken prisoner. Shortly after midnight on the twelfth, Cornwallis recrossed the river into Philadelphia with the forage wagons. Large numbers of cattle and sheep were taken, for which the farmers were reimbursed. Officers, upon taking an oath that such payments were made, were allowed to keep one bullock and two sheep. All others were to be turned over to the Commissary Department. Andre observed "the great disappointment of many people" because no cattle were distributed to the civilians.[20]

Cornwallis crossed the river again on the sixteenth and then, after a smart skirmish, withdrew. Although a large quantity of forage had been amassed, it would last only a short time. Howe therefore decided to personally command a large-scale excursion to sweep the country west of the Schuylkill. Taking a force in excess of 7,000, and accompanied by Grant, Grey, Leslie, and Erskine, he crossed the river on 22 December. Knyphausen was left in command of the city defenses. In the meantime, Sullivan and Stirling's Continental divisions were equally active between Valley Forge and Wilmington. The Americans devastated all farms, destroying whatever they could not carry off.[21]

Howe hoped to cover more territory than Cornwallis and to find areas the other expedition had missed. He blanketed the countryside with large parties of foragers protected by army detachments. The army encamped along a line which extended about four and a half miles near the main road out of Darby. Many farmers reportedly had hidden forage and livestock from American militia, both of which they would be willing to sell for British gold.

Washington entertained thoughts of striking Howe's scattered force or the weakened lines defending the city. Potter had almost hourly furnished headquarters intelligence on the movements of the British army. On Christmas day Washington prepared a plan for a surprise attack on the redoubts north of Philadelphia. The main attack was to be made by Stirling and Sullivan aided by Potter. Brigadier Generals Enoch Poor, James Varnum, Jedidiah Huntington, and the North Carolina brigade were to form the reserve; elements of Woodford's, Scott's, and Wayne's brigades were to take position on the west bank of the Schuylkill near the ferries and bridges opposite the city. This arrangement was mystifying, as the latter brigades would be advancing directly into the path of Howe's force. Soon after moving out of camp, the Americans encountered part of Howe's command and, after a sharp engagement, retired to their former positions. The main force approached the line of redoubts and exchanged a few cannon shot without inflicting any damage. After probing the line of redoubts, Washington considered the defenses too strong and retired to Valley Forge.

Howe returned to Philadelphia on the twenty-eighth with a large quantity of forage and livestock. It was estimated that he had obtained about one thousand tons of forage, which was believed to be sufficient for the winter. However, Howe's judgment was in error; in a few weeks there was a desperate need for hay. In April he excused his military inactivity on the need for green forage.[22]

Several weeks before leaving on the foraging expedition, Howe had ordered Robertson, the barrack master, to survey the city and assign quarters to the various regiments and battalions. Officers, except general or staff level, were to be housed within the perimeter of their commands. Upon his return, Howe, apparently dissatisfied with Robertson's performance, summarily relieved him of his duties and named Captain Benjamin C. Payne in his place. Robertson's brother, General Archibald Robertson, piqued over the dismissal, wrote that it was done without notice or hint. He then added, ''This Trait plainly shews the wide Difference of a Despotical and Monarchial Government Lord have Mercy on the Poor People that are allways subject to the peevish spleenitical [sic] whims of an unreasonably headstrong Despot." This was typical of Howe who, without consultation, usually asserted his right of prerogative and made unilateral decisions which incurred the wrath of associates and subordinates.[23]

Regardless of petty infighting, the army was quartered within two days. Baurmeister was astounded how twenty-six battalions could be housed, generals and their suites provided for, and all the space needed for hospitals and storehouses found in "the desolate city of Philadelphia" The troops were busy removing all boards and usable articles from their temporary huts and wigwams. These materials were used to build berths in their quarters, and the balance was used for fuel. Items not usable were left for the inhabitants. Complaints of unauthorized occupancy of houses continued to be registered at headquarters, and each regiment was ordered to submit a list of the owners' names and addresses to the barrack master.[24]

Measures were taken to provide clean habitations for the men. All barracks received brooms and scrappers. Because of the scarcity of blankets, the men's pallets were filled with straw, and this bedding was replaced as needed. In January, as straw became scarce, an effort was made to secure blankets and rugs. Merchants and residents were directed to submit a return of any of these items in their possession and establish a selling price. But under no consideration were they to sell to anyone but the barrack master. Repairs were ordered for all houses used as a barracks. As only a few chimney sweeps were available, the pioneers were instructed to keep the chimneys of all quarters swept clean. As Stephan Popp described, we "were quartered in old empty houses on Front St., the rooms were large, well papered, but very cold, having no stoves to heat them."[25]

Heat and light were of primary importance to the soldiers' comfort, with wood for fuel calculated at a quarter cord per week for each room. Baurmeister estimated that each fireplace consumed three-eighths of a cord per week. The army used 800 cords of wood each week. When candle requirements were considered for the 1778-79 winter, it was estimated that each regiment (612 privates, plus officers) required seventy-five rooms and a pound of candles for each room per week. Similar demands were presumably necessary in 1777-78.

Men received lower wages and a smaller ration in garrison than during active field service. Each sergeant was paid one dollar, corporals a half dollar, and drummers and privates a quarter dollar per week. Ewald said the Hessian army was well paid: a jäger company commander received one guinea plus booty, a jäger trooper twenty English shillings, and the Hessian infantryman and grenadier twelve shillings each month. They also received needed accoutrements. Each Wednesday sergeants were to visit the market and buy necessaries for the men and the mess, such as roots and soap. A strict accounting was to be kept, as the cost of all articles purchased was to be stopped out of the soldiers' pay. Regular rations were issued every seven days to the battalion commissary officers. The British and Provincial corps received theirs at Willing and Morris wharfs, while the Hessians and other departments of the army obtained theirs at the store on Carpenters' wharf, above Walnut Street. According to Ewald, the stoppage for provisions shipped from Europe was deducted from each officer, soldier, and servant at the rate of six shillings per month. However, no stoppage was made for produce or livestock taken from the enemy. An accounting of cash in the military chest on 1 March 1778 disclosed that for the month of February the amount stopped from the soldiers' pay was £4,740 15s. 6d. for subsistence and £2,814 4s. 6d. for extraordinaries.[26]

As an added incentive, soldiers who volunteered as woodcutters were paid five shillings a cord, payable with their monthly allowance. For the soldiers' personal comforts, Howe ordered company commanders to make a weekly inspection to make certain that each soldier had two good shirts and two pairs of shoes and stockings.

General and staff officers were quartered in private homes, usually with the reluctant acceptance of the householder. Some were considerate of the feelings and privacy of their host or hostess, taking care to give no umbrage. Others, especially some younger officers, were overbearing and arrogant. They ignored the sentiments or religious convictions of other occupants of the house. Elizabeth Drinker resisted having any officer stay at her home until it became apparent that she had little choice. As she heard that Major Crammond, her petitioner, was of good character, and fearful of having a Hessian officer, she consented to permit him to have the two front parlors. She had heard of several cases of rudeness and impudence and advised her husband that after eight weeks he "has behaved very well, is a sober young man, and incommodes us as little as can be expected." Many were bitter and distressed by the conduct of those residing in their homes. Mary Eddy had an officer who was insolent and abusive and "has a woman he calls his wife." Conversely, Phoebe Pemberton offered her house and use of the vegetable garden to General Pattison, possibly to protect herself from vandals.[27]

Public buildings which had previously been commandeered on a temporary basis were now taken over as permanent army installations. All churches except Christ, Saint Peter's, Catholic, and the Quaker meetinghouses were converted into hospitals, riding schools, or stables. A concession was made at Saint Michael's Lutheran Church, where services were permitted on Sunday afternoons. The sanctuary was always filled with Hessian soldiers, and Hessian chaplains assisted in the service. Many Hessians also attended Gloria Dei (Old Swedes), Christ, and the Catholic churches. Throughout the winter there were references to Hessian troops parading to church, usually termed a "Kirchenparade," which involved a strict personal inspection. The first British battalion held open-air services opposite General Maxwell's quarters.[28]

On 8 February, Howe issued new instructions concerning the hospitals, but excluded those operated by the navy. All new medical patients were to be taken to the German Lutheran (Zion) and Dutch Calvinist (Reformed) churches, "Churgical" to Dickinson's house and the college, and venereal to the Pennsylvania Hospital. The latter disease caused concern during the winter. Dr. Yeldall advertised regularly throughout the occupation that he had an "Anti-Veneral Essence":

This Essence not only cures the disease in all its degrees, and in such manner that the patient need not be hindered from his business, or his condition be made known to his most intimate acquaintance, but will also effectually prevent catching the infection: Proper directions will be given in print, so that no questions need be asked, (two dollars).[29]

The cavalry and the artillery, with multiple requirements for storage and space, appropriated many buildings and areas for stables, ordnance, and supplies. The light dragoons removed all sheds in the market house from Front to Third streets and converted the shambles into stables. Other troops of horse occupied the stables of taverns. One troop was headquartered at George's Inn on Second Street at Arch.

General Pattison was ordered to establish an artillery park for about one hundred pieces of ordnance in the walled court behind the State House. The college was set aside for the artillery hospital and received patients transferred from the hospital on Front Street. As soon as the majority of wounded American officers had been removed from the State House, it was equipped as the artillery barracks. Substantial sheds to store ammunition were constructed at a convenient distance to avoid any risk of a catastrophe. Pattison considered his assigned quarters the "Prize in the Lottery."[30]

Pattison was a strict disciplinarian, but even he was beset with the same problems that confronted other corps commanders. He insisted on a strict adherence to cleanliness in dress, with white shirts, black or white neckerchiefs, hair tied up and clubbed, no short hair allowed. Unfortunately, behind the scenes, the soldiers' carelessness created concerns. Cleaning utensils were issued to the barracks; however, as winter progressed, the men's personal habits and hygiene gave rise to sanitation and health problems. The admonishments of officers were ignored. These conditions unquestionably contributed to the filth and debris found in the city after the British evacuation. Pattison's order of 7 February offers a graphic portrayal of the slovenly behavior of the men:

Notwithstanding the Great care and attention that has been paid to Render the state house Barracks particularly Clean and Comfortable, some of the men have been so beastly as to ease themselves on the Stairs and Lower area of the House between doors, the Centry is therefore in future to be very attentive (particularly during the Night) to put a stop to such scandalous behaviour and immediately to Confine any man who shall presume to make use of any other place whatever than the Privy for his Necessary Occasions. The Tubs placed within doors for the conveniency of making water during the Night are to be Emptied down the Privy every Morning immediately after gunfiring, and set in some proper place to air during the day.[31]

Proclamations were promulgated and orders were issued to clean up the accumulated debris in the barracks and houses. A specific order of 22 March directed that "the Quarters of the Several Regts in Garrison are to be Thoroughly Cleaned immediately & the Dirt Rake'd up into a pile in the Street Opposite each Quarters to be carried away by the Scavengers, Fresh Mold is to be frequently thrown into the Sink."[32]

To further illustrate the amoral habits of some of the garrison — characteristics which led to the desolate appearance of the city on 19 June 1778 — a Hessian observed that when orders were received on 15 June to march, "the soldiers indulged in a scene which was cruel and ridiculous to behold. Everything in the rooms was thrown out of the windows, and other endless confusion ensued."³³

Pattison became a controversial figure as a result of his arbitrary attitude in making restitution for the use of private property. Through his aide, Brigade Major Edward Williams, he advised the church wardens of Saint Peter's, that the fence around the church and grave-yard was needed because of the scarcity of boards and promised the church reimbursement. Reverend Coombe and the wardens called to protest the fence's removal, but found it had already been taken down. Shortly before Pattison departed for New York, a committee called to seek the promised payment. He said no restitution would be forthcoming, as he had acted under orders of the commander in chief. No rebuttal was possible as Howe was already at sea on the way home. In a separate instance, Dr. Smith of the college presented a memorandum to Howe's secretary, Robert Mackenzie, asking reimbursement for use of the institution's property. Pattison was equally evasive to the secretary's inquiry. He acknowledged that certain facilities had been used as barracks and a hospital, but pleaded ignorance to the use of other property. Regardless, he did not believe the army should pay for any building occupied during the occupation; he would, however, defer to any express order from His Excellency. Clinton acted in the affirmative on the college's petition and ordered Captain Payne, barrack master, to pay Dr. Smith £140 as rent for using their facilities as a hospital.³⁴

The winter of 1777-78 was very cold with heavy snows. Temperatures rarely rose above freezing; Pemberton recorded only eight readings in the forties between Christmas and mid-March. Snow, sleet, and hail, with an occasional afternoon rain shower, were common. British and Hessian officers' journals are interspersed with comments on the severity of the weather. Late in March, a severe gale accompanied by heavy rain that lasted nearly twenty hours struck the city. Men-of-war were driven from their moorings, and one new brig was driven against a wharf and sunk. Howe was concerned by reports of carelessness on the lines. Sentries were not alert, but relied on the weather to keep American patrols in camp.³⁵

In early January, Howe received a communique from the colonial secretary's office along with a "Paper of Intelligence" received from France. Howe was cautioned to be on the alert for American agents in the city. According to this intelligence, many spies were in the city masquerading as loyal subjects of the king, but their real mission was to supply Washington with enough information to permit a

"Coup de Main." The report specifically mentioned Thomas Willing and Robert Morris, but with Morris absent from the city, Howe apparently accepted Willing's protestations of neutrality.[36]

This advice and other warnings compelled Howe to prohibit trade between the city and rural sections. He began preparations to ensure adequate steps be taken for the defense line. In the event of an impending attack, four cannon at Bettering House would be fired. At this signal the troops were to get under arms immediately and quietly. In case of fire at night, the bell in Christ Church would be tolled — all but one had been removed when Howe approached the city.

Troops were assigned specific sections of the line, with responsibility for designated redoubts. The three redoubts nearest the river were committed to the British guards, with the Queen's Rangers stationed a few hundred yards in advance at Kensington. John F. Watson claimed that Simcoe had advised him that he was commander of the area where the "Penn Treaty Tree" stood, and out of respect for William Penn and the tree's historical significance, he had placed a guard to protect it from the axe.

Redoubts four through eight were entrusted to the British 1st, 2nd, 4th, 3rd, and 5th brigades respectively, with the latter assisted by the 2nd Battalion of Anspachers. Stirn's Hessian brigade was stationed near redoubt nine, and Wolwarth was at ten. The jägers had a crude breastwork a short distance in advance of Wolwarth. Apparently this arrangement was modified on 25 February. Howe then ordered all duty at the redoubts be furnished by the grenadiers and light battalion companies, with the light infantry to cover the woodcutters.[37]

One Hessian officer declared that one thousand men were assigned to protect the line of redoubts. The garrison for each redoubt was a captain, two subalterns, and fifty men, who were to be relieved every twelve hours. The garrison on the lines was changed every forty-eight hours, and the tour of duty for officers was every eighth day.

Particular attention was given to the barriers, or gates, at all entrances through the lines. There were five barriers: the one farthest west was at Ridge Road; the next three, at Seventh, Fifth, and Third streets, eventually merged into Germantown Road; the easternmost was at Second Street or Frankford Road. Two sergeants were to be posted from reveille to sunset at each barrier and the new bridge to examine and search all persons and their baggage crossing the lines. Violators were to be reported to the field officer. Each sergeant received one shilling sterling per day for diligent execution of his duty. On 7 January all barriers were closed except those at Ridge Road and Second Street. Any goods seized were to be distributed evenly between the informer and the poor. Regardless of orders and proposed safeguards, the flagrant inattention to duty by many officers irked Howe. Barriers were not closed at night, but those closed were left unlocked and the abatis in front of the lines were left open.[38]

During this period Howe had several annoying administrative problems to solve. Regiments were transferring recently arrived recruits to undermanned battalions, but insisted on compensation. It was finally agreed that any regiment reassigning recruits was to receive £5 per man. Thus the 4th and 10th regiments paid the 9th and 47th regiments the designated rate.

A delicate controversy developed between the British and Hessian medical staffs. A critical shortage in medicines and hospital supplies at the Hessian hospitals had led to a request for assistance from British surgeons. Surgeon General Morris and other physicians petitioned Howe for guidance in answering the Hessian request. They were apprehensive that serious consequences would result among their wounded if they shared supplies with their allies. Unfortunately, Howe's answer is not known; however, the deficiency continued until supplies were replenished by a shipment from England.[39]

The majority of inhabitants were afraid to commit to writing anything relating to conditions in the city. Censorship of all mail made most fear that anything they wrote might be misunderstood and their political loyalties misinterpreted. Howe had imposed this restriction on civilian correspondence to prevent an intelligence leak to the Americans. Hannah Lloyd wrote James Pemberton, "You don't know the great difficulty there is in writing to you, many things may be lawful, but not expedient." Others, like Henry Hill, exercised extreme caution. Hill wrote several innocuous letters, but, fearing misunderstanding, did not send them. Then there was Edward Shippen, Jr., who notified his father after the British army evacuated the city that it had been impossible to answer his letters because "the British Commander towards the latter part of the time he possessed Philadelphia was very attentive to prevent every kind of Communication with the Country."[40]

Several officers, depressed by the distressed appearance of their men who had inadequate winter clothing, implored Howe for help. Shipments from New York had been halted by the embargo placed on water traffic between the two ports. Little relief could be expected until the ice in the river broke up sufficiently to allow ships to reach Philadelphia.[41]

Recruitment rendezvous were held throughout the city and on board His Majesty's ships in the harbor area. Appeals were made to "All Gentlemen Sailors or Volunteers" who wanted to be useful to their country. If desired, they were guaranteed service in American waters only. Desertions had been frequent, and losses in actions with the Pennsylvania galleys had been significant. Navy hospitals were filled with sick and wounded seamen. The *Vigilant*, the *Pearl*, the *Camilla*, the *Liverpool*, and the brig *Stanley*, belonging to the *Roebuck*, all sought recruits. Several galleys being built for the defense of the river and city needed seamen.[42]

Deserters arrived in the city daily. They were encouraged to enlist in the Provincial corps being raised or, if they preferred, they were offered free transportation to Europe. A report dated 25 March 1778, presumably compiled by Galloway, indicated that 1,134 soldiers, exclusive of militia, and 354 galleymen from the State fleet had entered the city and taken the oath of allegiance to the king. Of this number, only 283 soldiers and 75 galleymen were native-born, with England and Ireland furnishing 492 and 206 soldiers and 157 and 69 galleymen, respectively. The remainder came from Germany, Scotland, Canada, and France. As it became increasingly evident that the British were considering evacuation of the city, desertions decreased significantly. A later report reflected that from 30 September 1777 to 17 June 1778, 1,289 soldiers and 391 galleymen had deserted. This account also listed desertions by 603 militiamen.[43]

Comfortably ensconced in their winter quarters, British and Hessian officers took stock of their surroundings and offered varied opinions on Philadelphia. Ambrose Serle thought the city was "finely laid out in a pleasant Situation." He was moved by the "handsome Public Buildings and some Houses not inelegant." The Hessian von Jahr considered it "a large and beautiful city . . . a handsome Market Place with pretty gardens round about the city."

Others had a less charitable viewpoint and, like James Murray, thought it was "upon the whole somewhat of a stupid town." A Hessian captain, Johann Heinrichs, asserted, "If the Hon. Count Penn were to offer me the whole county of Pennsylvania, with the condition that I should live here the rest of my life, I hardly think I should accept it." One of the most vituperative judgments was expressed by

Lieutenant W. Hale. He wrote his parents that he "would exchange a dungeon in New York for the governor's house in Philadelphia . . . a most disagreeable sameness reigns throughout the streets . . . not a single public building to attract notice or attention of an European, the State House is mean, and at the same time heavy, piece of Architecture." He believed the only claim other buildings such as the hospital and Bettering House, had was their utility. Somewhat snobbishly, he deprecated the general appearance of the city, noting that "agreeable to the levelling principles of the Quakers, a man no sooner builds a good house, than three or four dirty hovels are run up close to him."[44]

During the last week of December one of those farcical events occurred that sporadically punctuated the somber aspects of war. David Bushnell, America's submarine pioneer, built a number of underwater mines, with which he hoped to destroy British shipping. The mines were connected with buoys or kegs, and the action of the water was expected to explode them against the hulls of ships. The project proved abortive, but was the subject of many ludicrous accounts. American letters painted the British as confused and running in wild disorder throughout the city. It was reported that nervous British soldiers fired volleys at the floating objects — and some shadows — much to the amusement of Americans. Francis Hopkinson immortalized the event in a famous poem entitled "The Battle of the Kegs." Little reference can be found for this incident in British or Loyalist sources.[45]

After 1 January 1778, encounters between British and American troops were largely minor actions involving British Provincials and American militia. Howe was fearful that after the Schuylkill froze over, Washington would attempt a surprise attack below the redoubts. A constant alert was maintained along the east bank of the river. However, virtually all action centered north of the city between the two rivers and in New Jersey. The latter state was the scene of two large-scale expeditions during the first quarter of 1778.

Washington entrusted to Potter's militia patrol the area west of the Schuylkill and to Lacey the area north of the redoubts. Some Continental units led by "Light Horse" Harry Lee, Daniel Morgan, and Allen McLane cooperated with the militia. Lacey, who was involved in most of the skirmishes, also suffered the greatest frustrations. He had to defend a vast countryside, which had a large Loyalist sentiment in Bucks County, with usually less than 600 men, of whom at one time only 140 had arms. Washington advised him to keep his command moving and to cover all roads leading into the city. With headquarters at Doylestown, he established rendezvous for scouting parties throughout the region at Flourtown, Jenkintown, Bustleton, Smithfield, Crooked Billet, Springhouse Tavern, North Wales, and Graeme Park.[46]

Howe assigned responsibility for protecting the roads leading into the city to different corps. The Queen's Rangers were stationed at Kensington and patrolled the Frankford Road as far as the hamlet of that name. Old York Road was committed to the light infantry, and Germantown Road to the line regiments; the jägers, quartered in the Neck, covered the east banks of the Schuylkill and north to Ridge Road. Provincial troops formed the bulk of the forces conducting raids into the interior sections of Philadelphia and Bucks Counties. Captain Richard Hovenden, with his First Troop of Philadelphia Light Dragoons, figured prominently in most engagements. Civilians familiar with the country guided these detachments on their forays.[47]

Partisan reports invariably colored the results and losses of these skirmishes. Little of consequence was resolved, except that the vicious predatory actions of irregulars on both sides intensified the hatred between Loyalists and Americans, especially in Bucks County. On the other hand, Ewald commended certain Continental detachments for their "discipline, courage and resolution," but criticized the militia.

The first major expedition of the winter was occasioned by Washington's orders to Wayne to forage in New Jersey and to collect all the livestock he could drive back to Valley Forge. When news of Wayne's presence in New Jersey reached British headquarters, Abercrombie was sent across the Delaware below Billingsport on 24 February to intercept the American. On the 25th Stirling, with the same objective, crossed at Cooper's Ferry with a detachment including Simcoe's Queen's Rangers and hurried toward Haddonfield. In the meantime, Wayne and John Barry, with armed boat crews, had been systematically destroying all hay that could not be carried off. The owners' names were taken for subsequent restitution. However, a large number of farmers had removed their cattle and hay into the deep pine woods rather than accept what they considered a worthless promise to pay. Passing quickly through the area, Wayne was north of Haddonfield when Stirling reached that village.

Their quarry having escaped, Stirling foraged in the Haddonfield area, and Abercrombie went as far south as Salem. They succeeded in gathering forage, but of greater importance was Abercrombie's recognition that forage was abundant in the lower counties of New Jersey.

Wayne had sent a detachment under Lieutenant Colonel Sherman to escort 150 head of cattle to Valley Forge. Reaching Bucks County, Sherman requested assistance from Lacey, but the militia officer was undermanned and refused. The unit proceeded, unaware that their drive was known in Philadelphia. A detachment of British dragoons and "embodied Refugees" overtook them about thirty miles north of the city and captured a few men and the cattle — British sources said 130.[48]

As the weather improved and the river became navigable, Hamond took steps to protect shipping in the bay and river. In cooperation with Howe, he developed a joint army and navy expedition to gather forage in the lower counties of New Jersey. On 10 March, Hamond ordered the *Pearl* to take station between Chester and Reedy Point and to destroy all rebel armed boats infesting the mouths of the creeks in the Wilmington area. Protection was to be offered to all boats bringing produce to Philadelphia markets. Captain Linzee was informed that Colonel Mawhood, with a body of troops, had embarked on several transports. They would be escorted by a flotilla of small armed boats and a galley commanded by Captain Watt. Linzee was to assist and escort the expedition and to ascertain the movements of American naval and army units.

Two days later, Captain Phipps, with the *Camilla*, was ordered to proceed down the river and patrol the area between Reedy Island and Bombay Hook. He was ordered to take station near the mouth of Cohansey Creek (Cumberland County, New Jersey), which was Mawhood's objective. Also, the *Zebra* was to take a position at the mouth of the Brandywine and offer any assistance necessary. Mawhood's principal escorts were to be the *Camilla* and the *Pearl*. Hamond warned Phipps that while patrol duty was important, the immediate objective was to cover Mawhood and provide a safe landing for him at Cohansey Creek.[49]

Mawhood's expedition had been planned for some time, probably based on information Abercrombie brought back to headquarters. It had been scheduled for early March, but because of several days of inclement weather and heavy snow, river traffic was brought to a standstill. Mawhood's command included the 17th, 27th, and 46th regiments, a force of about 900 regulars, plus Simcoe's Queen's

Rangers and the New Jersey Volunteers. With the Provincials, Mawhood probably had a combined force of between 1,200 and 1,300
men.[50]

General Robertson accompanied Watt on the sloop *Strumpet*.[51]
After five days they reached Reedy Point opposite Salem Creek. On
the fifteenth, the flotilla picked up the *Pearl*, which convoyed them
down the river. At this point, the original instructions to proceed
down the river to Cohansey Creek were countermanded, and a decision was made to cross the river to the Salem area. Howe undoubtedly gave Mawhood some discretion to change the landing place if
his Loyalist informants suggested a better foraging area than
Cohansey Creek. According to Simcoe, about three o'clock on the
morning of the seventeenth his rangers landed about six miles from
Salem. Robertson stated that the main body landed at 7:00 A.M. near
Salem Creek and marched directly to Salem.[52]

At Salem, Mawhood dispatched foraging parties, covered by
detachments of fifty to seventy soldiers, throughout the country north
of Alloways Creek. They were only moderately successful, and he
turned his attention to the area south of the creek, where, it was
reported, there was an abundance of hay and oats. The farms around
Salem and north of the creek had been swept fairly clean of forage by
Wayne, Abercrombie, and parties of Loyalist and American militia.

Three bridges spanned Alloways Creek. The American militia
crossed the creek, erected breastworks, and then removed the planks
of the bridges. Inferior in numbers and equipment, their resistance
could do little more than momentarily delay the British. The absence of artillery briefly delayed Mawhood's effort to dislodge the
Americans from their breastworks.

During the first few days, militia detachments were defeated at
Thompson's and Quinton's bridges. The Americans complained of
the savagery exhibited by British troops, especially the Queen's
Rangers. It was reported prisoners were brutally bayoneted after having thrown themselves on the mercy of their enemy.

On 20 March, Simcoe and his rangers were ordered to clear out
a pocket of resistance at Hancock's bridge. Most of the militia withdrew upon Simcoe's approach, but a party of twenty or thirty threw
themselves into Hancock's house. The rangers easily captured the
house and cruelly killed many of its occupants. No justification can
be ascribed to their conduct. Simcoe admitted, "Some very unfortunate circumstances happened here." Simcoe had no more control
over his partisan corps than any officer who commanded irregular

troops. He further observed, "Events like these are the real miseries of war." Normally, an action between armed opponents, regardless of their relative strength, cannot be classified as a massacre. At Hancock's house, however, no distinction was made between those who wanted to surrender and armed militia and civilians.

After four frustrating days and minor victories, Mawhood issued an ultimatum to the militia to disperse and lay down their arms. His fulminations of condign punishment infuriated the Americans and were certainly not a credit to a British officer. If they did not comply, he threatened to arm "the Inhabitants well affected called the Tories" and attack and destroy all the militia who continued to resist. This was a curious statement, as he knew that many local Loyalists had already joined the Rangers and New Jersey Volunteers. He proposed to burn their houses and other property and reduce them and "their unfortunate Women and Children to Beggary and Distress." To further emphasize his determination, he appended a list of men who would be the first "to feel the Vengeance of the british nation."

After the massacre at Hancock's house, the foraging parties worked feverishly throughout the country south of Alloways Creek. The nearest American force of any consequence was regrouping in the vicinity of Cohansey Creek. Rather than advance to attack these Americans, Mawhood decided to load all the forage on board the boats and return to Philadelphia. One officer said he returned with thirty sail loaded with hay and oats. The same officer saw five American officers and 107 privates brought back as prisoners; however, he acknowledged thirty-one British casualties — a mute testimony to the American resistance.[53]

Throughout the winter, other nagging situations beset the commander in chief and the civilian population, with some of a personal nature adding to the discomfiture of Howe.

The army's presence in the city was a constant source of dismay and concern to inhabitants having slaves or indentured servants and to a number of husbands whose wives deserted them for British officers. Elizabeth Drinker noted that a British officer stole her servant girl "over a fence" and apparently discarded her later.

Ewald prided himself on being a humanitarian and a strict disciplinarian. His efforts to protect the property of the residents near his bivouac had endeared him to a number of well-known Quakers. He visited their homes and, on at least one occasion, accompanied a Quaker friend to a meeting "partly out of curiosity and partly just to hear something good once again." He described the solemn religious

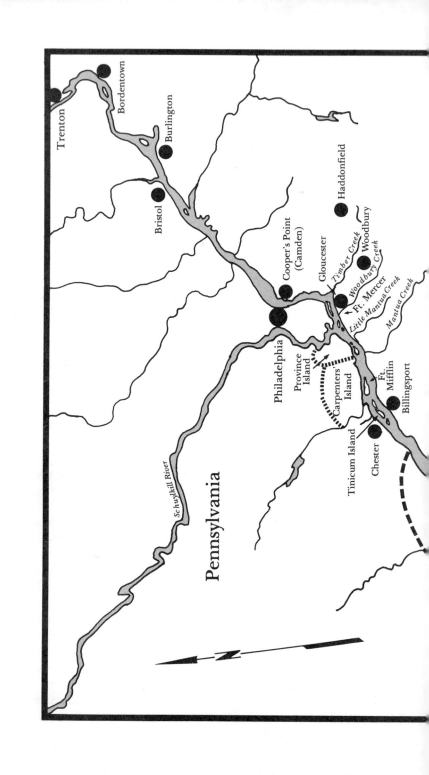

Trenton

Bordentown

Burlington

Bristol

Haddonfield

Cooper's Point
(Camden)

Gloucester

Timber Creek

Woodbury

Woodbury Creek

Ft. Mercer

Little Mantua Creek

Mantua Creek

Philadelphia

Province Island

Carpenters Island

Ft. Mifflin

Billingsport

Tinicum Island

Chester

Schuylkill River

Pennsylvania

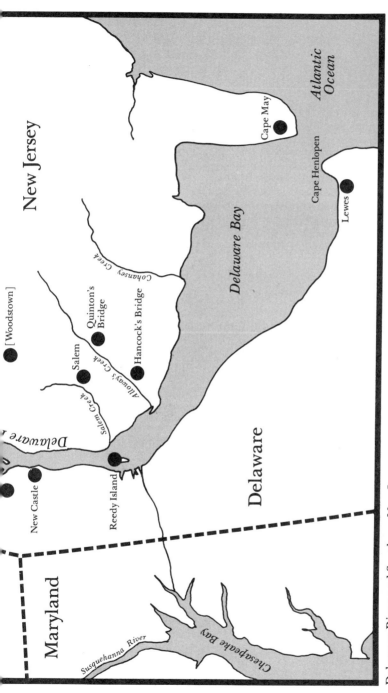

Delaware River and Southern New Jersey

service, and as he was about to leave, an aged woman arose and said the "Holy Spirit" had inspired her to admonish the meeting with a warning

directed to my sex. I hear during these frightful times — which we have earned through our sins — when our whole region is swarming with all sorts of foreign peoples, very bad things about our women and their daughters. Women and girls are said to be exchanging visits with these warriors. I know that some have made light of their shame so much that they stroll about with these people in broad daylight.

I beseech you — mothers and fathers — to stop these depravities. Remember that these people have a wandering foot, that you cannot prosecute them under our laws when your daughters go too far with them. But bear in mind — to your own disgrace — that you must accept what they leave behind. Think! — no good can come of this!

The large attendance sat in a stunned but devout silence for a while and then quietly filed out of the meetinghouse. Ewald returned to his quarters with his curiosity satisfied, but "little edified."[54]

The scarcity of provisions and the exorbitant price for most commodities created a fear among the city's Quakers that they would be without many essential staples before the end of winter. Howe had forbidden commerce with the country, and the lack of gold or silver convinced the Quakers that an appeal must be made to their brethren in England and Ireland. An open letter was addressed to Ireland asking for a large shipment of beef, pork, butter, biscuit, meal, peas, cheese, coal, and other items. Full restitution was promised as soon as affairs in Philadelphia permitted. Troubled about the plight of the city's poor, they suggested that any charitable contributions for their benefit would be gladly accepted. In this regard, a committee of Philadelphia Quakers had been formed to distribute money to the poor, and as time passed, additional funds were raised.

London and Irish Quakers responded generously and sent a shipment of the needed articles valued at £5,000 on the *Mary and Charlotte*. James Woods, on 10 February, and Robert Barclay, on the sixteenth, advised Dr. Thomas Parke that the ship had sailed for America. Unfortunately, the vessel did not arrive in Philadelphia until early June. Having been stored in the hold for seventeen weeks, her cargo was badly damaged by heat. Normally the loss would have caused grave concern, but with the British soon to leave the city, there was much joy among the Quakers because fresh provisions were soon expected to arrive.[55]

Other churches were equally concerned with the condition of the poor. Charity sermons were held at Christ Church on 11 January and at both Christ and Saint Peter's on the eighteenth. A sum of £97 8s. 11d. was distributed to the city's needy, and £50 1s. 10d. in Continental money to those who could dispose of it.[56]

To boost Loyalist morale, publishers of Philadelphia newspapers editorialized about the helpless situation of the Americans contrasted with the plenty of His Majesty's subjects. On the other hand, publishers who had fled the city and set up shop in Lancaster and York devoted considerable space to editorials and letters vilifying Galloway and the British authorities in Philadelphia.[57]

Towne and Humphreys used editorials to counteract rumors of an American alliance with France. Towne warned Americans not to be deluded by vague tales, but to judge for themselves by consulting *"authentic letters* and *affidavits,"* which can "be seen by any candid enquirer." On 7 February, he published a disclaimer assuring his readers that "the court of France has positively determined they shew no countenance whatever to the rebellion in America." Three days earlier Humphreys had made the same observation, adding that the people at York were so chagrined they had confined the courier, a Continental army captain, in the local gaol. The editors continued their tongue-in-cheek propaganda by declaring that France was closing its ports to American ships.[58]

An insidious charge directed against the British authorities during the winter was that they were counterfeiting Continental money. Earlier in the year, an advertisement appeared in New York newspapers which flagrantly offered "persons going into other Colonies . . . any number of counterfeit Congress-Notes, for the Price of the Paper per Ream." The announcement proclaimed the fake money could not be distinguished from the genuine and had already had a successful circulation. Whether this effort had Howe's official sanction cannot be ascertained, but the widespread distribution throughout the war lends credence to, at least, his tacit endorsement of the practice. Conversely, citizens of Philadelphia were warned in February that counterfeit dollars were in circulation — one issue made of copper and difficult to detect, another made of a soft metal and easily bent.[59]

Toward the end of the first quarter, Howe encouraged the inhabitants to plant vegetable gardens and hay for forage. Peebles rode down into the Neck in late March and observed that residents were building fences and enclosures. It was his opinion that the entire area below Bettering House would be fenced in from river to river for hay fields.[60]

A few days previously, Howe had ordered a survey of all ground fit for pasture land in the territory under protection of the British army.

As the winter drew to a close, Philadelphia settled down to life as a garrison city. Howe established a civil government, subject to certain restrictions. Unfortunately, as the winter progressed a schism developed between the commander in chief and Galloway, the civil head, which made cooperation impossible. With starvation facing the poor and provisions and forage never adequate for military or civilians, Howe was forced to impose regulations to control the distribution of the meager supplies reaching the city. As month succeeded month, a frustrated Howe looked to the east for a royal communique granting his request to return to England.

CHAPTER X

MILITARY JUSTICE

ASIDE FROM THE perplexities of quartering the troops and organizing the defenses of the city, Howe's most serious problem was discipline. He first directed his attention to a dual justice system of civilian and military tribunals. It soon became obvious that all criminal offenses had to be handled by general or regimental courts-martial. Although it is difficult to determine the full extent of the superintendent general's and the magistrates' of police participation in legal matters, they were involved in some civil lawsuits.

The unarmed city watchmen commanded little respect from military personnel or the city toughs who patronized waterfront dram shops and tippling houses. These questionable houses of entertainment and refreshment, also frequented by the military, caused embarrassment to the corps commanders and were the principal contributors to the breakdown in discipline. Orders were issued to all quartermasters to survey all houses selling liquor without a license and to confiscate their stock. The appropriated liquor kegs and casks were to be ''stav'd'' and the shop owners arrested and sent to the provost guardhouse.

Concurrent with this order, Howe received complaints from the magistrates of police that some officers of the army were guilty of ''Shamfull & UnGentleman Like treatment . . . to wretched Unarm'd Watchmen in the Execution of their Duty.'' Howe was aghast and could ''Scarsley believe that Officers and Gentlemen are Capable of Being Guilty, of Such Horrible Outrages.'' However, he promised to bring to public trial the first officer or soldier ''Detected in Such Unwarrantable Practices.''[1]

To protect the inhabitants, each regiment was to send patrols throughout their districts from tattoo to reveille. The 16th and 17th dragoons were ordered to complement the regimental patrols by having mounted detachments move all night through every section of the city. All patrols were to make a tour of duty at least once every hour and apprehend disorderly persons or straggling soldiers who did not have passes signed by their company commanders. The patrols were only moderately successful, as they probably ignored stragglers and merely picked up soldiers or civilians engaged in actual crimes. This condition became apparent as Howe received numerous remonstrances protesting the unsafe condition of the streets and depredations of private property.[2]

Repeated admonishments to corps commanders to intensify the patrol activity were supplemented by a demand that company officers maintain a constant vigil over the activities of their men. Officers were to make certain that barrack houses were not overcrowded. They were to visit the soldiers mess every day at 1:00 P.M. and visit the barracks each night. Roll calls were to be taken frequently and at irregular intervals. It was hoped that these and other efforts to provide for the soldiers' comfort would raise the garrison morale. Regimental officers were to pay particular attention to the health and safety of their men by extinguishing all barrack fires every night. If the rooms were too warm, it would be harmful to the soldiers' health if they were suddenly called to march during a cold night. Howe believed that high morale and good health would contribute to a contented and better disciplined garrison.[3]

Howe was especially annoyed at the reports of plundering and destruction of private property. He had hoped to avoid having to make indemnification to residents for the willful vandalism of his soldiers. Daily complaints were received, and he was "mortified" that it was necessary to again admonish corps commanders about conduct so "Absolutely Repugnant, to all Military Order & Discipline [and] Shamefull and Unsoldier like Behaviour." Fences and houses were pulled down throughout the city, and other houses were stripped of all wood. Furniture and other articles of wood were burned or destroyed in the guardhouses. Elizabeth Drinker observed that soldiers and children were tearing down sheds, gates, and everything made of wood.[4]

The commander in chief was determined to make an example of the first culprits apprehended. On 22 December, two soldiers were executed according to Howe's orders. Finally, the provost marshal was ordered to make frequent rounds of the city and to execute on the spot any soldier or follower caught marauding, pulling down houses, or possessing plunder. All suspicious persons were to be brought in for questioning. No one was to be out after 8:30 P.M. without a lantern until reveille. To keep abreast of disciplinary violations, Howe ordered the captain of the main guard to report directly to him.

Vandalism was not limited to the private soldier. Officers at least condoned, if not actually participated in, such acts. When two companies selected the same property as their prey, an occasional confrontation occurred. At least one duel was fought between officers. Colonel Hyde and Captain Watson, of the guards, fought over the rights of their men to pull down an old house for firewood; Hyde was run through the right arm. Peebles observed that "most quarells rise from triffling causes." Officers were reprimanded for the unauthorized shifting of their quarters. Others practiced with firearms near private property and attempted to excuse their actions by claiming they were preventing depredations. Threatened with exposure to Howe, they vaulted fences and continued target practice in private gardens.[5]

The woodcutters, under strong escorts of two hundred or more, ventured out daily to gather fuel for the garrison. As one area was cleared of all trees, they shifted their location. By late spring, the region between the redoubts and Germantown, or Frankford, was almost denuded of timber. A serious disciplinary problem arose as the returning wagons (during snowy weather sleighs were used) entered the lines: Soldiers swooped down and pilfered significant quantities of their contents. The men retained some of the wood for personal use, but sold the bulk of their plunder to inhabitants. Apparently, this practice became very lucrative, and as the winter became very cold, organized groups of soldiers stole wagons and carts to go out of the lines to the main wood yard and returned with full loads of wood to sell. Sentries were strictly enjoined not to permit wagons to cross the lines without a certificate. Patrols of a sergeant and twelve soldiers were ordered to conduct wagons to the wood yards. All malefactors were to be summarily punished, but no evidence exists to show that anything more than a possible reprimand was given.[6]

Until January, small stands of timber remained in the lower Neck and at a few locations along the east bank of the Schuylkill, as they were reserved for army use. Wood yards were set up at convenient locations in the city, with the principal one being just outside the northern defense line; one was on the banks of the Schuylkill, and another near the new gaol. Coal was brought in by ship and used in limited quantities.

Virtually every issue of the Philadelphia newspapers carried notices of robberies and crimes. Most announcements appeared in the form of an advertisement offering a reward for the apprehension of the thief or recovery of the stolen articles. The publishers carefully avoided any editorial comment on the licentious or criminal behavior of officers or soldiers. An occasional letter to the editor belittled accusations of rapine leveled at British officers as being fallacious and the product of American propaganda. One Loyalist correspondent scoffed at the charges that British officers were committing rape. Rather, he claimed, all Quakers and other inhabitants were unanimous in their opinion that "the city never enjoyed such uninterrupted regularity, as since the British conquest [occupation]."[7]

Elizabeth Drinker epitomized the civilian concern over personal security, recording, "These are sad times for thieving and plundering, 'tis hardly safe to leave the door open a minute." She commented on the vandalism of the rioting British troops, noting that "things wear a very gloomy aspect." Concerned, but obviously grateful for the presence of her officer lodger, she witnessed men scaling fences and soldiers carrying bundles which proved to be clothes stolen from a neighbor through an alley.

Although the items stolen were typical of robberies in any city, there was a significant increase in the number of such incidents. Jewelry, watches, silverware, household and dry goods, clothing, horses, cows, and carts were among the articles taken. British officers and surgeons reported losing regimental pistols and jackets, saddles, bridles, and a silver flute in its box. Occasionally jewelry and other valuables stolen in Newport and New York were sent to Philadelphia for disposal. One of the most atrocious crimes committed against the civilian population was plundering homes of everything portable, usually under the pretext of military sanction. Even more heinous were the cases of rape; it is impossible to determine if all such incidents were reported.[8]

Other crimes that involved military personnel included desertion, joining the rebel army, striking an officer, and corresponding with the enemy. A review of the courts-martial records clearly shows that each board of officers used a different set of standards in judging and sentencing accused prisoners. Unfortunately, the records of some court-martial proceedings are incomplete. However, it is obvious that most officers considered the youth, inexperience, past record, and, in some cases, the attitude of the prisoner while in confinement in handing down a verdict or in determining the severity of the sentence. In a number of verdicts in which the death penalty was imposed, Howe, using similar criteria, appealed for royal clemency.

Punishments varied. For desertion and joining the American army, men suffered from three hundred to one thousand lashes "on bare backs with cats of Nine Tails." For robbery, rape, striking an officer and murder, the penalty was five hundred to one thousand lashes or death. In addition to the physical punishment, civilian employees of the army, followers, and inhabitants, were humiliated before their peers by being drummed out of the lines. In some instances, the punishment seemed too severe to fit the crime. Many of the accused were pathetic figures or young boys. Others were hard-bitten toughs who inspired little pity. Soldiers were punished at the head of their respective corps, with the sentence of camp followers carried out by the provost marshal's executioner.[9]

Courts-martial were constantly in session all winter at the State House, Pennsylvania and regimental hospitals, the old gaol, the orderly room, and various taverns. These tribunals usually comprised three general officers and ten captains. A few trials illustrate the degree of military justice.

The court-martial of Captain Alexander Campbell[10] occasioned considerable comment and was mentioned in more officers' journals than any other trial during the occupation. Campbell was accused by Mary Fygis (or Figgis), sixteen years old, of using her to carry intelligence to the Americans. Howe's orders called her a spinster; however, all others referred to her as a young girl. After a trial in which much sympathy was expressed for the defendant, he was acquitted. Peebles said the young girl recanted her testimony. His statement appears accurate, as she was later tried for perjury; but the case was dismissed because of her age, and she was eventually turned out of the lines. Sir John Murray believed that Campbell would suffer in character and fortune regardless of the outcome of the trial, "a victim of the malice and depravity of an abandoned little wretch." Howe apparently agreed that Campbell's reputation would be damaged, as he had a notice inserted in all regimental orderly books showing his agreement with the verdict: "the innocence of Captain Alexander

Campbell . . . in justice to his character [and] . . . to signify his entire approbation of the fidelity & diligence with which [he] has executed the several duties committed to his charge."[11]

More tragic was the trial of Corporal John Fisher. The young soldier was a baby-sitter for a British soldier and his wife when he committed "a Reap on ye Body of Maria Nicklos [Nicholls] a Woman Child of 9 years of Eage [age]." He was adjudged guilty and ordered "hang'd by the Neck until he is Dead." Peebles recorded that Fisher was reprieved. An interpolated note in Peebles's journal said this was done through the intercession of Miss Franks, probably Rebecca Franks, one of the belles of the Meschianza and a noted Loyalist wit. Miss Franks may have appealed to the commander in chief; the same day, 23 March, Howe wrote Germain confirming the sentence but requesting royal clemency for Fisher. However, other than Peebles's statement, there is no indication that a pardon was granted.[12]

Somewhat mystifying was the severity of the sentence of Thomas Murphy, a civilian, convicted of stealing a piece of linen. He was to receive "500 lashes in the most public manner and drummed out of the garrison with a halter around neck." In another case, a negro, Anthony Cuff, was charged with buying a pair of shoes from a soldier of the 63rd Regiment. His penalty was to pay £5 or suffer six months' imprisonment. Soldiers were constantly selling or spoiling their clothes, which caused great concern to their officers.[13]

Private John Rowland, another soldier, and a negro man were accused of tearing down a house belonging to Lieutenant George Spann. However, there is some question about Spann's legal ownership of the house. According to the soldiers, they were acting under orders of Captain Harrison, who had instructed them to gather wood. A disagreement ensued, and after a heated exchange, Spann called Rowland a rascal, broke a lath over his head, and then picked up another board and struck him again. At that instant Rowland retaliated and struck the officer. Regardless of his orders or provocation, the private was sentenced to death. Howe appealed for clemency, and Rowland was pardoned because of his exemplary conduct while a prisoner.[14]

This incident typifies some of the bitterness that arose between the various regiments over trifling matters. Howe was bombarded with protests over officers and men pulling their houses apart for fuel. As late as 4 April, he was charging officers and noncommissioned officers of the guards with responsibility for this type of complaint.[15]

Catherine Stone and a negro girl, Isabel Mitchell, were walking on the street between eight and nine o'clock at night when they were accosted by three men. The men, one in uniform, said they were a patrol and the girls would have to accompany them to the guardhouse. On the way the Mitchell girl escaped, and the three men dragged Catherine Stone toward the doorway of the Southwark Theatre, where she was ravished by one of the men. After her ordeal she sought refuge in a nearby house, but the occupants were afraid to give her sanctuary. Later they testified they thought she was a disorderly woman and, because of the frequent riots, refused her assistance and insisted she leave their property. Some days after her harrowing experience, she saw two of the men, Robert Brown and John Dillon, wagoners, on the street. They were arrested, tried, and convicted. Each was to receive 1,000 lashes and drummed through the city with a rope around his neck and then turned out of the lines.[16]

A number of robbery trials have some resemblance to the case of private Cornelius Dunn. He dragged a negro woman from the middle of the street into a doorway and was robbing her when arrested by Lieutenant John Howse of the 38th Regiment. Dunn was searched and found to possess a ring, spoons, a tablecloth, and other articles. Convicted, he was sentenced to receive 500 lashes. A favorite pretext for soldiers intent on robbery was "rooting parties." On 26 December, four sergeants and two acting sergeants were relieved of their duties "for irregular behaviour on a rooting party." One sergeant was acquitted. Four days later, three privates were accused of plundering a private house while out looking for roots. One received 500 lashes, while the other two were adjudged not guilty.[17]

Many cases are described in the general courts-martial records. For example, Private Michael Finnerty was convicted of stealing money from Captain Cathcart and sentenced to death. Any crime committed by a private in which the plaintiff was an officer always seemed to carry a harsher punishment. Numerous incidents of plunder were charged to soldiers on foraging expeditions. Three sailors on an army victualling ship were accused of embezzling part of the ship's cargo, to wit several bags of oats. Their defense was that the bags taken were nothing but the sweepings from the floor. The court apparently believed them, as they were acquitted. Being drunk, afraid, or, in at least one case, having a language difference were frequent alibis offered by suspects.

One of the few robberies carried in the columns of the newspapers was the tale of three suspected "rebels." The *Royal Pennsylvania Gazette* stated, "On March 18 — 3 rebels . . . villains received their discipline of the cat at the end of the market, for (like their brethren) making too free with the property of honest people; after being thus duly qualified for the service of Congress, they were escorted out of town, by a number of drums and fifes, with music suitable for the occasion."[18]

An interesting aspect of military justice during the occupation is contained in Howe's Orders of 6 January: "The Quarter Master is immediately to Cause a Guard bed be fixed in the Black Hole, is also to Provide a Verry Strong Sack for the Door & Everything that is Necessary for fastening of it Properly." The location of the "Black Hole" is uncertain, but it was undoubtedly the place of confinement for prisoners sentenced to death and for hardened criminals.[19]

CHAPTER XI

HOWE'S STROLLING PLAYERS

L*ITTLE CONSIDERATION WAS* given to organized diversions or amusements until the army went into winter quarters in late December. As many of the officers had participated in amateur theatricals in New York; they naturally looked upon the Southwark Theatre on Cedar (South) Street as an ideal setting for their thespian endeavors. A. H. Quinn said it was a red brick and wooden building. Oil lamps without glasses were used to light the stage. For part of the audience, the view was obstructed by pillars which supported the roof and gallery. For a short time after the battles at Brandywine and Germantown, the theatre was used as a hospital. Undoubtedly with the concurrence of the fun-loving Howe who had been a devotee of the theatre in New York, a group of officers were allowed to use the facility to offer a series of plays for the entertainment of the garrison city.[1]

Programming, production, recruiting actors and actresses, and administration were entrusted to young officers, including the imaginative John Andre and Oliver Delancey. The first public notice of the dramatic group was to employ civilians with specific talents. Advertisements in the *Pennsylvania Ledger* on 24 December 1777 asked for personnel ''Wanted for the Play-house, a Person who writes quick, and a legible hand; also a Person well versed in accounts, to act as Clerk and Vice-Treasurer. Any people that have ever been employed about the Play-House, as carpenters or scene-shifters, may get employment by applying to the Printer [James Humphreys, Jr.].'' A Mr. Smith was obtained presumably to act as the theatre manager.

Most authorities agree he was the proprietor of City Tavern on Second Street at Walnut. His theatre office was established on Front Street below the drawbridge (over Dock Creek) and a few doors below Peter Suter, Hatter.[2]

The precision of the announcements offering tickets for sale, stating rules governing admission, and reserving seats smacked of military orders. Before the first performance, tickets could be purchased from James Humphreys, Jr., the printer; at the Coffee House, the Pennsylvania Farmer, and John Richmond's on Front between Chestnut and Walnut streets; at the Turk's Head, Water between Race and Vine streets; or from Mr. Smith at the theatre office. Later, ticket locations were reduced to the printer, the Coffee House, and the Pennsylvania Farmer "and no where else." Tickets sold for one dollar for boxes and the pit, and a half dollar for the gallery. No money was accepted at the door "on any Account." Officers and other gentlemen were admonished not to attempt to bribe the

Southwark Theatre, used as a British army hospital after the Battle of Germantown. It later became the British officers' theatre. *Free Library of Philadelphia*

Major John Andre: self portrait engraved by W. G. Jackman. *Kean Archives, Philadelphia*

doorkeeper. In January a notice was seen in the *Pennsylvania Ledger* requesting "The Foreign Gentlemen [Hessian officer] who slipped a Guinea and a Half into the Hand of the Box-Keeper, and forced his way into the House is desired to send to the office of the Theatre in Front Street, that it may be returned." A study of Humphreys' handbills and other memorabilia has revealed that 1,000 handbills and 660 tickets were printed for each performance.[3]

Patrons seeking box seats were cautioned that "Places for the

Boxes to be taken at the office of the Theatre in Front-street, between the Hours of Nine and Two o'clock; After which Time, the Box-keeper will not attend. Ladies or Gentlemen, who would have Places kept for them, are desired to send their Servants to the theatre at Four o'clock, otherwise their Places will be given up." Theatre-goers were warned that no one would be permitted behind the scenes.

The proceeds of the theatre were used to benefit the widows and orphans of British soldiers killed in action and any other charity designated by the managers. This humanitarian gesture was not un-common among the military and civilian population, who made many efforts to ease the suffering of the poor.

Attention was quickly directed to obtaining scenery and props for the forthcoming productions. Andre, along with Delancey, has been credited with painting the scenery. One scene ascribed to Andre depicted a rural countryside with a small stream meandering from the foreground into the distant background. In the center foreground was a beautiful cascade of water falling amid a grove of majestic trees. The entire scene was one of calm and serene beauty. Unfortunately, when the theatre burned in 1821, this memento of the military theatre of 1778 was destroyed. An interesting advertisement appearing in the newspapers toward the end of December seems to have been in-tended for the use of the theatre: "Wanted a Carpet — from thirteen feet to nineteen and a half in length, and from eleven to twelve feet wide. Any person having such to dispose of may hear of a purchaser by applying to the Printer."[4]

Assembling a repertoire was a major concern. Local bookstores and libraries, both public and private, were scanned for appropriate plays. As Philadelphians had generally frowned on the theatre as amoral, books of plays were not abundant. Several desired titles were requested in advertisements, sometimes requiring three insertions before meeting with success. It seems some of the plays were rewritten for the theatre. *Douglas,* written by Dr. John Holme, was apparently adapted for the 19 May performance by Major Gordon of the 26th Regiment. A copy was not readily obtainable, and as the play had been used previously by military actors, Gordon may have borrowed on his knowledge of the original. A comedy or a farce and a tragedy or a serious work were presented at each performance.[5]

The first presentation was announced for Monday, 19 January, with a performance planned for each Monday thereafter. However, circumstances made certain changes necessary. The first play started precisely at 7:00 P.M. Thirteen evenings of entertainment were held during the winter for devotees of the theatre. The plays and dates presented were:

Monday, 19 January 1778
No One's Enemy but His Own
The Deuce is in Him (farce)

Monday, 26 January
The Minor
The Deuce is in Him

Monday, 9 February
The Minor
Duke and No Duke (farce)

Monday, 16 February
Constant Couple
Duke and No Duke

Monday, 2 March
Constant Couple
Mock Doctor (farce)
(Announced, but postponed ''for very particular Reasons.'')

Monday, 9 March
The Inconstant
Mock Doctor
(Tickets sold for March 2 will be honored this night. ''After the . . . performance the House will be entertained with a beautiful Exhibition of *Fire-Works.*'')

Monday, 16 March
The Inconstant
Lethe (farce)

Wednesday, 25 March
The First Part of King Henry IV
Mock Doctor

Monday, 30 March
The First Part of Henry IV
Lethe

Friday, 10 April
The Wonder, A Woman Keeps a Secret
A Trip to Scotland (farce)
(Postponed because of the indisposition of one of the actresses.)

Monday, 13 April

The Wonder, A Woman Keeps a Secret
A Trip to Scotland
(Postponed to April 20 because of Passion Week.)

Monday, 20 April

(Program postponed from 10 and 13 April.)

Friday, 24 April

The Wonder, A Woman Keeps a Secret
Mock Doctor

Friday, 1 May

The Liar
A Trip to Scotland

Wednesday, 6 May

The Liar
Duke and No Duke

Tuesday, 19 May

Douglas
The Citizen (farce)[6]

Before the first performance on 19 January, a member of the ''society of Gentlemen of the Army and Navy'' delivered a prologue. It has been claimed the speaker was Major Robert Crewe:[7]

> Once more ambitious of theatric glory,
> Howe's strolling company appears before ye
> O'er hills and dales, and bogs, thro' wind and weather,
> And many a hair-breadth 'scape we've scrambled hither —
> For we, true vagrants of the Thespian race,
> Whilst summer lasts, ne'er known a settled place;
> Anxious to prove the merit of our band,
> A chosen squadron wander through the land.
> How beats each Yankie bosom at our drum,
> ''Hark! Jonathan, zounds, here's the strollers come'' . . .

Before the prologue a short statement announced that the theatre was for the ''laudable purpose of raising a supply for the Widows and Orphans of those who have lost their lives in his Majesty's service, as well as for such other generous charities as their funds may enable them to perform.''

The performers were army and navy officers , at least one army surgeon, "& some kept Mistresses" Peebles thought "the gentlemen do their parts very well, but the Ladies are rather defficient." The captain, sometimes accompanied by ladies, attended several plays and is the principal source for the names of a number of actors and actresses. He was also free in his comments on the merits of their performances.[8]

Captain Charles Phipps, of the frigate *Camilla*, played the *Mock Doctor* very well and gave a good performance as Percy in *The First Part of King Henry IV*. In the latter production Captain Stanley of the dragoons played the king, and Captain Madden of the guards played Falstaff, each offering "very good" impersonations. Dr. Hamond Beaumont "of ye Hospital" was the old man and Lord Chalkstone in *Lethe* and later "shin'd" as the *Mock Doctor*. Peebles thought that Lord Cathcart performed in the *Inconstant* and *Lethe* on the same evening, "with more propriety in speech than in some parts chosen — ridiculous in a man of his Rank & fashion to play the part of a Valet & suffer the ceremony of being kick'd [Peebles' displeasure is further displayed]. . . . Play full of bawdy Sentiments indelicate to a modest ear, but most women can bear a little either very Publickly or very privately." On 19 May Mrs. Williams did very well as Lady Randolph in *Douglas*.[9]

Mrs. Williams may have been the wife of Major Williams of the artillery. The major had portrayed the tragic hero in both *Richard* and *Macbeth* in New York and was now in the garrison at Philadelphia. It is probable that he was a member of the thespian group. Charles Durang related a conversation he held with John North, who had been caretaker of the Southwark Theatre. North said that a "Miss Hyde sang and acted with the British officers during the war. . . . She sang 'Tally Ho' between the play and the farce. Many of the soldiers' wives helped the officers on the stage. They were generally of no character. They and the officers were about the theatre all day. When any piece was to be rehearsed, they all would flock about the back door, or the side lot."[10]

Many inhabitants rebelled at the wickedness of again having a theatre in their midst. The Quakers were particularly offended and were appalled by the effect it would have on their youth. They were convinced that the attractiveness of amusement and diversion "promoted by the military" would lead to a "Spirit of Dissipation Levity and Profaneness." All were admonished to avoid such "vain and Wanton Exhibitions." A committee was appointed to present a

THEATRE.

On ACCOUNT of the INDISPOSITION
of one of the ACTRESSES,

The Play,

Which was to have been Performed

ON FRIDAY,

The Tenth Inſtant,

Is obliged to be

POSTPONED.

APRIL 8th, 1778.

❊❊❊❊❊❊❊❊❊❊❊❊❊❊❊❊❊❊❊❊❊❊❊❊❊❊❊

PRINTED by JAMES HUMPHREYS, JUNR. in *Market-ſtreet*, between *Front* and *Second ſtreet*.

MONDAY, *FEBRUARY* 16, 1778.

BOX, ONE DOLLAR.

CONSTANT COUPLE.

The Doors to be open at FIVE, and Play
to begin at SEVEN o'Clock.

TUESDAY, MAY 19, 1778

BOX, *One Dollar*.

DOUGLASS.

The Doors to be open at FIVE, and Play
to begin at SEVEN o'Clock.

6 60

Theatricals of the British Army in Philadelphia, with the box tickets used

---

Announcement of postponement of a play. *American Historical and Literary Curiosities, Second Series,* Smith and Watson. *American Philosophical Society*

On MONDAY Next,

The THIRTEENTH Day of APRIL, *1778*

At the Theatre in Southwark,

For the Benefit of a PUBLIC CHARITY,

WILL BE REPRESENTED, A COMEDY CALLED

The Wonder,

A Woman keeps a Secret!

TO WHICH WILL BE ADDED,

A TRIP to SCOTLAND.

The CHARACTERS by the OFFICERS of the Army
and Navy.

TICKETS to be had at the Printer's; at the Coffee-houfe in Market-
ftreet; and at the Pennfylvania Farmer, near the New-Market, and
no where elfe.

BOXES and PIT, ONE DOLLAR.—GALLERY, HALF A DOLLAR.

Doors to open at Five o'Clock, and begin precifely at Seven.

No Money will, on any Account, be taken at the Door.

N. B. Places for the Boxes to be taken at the Office of the
Theatre in Front-ftreet, between the Hours of Nine and Two o'clock:
After which Time, the Box-keeper will not attend. Ladies or Gentlemen, who would have Places kept for them, are defired to fend
their Servants to the Theatre at Four o'clock, otherwife their Places
will be given up.

☞ No Perfon can be admitted behind the Scenes.

TICKETS delivered for the 10th inft. will be taken.

PHILADELPHIA: Printed by JAMES HUMPHREYS, JUN.
Theatricals of the British Army in Philadelphia

Theatre program. *American Historical and Literary Curiosities, Second Series,*
Smith and Watson. *American Philosophical Society*

remonstrance to Howe, but, upon learning of his imminent departure for England, decided to wait until Clinton arrived. The committee did protest to Clinton, but by that time the theatre, gaming rooms, and ballrooms were already closed.[11]

Equally disturbed was the Reverend Henry Melchior Muhlenberg, a Lutheran minister in the village of Trappe. He lamented the theatre and other entertainments engaged in by British officers, but in keeping with the strict moral code of many clergymen of the eighteenth century, he deplored his countrymen's participation in similar activities while American and British soldiers were suffering in prisons:

In the midst of this terrible war, this last winter indeed, we read in the newspapers that various prominent British military heroes in Philadelphia played in comedies, held balls and *assemblies,* and danced with the ladies in accord with the morals customary in the world of society; and some of the so-called Sons and Daughters of Liberty who had fled from Philadelphia to Lancaster published in the English newspaper of Lancaster that they, too, had held *assemblies* and dances at night, at the very time when hundreds yea thousands were languishing in prisons, suffering hunger and cold.[12]

The theatre's demise after the performance of 19 May happened without comment. However, an announcement that had appeared in the newspapers in late April and early May should have warned patrons that the season would soon end. Mr. Smith requested that any persons having demands against the theatre should bring them to his immediate attention. It is, nevertheless, unlikely that the managers planned to offer any performances after mid-May. As Southwark Theatre was poorly ventilated, audiences attending plays in early May were already very uncomfortable. Before the last presentation on 19 May, it was announced that "every method will be taken to render the house as cool as possible."[13]

It is probable that interest in Howe's strolling players waned as rumors circulated among the officers' clubs and barracks that Philadelphia was to be evacuated and Howe replaced by Clinton. Most actors were members of Howe's coterie of young officers and not particular favorites of Clinton. Even if by some fortuitous circumstance the peace commissioners reached an accommodation with the American Congress; it was apparent that the presence of the British army and the military theatre were nearing an end.

At least two weeks before the theatre's final performance,

Howe's partisans had started to direct their energies elsewhere — to designing an elaborate entertainment to honor their departing chief. The theatre was neglected in order to produce the extravaganza to be called the Meschianza. Thus the British military theatre in Philadelphia of 1778 quietly faded into oblivion.

CHAPTER XII

CONVIVIAL INTERLUDES

DURING THE WINTER of 1777-78, Philadelphia has been described as the scene of continual debaucheries and gaming. Many of the activities criticized, such as the theatre, were neither unnatural nor immoral diversions. Howe was fully cognizant of the danger to the morale of his officers if they were not provided relaxation and entertainment. Therefore, he gave tacit approval to a festive winter. Then the general's preoccupation with his paramour, Mrs. Loring, and the convivial board caused him to overlook their excesses. The fertile imaginations of the debonair, but ill-fated, Major John Andre and a small coterie of officers who conceived entertainments such as the Meschianza have placed all merrymaking out of focus. While no excuses can be offered for the compulsive gambling of certain officers whose participation at the tables ruined their army careers, most of the intemperate actions were a fact of life in all eighteenth-century garrison cities.

Amusements varied according to the background and desires of individual officers. Most deplored the action of the gaming tables, but considered the theatre, horse races, and cricket matches acceptable diversions. Many officers used the winter to improve their knowledge. Lieutenant Hale, for example, was "fully employed in learning the German language."[1]

Camaraderie was frequently witnessed at the nightly dinners given by individual officers and at regimental messes. All officers above regimental commander were expected to provide a lavish board. Hamond considered it mandatory to maintain excellent inter-service relations. He observed that "as in all great Garrisons a considerable degree of Disruption frequently prevails, such was the case here to a great Extent, throughout the whole winter, Every Officer of Rank being provided with a furnished House, and giving frequent Entertainments." Some regimental commanders maintained private boards. However, most attended their own messes, often the occasion of good will, fun, and fellowship.[2]

Captain John Peebles maintained an almost daily account of his dining habits and furnished a fascinating portrayal of the regimental mess. No comments were found on conditions at the field mess at the redoubts or new gaol. The captain sometimes dined with companions at a tavern or was the guest at headquarters or of another officer. Most frequently he joined brother officers at the regimental mess. He was unhappy with tavern dining because the meals were too expensive; he mentioned one dinner that cost three dollars.[3]

Most dinners were merry and spent with congenial companions. Frequently, officers of the grenadier battalions, the "Light Bobs," or the colonel joined them. All imbibed freely, and on one occasion Captain Peebles noted, "Our Light Bobs din^d with us today we got all hands very merry." Another time he mentioned company at the mess "which always ends in hard drink, contrary to the primary intention of the Mess." The conviviality of their dinners is apparent in his entry for 17 May: when the mess wine ran out "we have drank 36 dozen since the Mess began vizt 11th Janu^ry 18 weeks."[4]

Some gatherings were less pleasant, especially when the colonel came to dine. He visited Peebles' mess on 5 February, and although they thought "mirth & good humor presided," it appears to have been a dull evening. As a footnote to the meal, the captain added a bit of doggerel:

> Some people shines at the table some in the field,
> some fills their purse & some the Baton wield —
> But happy the man who Sleeps at ease, nor stung
> by conscience, nor yet bit by fleas.

On 21 March Peebles again dined with the colonel and some ladies and lamented, ". . . not much fun there."[5]

In early April Peebles had company for dinner. Sir James Baird and Lieutenant Campbell joined the fun-loving diners; however, the captain was puzzled because "we can't find out who's guest they are." Occasionally, a tragic note was struck. After one meal, one of the guests was forced to sell his commission for 1,600 guineas and return to England.[6]

Peebles particularly enjoyed his visits to other messes and, more rarely, the evenings spent with congenial companions in a tavern. On 5 January he joined the officers of the 3rd Battalion of grenadiers at the Indian King to commemorate the anniversary of the corps. The fifteen men present had an "elegant dinner & good claret."[7]

A strange entry in Peebles' journal for 7 May indicates that all dinners did not end on a cordial note: "Remember you had some words to day at the table which obliged you to take a Step you did not like." Whether these harsh remarks led to a duel or whether the captain was able to satisfy his antagonist cannot be ascertained; nevertheless, the next day he recorded, "Went out & settled that affair better than I expected." As Peebles had remarked earlier, many differences occurred over trifling matters.[8]

Toward the end of the occupation period, as board became scanty, the colonel proposed that the battalion mess with the sutlers. The officers agreed to give six shillings sterling and their current rations, reserving "half ye Bread & all ye Rum." During this time it cost two dollars a gallon for good spirits and two shillings six pence for a bottle of port.[9]

While all taverns were patronized by British and Hessian officers, City Tavern was the center of the social whirl and the principal gambling casino of the festive season. In early January a group of officers, chiefly colonels and majors, were named managers of the rooms open at the tavern. After several meetings of the managers, "The City Tavern was . . . fitted up & open'd to receive comp^y in the style of Public Rooms, every Even^g (except Sunday & a Ball every Thursday)." The expense of operating the rooms was to be defrayed by a charge of two days' pay from each subscribing officer and an admission fee of half a guinea for ball tickets. Coote recorded that the daily rates for junior officers were: captains, 10s.; lieutenants, 4s. 8d.; ensigns, 3s. 8d.; surgeons, 4s.; and surgeons mates, 3s. 6d. He added that dollars were exchangeable at the rate of 4s. 6d.[10]

The first assembly room was opened at 6:00 P.M. on Friday, 23 January. To prevent any disorders, an officer's guard from the grenadiers was mounted at the rooms every evening but Sunday. Hale said tea, coffee, lemonade, and Orgeat were the only liquids allowed except on ball nights, when Negus was served. Coffee and tea cost a half dollar, instead of the quarter dollar as subscribers had been told.

About the same time a "Pharao [faro] Bank" was opened by a Hessian officer, Captain Wreeden of the jägers. Ewald asserted that

City Tavern was the largest of the gambling clubs; its bank always consisted of 1,000 guineas. Observers noted an "extravagant rage for play" and believed that high-ranking officers encouraged younger officers to gamble for high stakes, sums they could not afford to lose. Ewald said, "More than once I have seen 50,000 dollars change hands—where some made their fortune but many their ruin." Peebles visited the rooms and "saw much gambling going on as usual, a great deal of money lost & won this winter." Peebles, a small time gambler, admitted playing dollar whist at the room and winning eight dollars. Colonel von Wurmb reported, "We have parties and gamble, whereby every night 700 and 800 pounds are lost and won." Apparently as a gesture, the bank permitted the players to win all the money on the table on the final night of play, 30 April. Peebles said the bank's net winnings for the season were £7,000.[11]

City Tavern, on Second near Walnut Street. The tavern was reopened in 1976. *Independence National Historical Park Collection*

The harmful effect of gambling on the British army was evidenced by the ruin of many officers. Deeply in debt as a result of their losses, they were forced to sell their commissions, usually to less qualified individuals. Ewald said, ''Some even shot themselves out of desperation.'' Charles Stedman, a native Philadelphian and British officer with a deep-rooted prejudice against Howe, deplored the loss of numerous honorable officers who might have rendered great service to Great Britain.[12]

On Thursday nights games were suspended, as a ball was held in the tavern. Elaborate preparations were made to hold the first ball on 29 January. Three officers were to act as managers at each ball. After a consultation, it was decided to increase the number of tickets to 300 and retain the admission charge of half a guinea. All tickets were to be delivered to the army and navy on the Tuesday or Wednesday before each ball, with the unsubscribed tickets to be placed on sale on Wednesdays at the tavern. No tickets would be sold on the day of the ball, and money would not be accepted at the door. Colonel Howard, Lieutenant Colonel Abercrombie, and Major Gardiner managed the first ball. In all, thirteen balls were held. The final one, on 30 April, witnessed the closing of all the rooms. An advertisement in the *Pennsylvania Ledger* on 9 May indicates that the tavern discontinued all operations: ''The City Tavern to be let and entered upon the 1st of May — For terms enquire James Allen, Walnut above 3rd.''[13]

General officers gave private balls, dances, and concerts at their quarters. At least two great balls took place at Howe's headquarters.

The most graphic portrayal of the dizzy pace set by the belles of Philadelphia society was put forth in Rebecca Frank's oft quoted letter to Anne Paca, the wife of a Maryland delegate to the Continental Congress. Imploring Mrs. Paca to visit her for a week or two, she described her daily whirl of merrymaking:

You can have no idea of the life of continued amusement I live in. I can scarce have a moment to myself . . . I am but just come from under Mr. J. Black's hands and most elegantly am I dressed for a ball this evening at Smith's where we have one every Thursday. You would not Know the room tis so much improv'd.

. . . I spent Tuesday evening at Sir W[m] Howes where we had a concert and Dance.

. . . The Dress is more ridiculous and pretty than anything that ever I saw — great quantity of different coloured feathers on the head at a time besides a thousand other things. The Hair dress's very high . . .

No loss for partners, even I am engaged to seven different gentlemen for
you must know 'tis a fix'd rule never to dance two dances at a time with the
same person. . . . I know you are as fond of a gay life as myself — you'd have
an opportunity of rakeing as much as you choose either at Plays, Balls, Concerts or Assemblys. I've been but 3 evenings alone since we mov'd to town. I
begin now to be almost tired. . . .
     . . . I must go finish dressing as I'm engaged out to Tea.[14]

Rebecca Franks, a self-willed and ardent Loyalist, was noted for
her repartee. An item attributed to her appearing in the *Pennsylvania
Ledger* on 24 December 1977 revealed her trenchant wit: "Before this
city was in the possession of the British troops, a rebel officer asked a
sensible and witty young lady, if their arms had not been crowned
with great success, since the commencement of the War? To which
she replied that she knew nothing as to their arms, but their legs had
surprisingly — in running away." Miss Franks later married Colonel
Sir Henry Johnson and moved to England, but always retained a
nostalgic affection for her native city.[15]

Officer's dining clubs met once a month. The most popular dining rooms were at the Bunch of Grapes and Indian King taverns.
Dinner was served at 4:00 P.M., which permitted members to spend a
companionable evening at cards or conversation or the freedom to attend the theatre or gambling tables at the City Tavern.

The Friendly Brothers and the Yorkshire Club regularly pub-
lished notices of their meetings. At each dinner one officer was
chosen to preside over and moderate the proceedings. John
Montresor, our engineer friend, and H. F. Brown officiated at some
Friendly Brothers dinners, while the only name on record for the
Yorkshire Club is a Major Strawbridge. The Friendly Brothers al-
ways footnoted their announcements with their motto, *Quis Separabit.*
A Loyal Association Club met at Clark's Tavern, opposite the State
House on Chestnut Street. Other nonmilitary groups, such as a
Society of Journeymen Tailors and the Amicable Fire Company,
plus cultural organizations such as the Library Company, held stated
meetings.[16]

Like Peebles and Coote, a significant number of officers enjoyed
congenial evenings at their quarters, the regimental mess, or a local
tavern. Many officers preferred the individual companionship offered
in the taverns to a club. In a few instances, new or vacant taverns
were opened at the behest of "merchants and gentlemen of the navy"
and army. In mid-April Peter Lenox reopened the popular Indian

King and renamed it the British Tavern. He planned to provide dinner every afternoon at 2:30 P.M., and for those unable to attend at that hour, a cold collation would be available at noon. Fox and LeMayne, occupying the former quarters of Austin's New Ferry at the lower end of Arch Street, converted it into a dining room. They planned to serve a "genteel dinner" at 2:00 P.M. in a commodious room which had a beautiful view of the river and the "Jersies." Entertainment was available for private parties, and boats were for hire if good security was given.[17]

Typical of the times, liquor flowed freely and the officers enjoyed discussing the political situation in America, the strategy of Howe, and the inability of Europe's leading military power to defeat the tatterdemalion rebels. Others dwelt on the nostalgic past in their homeland. Many sought diversion in card games. While there was much gambling, the losses were more moderate in these private games. The extent of card playing as an amusement is obvious in the numerous advertisements offering decks of cards such as Merry Andrew, Henry the VIII, the King's Patent, and Falstaff as "so much esteemed and used in polite companies." They were offered for sale by the gross and dozen.[18]

Unlike Rebecca Franks and John Andre, some officers enjoyed quiet visits with the townspeople, conversation, cards, and punch. Peebles mentions that he attended church with the ladies. On one occasion he found it crowded with Hessians; on another the parson had a bad voice. Several calls were made on friends; once he "got a great dish of chat, how some women talk." His fondness for the ladies is obvious, as at another time he had an agreeable party for two hours with Mrs. Morgan, Mrs. and Miss Inglis, Mrs. McCall, and Miss Swift. A pleasant evening visiting friends often included "much cards and punch." A few days before the evacuation, he soliloquized, "I had a walk with little ———— in the Even^g again who is always so agreeable that I wish I may not be too particular there."[19]

Peebles had a strong penchant for footnoting his activities and observations with little ditties. When John Allen, a prominent Philadelphian, died, he noted the sad event in his journal on 3 February, 1778 and then added:

> Let death attack us in the bed or field
> All Ranks & ages to his force must yield
> Happy the Man Who meets the foe unafraid
> For death or his Enemy never unprepar'd

To relieve the boredom of garrison life, some of the more sporting officers engaged in cockfighting, cricket, and horse racing. Privates, on at least one occasion, took part in a footrace. Still, little is known about these activities. The first cockfight apparently was staged on 28 March at a cockpit in Moore's Alley off Front Street, near Carr's store. Thomas Wildman, of the 17th Dragoons, took care of the cocks. Owners were advised that their cocks could fight in mains or battles; the former fought for 100 guineas. There is little question that considerable sums were wagered on the side. Repeated appeals were made for any person acquainted with the making of cricket bats and balls. Lieutenant von Kraft's journal makes a mystifying reference to a bowling alley in the northern section of the city.

Horse races were held near Centre House or the central commons. Peebles commented on walking the ladies to see a horse race at the commons. Jacob Coats recalled that as a small boy he saw a footrace between the champions of the First and Second battalions of light infantry. Fully accoutred, the men raced on a course set near the Schuylkill. It started near the northern defense lines and finished in the Neck, a distance of about three miles. The First Battalion runner won "by a very short distance." Other regiments selected their favorite, and it is likely that the men wagered heavily on the outcome.[20]

Public holidays were not forgotten, although little mention of Christmas can be found. As the army was then on a major foraging expedition and the garrison was busy preparing winter quarters, 25 December was probably honored as Peebles noted: "Xmas not intirely forgot." Other holidays were celebrated by parades and special festivities. Saint Patrick's Day was observed as "the Hybernians mounted the Shamrogue [shamrock] & an Irish Grenad[r] Personated St. Patrick in a Procession thro' the Streets with a prodigious mob after them — the friendly Br[s] & several other Irish Clubs dine together & dedicate the day to the St. & the Bottle." To honor the day, deserters coming in from Valley Forge were seen wearing shamrocks in their hats.[21]

On 23 April grenadiers celebrated Saint George's Day by making a procession through the city with a replica of the saint. When they arrived in front of Howe's headquarters, he ordered rum distributed to the marchers. A story circulating in the Hessian quarters was that the Americans also celebrated Saint George's Day. On a large board they reportedly painted a picture of George III, with sword in hand, kneeling before the standing figure of Washington. The king was humbly presenting his latest proposal, to which Washington replied, "My dear King, if you wish to beg for something, bend your knee, then let me speak." Ewald was aghast that the American general would tolerate such a disgraceful exhibit, as he was highly respected by Hessian officers. Late on 4 June, a royal salute was fired in honor of the king's birthday. Peebles was disappointed that fireworks were not allowed that night. He attributed it to the gloom pervading the camp because of the impending evacuation: "These things out of fashion in this Country now."[22]

Probably the most unique procession was one described by a Hessian soldier:

There were walking tours in society to nearby places as Germantown and Frankford where one attended to his entertainment with shooting and bringing in hay. But this bringing in the hay is not to be understood as it happens by us [in Germany] in the month of July out in the fields and meadows. Rather, it is concerned only with such hay and forrage as the officers bought in the neighboring places and bothered to transport themselves for the fun of it, since in America during the winter grass grows as little as it does in Germany. But it was funny to see the soldiers (who were sent out for this purchase) when they pulled into the city practically in caravan fashion; often 200-300 wagons drove so closely packed behind one another that not even one man could pass in between. The main load consisted of hay, straw and grain; the other loads of chicks, geese, chickens, pigs and the like. And it was often funny to see the Negroes (who were by the wagons) with solemn intentions leading the horses to the hay wagons — with the bridle in the right hand, but carrying under the left arm one or two young pigs which were grumbling about the hard times and their fate and loudly crying.[23]

Officers and their ladies enjoyed sleigh rides, and when the ground was clear of snow, horseback riding was a popular pastime. Another minor diversion was band concerts performed by the regimental bands at churches and upon the different commons.

Many officers occupied their time with cultural attainments. They frequented bookstores, attended occasional book auctions at Robert Bell's bookshop on Third Street, or subscribed to lecture series. A course of lectures in natural and experimental philosophy given at the college was so oversubscribed that at its conclusion a second series was offered. The course consisted of twenty-five lectures, daily except Sunday, at one dollar per lecture. Classes were also offered on electricity, and guided tours could be taken to David Rittenhouse's orrery. Officers and civilians attended classes in foreign languages. Teachers proposed to instruct anyone interested in various musical instruments.[24]

There was more to life during the winter than balls, assemblies, and supper clubs. Under the most adverse conditions, inhabitants were endeavoring to adjust to life in a garrison city. Despite the presence of the British army, property was sold and rented; personal articles of all descriptions were lost and found; slaves were sold and the services of indentured servants were transferred. Clerks, wet nurses, apprentices, and tradesmen sought positions. Poignant advertisements covered the loss of pets — from Captain Moyle's fat little brown and white spaniel with a scar over one eye and the front teeth on his upper jaw gone to a tame mocking bird that fled from its cage and could be easily taken.[25]

With the advent of spring, all activities gradually ended and a more sober note was heard. The military as well as the citizenry were apprehensive over the rumors of change in command and how those changes might affect the future status of the army in Philadelphia.

CHAPTER XIII

CHANGE OF COMMAND

*T*HE RELATIONSHIP BETWEEN Howe and Germain worsened as the winter progressed. The decorously polite exchange of letters with their thinly veiled acrimony had not escaped the king's notice. On 10 January, George III wrote the prime minister, Lord North, that to retain the Howes in command would be difficult, inasmuch as Germain's letters had been "so cold and dry in respect to Sir W. H.'s successes in Pennsylvania." Three days later he observed that it would be awkward "to get Sir W. Howe to remain, and not less so to get Ld. G. Germaine to act in such a manner towards him as will make the efforts of others not prove abortive on that head."[1]

Germain endeared himself only to a few close political associates and sycophants while he engaged in political infighting with Parliament and the Ministry. The king reluctantly recognized that unless he removed the secretary, a recommendation he vowed he would never make, he would have to accept Howe's request to return to England. Germain was advised of the king's acquiescence on 4 February and with obvious satisfaction notified Clinton to succeed Howe as commander in chief in North America.

Perplexed and beset by uncertainties, the king carried on a daily correspondence with North in an obvious effort to convince him to remain in office. The alternative to North was to accept the despised Lord Chatham (Pitt) as the only statesman capable of unifying the country in the face of a possible war with France. A short time later the king considered Germain's recalcitrance a blessing in disguise and wrote North, "I think Ld. G. Germain's defection a most favourable Event. He has so many enemies. . . ."[2]

As early as January, rumors and intelligence received from

George III. Painting by Benjamin West. *Historical Society of Pennsylvania*

France indicated that a treaty with the Americans would soon be negotiated. Shortly thereafter, the French ambassador in London openly boasted that a treaty of amity and commerce had been signed "with the rebel agents in Paris." Apprehensive that this would soon be followed by a declaration of war, the king suggested a possible withdrawal of "troops from the revolted provinces." He held several councils with his ministers and on 21 March ordered Germain to send Clinton secret instructions on the future conduct of the war. Germain opened his communique with a denunciation of the French king, noting "that contrary to most solemn assurance, and in subversion of the Law of Nations, hath signed a Treaty . . . with our revolted subjects in North America."

The instructions stated that it was the king's wish that a competent officer be given command of 5,000 men to invade Saint Lucia in the West Indies. A second detachment of 3,000 was to move against Saint Augustine, Florida. Both expeditions were to have proportionate auxiliary forces of artillery and other ordnance. After the departure of these units, it was the king's pleasure that Clinton evacuate Philadelphia, return to New York, and await the outcome of the peace commissioners' efforts. Should they be unsuccessful, Clinton was to abandon New York and possibly Rhode Island, if that post was not defensible, and proceed to Halifax. The instructions detailed garrison requirements, defenses for Canada, and possible reinforcements from England. All were predicated on the assumption that war with France was inevitable.[3]

Unfortunately for the king, the course of events forced his plan to be aborted. War was declared, and with the appearance of a French fleet in American waters, any large scale withdrawal by sea became too hazardous. Later rumors warned of a French army detachment being sent to America.

In addition to the Howe brothers, the Peace Commission was to include William Eden, George Johnstone, and Frederick Howard, Earl of Carlisle, as chief spokesman. They were empowered to make certain concessions to the Americans, short of independence. If Howe had already departed for England, Clinton was to replace him on the commission. However, the king privately contended that "neither the Generals nor Admiral . . . need be in the commission, but Peers and Commoners from hence." Frustrated by dissension in his ministry, opposition in Parliament, war with France, and the almost hopeless task of the commission to placate the Americans, the

king plaintively advised North, ''I am still ready to accept any part of
them [Parliament] that will come to the assistance of my present
efficient Ministers; but whilst any ten men in the Kingdom will stand
by me, I will not give myself up into bondage.''[4]

April dawned on a garrison plagued with rumors and busy with
increase in military activity. Morale declined as reports circulated of
Howe's possible recall to England. Frustrated and disappointed, the
officers were further depressed by the story that the army would soon
abandon the city. The loss of hundreds of men and many beloved
fellow officers seemed a wasted gesture if, after their sacrifice,
Philadelphia was to be turned over to the rebels without a fight. Yet,
as Howe increased his sorties and excursions into the surrounding
countryside, hopes grew that at last a major attack would be made on
Washington's army.

Stepped-up military operations, from small scouting parties to
battalion-strength reconnaissances, were conspicuous around the
city's perimeter. The jäger corps was assigned the land to the west,
across the Schuylkill. Patrols, and sometimes the entire corps,
combed the area seeking American positions. Daniel Morgan's
riflemen became their principal adversaries, and, according to Ewald,
a cat-and-mouse game developed. The jäger captain tacitly respected
the ability of the backwoods American. It became impossible to trap
or force either antagonist into action unless an advantage was obvious. Each came to recognize the movements and tactics of the other.
Ewald finally devised a plan to use his patrols or reconnaissances in
echelon: ''One thus covers his rear, and if you withdraw before a
superior enemy, you always become stronger while the enemy
becomes confused. This is the safest way of all, particularly in cut-up
areas: one cannot be defeated.'' But the tactic was to no avail, as the
wily Morgan refused to be baited.

The area north of the city posed a greater threat to the security of
Philadelphia. Howe was concerned about the vulnerability of the
defense line. Throughout the winter he had admonished the officers
and men on duty at the redoubts for their carelessness and inattention.

Quick striking forces constantly moved along Germantown and
Ridge roads to intercept bands of American militia. These troops
were usually light dragoons and light infantry (sometimes the latter
were mounted) and an occasional troop of Provincial dragoons. They
were chiefly engaged with raw American militia recruits, many

unarmed, who in most instances offered little resistance. British accounts rarely mentioned a setback for their detachments, but described the complete rout of the Americans. The Americans reportedly suffered heavy casualties, while British losses were insignificant. Similarly, the Frankford Road as far as Bristol was the scene of skirmishes between Provincial dragoons and American militia. In addition to these lightning-like thrusts into the country, regular infantry contingents furnished daily escort for woodcutting expeditions.[5]

Excursions of British and Provincial troops of battalion, or greater, strength combed the region of New Jersey comprising modern Camden and Gloucester counties. Passing over the Delaware River at Cooper's Ferry or Gloucester Point, they were to rid the area of American militia. At the same time, parties of Loyalist and American partisans were engaged in a bitter internecine conflict. Loyalists used their station at Billingsport as a base for marauding expeditions north to Haddonfield and Timber Creek and south to Swedesboro. Americans retaliated by stripping Loyalist farmers of their livestock and produce and by cutting off small parties of their partisans.[6]

The woods close to the city had been stripped of most stands of timber. Accordingly, the British command concentrated on the heavily forested area on the east bank of the Delaware, where a permanent post would be necessary to protect the woodcutters. Brigadier General Sir William Erskine and Montresor were instructed to survey the area in the vicinity of Cooper's Ferry as a possible site. On 28 April, they accompanied the 1st Battalion of light infantry and a woodcutting party for this purpose. Five days later the 55th and 63rd regiments, with a troop of twelve light horse, were ferried over to the confluence of the Cooper and Delaware rivers to begin work on the proposed fortifications. The galley *Cornwallis* covered the party from the water side. By 6 May the works were completed, and on the following day Allen's and Clifton's Provincial corps were added to the garrison at Cooper River.[7]

All winter Brigadier General John Lacey and his militia had been a thorn in the side of the British patrols. The militia was small in numbers, rarely exceeding 500, and many were without firearms. Still, they were expected to patrol all roads north of the city and those between the Delaware and Schuylkill rivers. On 30 April, intelligence reached the city that Lacey would be encamped at Crooked Billet Tavern (Hatboro) that night. The Loyalist sympathizer who provided this information also described the countryside, roads, and woods so that a perfect ambuscade could be planned.

Howe's aide, Lieutenant Colonel Nisbet Balfour, summoned Simcoe and advised him of the plan. As Simcoe knew the area, he was ordered to assemble his corps and join the attack. Lieutenant Colonel Abercrombie was given command of the column, which included fourteen companies of light infantry, two troops (120 men) of the 16th and 17th dragoons under Major Crewe, Simcoe's Queen's Rangers (430 strong), Captain Hovenden's Philadelphia light dragoons, and Captain James's Chester County dragoons. They were to muster between the first and second redoubts and march north on Second Street.

Maintaining the utmost secrecy, Abercrombie advanced under the cover of darkness and proceeded to Huntingdon Valley, where the command divided. Abercrombie, with the main force, moved west to Old York Road to take Lacey's camp in the front. Simcoe was to march north a short distance, cross above the American camp, and attack Lacey on the rear and flank.

As in most attacks involving separate detachments, the British units did not arrive in their assigned positions at the expected hour. Even with the guides,[8] it was difficult to move quickly over the night-shrouded roads. Upon nearing his objective, Abercrombie detached Crewe, with his dragoons, to reconnoiter the area near Crooked Billet and locate the American patrols and outposts.

Lacey said his camp was surprised in the early morning hours. He charged that his scouts neglected their rounds during the night, thus allowing the British to approach undetected. One of Lacey's lieutenants alibied that the British dragoons were so close that he anticipated being cut to pieces if he fired at them. Instead, he dispatched a scout to warn Lacey, but the courier ran away. The advance party he encountered was probably Crewe's dragoons. British accounts agree that their impetuous major attacked prematurely.

The surprise was complete, and the American troops were soon driven from their camp while Lacey slept in a nearby farmhouse. Some segments of the battalion made a brief stand, but with the approach of the main British force, all resistance soon ended.

Of all engagements fought during the winter, the Battle of Crooked Billet witnessed the most shocking blot on the honor of the British army, even surpassing the brutality exhibited at Hancock's Bridge. Lacey's report to the Pennsylvania Executive Council described the atrocities committed: "Some were Butchard in a manner the most Brutal Savages Couldnot equal, even while Living Some were thrown into Buckwheat Straw and the Straw set on fire, the Close [clothes] were Burnt on others, and scarcely one without a Dozen Wounds with Byonets or Cutlasses."

Residents of the area who visited the battlefield were appalled at the sight which greeted them. Their depositions concurred with Lacey's report, with the exception of a statement by one deponent who was advised by British soldiers that gunpowder from American muskets had started the fire. British and Hessian accounts are strangely silent about this savagery; Baurmeister alone recorded that "several grenadiers [light infantry] were so embittered they burned nine rebels." If the Hessian major was right in stating that embittered light infantrymen perpetrated this horrendous act, then it was probably done in retaliation for the brutality of Wayne's men at Germantown. Just as British savagery at Paoli begot reprisals at Germantown, Wayne's butchery at Germantown in turn begot retribution at Crooket Billet.

Reports of American casualties varied between eighty and one hundred killed and wounded, with fifty or sixty taken prisoner. Ten to fourteen wagons loaded with baggage, flour, salt, and whiskey were captured, and three were burned. British losses were about six men wounded.[9]

After the river defenses had fallen, American ships were moved up the Delaware and anchored in the mouth of creeks between Burlington and Trenton. Washington was convinced that the State galleys could offer little opposition to any British naval force that might move upstream. He therefore recommended that the Pennsylvania fleet be scuttled to prevent its falling into British hands. When intelligence reached Howe that the galleys were out of commission, he realized the Americans would be unable to deter an expedition launched against the rebel shipping. Howe anticipated no problems in seizing the two unfinished American frigates, *Washington* and *Effingham.*

Howe ordered a joint army and navy expedition to move to the Bordentown area and destroy all ships and boats they would locate. Major John Maitland, with the 2nd Battalion of light infantry and two field pieces, embarked on eighteen flatboats. They were escorted by Captain John Henry with a flotilla of four galleys, two armed schooners, and four gunboats, hardly a match for the Pennsylvania galleys if they had been afloat. The combined expedition left Philadelphia early in the evening of 7 May and moved upstream to Rancocas Creek. Their movement was hampered by heavy winds and rain which forced a layover until the next morning. At about 5:00 A.M., a change in the weather permitted them to resume their voyage up river to Whitehill, about two miles below Bordentown.

The *Washington* and the *Effingham* were anchored at Whitehill. Against the wishes of Washington, instead of being scuttled they had been converted into quarters for idle Continental seamen. Apparently the seamen had abandoned the frigates as the British met no opposition. Maitland burned both frigates plus other small craft at the anchorage.

Maitland then sent his light infantry in motion along the east bank of the Delaware. A short distance below Bordentown, they dispersed a detachment of New Jersey militia. Upon arriving at the town, they proceeded to burn warehouses and, regrettably, the private residences of well-known Americans. Although British officers deplored the wanton destruction of private property, this does not excuse them for the undisciplined conduct of their men.

On 9 May, the combined force moved up and down the river, destroying everything afloat and an occasional residence. Their attempt to destroy the magazines and stores at Trenton was thwarted by General Philemon Dickinson of the New Jersey militia and a two-gun battery. Maitland and Henry feared that Washington might send a superior force, including artillery, to cut off their retreat. Thus, with their mission only partially successful, they withdrew and arrived back in the city by early morning of the tenth.[10]

On 18 May, Howe received intelligence that a sizeable detachment of American troops, commanded by Lafayette, was in the vicinity of Barren Hill, about eleven or twelve miles north of Philadelphia. Preoccupied with the plans for his farewell extravaganza, the Meschianza, Howe took no action until the nineteenth. Grant was finally ordered to march out that night and attempt to get in the rear of the American contingent. Howe assumed personal command of this attack, as it was his final bid for victory. Simcoe asserted that throughout the army a hope prevailed that Howe would attack Valley Forge before leaving for England. Baurmeister called it "Howe's last and likewise unsuccessful expedition." Parker said that "It seems Gen¹ Howe claims the command until his departure." The statements of other officers also indicated that Howe was in command of the expedition. However, because Howe had officially turned command over to Clinton on 11 May, some American versions assumed Sir Henry was in charge.

A 20 May return of British and Hessian rank and file in Philadelphia showed 14,420 men fit for duty, in addition to 1,343 Provincials. Grant's column consisted of approximately 6,000 rank and file.[11]

Howe was to command the main detachment of about the same size.[12] Howe placed General Leslie in charge of the city's defenses and left the British 3rd Brigade, the 26th Regiment, and Wolwarth's Hessian battalion, about 2,300 rank and file, with him. Interestingly, Baurmeister contended that only Wolwarth's battalion was in the lines.

These assignments leave two questions unanswered. What happened to the detachment supposedly sent out under Grey? And what about the use of over 1,000 Loyalist troops, excluding the Queen's Rangers with Grant? Stedman appears to be the only contemporary authority who mentioned that Grey moved out during the night with a strong detachment. He crossed the Schuylkill, marched up the west bank, and took post at a ford two or three miles below Lafayette's position at Barren Hill. American scholars have accepted Stedman's statement, but they place Grey on Ridge Road. Some state that his force was composed of grenadiers; but these troops were all with Grant. Ewald disputes Grey's presence on Ridge Road, claiming that at 10:00 A.M., he was ordered to the Falls of the Schuylkill with 150 dismounted jägers and twenty horse to demonstrate along the Ridge Road and push back all American patrols. Ewald had the only British detachment operating along Ridge Road. It is more likely Grey accompanied Howe and had command of the column's vanguard.

No mention is made of the 1,000 Provincials remaining in the garrison.[13] Howe's favorite Loyalist corps, the Queen's Rangers, were with Grant. He probably continued to consider the other Provincial units auxiliary troops to be used only on scouts or patrols. In addition, Howe was uncertain of the loyalty of some Provincial corps, as many were deserters from the American army. With Simcoe's rangers gone, the corps was probably assigned to patrol the roads leading to Frankford and the northeast to guard against a surprise attack from that direction.

A certain mystery surrounds the employment of virtually the entire British army to trap a small American detachment of 2,200 men.

American historians contend the prize was Lafayette and that elaborate plans had been made for a gala celebration in the city to honor his capture. Lord Howe, Clinton, Knyphausen, and almost every general except Leslie attended Sir William in his hour of expected triumph. Tradition claims Clinton had issued invitations to leading citizens to be his guests at a reception for the marquis. Another possibility for the action was Howe's desire to vindicate his lackadaisical performance during the winter. Rumors in Philadelphia claimed that Washington's army was weak and that he was impatiently waiting for spring to bring in reinforcements. Howe may have believed that a general engagement, if fought under favorable conditions, could silence his critics.

At 9:00 P.M. of the nineteenth, Grant marched out of the lines and up Old York Road. At the junction with the road to Whitemarsh (probably Church Road), he filed to the left. He knew this road well, as it was here that he had maintained a leisurely pursuit of Greene after the Battle of Germantown. At the intersection of Bethlehem Road and Skippack Pike, he moved northwest to Broad Axe,[14] turning left over modern Butler Pike to the vicinity of that road and Ridge Road (near modern Conshohocken). This would place him in the rear of Lafayette's position. Unfortunately for the British, Howe had entrusted this column to the most inept general in his command, a man who was overly cautious and usually wasted valuable time in indecision.

On the march Grant ordered Simcoe's advance to maintain the slow pace of two miles per hour. It was a tiresome march for the rangers, but the pace especially fatigued the heavily accoutred regulars. Instead of keeping well in advance of the main column, Simcoe was forced to halt frequently to permit his tired regulars to close up the column. His inability to throw out scouting patrols in advance of Grant permitted American scouts to approach the British force undetected. Sullivan, who was with the column, mentioned that shots were exchanged between British dragoons and American horsemen, with a few casualties on both sides. In contrast, Simcoe claimed the Americans took to their heels whenever he tried to close with them. But the damage was done, as patrols had sighted the British and alerted Lafayette of the force in his rear.

Howe's column left the city about 5:30 A.M. on the twentieth and marched directly to Germantown. His presence in the village completed the blockade of every avenue of escape for Lafayette except over Matson's Ford (Conshohocken). As Grant's position on Ridge Road was closer to the ford than Lafayette's, this avenue could be blocked. Lethargic as usual, Grant neglected to send a strong detachment to the ford to prevent passage by the young Frenchman. Instead, he marched his command south on Ridge Road toward Barren Hill. Upon arriving there, he found his quarry had sprung the trap. Lafayette, having been forewarned, had filed to the right and, under cover of the thick woods, made his way to the unguarded ford and crossed to the west bank of the Schuylkill.

When Howe had advanced about one and a half miles beyond Germantown, he was met by Grant's courier, General Erskine, who apprised him of Lafayette's escape. Thereupon the commander in chief ordered all detachments to return to Philadelphia. His column reached the lines about two o'clock and toward evening was joined by Grant. All were chagrined, and Grant's troops, after a march of nearly forty miles in hot weather, were exhausted.

One incident in the affair at Barren Hill supposedly involved a confrontation between British dragoons and a detachment of Oneida Indians which was with Lafayette. The popular version depicts both parties fleeing in terror. The Indians were startled by the brilliant red coats of the dragoons, and the British were horrified by the war whoops of the Indians. Where this burlesque took place is unknown, although most, if not all, of the dragoons were a part of Grant's column. Most surprising, however, was the contention that there were any Iroquoian Indians who had not previously seen British soldiers.

The casualties on each side have been exaggerated. Some British accounts state that over one hundred Americans drowned in crossing the river. Washington advised Congress that American losses were nine killed. British losses were insignificant. According to Hale, a number died of heat exhaustion on the march back to the city.[15]

In the meantine, many inhabitants, in dire need of fuel, were detected going out of the lines and bringing back wood that had been cut for the army. At first a strict prohibition with severe penalties was threatened. After a number of residents importuned the barrack master to lift his restrictions, he relented and said the inhabitants could have timber measuring up to eight feet; all other lengths were for His Majesty's troops.[16]

Charles Blagden, an army physician, related an incident which demonstrated to what extent each army would go to cut off food supplies destined for its enemy. With the advent of spring, soldiers were instructed to block the efforts of fish, mostly shad, to get up the Schuylkill to Washington's camp at Valley Forge. No record exists to describe the method used to prevent the shad from swimming upstream, but Blagden intimates the efforts succeeded.[17]

Always concerned for the welfare of the less fortunate, Howe proposed a lottery to aid the poor. Six thousand tickets were to be sold at $3 each, with L1,012 10s. to be allotted to the poor and the balance awarded to the holders of 2,185 prize tickets. In view of the impending evacuation of the city, it is interesting that prizes were to be drawn the first Monday in July.[18]

Tentative plans were underway to abandon the city in late May. However, when it was learned that the king's peace commissioners were sailing for Philadelphia, evacuation was postponed until they accomplished their mission. To confuse Washington, Howe decided to create the impression that the British intended to remain in the city. To create the illusion, the commander in chief was conspicuous in surveying his defense lines. On 22 April, he accompanied Montresor on an inspection of the defenses and proposed that he build several new fortifications. Two days later work was begun on two semicircular redoubts. One, on Ridge Road, about five hundred yards in front of the barrier, was to support a garrison of one hundred men. A smaller one, for fifty men, was laid out to the right, with a curtain connecting the two bastions. Later, on 10 May, by Howe's order Montresor laid out several additional breastworks ''picketted and Lock spitted, in order to make appearance only to the Enemy to answer certain purposes.'' Montresor also recommended blowing up Mud Island; but Howe feared this would alert Washington to the real British intentions. Such camouflage tricks were actually unnecessary, as rumors that the British were leaving the city had infiltrated both Valley Forge and the halls of Congress. Nevertheless, work on the lines continued unabated until the evacuation.[19]

As early as 16 April a frigate arrived from England with a draft of a conciliatory bill to be offered to the Americans. Two weeks later reports circulated that Congress would not entertain thoughts of reconciliation that did not recognize American independence.

As the weather improved, reviews of the various army corps were conducted at the central commons. The Royal artillery made a fine display on 28 April: ''. . . went thro the old fashion'd things in Battalion with 2 6 pdrs on each flank.'' On 7 April and 4 May, Knyphausen proudly paraded the entire Hessian corps for Howe's benefit. They made an impressive appearance, but the commander in chief met with an accident that, fortuitously, ended on a happy note: "In marching past the Gen^ls horse started at the Colours & his Ex: came down but was not hurt, & quickly mounted again."[20]

Clinton arrived in the city on 8 May. On the same day the sloop-of-war *Porcupine* brought word that France had openly espoused the American cause and an official declaration of war was imminent. Incredibly, before this date many British officers chose to ignore the possibility of a war with France. Washington had celebrated the alliance with France on 5 May at Valley Forge. Parker heard a *feu de joie*, followed by thirteen cannon fired three times from the direction of Valley Forge, but made no other comment.[21]

While Howe officially turned command of the garrison over to Clinton on 11 May, he actually relinquished little authority until his departure thirteen days later. A field day was held on the eleventh. At that time Howe's official, although somewhat tongue-in-cheek, orders were read to the army:

Genl Sir Wil^m Howe having obtain'd his Majesty's permission to return to Europe, the King has been pleas'd to appoint His Excellency Sir Henry Clinton to succeed him upon his Departure as General and Commander in Chief of the army in this district of America & all orders issued by Genl Sir Henry Clinton are to be obey'd — Genl Sir Wm Howe cannot think of taking leave of the Army without expressing in the strongest terms the very high sense he entertains & ever shall entertain of the distinguishing spirit alacrity & Unanimity exerted upon all occasions by every officer & soldier he has had the honor to Command as well Foreign as British in the course of a service attended with much fatigue & hardship — at the same time he feels a real satisfaction in being able to congratulate the army on his being succeeded in so important a Command by a Genl who he is fully persuaded, will not only add lustre to [His] Majestys Arms but acquire great honor to himself and to the army under his Command.[22]

The next day Clinton released to all governors and garrison commanders in North America a communique announcing his assumption of the command of the army. However, life in the tension-packed atmosphere of Philadelphia was decidedly uncomfortable for the querulous Clinton. The day before Howe sailed, Clinton wrote his cousin, the Duke of Newcastle:

I must confess at any rate I should have wished to avoid the arduous task of attempting to Petrieve a Game so Unfortunately Circumstanced I felt myself however called upon by my Country to Exert myself I cannot flatter myself that my efforts would have been successful but I hope they would have been becoming. A private letter, to a friend which came with my first instructions gave me hopes of being dealt with liberally, that I should not be tied down by instructions, with those I received from L.G.G. [Germain] I was satisfied, but those which I received by the porcupine [*Porcupine*] have altered my satisfaction exceedingly, My Command is now very unenviable indeed, I have a task to per form full of difficulty and perhaps danger without the least prospect of reputation to alleviate the weight. I do not however shrink besides it, but in hope of soon being relieved from a station which anyone may fill as serviceably as myself I shall while I remain in it cheerfully and zealously exert myself in every point that may benefit the State.[23]

Clinton deplored the lack of discretion granted him as commander in chief. He had always opposed Howe's move to Philadelphia, and now it appeared he was being ordered to rectify Sir William's mistake. Little credit was to be gained from a successful evacuation, and the dangers inherent in removing an army, thousands of civilians, and tons of materiel were great.

Clinton anticipated a withdrawal soon after Howe left for England. On 14 May, it was ordered that all heavy baggage should be ready to be placed on shipboard at a moment's notice. Clinton realized that sufficient shipping was not available to evacuate the entire army and all others who desired to leave. It would be necessary for the bulk of the army to go overland to New York. Howe accordingly recommended to all officers that they lighten their baggage for the field.[24]

Before his departure, Howe evinced concern for the safety of loyal citizens and officials who had faithfully administered the affairs of the city during the occupation. He knew most would be forced to leave the city with the army and perforce leave behind all their non-portable possessions, which would be confiscated by returning Americans. He submitted, among others, the "Establishment of the Police" to Germain for special consideration and protection. He especially suggested that their salaries be continued so that they could support their families wherever they moved in Great Britain or America.[25]

While the army remained his first concern, Howe was also interested in the welfare of Loyalist residents, who reciprocated by their concern for him. Daniel Coxe, in New York in December 1778, emphasized the affection Loyalists felt for the brothers Howe. In a letter to Galloway in London, he expressed sentiments that must have galled the exiled Philadelphian, requesting he give "my respectfull compliments to Sir William Howe & all the gentlemen of his Suite

Caricature called "John Bull Triumphant." Occasionally described as symbolic of Howe's taking Philadelphia in 1777. Published by W. Humphrey, 1780. *Historical Society of Philadelphia*

that we had the honor of knowing in Philadelphia. The civilities and attention of the noble Brothers to many of us at Philad'a. ought never to be forgot. The contrast of the present is too glaring not to regret the change for many reasons."[26]

As touched upon earlier, a number of officers had been unhappy with what they considered Howe's arbitrary handling of the army and his favoritism for a small circle of officers. Nevertheless, most officers, notably lieutenants and captains, respected and loved him, even though several disagreed with his strategy. Hale expressed the feelings of the majority in writing his parents, "Whether you can send a better Gen. than Sir William Howe, I know not, one more beloved will with difficulty be found."[27]

Thomas Stirling revealed an officer's frustration and bitterness with conditions in the army, but not with Howe. "No sense could bribe one to undergo two such years as I have done, the profitable part of it can be no object for in that light I shall be better when out, I can get 5000 Guineas if not more whenever I please my pay does not exceed £300 per an. there is no comparison, and by Lord Barringtons rule I shall be lucky if I have pretension to ask a Regt these 10 or 12 years, and during that time shot at, starved, cold, hot, wet and dry, it is a sad prospect." Two days later he added to his letter, "O but we have now received such heartbreaking news of the recall of Genl Howe & of the submissive terms you offer the Americans that unhinges everybody here."[28]

With a grand entertainment planned for his farewell, Howe did not sail until 24 May. As he boarded the *Andromeda* a salute was fired along the city waterfront.[29]

The coolness that existed between the two generals did not interfere with Clinton's purchasing some personal items and delicacies from Howe. An interesting receipt for these purchases was signed by T. Hill, steward:

A fine gelding		L73: 10: 0
12 lb Hartshorn shavings	@ 1/6	0: 18: 0
Box sittron [citron] 4 lbs	@ 1/6	0: 6: 0
12 lb Gordon Almonds	@ 1/6	0: 18: 0
6 garrs [jars] Pickels	@ 2/6	0: 15: 0
2 doz Wine glasis	@ /6	0: 12: 0
2 doz gelley Dº	@ /3	0: 6: 0
1 doz Sweetmeet glasis	@ /6	0: 6: 0
1 Parmagon [parmesan] cheese 38 lb	@ 1/8	3: 3: 4
6 Quarts Spanish ollivis	@ 2/	0: 12: 0
2 Doz Dayleas [doilies]	@ 1/	1: 4: 0
		L82: 10: 4

The denouement of Howe's colorful career in America thus involved a bit of trivia — a personal transaction with his archrival and military critic.[30]

CHAPTER XIV

MESCHIANZA

THE KING HAD granted Howe's request to return to England. No citation exists which indicates the precise date when the officers first entertained an idea for a gala farewell to their commander in chief. It was probably conceived over a convivial glass at the City Tavern or at one of the other hostelries popular with the military.

A cadre limited to twenty-one or twenty-two officers was formed.[1] Each officer agreed to subscribe L140 to defray the expenses of the proposed fete. The exact cost of the Meschianza cannot be determined. However, in addition to the reported contributions of the officers, Peebles said the banquet cost L900, and Baurmeister asserted that two English merchants, Coffin and Anderson, sold silks and other fine things valued at L12,000 to the managers. This mercantile house was located just north of Christ Church on Second Street.

After further deliberation the officers selected four of their number to manage the entertainment: Sir John Wrottesley, Sir Henry Calder, Colonel Charles O'Hara, and Captain John Montresor. Captain John Andre in his account substituted Major Gardiner for Sir Henry Calder. Unquestionably, Andre was a member of this band, but not the sole architect of the program. His devotion to Howe and his known artistic talents made him a logical participant in the fete's production.

As an extravaganza, the Meschianza had no peers in eighteenth-century America. It was finally concluded that the affair would encompass a series of events. First, a procession of decorated watercraft would move along the waterfront; then a joust or tournament of knights, followed by an elaborate banquet, dancing, and a colorful display of fireworks. This hodgepodge suggested a mixture, or medley, and thus was called the Mischianza or Meschianza.[2] Andre favored the former name, whereas most officers' correspondence and journals cited the latter.

Andre, the most articulate member of the cadre, is also credited with being the principal innovator of the event. Many circumstances placed Howe's colorful subordinate in the forefront of the day's happenings. His two versions of the fete vary in some detail, but have been accepted as the official description of the Meschianza. Andre's involvement with "Howe's strolling players" has intrigued historians for two centuries. So much of his participation in the activities of the winter has been prefaced with "attributed to" that it is at times difficult to distinguish between his actual performance and tradition. His vague romantic involvement with Peggy Shippen and his tragic death have added to the aura that surrounds his name. There is, however, no reason to question his devotion or contribution to the pageant. His major effort, ably abetted by young DeLancey, seems to have been in the design and production of settings, costumes, and banquet hall decorations. The majority of officers in the coterie were senior to Andre and, with their appointment as managers, assumed full responsibility for the Meschianza.

The last two weeks of April were frantic as the managers became engrossed in research and plans for the fete. Books and records were investigated to obtain costume designs and to learn the rules and conduct of knights at jousting tournaments. The city was scoured for boards and scantlings needed to build a huge banquet hall and contingent pavilions. Merchants and civilians were asked to provide materials for costumes, drapes, and bunting for the boats. Mirrors, chandeliers, and rugs to grace the banquet and dance halls were borrowed from householders. The late Joseph Wharton's mansion near the old battery, was chosen as the site for the pageant. A broad sloping lawn stretched several hundred yards from the house to the river. With all preliminary planning having been completed, construction began in late April. The date of the affair was set for Monday, 18 May.

A note by James Parker on 6 May records one of the first views of activity at the site: "Great works are erecting at the large house of Mr. Wharton near the south end of the Town for a fête champêtre. A space 180 feet by 30 is building with an arched roof covered with canvas & floored with plank." Six days later, Captain Peebles noted "Great preparations going on for an Entertainment to Sir Wm.

Peggy Shippen (Mrs. Benedict Arnold) and son. Painted by Daniel Gardner. *Historical Society of Philadelphia*

Howe by a select No. of Field officers." Again on the sixteenth, he "went to see the preparations for this Grand Entertainment which is call'd a *Meschianza*, which signifies a Meddly." The next day, accompanied by some ladies, he again visited the mansion, but was forced back by rain. Parker, on the same day, was aghast at the pomp and ostentation of the next day's spectacle and compared it with "pueril [sic] stories in the twopenny books."[3]

Although the main social event of the winter was the Meschianza, Howe's imminent departure inspired several private parties and balls. The commander in chief, always amenable to a gay evening, gave two or three balls at his headquarters, and other officers reciprocated. Hamond gave a lavish party in Howe's honor: "Previous to the fete called the Mesquienza I gave the General a Ball and supper on board the *Roebuck*, where 200 Ladies and Officers sat down to supper and danced until Day light in the morning — the ship was hauled to the Wharf for the occasion."[4]

The Meschianza was to include a sumptuous board for 400 officers and their ladies.

Each guest received an elaborate invitation emblazoned at the top with a large crest of the Howe family and the quotation, *Vive, Vale.*

Walnut Grove (Wharton Mansion), site of the Meschianza. *Free Library of Philadelphia*

Meschianza ticket and sketch of costume. *American Historical and Literary Curiosities,* Smith and Watson, *American Philosophical Society*

The center of the ticket featured a sun setting into the sea, and mounted within a streamer was the motto, *Luceo Discendens* (with the first n crossed out) *Aucto Splendore Resurgam.* A composite translation could read, ''He is shining as he sets, but he shall rise again in greater splendor — or more luminous.'' A laurel wreath, symbolic of Howe's supposed accomplishments, encircled this scene. In the background was a galaxy of military equipment, such as field cannon, shot, powder keg, flags, swords, ramrods, shields, drum and an espontoon, or halberd. The symbolism of the ticket has been the object of derision by detractors of the fete.

The back of the ticket was a personal invitation with the inscription, ''The Favor of Your meeting the Subscribers to the Meschianza at Knight's Wharf near Poole's Bridge to Morrow at half past Three, is desired.'' Each was dated Sunday, 17 May, and was signed by Henry Calder. The date, one day before the actual celebration, may appear unusual, but it must be assumed that all guests had received some form of personal invitation at an earlier date.[5]

Fortunately for the managers, after a rainy seventeenth, the day of the fete dawned fair. The weather remained moderately comfortable except for somewhat gusty winds. As noted on the invitations, all guests were to gather at Knight's Wharf [6] at three-thirty in the afternoon to board the boats. Along the wharf were three separate flotillas, or divisions, of ten barges or flatboats, headed by a galley as the flagship. The galleys were to carry the guest of honor and the general officers.

For the festive occasion, each boat and galley was gaily bedecked with bunting, streamers, and flags and became, as Andre phrased it, a ''Gaudy Fleet.'' Guests attended the departure with some impatience. The first division, led by the galley *Ferret* with several general officers and their ladies, pushed off at four o'clock. This division was followed by three barges with bands of music. The second flotilla, with Sir William Howe and Lord Howe in the galley *Hussar,* was soon in motion. It is believed that Sir Henry Clinton and Howe's paramour, Mrs. Loring, were present on the *Hussar.* [7] The last division, with Knyphausen on the *Cornwallis,* closed the rear of the water pageant. An account ''By one of the Company'' placed Knyphausen in the first division rather than the last.

For over a mile along the waterfront, wharves and houses were adorned with colorful bunting. Cannons were placed at intervals to salute the passing pageantry. Ships at the wharves were also decorated with maritime streamers and flags. People lined the waterfront and roofs of buildings and enthusiastically cheered the boats on.

The *Vigilant* was stationed off Knight's Wharf and served as starter to ensure that the divisions followed in an orderly arrangement. Near the Market Street wharf, the *Fanny,* an armed sloop, was stationed, and further downstream was Hamond's *Roebuck.* As Howe's galley neared the *Fanny,* which according to Andre was covered from the water's edge to her masthead with streamers and ensigns, the procession was halted. A thunderous din rose from the shore and the deck of the *Fanny* and was returned by sailors rowing the boats and galleys. The music boats closed up to the *Hussar* and played ''God save the King.'' It was so crowded on the water that six armed barges were employed to keep the swarm of small boats hovering on the flanks of the regatta from disrupting its progress.

In his first account Andre mentions that near Market Street the ''flood-tide'' became so rapid that it was necessary to abandon the galleys and transfer the guests to different barges before proceeding to the place of debarkation. As they passed the *Roebuck*, they received a salute of nineteen guns. At about six o'clock officers and their ladies landed near the old Association battery. The water pageant had taken more than two hours to cover about one mile.

On the lawn that sloped down to the water's edge were two arches. Nearest the river was a naval arch embellished with naval decorations. At the top was a figure of Neptune with a trident and a ship. Inside, captions on the columns described the characteristics of the god of the sea. On the entablature was the inscription *Laus illi debetur, et a me gratic major.* In a niche on each side of the arch, a sailor stood with his sword drawn. This arch was intended to be a tribute to Lord Howe.

About 150 yards beyond, a second arch was "decorated with military Emblems and Devices." The figure of Fame was on the pediment, and, on the inside, a plume of feathers and military trophies. The motto was *I bone quo te virtus tua de vocat I pede fausto.* Two grenadiers stood guard under this arch.[8]

Open ground between the river and the naval arch was selected for the tournament of knights. Andre called the event a "Carousel." On each side of the area a small pavilion in the shape of an amphitheatre[9] had been built for the knights' ladies. Seven young ladies were chosen by each company of knights for their "youth, beauty and fashion."

After the ladies had taken their seats, the other guests moved into position around the field to see the knights joust. Further back "spectators not to be numbered darked the whole plain around." Troops, probably the grenadiers, were stationed at various posts to keep the curious from mingling with the guests.

Andre described the ladies' dress as being fancy. "They wore gauze Turbans spangled and edged with gold or Silver, on the right Side a veil of the same kind hung as low as the waist and the left side of the Turban was enriched with pearl and tassels of gold or Silver & crested with a feather. The dress was of the polonaise Kind and of white Silk with long sleeves, the Sashes which were worn round the waist and were tied with a large bow on the left side hung very low and were trimmed spangled and fringed according to the Colours of the Knight." Pierre Eugene du Simitière painted a water color of Miss Smith in the dress she wore at the Meschianza. He portrayed her wearing a "high turban and veil ornamented with black feather jewells, gold lace & Spangles a white silk gown and mantua flowered

& Spangled and a Sash around the waist of white Silk also tied with gold strings and tassells."[10]

Andre included a vignette on the habiliments of the white knights:

Their dress was that worn in the time of Henry the 4th of France: The Vest was of white Sattin, the upper part of the Sleeves made very full but of pink confined within a row of straps of white sattin laced with Silver upon a black edging. The Trunk Hose were exceeding wide and of the same kind with the shoulder-part of the Sleeves. A large pink scarf fastened on the right shoulder with a white bow crossed the Breast and back and hung in an ample loose Knot with Silver fringes very low under the left hip, a pink and white Sword belt laced with black and Silver girded the waist, Pink bows with fringe were fastened to the Knees, and a wide buff leather boot hung carelessly round the ankles: The Hat of white sattin with a narrow brim and high crown, was turned up in front and enlivened by red white and black plumes, and the Hair tied with the Contrasted Colours of the dress hung in flowing curls upon the back. The Horses were caparisoned with the same Colours, with trimmings and bows hanging very low from either ham and tied round their Chest. The Esquires of which the chief Knights had two and the other Knights one were in a pink Spanish dress with white mantles and sashes: they wore high crowned pink hats with a white and a black feather and carried the lance and Shield of their Knight. The lance was fluted pink and white with a little banner of the same Colours, and the Shield was silvered and painted with the Knights device.

A blare of music from the combined bands opened the "Ceremony of the Carousel." A herald (Dr. Beaumont) with his trumpeters[11] entered the quadrangle from the left and proclaimed the entry of their knights, whose motto was "We droop when separate." The herald's symbol, a white and red rose entwined with a stem, was emblazoned on his coat and on the trumpet banners.

Led by Lord Cathcart, the white knights galloped onto the field and for their ladies gave an exhibition of their equestrian prowess. They styled themselves the "Knights of the Blended Rose." Each knight was preceded by his esquire on foot. Knights spaced at designated intervals moved around the field in an orderly procession. Passing the pavilion, they saluted the "Ladies of the Blended Rose" and the guest of honor. They then filed to the left, formed in line with the chief knight in the center, and advanced slightly to the front.

The herald and trumpeters moved to the center of the field of action. The trumpets roared defiance and the herald issued a challenge in accordance with the rules of knighthood and chivalry:

The Knights of the Blended Rose, by me their Herald proclaim and assert, that the Ladies of the Blended Rose, excell in Wit, Beauty and every Accomplishment, those of the whole world, and, should any Knight, or Knights, be so hardy as to dispute or deny it, they are ready to enter the lists with them and maintain their assertions, by deeds of Arms, according to the laws of ancient Chivalry.

He repeated his challenge to the assembled guests, the black knights and their ladies on the right of the field; and then returned to the left and solemnly repeated it to the white knights.

The Knights of the Blended Rose (the white knights), their squires, and their ladies were:

Chief knight, Lord Cathcart, 17th Dragoons; his squires, Captain Hazard, 44th, and Captain Brownlow, 57th. His shield was "Cupid on a Lion"; motto, "Surmounted by Love"; and his lady; Miss Auchmuty.

Honorable Captain Cathcart, 23rd; squire, Captain Peters; shield, "A Heart and a Sword"; motto, "Love and Honour." He apparently did not represent a lady at the joust.[12]

Lieutenant Bygrave, 16th Dragoons; squire, Lieutenant Nicholas; shield, "Cupid Tracing a Circle"; motto, "Without End"; lady, Miss J. Craig.

Captain Andre, 26th; squire, Lieutenant Andre,[13] 7th; shield, "Two Game Cocks Fighting"; motto, "No Rival"; lady, Miss P. Chew.

Captain Homeck, Guards; squire, Lieutenant Talbot, 16th Dragoons; shield, "A Burning Heart"; motto, "Absence Cannot Extinguish It"; lady, Miss N. Redmond.

Captain Matthews, 41st; squire, Lieutenant Hamilton, 15th; shield, "A Winged Heart"; motto, "Each Fair by Turns"; lady, Miss Bond.

Lieutenant Sloper, 17th Dragoons; squire Lieutenant Brown, 15th; shield, "A Heart and Sword"; motto, "Honour and The Fair."

As soon as the herald of the white knights completed his pronouncement, the herald of the black knights (Lieutenant Moore) and his trumpeters entered the quadrangle. They were closely followed by the seven black knights, who were dressed "in black Sattin contrasted with orange and laced with gold according to the stile of dress of the White Knights; Their Horses were black and likewise ornamented with black and orange. The Esquires were in orange coloured silk with black mantles and Trimmings." They called themselves "Knights of the Burning Mountain," and their herald and trumpeters displayed their motto, "I burn for ever."

The Knights of the Burning Mountain (the black knights), their squires, and their ladies were:

Chief knight, Captain Watson, Guards; squires, Captain Scott, 17th, Lieutenant Lyttleton, 5th; shield, "A Heart and a Wreath of Laurel"; motto, "Love and Glory"; lady, Miss Franks.

Lieutenant Underwood, 10th; squire, Ensign Havercam; shield, "A Pelican Feeding Her Young"; motto, "For Those I Love"; lady, Miss N. White.

Lieutenant Winyard, 64th; squire, Captain Boscawen, Guards; shield, "A Bay Leaf"; motto, "Unchang'd."

Lieutenant Delaval, 4th; squire, Captain Thorne; shield, "A Heart Aimed at by Several Arrows and Struck by One"; motto, "One Only Pierces Me"; lady, Miss B. Bond.

Monsieur De Montluivant, Chasseurs; squire, Captain Campbell, 55th; shield; "A Sunflower turning to the Sun"; motto, "Je vise a vous"; lady, Miss B. Redman.

Lieutenant Hobart, 7th; squire, Lieutenant Briscoe; shield, "A Mariner's Compass"; motto, "To The Fairest"; lady, Miss S. Chew.[14]

Brigade Major Tarleton; squire, Ensign Hart; shield, "A Light Dragoon"; motto, "Swift, Vigilant and Bold"; lady, Miss W. Smith.

The black knights promptly expressed their determination to demonstrate the superior worth of their ladies and to disprove the assertions of the white knights. Like the white knights, they proceeded in a stately procession around the field, exchanged a salute with their adversaries, and then paid their respects to the gathered assemblage.

Their herald was directed to issue a counter ultimatum:

The Knights of the Burning Mountain enter these lists not to contend with words, but to disprove by deeds of Arms the vainglorious assertions of the Knights of the blended Rose and to shew that the Ladies of the burning Mountn as far excell all others in Charms as the Knights themselves surpass all others in prowess.

The trumpets blared forth for a parley, and the two lines of knights sheathed their swords and met midway in the quadrangle. Lord Cathcart threw down his gauntlet in defiance. A black knight's squire picked it up and returned it to Cathcart, thus accepting the challenge. The squires presented their knights with shields and lances, and after a gallant salute with their lances, the knights resumed their stations ready to give battle.

Andre's description of the tournament included the major elements of all contemporary accounts:

The Signal for the Charge was next sounded when the Tilt took place with great rapidity and dexterity, each Knights Spear appearing to be shivered against his Antagonist, the Charge back again was immediate and with the pistol, which was fired in passing, the other pistol being produced, a third Charge was made; The Knights then drew their Swords and rode again at each other striking as they passed. The Whole now advanced against each other at once and closed, each Knight to his adversary, fighting hand to hand, and circling round, to direct their blow, till on a Signal they desisted to admit of a Single Combat between the Chiefs. These whilst fighting furiously, were parted by the interposition of the Judges of the Field, who doubtless deemed the Ladies so fair and the Knights so brave that it wou'd have been impious to decide in favour of either.

The honor of the ladies having thus been upheld, the knights and their retinue passed through the naval arch and formed a line on each side of a wide avenue leading to the military arch. This court was approximately three hundred yards long and thirty-five yards wide. Also in line were twenty men and one officer from each regiment in the garrison and the regimental bands, which according to Peebles included one hundred musicians. The avenue of color — flags of each regiment, gaily caparisoned knights with their entourage, and the arches with their brilliant decorations — delighted the strolling guests. As the guests walked through the long line of martial splendor, they were saluted in turn by each knight and squire.

Upon emerging from the military arch, guests entered a beautiful flower garden. A gravel walk led to the steps of the mansion. As they approached the mansion, many were awed by the elaborate fireworks display which Montresor had installed near the front of the house. Everyone ascending the carpeted steps was greeted at the door by the principal managers, Sir John Wrottesly, Sir Henry Calder, Colonel O'Hara, and Captain Montresor.[15]

The folding doors opened into a large hall, thirty by twenty feet, brilliantly illuminated with "spermaceti," fine white candles. Floors were covered with green baize. Each wall was paneled and painted "in imitation of Sienna marble," which enclosed festoons of white marble. The surbase was painted black. In the hall and two rooms adjoining it a light collation of coffee, tea, lemonade, punch, sangaree, wine, and various kinds of cakes was served. Tables covered with green baize and chairs were placed around the sides of the rooms and the hall. On each table exquisite china was heaped with choice delicacies. Over the fireplace chimney in each room a panel had been painted with a cornucopia which was "exuberantly filled with flowers of the richest colours." Shrunken cornucopias, inverted and emptied, were painted atop the doors. Later one of these rooms was cleared, and a faro bank was installed which was run, it was said, by three Hessian officers.

As the company enjoyed refreshments, the knights entered the hall and knelt before their ladies to receive their favors. Soon everyone mounted the stairs to what one guest described as a large entry flanked by four rooms. Opened, the rooms provided a large ballroom. In the entry at the head of the staircase an orchestra was seated to furnish music for the dancing.

Andre wrote that the upstairs rooms were

decorated in a light elegant stile of painting. The ground was a pale blue, pannelled with a small gold bead, and in the interior filled with drooping festoons of flowers in their natural colours. Below the surbase the ground was of rose-pink, with drapery festooned in blue. These decorations were heightened by 85 mirrours, decked with rose-pink silk ribbands, and artificial flowers; and in the intermediate spaces were 34 branches with wax-lights, ornamented in a similar manner.

The mirrors were so placed that they "multiplied every object."

The ball was opened by the knights and their ladies. The ladies then danced with the squires, after which the entire company joined the soiree. At about ten o'clock, windows were thrown open and a "magnificent bouquet of rockets began the fireworks." Twenty different exhibitions could be viewed by the entire assemblage and, most likely, also by the many residents who still ringed the grounds. For the conclusion, the triumphal military arch was

illuminated amidst an uninterrupted flight of rockets and bursting balloons. The military trophies on each side assumed a variety of transparent colours. The shell and flaming heart on the wings sent forth Chinese fountains, succeeded by fire pots. Fame appeared at top, spangled with stars, and from her trumpet blowing the following device in letters of light, *Tes Lauriers sont immortels.* — A *sateur* of rockets, bursting from the pediment, concluded the *feu d'artifice.*

With the fireworks over, the company returned to dancing. In the interim the faro bank had opened, and a goodly number decided to try to break the bank.

At midnight, when supper was announced, large folding doors were opened, revealing a large salon, 210 feet long, 40 feet wide, and 22 feet high. The salon, or banquet hall, connected to the mansion, had been constructed especially for the fete. Canvas was stretched over a sturdy arched frame; three alcoves on each side served as sideboards and were well stocked with liquors. The canvas walls and ceiling had been painted a light straw color, with vine leaves, some a bright and others a dark green, and festoons of flowers. Several doors were cut in the canvas to provide guests with quick egress and ingress to the banquet hall.

The walls were also covered with chandeliers, girandoles, and fifty-six large pier glasses ornamented with green silk, artificial flowers, and ribbons. They were entwined with garlands of flowers and festoons of green silk and ribbon. Eighteen lustres, each having twenty-four spermaceti candles, were suspended from the ceiling.

At two long tables extending the length of the salon, 430 places were set with 1,200 dishes. On the tables were fifty luxurious pyramids with jellies, sillabubs, cakes, and sweetmeats. The tables were adorned with 300 tapers. All the guests were served a cold supper, except for several tureens of soup. Courses included chicken, lamb, buttered hams, Yorkshire pies, veal, several varieties of pudding, and other delicacies. Twenty-four negro men garbed in oriental costumes served the supper. They were dressed in white shirts with blue silk sashes, silk turbans, and tin or silver collars and bracelets.

Toward the end of the supper, the herald of the Blended Rose and his trumpeters entered the banquet room and, sounding their trumpets, proclaimed the king's health. After the toast the band played "God Save the King," and the entire company joined in song. Other toasts followed for the queen and royal family, the army and navy and the commanders, the knights and their ladies, ladies in general, and the founders of the Meschianza. At the conclusion of these toasts, Hessian officers rose and gave a toast, "God Save the King, and success to his Majesty's Arms." Each toast was followed by a musical salute and three cheers.

After the toasts, the majority of the guests returned to the house, where they danced until daybreak. However, a party of gentlemen "remained at the table, determined to devote the rest of the night to Bacchus." As the sun rose, all guests but the gentlemen at the table had gone home.

While the festivities took place, a few Americans in the city were busy. McLane apparently planned to upset the entertainment with an annoying demonstration at the defense lines. According to one version, McLane divided his command into four detachments of twenty-five men and one lieutenant who were to be supported by Major Clough's dragoons. The men carried kettles filled with combustibles. At the proper signal, they were to set fire to the abatis in front of the lines. McLane reportedly hoped to distract the merrymakers and add to the fireworks display. British accounts mention little or nothing of this disturbance. However, a drum roll was heard along the line, from river to river, when the abatis was fired. British mounted patrols pursued the intrepid McLane to the Wissahickon. It is impossible to evaluate McLane's objective, other than being a nuisance. Yet it was known a major break out of the new gaol was planned by American prisoners for the night of 18 May. Possibly McLane's real intent was to create a diversion, inasmuch as a number succeeded in making their escape.[16]

What happened to the fair ladies of the Meschianza? In 1782 Rebecca Franks married Colonel Sir Henry Johnson and moved to England, but she always retained a fond attachment for her native America. Rebecca Redmond (or Redman) married Colonel Elisha Lawrence of New Jersey in 1779; however, the later life of her sister Nancy is unknown. Some authorities state that Miss Auchmuty, the daughter of the rector of Trinity Church in New York, married Captain Montresor; others assert he married her sister. Wilhelmina Bond married General John Cadwalader of Philadelphia in 1779. Her sister Becky went to England, but never married. Peggy Chew married Colonel John Eager Howard of Maryland, and her half sister Sarah Chew married her cousin John Galloway of Maryland. Miss W. Smith married Charles Goldsborough of Maryland. Janet Craig never married, and little is known about the future of Nancy White. Of the eleven beauties at the fete, only three are known to have moved to England — Rebecca Franks, Becky Bond, and Miss Auchmuty. Eight ladies remained in the new country, and all treasured fond recollections of 18 May 1778. Peggy Chew Howard, years later at her home in Baltimore, nostalgically said, "Major Andre was a most witty and cultivated gentleman." It is said her valiant husband, huffed at the remark, thundered, "He was a damned spy, sir; nothing but a damned spy."[17]

Reams have been written condemning the lavish Meschianza. The *London Chronicle* called it "nauseous." Others styled it a "silly exhibition" or a "ridiculous farce." Elizabeth Drinker said it was a day to be remembered for its many "scences of Folly and Vanity." Never a devotee of Howe, the *Chronicle* charged that the general preferred "the pleasures of indolence and dissipation to a discharge of his duty to his country." Criticisms of the Meschianza can be found in journals, letters, newspapers, pamphlets, and the works of early historians. Much of the vituperation heaped on Howe was simply the personal vilification of his enemies. Some, for religious reasons, were aghast at the ostentatious spectacle. A greater number felt that the pomp and frippery was not merited in view of Howe's meager accomplishments. They sincerely believed that any demonstration should only be celebrated when victory graced the British army.

Most promoters of the Meschianza were members of Howe's coterie of officers. As leaders in the social activities of the winter, they had also been the managers of City Tavern and its balls, assemblies, and gambling rooms. Many of these officers organized and performed with "Howe's strolling players" and usually attended the private balls given by leading officers. Their penchant for pageantry was well-known. They were unquestionably indifferent to the criticisms of others. Andre, expressing the sentiments of the fete's managers, observed that Howe would be grateful for the Meschianza because of "the spirit and motives from which it was given." In contrast, the opinions of those officers not actively engaged in the Meschianza was aptly stated by Serle: "Every man of Sense, among ourselves, tho' not unwilling to pay a due Respect, was ashamed of this mode of doing it."

The next day, 24 May, Andre witnessed Howe's departure for England and commented on the show of affection given at "waterside," saying it was even "more flattering testimony of the love and attachment of his army, than all the pomp and splendor of the *Mischianza* could convey to him."[18]

The denouement of America's most brilliant and picturesque spectacle occurred five days after the event, when a notice appeared in the *Pennsylvania Ledger* offering for sale "at the house where the entertainment was held on Monday last, a large quantity of *Boards* and *Scantling*."[19]

CHAPTER XV

THE DENOUEMENT: EVACUATION

EVEN BEFORE SIR William Howe boarded his ship to sail home, a feeling of uneasiness prevailed in Philadelphia. The countenances of many civilians had a look of hopelessness. Information that the city would be abandoned had been bruited around town for some time. A number of officers chose to ignore the significance of orders to place all heavy ordnance and excess officers' baggage on board ships in the harbor.

It was natural that most civilians and officers tried to remain optimistic and turned a deaf ear to disheartening rumors. However, what hope remained was suddenly dashed by a report that circulated the city a day or two after the Meschianza. The disheartening news emanated from a conversation between Howe and Shoemaker, one of the magistrates of police. At the latter's headquarters, the magistrate remarked that the people were disconsolate and afraid of the vengeance of the rebels. Howe answered that the imminence of a war with France would probably mean the army would be withdrawn from Philadelphia. He advised that all loyal subjects should attempt to make peace with the Congress. This recommendation placed a damper on those who had sacrificed everything for their king. Ambrose Serle, secretary to Lord Howe, was chilled and horrified, and said most friends of government thought there was "a rope around their necks and their property confiscated." There were so many stories circulating that Parker called it "the whisper of the day."[1]

On 22 May, Sir William Erskine was dispatched to notify Galloway officially of the decision to evacuate the city. Although the

Loyalist leader's emotions can only be conjectured, he castigated Howe privately for abandoning the friends of Great Britain. For two days Galloway and Serle held confidential meetings and decided to wait for Howe's departure before presenting to Clinton the plight of the Loyalists with reasons why the army should remain in the city. Serle said that he put in writing thirteen cogent reasons for Galloway to offer Clinton.

Galloway obtained an audience with Clinton on 25 May and, after a long conference, returned to his quarters to consider the details of their conversation. Apparently he had second thoughts, as later in the day he reappeared at headquarters for another long conference. Clinton promised that no imprudent steps would be taken. Up to this time Clinton had not revealed his orders from the king, which stated that the British were to leave Philadelphia. However, he realized that unless these instructions were revealed, he personally would be blamed for making a unilateral decision to quit the city. Aware of his untenable position, Clinton sent Erskine to Galloway early the next morning to disclose the orders from London. Aghast, Galloway quickly hurried to headquarters and remonstrated discreetly, but to no avail. The element of panic was added to the despair already evident. Most Loyalists hastily made preparations to leave with the fleet.

Regardless who gave the order to quit the city, Galloway thought his fortune was lost and he would have to "wander like Cain upon the Earth without Home, & without Property." On the twenty-third, he advised the stunned magistrates of the unhappy news. Nevertheless, he remained convinced that after Howe had gone he could convince Clinton to keep the army in Philadelphia. Serle, in an effort to strengthen his friend's position, interceded on his behalf with Lord Howe; unfortunately, the admiral reiterated his brother's advice — make peace with the Americans. The Admiral also said that haste was necessary so that all Loyalists who desired to leave with the army could be accommodated on the transports. Galloway apparently followed this recommendation, as he instructed all who intended to leave the city to register at his office and indicate the number in their family.[2]

Galloway's continued despondency caused his friend Serle concern. He counseled the Loyalist to contact the Continental Congress and make his peace. Appealing to Galloway's devotion to the crown and his vanity, Serle pointed out he could "when the madness of the Times was abated, . . . be a mediator between the two Countries."[3]

Before leaving Philadelphia, Serle was instrumental in persuading Galloway to prepare a paper on the reasons why the city should not be abandoned. Both men were aware that the presentation would have no effect on the decision to leave the city, but they felt it would demonstrate to Great Britain the importance of Philadelphia. The arrival of the peace commissioners on 5 June temporarily buoyed the Loyalists' hopes and probably delayed the mailing of Galloway's memorials. They were finally forwarded to Lord Dartmouth on 17 June, one day before the withdrawal of the last contingents of British troops.

First Galloway offered a detailed argument against abandoning Philadelphia. He realized that any appeal to England would be impossible to implement, even if favorably received. His letter was on the outgoing ships, and by the time it reached England, the recommendations would be academic. Nevertheless, it provided him with a platform to register opposition to what he considered the misuse of British power in America.

Galloway considered Philadelphia to be the hub of all commercial and industrial activity in the colonies. Whoever had possession of the city could readily be supplied with the sinews of war. All materials were found in abundance in this area and could usually be procured much cheaper than elsewhere in the colonies. Once Pennsylvania was in British possession, the army could effectively sever all contacts between the northern and southern provinces. With the fleet controlling the waters, the various parts of the country could be conquered in detail. The main army under Washington was so weak that it would simply require an aggressive effort on the part of the superior strength of the British army to destroy or disperse the Americans. After the enemy was defeated, the faithful inhabitants with a small regular force could defend the city at the line of redoubts — a tacit acknowledgment that American units would still be hovering near the lines.

A second memorial outlined a method to reduce the countryside as the British army pursued Washington. Messengers should be sent into all districts urging ''Men of Weight and Influence'' to raise the ''King's Standard.'' All disaffected persons should be secured and disarmed. All loyal subjects should be promptly and properly armed. To expedite this arrangement, a ''Brigadier or General'' in whom the people had confidence must be given command of the Provincial corps (naturally Galloway's modesty forbade any recommendation).

He estimated that twenty counties adjacent to Philadelphia in Pennsylvania, New Jersey, Delaware, and Maryland, plus two on the eastern shore of Virginia, would each raise a minimum of 500 men, some 1,000. The British were thus assured of no less than a corps of 10,000 men. Ironically, Galloway had predicted an identical response by area residents in the early months of 1777. Andrew Allen echoed these prognostications, and the two for the balance of their lives sincerely believed, or convinced themselves, that nine out of every ten Americans would flock to the royal standard if guaranteed British army protection. All this would be used as ammunition in his acrimonious confrontation with the Howe brothers in 1779.[4]

Despair was written on the countenance of almost every officer. It was inconceivable that the powerful British army would not strike Washington's inferior forces. When Erskine realized that the British were quitting the city like whipped dogs, he went to headquarters and remonstrated with Clinton. He urged the commander in chief to attack the rebels, saying it would soften the grumblings in the ranks and would put a stop to the increased desertions. Erskine attributed the discontent among the men to the humiliation of running from a weak and despised enemy.

After an unsuccessful conference with Clinton, he met for dinner with a group of officers, including General Sir Charles Grey, Colonel James Patterson [Paterson], and Serle. Grey and Erskine dominated the conversation at the table. The idea of letting the rebel army escape unscathed infuriated them. Erskine was so miserable he said he was ''ashamed of the name of a Briton.'' The two generals said a vigorous attack would drive Washington over the Susquehanna River within forty-eight hours. Serle commented that while the others present said nothing, all tacitly agreed with the generals' recommendations.

Boudinot, who had been in Germantown negotiating an exchange of prisoners, heard of an incident which reflected the wrath of the rank and file. ''The [Peace] Commissioners had like to have been mobbed by the british light Infantry two Nights ago [9 June] — They hung Lord North in Effigy with the two Acts of Parliament in his Hands — They cannot bear the thoughts of Peace.''[5]

During the entire period of preparations, a depressed commander in chief had been taking stock of his unenviable situation. At first a shortage of shipping had delayed the move. Lord Howe advised him the fleet was dispersed on a variety of necessary services and there were not enough men-of-war to convoy the garrison and stores to New York. For some unknown reason, the admiral also confided that if Clinton wished to send part of the garrison back on the available transports, they would have to embark at Newcastle. Clinton was appalled at the thought of marching forty miles to the Delaware port town unless with "the whole army," thus marooning a part of the army at that port until additional ships arrived.

He also realized the danger of a delay. A French fleet was expected in American waters, and he wished to avoid being trapped at sea. He wrote to Germain on 23 May, saying he did not consider it expedient to move only part of his army, but would wait for additional naval support.

The decision became moot when it was announced that the commissioners were coming. Hamstrung by orders and circumstances, Clinton bared his emotions to his cousin, the Duke of Newcastle: "I am ordered to Evacuate this place and proceed to New York, my orders are clear, and positive, not to be misunderstood or disobeyed, had I however followed them exactly by embarking in the river, I might have lost New York & must have made a most disgraceful retreat."

On 11 July, safely ensconced in New York, he somewhat smugly wrote, "Had I followed my instructions as to the manner of quitting Philadelphia — bad consequences might have followed." He noted that French men-of-war were sighted off the Delaware capes and then plaintively added that he wanted to return home.[6]

For several weeks, rumors that the British planned to evacuate Philadelphia had infiltrated the American camp and Congress. Washington believed the reports, but wondered when they would leave and what their destination would be. Howe, and later Clinton, endeavored to camouflage their intentions by increased activity at the lines. The new redoubts started by Howe were strengthened by 300 men toiling every day. Work on the lines also continued, and the ditch in front of the abatis was filled with water and dammed, "forming a kind of Liquid abattis."[7]

Whatever the British commanders planned, their subterfuge at this time did not deceive the American patrols or agents in the city. Regardless, it was necessary to maintain a posture of defense until a safe evacuation could be effected.

On 20 May, Clinton ordered Pattison to remove from the lines and city, all artillery and stores except those to be carried by the army on its march across New Jersey. The heavy ordnance on the lines were to be replaced by regimental field pieces. One erroneous report said wooden cannon were placed in the redoubts to deceive the Americans. Pattison was allowed only two weeks to complete the embarkation. Irritated because he had been working his men day and night in anticipation of such an order, he doubted it could be accomplished in the allotted time. In addition, Lord Howe refused his request for navy ships, thus forcing him to commandeer commercial vessels. Pattison was fortunate to find seven ships downstream that had been stopped by the embargo. Howe had imposed an embargo on all shipping to ensure adequate tonnage would be available for the evacuation of the army, merchants, and civilians. Pattison wrote exultantly that in spite of the fatiguing work, his men had cheerfully labored fifteen hours a day and had fulfilled their mission in twelve days.[8]

The British continued their attempts to further mislead Washington. Large detachments made frequent forays as far as Chestnut Hill and Bebberstown. These excursions continued until at least 10 June. A Germantown resident observed a visit by the commissioners on 10 June, but thought the only object of the troops was to rob gardens.[9]

Initially Washington had been puzzled by the apparent indecision of the British commanders. However, he kept his small army mobile and on 1 June issued marching instructions to counter any move by Clinton. The only question was whether Clinton would go by sea or march across New Jersey. On 10 June, Washington advised his brother that he had expected the enemy to leave the city "for upwards of 14 days" and had been at a loss to understand their actions until he learned that the peace commissioners had arrived. He believed their presence would delay the army's departure for several days. In writing to Congress on the morning of 18 June, he said he had put six brigades in motion, but was still uncertain which route Clinton's army would take. He assumed that their destination was New York. Some of his staff were of the opinion that the British troops' presence in New Jersey was a disguise and that they actually intended to march down the Jersey shore (Delaware River) and embark. In Congress, Henry Laurens wrote he considered the British position in New Jersey carried "the aspect of stratagem."[10]

Intelligence reports from New York seemed to confirm that city as Clinton's goal. One report said several hundred houses were being cleaned to receive British troops, while another rumor disclosed that camps were being prepared to accommodate refugees from Philadelphia.[11]

While the commanders in chief tried to counter each other's move, Loyalists and merchants in Philadelphia were in a ''Continual scene of Terror hurry & Confusion.'' One Loyalist officer wrote, ''Such as have been active in favour of Govn^t or have any way favoured the army seemed depressed beyond expression.'' Adding to their distress was a rumor that the British might burn Philadelphia. Even though this fear was quickly dispelled, it had deepened the anguish of the inhabitants.[12]

Despite the bellicosity and bluster of a few Loyalists, evidence indicates that many more had little desire to leave their homes and face an unknown future. Those guilty of having abused the Americans realized they had little choice but to leave with the British army. When it became obvious that the decision to evacuate the city could not be revoked, leading merchants and citizens called a meeting to determine their future course. On 25 May, they met at the British Tavern (formerly the Indian King) in Market Street.

As a result of the meeting, they elected to seek an accommodation with the new government. This must have been a bitter decision for many who, like Galloway and the Allens, had worked faithfully to preserve the royal government in Pennsylvania. Galloway was selected as their spokesman and was empowered to request Clinton's permission for them to treat with Washington or Congress.[13]

Sometime after 25 May, Galloway met with Clinton and Lord Howe and asked permission to approach Washington. Lord Howe suggested that if Clinton had no objection a flag of truce should be sent to the American commander. Clinton was adamant, stating that he would never consent to anyone treating with the rebels. He considered the flag as evidence of his condoning a treaty.

Lord Howe, whose compassion for Americans was well-known, then suggested sending a private emissary to negotiate with Washington. Clinton was again unyielding. His position was that almost half the garrison at New York were Loyalists, and if these troops heard that Philadelphia Loyalists had received favorable terms, they might be induced to seek an equally beneficial arrangement. This would jeopardize the safety of New York as a garrison town. He also believed that any agreement with Washington would impede the negotiations of the commissioners. However, after he returned to New York and had secured that post, he might entertain a suggestion for a flag to treat with the Americans. The meeting ended with Lord

Howe's saying he appreciated Clinton's position; however, evidence shows that his private opinions were to the contrary.[14]

Whether Washington was apprised of this meeting is uncertain; nonetheless, he deplored the ineptitude of Congress in not taking the initiative to offer at least a conditional amnesty to most Pennsylvania Loyalists. He wrote Laurens, ". . . many hundreds nay thousands of valuable artisans and their goods . . . will leave with the departing British for fear of their property, honor and fortune." Washington was not alone in this opinion. As John Laurens, for example, advised his father, "The inhabitants anxious to know whether their persons and property will be protected from the rage of American Soldiery — if they could be sure of protection, it is thought much valuable merchandize would be retained in the city, which otherwise will be sent away." Boudinot also criticized the American indifference: "The Want of an Act of Indemnity have forced away several hundreds of valuable Tradesmen & Manufacturers, who are cast upon the mercy of the british Army & Scarcely know where to get a meal of Victuals — They exocrete [excoriate] our barbarous Severity in the bitterest & most poignant Terms of agony & Woe."[15]

A member of Congress related an anecdote that typified the dilemma of the average Loyalist in late May 1778. He said the narrator had overheard the conversation, but would not reveal the Loyalist's name:

It seems a cowardly Tory of large landed estate in York County [Pennsylvania] had fled to the enemy in Philadelphia the winter past, & when he discovered the movement of the enemy shipping their stores, baggage &c. of late; indicating their departure, he applied to their General to know what he should do, the General replied he was busy & sent him to an under officer: The Tory with enxiety asked the officer what he should do as he perceived they were going away. The officer told him he must do as they did when in difficulty make the best shift he could, the Tory still dissatisfied told him all this was come upon him for being loyal & faithful to the King & queried what shall I do. I expected protection, the officer replied go seek a passage on board some vessel &c the Tory with vehement anxiety, queried, but what the Devil shall I do with my estate, the officer replied, Damn you why did you not stay at home & fight to defend it with your Country, and so dismissed his applicant.[16]

At the same time, other memorialists were petitioning Clinton for losses sustained because their business properties had been taken over by the army and navy. Many owners of wharves and stores lamented the loss of revenue and requested restitution. Unfortunately, there is no evidence that their appeal was honored. British general officers usually maintained that as facilities occupied by the army were royal business, no compensation should be forthcoming unless specifically authorized by the commander in chief.

In fairness to Howe and Clinton, one record of payment has survived. Captain Payne, barrack master, paid Susanna Rakestraw £24 13s. 4d. for the use of six houses as barracks. In addition, for varying periods troops had occupied two houses on Third Street owned by David Potts. He was paid £28 20s. Turner or Tanner Allen, whose house was occupied by Lord Howe after his return from Rhode Island, received £56 10s. rental. Earlier, £140 was paid to the college for its use as a hospital. Although records of other disbursements could not be found, the fact that these rental payments were made suggests that other property owners also received compensation.[17]

Beset with frustrations and seemingly not welcomed by either side, many Loyalist and neutral merchants and artisans frantically applied to sail with the fleet. Householders placed their furniture and personal articles on the pavement by their homes and then searched hopelessly for a conveyance. A number of carts, drays, and wagons were finally procured. However, few horses were available, as most, belonging to the army, had been sent aboard the horse ships. The army and navy made a number of transports available. One lady observed the chaos and said ''her head grew dizzy with the bustle and confusion . . . carts, drays, and waggons, laden with dry goods and household furniture, dragged by men through the streets to the wharfs, for want of horses; beds, boxes, trunks, chairs, tables etc. turned out in the utmost confusion and haste.'' Ewald confirmed that pandemonium existed on the streets. Typical of every exodus, each person attempted to take more than could be accommodated, thus adding to the confusion. One American intelligence agent reportedly witnessed some of this furniture being thrown off the ships to make room for military stores.[18]

The countenances of the inhabitants revealed their political sympathies. One woman observed ''joy sparkling in the countenance of the Whigs, and consternation painted in those of the Tories.'' Ewald, slightly more caustic, noted, ''So well pleased do the opposite-minded people now appear that everyone already shows their delight very boldly, yet they regret it because our hard money leaves with us.''[19]

It has been generally accepted that the number of refugees who boarded the transports totaled 3,000. Ewald said about 1,500 families embarked on the ships, and Eden stated there were 5,000 Loyalists on the transports. In early June, upwards of 300 merchant ships and transports were anchored off Reedy Island. The distressed refugees on these ships were destined to remain at their anchorage until the third week of the month. As their food supply was dwindling, they waited impatiently for a signal to sail. Commissioner Eden, on board a ship with the fleet, saw "Crowds of wretched families in the Transports all round us are incredible — It will not be easy for us to feed them."[20]

Upon their arrival in New York, most of the pitiful expatriates would be dependent on the largess of the British occupation forces. Others, more fortunate, would take residence on Long Island or sail for England. An eighteenth-century account described the plight of those forced to remain in New York during the winter of 1778-79:

The situation of the Refugees with the British army in New-York, has afforded through the course of the present winter, a miserable spectacle. The barracks, hospitals, and public buildings have been occupied by the king's troops, while the miserable wretches who have followed them, are under the necessity of seeking shelter in the market-houses, in the stables with a fire before the door to prepare their victuals, or amongst the ruins of the burnt buildings, in the angles of the standing walls and chimneys.

The writer was obviously referring to the disastrous fire of 1776 that destroyed a large part of the city.[21]

Thousands of Loyalist sympathizers remained in Philadelphia and its environs. Most had given little umbrage to American partisans and were gradually absorbed into the mainstream of life in the new republic. Moderate Americans hoped to prevent radicals from wreaking vengeance on any inhabitants who had taken an oath of allegiance to the king or served the British army in a civilian capacity. Unfortunately, they were only partly successful. Two or three Loyalists or neutrals who had served as guides for army detachments or had identified American partisans in the city were tried and executed despite the protestations of numerous Americans. Each day New Jersey Loyalists could be seen crossing the Delaware to Billingsport. They hoped to receive amnesty from local authorities and then return to their homes.[22]

With the arrival of the peace commissioners, Clinton and Lord Howe assumed their places on the delegation. The general and admiral held a meeting with Eden, Carlisle, and Johnstone. After a lengthy conversation, an abashed Carlisle emerged incensed at the limitations placed on the commission. He was embarrassed because Clinton was "under the irresistable influence of *positive* and *repeated orders.*" Apparently these orders had been issued by the king sometime before the commissioners sailed, but had not been transmitted to them. Eden thought Clinton should have been given some discretion.[23]

The commissioners agreed that evacuation should be delayed until they had contacted the Continental Congress. Eden believed it would make little difference, as the American position was well known: No proposals would be entertained that did not acknowledge American independence. However, Eden was hopeful that it might be possible to negotiate as long as the British army remained in Philadelphia. Any implied threat to destroy or devastate the city would place the commission at a disadvantage if the army abandoned the area.[24]

Amid the chaos and diplomatic disappointments which ensued, preparations went forward to pull out of all military installations. Partly in anticipation of the annual spring offensive, there had been a buildup in military ordnance and supplies. The entry of France into the conflict made it necessary to concentrate and secure the army in New York, thus scrapping all plans for a 1778 campaign. Clinton and his staff and departmental heads were aware that a significant quantity of specific ordnance must be destroyed rather than permitted to fall into the hands of the Americans.[25]

Destruction of the various installations went on apace, including the demolition of some of the new redoubts that had been started on 3 June. The same day, Washington was the recipient of information that "a number cannon broke & thrown off wharf — likewise thousands of broken muskets — a large number of barrels of pork & beef also thrown over — not less than 4,000 blankets burnt that came out of the hospital."[26]

All ships under construction were ordered burned. Shipyard stocks in Southwark near Gloria Dei Church and in Northern Liberties and Kensington were set to the torch. The flames were seen throughout the city and, fanned by high winds, burned furiously for two days. Regretfully, the flames spread and consumed several houses occupied by poor families.[27]

Large quantities of provisions were left behind by Commissary

General Wier; one ration return acknowledges that 26,080 pounds of flour and bread and 16,640 pounds of pork were "lost." What disposition was made of these and other provisions cannot be ascertained. Enoch Story reported that large quantities of prohibited goods were to remain in the city. These goods included 700 hogsheads of rum, 10 of brandy, 40 of Geneva, 20 of molasses, 38 packages of medicines, and 12,000 bushels of salt. Elizabeth Drinker said the army was "giving ye remainder of their stores of Wood and Hay to ye poor." She considered this evidence of the imminent withdrawal of the British from the city. However, Peebles had a different version, at least in part, of the disposal of the army's surplus wood. He claimed the regimental quartermasters were drawing their allotment of wood and selling it in the town.[28]

Even if Clinton succeeded in nothing else, he did confuse members of the Continental Congress. On 9 June, James Lovell wrote Gates: "Here we are still the Sports of Lyars. One Day we are told the Enemy are filling the Ditches and preparing to leave Philada., en Ami; in the next we are informed of new Works and fresh arrived Troops." The next day John Wentworth, Jr., expressed similar uncertainty: "The enemy at Philadelphia for three weeks past have been doing and undoing — one day extremely busy in fortifying and the next in demolishing — in short their manoeuvres are so various as to render it utterly impossible to guess what measures they mean finally to pursue." Clinton's intention to create confusion among Americans had obviously succeeded.[29]

He had been given an unenviable command; his orders were to evacuate 20,000 troops, army ordnance, and stores — a monumental task. Added to his quandary were several thousand refugees and camp followers with their possessions. About 300 ships were employed to transport them, the surplus army supplies, sick and wounded soldiers, and American prisoners. The Anspach regiments were also ordered to sail with the fleet, as it was thought they might desert on the march. A Lutheran minister said that to facilitate loading of ships, the British were actively engaged in recruiting and impressing young townsmen as laborers. Once the ships were ready to drop down to their rendezvous at Reedy Island, Clinton was able to concentrate on plans to evacuate the main army.

Fortified bivouacs and posts were established in New Jersey to receive the corps marching across the state with Clinton. A steady procession of flatboats manned by 500 sailors was brought up from

Caricature called "La Grande Bretagne mutilée" represents Great Britain in 1778 with shipping idle in the harbor, New England lost, and Philadelphia reclaimed by the rebels. *American Philosophical Society*

the men-of-war. They ferried troops, field artillery, stores, provisions, wagons, and horses over the Delaware. From the fifteenth through the seventeenth, British and Hessian battalions crossed the river from the wharf near the northern edge of the city to Cooper's Ferry; others left from Gloucester Point, south of the city, to the area around modern-day Gloucester City.[30]

Late on the afternoon of the seventeenth, the British light infantry, grenadiers, and guards were moved up to the area in back of the redoubts, where they laid on their arms all night. At daybreak they withdrew, joined the battalions remaining in the city, marched to Gloucester Point, and crossed the river. Andre said the *Vigilant* was stationed near the point of embarkation to support their withdrawal. A few straggling officers and at least one small detachment were cut off by American patrols and captured.[31]

Anticipating a need for provisions and forage on the march across New Jersey, Clinton issued a proclamation on 13 June asking all inhabitants to bring those commodities into camp or to the marching column, a curious petition after Wier reported the wasteful loss of tons of provision. All who complied were to be given their full value in gold or silver. In addition, he guaranteed that neither their persons nor property would be molested. This promise must have had a hollow ring to those who had suffered losses on previous marches by the British army. He concluded by admonishing all who might consider hostile action against the column "that they must abide by the Consequences," a final gesture of futility.[32]

CHAPTER XVI

A DEVASTATED CITY

THE FIRST AMERICAN troops to enter Philadelphia re-
sembled a raiding party. They took a few prisoners and then withdrew to the northern perimeter of the city to await the arrival of
General Benedict Arnold, the newly appointed military governor of
Philadelphia. Washington had offered Arnold a field command, but
the latter had begged off, claiming his leg, wounded at Saratoga, was
still painful and would handicap him in active service. A steady
stream of civilians preceded the military into the city. This trickle of
joyful humanity increased over the next several months, eventually
numbering in the thousands.

While 18 June was a day of homecoming for some refugees, it
was tempered by despondency when they saw the ruinous condition
of their homes. Loyalist sympathizers, Quakers, and other neutrals
wisely refrained from appearing on the streets. Stores were closed,
locked, and, in some cases, boarded up. The loss was irretrievable for
those who, following their conscience and convictions, had remained
loyal to their king and were now crowded on board the transports
headed down the river and bay. To these unfortunates, the sight of
the disappearing shoreline must have evoked poignant memories of
happier days. For a few, the separation would be temporary, as over
the next twenty years some would return to attempt to resume their
old lives in the new country.

The anger of returning Americans increased as they saw the
debris and filth that littered the city's streets. With the British army
gone, the logical targets for censure or revenge were the hapless
Loyalists. Moderates and radicals among the Americans agreed that
all Loyalists who had consorted with or joined the British army or

navy were guilty of treason, and that their estates should be confiscated. Less than 50 of the 453 Pennsylvania Loyalists attainted of treason were on the transports — not more than ten percent. In the fall the possessions of fleeing Americans had been disposed of at public vendue. Now, with the Americans returning, conditions were reversed, and sales of the effects of the departed "notorious" Loyalists were conducted.[1]

As the majority of Americans returned by roads from Frankford, Germantown, and other hamlets in the north, a scene of widespread desolation greeted them. Few houses were left standing in the northern section of the city. Those remaining were gutted and were missing doors, windows, or roofs. France's first minister to the United States, Conrad Alexander Gerard, wrote that "600 houses were destroyed."[2] Walking down any north-south street, piles of filth, garbage, and excrement could be seen in every intersecting alley and court. By comparison most of the main thoroughfares were relatively clean.

Upon entering their front doors, the refugees were nauseated by the effluvium which emanated from every corner of the house. This was particularly true for hundreds of householders whose homes had been used as barracks. In many cases the soldiers had cut holes in the parlor floor and pushed their excrement and trash into the cellar.[3] The filthy habits of the British soldier had been a constant source of concern. General Pattison had earlier admonished his artillerymen for relieving themselves on the staircase or behind doors at the State House. Regardless, a large number of junior officers had tolerated these conditions by ignoring orders to visit or police the quarters allotted to their companies. Similarly, officers and men had ignored Galloway's proclamations ordering all trash and debris to be placed at the curbside at stated times for the scavengers to pick up.

It appears that when the men could no longer stand the stench, they shoveled the refuse that had accumulated in the cellars onto the streets. While an indefensible filthy habit, it should be remembered that there were no modern sanitary facilities and that the houses were not intended to quarter the number of soldiers assigned to them. Furthermore, unless on duty, the men were forbidden to leave their quarters without a pass.

Before members of Congress and the inhabitants could resume a normal pattern of life, the city had to undergo a general housecleaning. Richard Peters complained of being ill for two or three days and attributed it to "the foul & abominable atmosphere of the Place." Dr. Benjamin Rush did not return to Philadelphia until 21 July, but he observed "the filth left by the British army in the streets created a good deal of sickness." Most houses that had been used as barracks were polluted and infectious, and all required considerable time to cleanse. Many returning inhabitants were annoyed by swarms of "flies which are here in the greatest possible Numbers that one Hand is employed in brushing them away while the other is writing." Peter S. Duponceau, aide to Steuben, went to have tea with his commander, but the filth was so loathsome that they could not enjoy their tea because "as fast as our cups were filled, myriads of flies took possession of them; and served us as harpies did the poor Trojans in the Eneid."[4]

John Maxwell Nesbitt's face was a picture of abysmal dejection when he first viewed the damages to his house and store. He described the trauma typical of all returning householders: "My house I found in a wretch'd Condition, — not fit to live in & am getting it cleaned &c. The Stores back are in a great measure destroy'd & everything left in & about the House gone, a few chairs & a Couple of Tables excepted. . . . The Town excessively Dirty & disagreeable, stinks Intolerably. . . ."[5]

Public buildings suffered despoliation similar to that experienced by churches and private dwellings. Congress was compelled to hold its sessions at the college because of the "offensiveness of the air in and around the State House, which the Enemy had made an Hospital and left it in a condition disgraceful to the Character of civility. Particularly they had opened a large square pit near the House, a receptacle for filth, into which they had also cast dead horses and the bodies of men." Another member of Congress noted, "The State House [was] . . . in a most filthy and sordid situation, as were many of the public and private buildings in the City."[6]

Artisans and shopkeepers were quick to take advantage of the needs of homeowners to restore their properties. William Rush advertised "to inform those who have been so unfortunate to have their houses or other buildings burnt, or otherways destroyed, that there is a large quantity of hinges, some chains for chimnies, and sundry other articles" for sale at his store in Front Street.[7]

British dragoons had left the interior of the shambles (market house) in a ruinous condition. Butchers advanced money to restore the stalls so the market could be reopened.[8]

All along the waterfront were the scarred remains of small boats. According to a returning ship's carpenter, only one vessel was found unscathed, and that was on the New Jersey shore.[9]

Virtually every absent American lost some personal articles or furniture. Benjamin Franklin reported the loss of a painting, books, a printing press, and other items. Andre and other officers had occupied the philosopher's house during the winter. Du Simitiere, the young miniaturist, had been stunned to see the dashing Andre pack Franklin's personal possessions, including the Wilson portrait, and remonstrated, but to no avail. The painting was a gift to his superior, General Grey, and the portrait hung in the Grey ancestral home until 1906, when it was restored to the United States. In contrast to the light-fingered proclivities of Andre was the honorable conduct of Knyphausen, who occupied the home of General John Cadwalader. Upon moving into the house, the Hessian commander had his steward prepare an inventory of all Cadwalader's property and upon vacating the premises had Cadwalader's agent check the list. Every item was found in place, even some wine in the cellar. In addition, Knyphausen paid rent for the use of the house.[10]

It is not possible to assess the extent of personal property losses. Most pilferage was committed by members of the military for their personal use or gain through private sale. Occasionally a civilian perpetrated similar thefts. For example, James Robertson, publisher of the *Royal Pennsylvania Gazette*, abetted by Christopher Sower, appropriated the printing press of the German-American printer John Henry Miller. Robertson justified this act stating that the Americans had taken his press.

Newspapers listed the specific items lost by the returning Americans. Advertisements were inserted to locate every conceivable article of furniture or personal property, including slaves and apprenticed servants.[11] A typical announcement of lost property was placed by Robert Porter, a saddler who believed his stolen articles were still in or near the city and offered a reward for information on their whereabouts. But he warned any person who concealed intelligence or who possessed the items after the public notice with prosecution under the law.

Was taken out of the subscriber's house, in Market-street, opposite the Gaol, last fall, while the British army were in possession of this city, the following goods, viz. three feather beds, six walnut chairs with flowered worsted bottoms, one walnut dining table, one walnut writing desk, one walnut double corner cupboard, one bedstead painted green, and sacking bottom, one set of iron rods for a bed, three windsor chairs, one tin plate stove and pipes, one nest of drawers, one pair of large andirons with brass heads, one Dutch oven frying pan, and warming pan, one large china bowl, one tureen, one iron tea-kettle and iron pot, one pair of tongs and two fire shovels, two six-quart bottles, one large pewter dish, two brass and one iron candlesticks, one cedar tub, one ditto for meat, and a gridiron.[12]

Joseph Turner, owner of a beautiful country seat in the Neck, offered similar admonishments to anyone with knowledge of any item on his list of missing property:

Six mahogany chairs, claw feet, leaf on the knees, open backs, and crimson damask bottoms; one half dozen walnut ditto, claw feet, shell on the knees and backs, compass bottoms covered with plain horse hair, and irons on the backs as strengtheners to the top rails; one close stool chair and pan, black walnut, claw feet, compass back; one mahogany easy chair, claw feet, leaf on the knees, covered with crimson damask; one common black walnut tea table; one large English bible; one mahogany desk, carved furniture, with a bird's head in the middle of the furniture.[13]

Other notices named the suspected culprit. Whitehead Humphreys, operator of a steel furnace, charged Joseph Fox, ''a noted traitor,'' with carrying away four tons of blistered steel and all its appurtenances. While serving the militia, John Hewson's linen printing factory in Kensington was broken into by Nathaniel Norgrove and William Grant of Northern Liberties. They were seen unlawfully removing a large wooden machine and other materials used in linen printing work.[14]

The excitement, anticipation, and pathos of this time produced many human-interest stories. For example, one incident represented the tribulations of the Reverend Michael Schlater, or Schlatter. The Reverend, known as an ardent patriot, was arrested when Howe arrived in the city. Schlater was considered inimical to the British cause. After several months' confinement, and with his family in dire straits, he humbly petitioned Howe for a pardon. His memorial stated he had ''taken the Test Oath to the State of Pennsylvania'' because he had been defrauded in the sale of a farm and wanted to avail himself of the protection of the state laws. He acknowledged that his son had served in the local militia, but beseeched Howe not to hold him accountable for the actions of a child. After outlining the purity of his ministerial intentions, he implored Howe to permit him to renew his allegiance to "His Sovereign" and receive the protection of the British authorities. There is reason to believe that the Reverend's repentance may have been a tongue-in-cheek effort to obtain his freedom.

It appears that after the British left the city he made his peace with the Pennsylvania Assembly. On 2 January 1779, he ran an announcement asserting that his "dwelling house on Chestnut Hill was most cruelly plundered by the British troops on the fifth of December [1777]." His enumerated list of stolen items included a library of nearly one thousand volumes, the wearing apparel of his family, kitchen utensils, several tables and chairs and "other things too tedious to mention." Like most of the crestfallen residents, it is unlikely he retrieved more than a handful of his effects.[15]

Another vignette concerned the confrontation between Howe and Israel Pemberton just before the former boarded ship to sail to England. Pemberton, the "King of the Quakers," "it is said, waited on him for payment of damages done to his property to the amount of several thousand pounds; that being refused any compensation he told the General that he was determined not to put up with the loss, and would follow him to London." This out-of-character fulmination by the venerable Quaker, if true, never reached fruition. In October 1778, his wife died and his grandson was dying. Israel himself died in April 1779.[16]

Americans who returned to their homes and stores not only found most of their personal possessions were missing but, conversely, found personal items, furniture, and household effects that did not belong to them. During the winter officers and soldiers had taken everything of value that was portable. Officers fitted their quarters with anything that appealed to their fancy, while privates pilfered anything they could sell. Greed and avarice prompted some to keep items of value. Another group of citizens, those who had remained in the city during the occupation, purchased any articles offered with the intention of restoring them to the owners. One compassionate "young Gentleman" had "purchased last winter of the British soldiery for a trifling consideration . . . with the thought of restoring them to their owners, two eight-day clocks." Proof of ownership and a "few inconsiderable charges" was all the young man asked for his trouble.[17]

As evidenced by some notices, a number of residents who had returned adopted a fatalistic attitude toward their losses:

There were brought to the Northern Liberties of Philadelphia by a party of the British army some time before they evacuated the city, and exposed to sale something under value, and being supposed to be plundered goods were purchased in order to be returned to the right owners, the following Articles, viz. one dark flowered chintz gown, one small spotted cotton bed spread, one bed spread of coarse stamp linen, with the name of David Weatherby stamped in the cloth, one long white superfine cloath cloak without a hood, and one black paduasoy ditto lined with black silk mode. It was expected that the owners of the above things would have proclaimed their loss before now, otherwise they would have been advertised sooner. Whoever has lost said articles, by proving property and paying full charges may have them again. Enquire of the Printer.[18]

Merchants and tradesmen in a garrison city were always confronted with an accumulated indebtedness incurred by the military. A report circulated that departed British officers owed local businessmen £10,000.[19]

In August 1778, residents of Philadelphia presented a petition to the State House of Representatives "praying" to be reimbursed for losses sustained by enemy plunderings. A bill passed on 21 September 1782 instructed county commissioners to obtain an accurate account and estimate of damages done by British and Hessian troops. It was thought these calculations would be a useful tool for the government to have in any peace negotiation with Great Britain.[20]

It is impossible to ascertain if the commissioners of Bucks, Berks, and Chester counties submitted a statement of losses. However, several individual demands in these counties have been located, which confirms that area residents suffered extensive damages. A few of these claims appear to have been presented to Howe by Quaker farmers and honored.[21]

Any effort to estimate the losses in counties adjacent to Philadelphia is complicated by depredations committed by American troops. The losses reported for Philadelphia County outside of the city unquestionably represented property owners' attempts to collect from the state regardless of the depredator.

Fortunately, the record of reported losses for Philadelphia County and City has been preserved. They are, however, incomplete as they do not include the repairs to churches, public buildings, and those sustained by many leading citizens, especially Quakers. Many institutions and individuals preferred personally to finance the cost of restoring their property. Therefore, they refrained from filing a loss

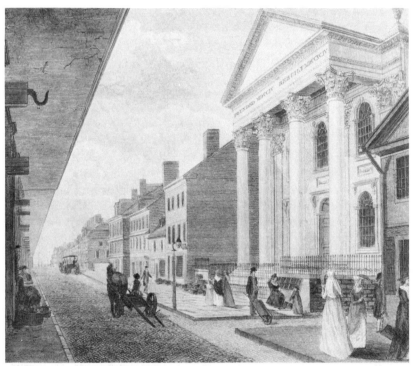

High (Market) Street with the rebuilt First Presbyterian Church on the right and the market on the left. Engraved by William Birch, 1806. *Independence National Historical Park Collection*

schedule with the county commissioners. Some 127 individuals and public buildings reported losses totaling £55,343 17s. 7d. in the city. In the balance of the county there were 673 claimants reporting damages of £155,719 14s.[22]

Some depredations not included in the county commissioners' figures have been obtained. All churches whose congregations were known to be partisans of the American cause experienced extensive damage. This was particularly the case with the four Presbyterian, two Lutheran, the Baptist, and the Dutch Reformed churches. Other churches did not escape unscathed, but were not as extensively damaged. In this category were Saint Paul's Episcopal Church, used as a hospital, and Saint George's Methodist, which became a drilling school for British dragoons.

The First Presbyterian Church (frequently referred to as the Buttonwood Church because of abundance of trees of that species), located at Market and Bank streets, retained the most complete record. The lower floor and gallery were stripped of all pews, all windows were broken, and the walls and floors were desecrated. After the evacuation, a committee was appointed to restore the sanctuary, with a subcommittee of three selected to purchase the necessary materials, employ workmen, and supervise the restoration. Work was begun immediately, but the demand for carpenters and artisans was so great throughout the city that church restoration was delayed. All renovations, which included pews, chandeliers, and whitewashing the entire church, were finished by about 1 March 1780. Cost estimates constantly increased. The final expenditure came to £14,763 3s. 3d. The pewholders subscribed to cover the entire cost.[23]

For the Second Presbyterian Church on Arch Street, repairs were £202 7s. 7d. for pews, chandeliers, and a fence around the graveyard. These may be only the preliminary costs, but, unfortunately, no additional records survived. Zion Lutheran Church lost all its pews, which had originally cost £2,000, exclusive of materials. Other churches experienced similar damages, but costs of restoration are either incomplete or not extant.[24]

Despite the war and all the destruction it brought, the majority of Philadelphians looked forward to resuming a normal life. It would take years to mend the cleavage caused by the bitterness and hatred of the civil conflict. The atrocities committed by both sides had left deep scars that only time would heal. In the meantime, with peace still five years in the future, suspicion and uncertainty dominated the thoughts and actions of many Americans.[25]

The British occupation of Philadelphia and its subsequent withdrawal represented the tragic end of Sir William Howe's colorful career in America. A controversial character, Howe was the subject of numerous vituperative attacks as well as outspoken expressions of affection. A rather harsh epigram was written which, in the eyes of many disgruntled Loyalists and some Englishmen, epitomized his performance in America:

> When mighty Caesar triumphs o'er his foes,
> Three words concise his gallant acts disclose;
> But Howe, more brief, comprises his in one,
> And *vidi,* tells us all that he has done.[26]

The Population of Philadelphia in 1777

No precise figure is available for Philadelphia's population before 1790, when the first federal census was taken. To arrive at the city's population in 1777, this study will use a simplified formula — multiplying the number of dwellings by the estimated average number of residents in each household.

Sources include records in the archives of the city of Philadelphia; county tax assessment ledgers for Philadelphia County, 1774 and 1775; Provincial Tax Duplicate, Philadelphia County, 1775; constable returns for the city, 1775 and 1780. The *Pennsylvania Archives*, (Third Series, vol. 14) was also used, but in all instances revealed the omission of several hundred householders who were not taxable, e.g., widows. Helpful comparative data was found in Benjamin Davies, *Some Account of the City of Philadelphia, 1794.* Joseph Galloway's census of buildings taken for Cornwallis and Howe shortly after the British occupied the city is especially pertinent to this study.

Although the various returns compiled by constables were a source of constant criticism and embarrassment to the Assembly, they remain the basic statistic on occupations and population. They have been used in conjunction with Galloway's census to establish a dwelling count. In 1777, Galloway reported 3,861 houses in the city and 2,196 in the districts of Southwark and Northern Liberties. The tax returns for the year 1775 (the last extant until 1779) recorded 3,693 for the city and 1,231 in the two aforementioned districts and the townships of Moyamensing and Passyunk. The slight increase of 168 in the urban area can be attributed to normal growth, even in wartime. This increase was almost entirely in Dock ward. It is impossible to account for the suburban increase unless, possibly, this is another example of the clerical mistakes found in certain constable's returns.

Galloway's return indicated "Number of Houses" and "Empty Dwelling Houses." If the first designated column is taken to mean the total houses in the city, it would be significantly under the number reported by the constables. This is consistent on a ward-by-ward comparison. Also, it would reduce the city's population by nearly 4,000. This study has accepted the premise that they represent two distinct classifications, namely occupied and unoccupied houses, and has estimated the population of urban and metropolitan Philadelphia on this basis. A contemporary manuscript, "A State of the circumstances of Philadelphia when the British took possession &c," is in the Sackville-Germain Papers, vol. 6, William L. Clements Library, University of Michigan. This document considers them as separate figures showing 5,460 inhabited houses and 597 uninhabited houses (for metropolitan Philadelphia), or a total of 5,957 — note the error of 100 in addition.

Galloway's return was entitled "An account of the Number of Houses and Inhabitants &c in the City of Philadelphia, The Northern Liberties, and district of Southwark" dated Philadelphia 9 October 1777:

		Number of Houses	Empty Dwelling Houses	Stores		Males		Females Generally
				Empty	Occupied	Under 18 Years	Above 18 and Under 60	
Mulberry	Ward	993	114	16	3	887	800	2,293
Upper Delaware	do	225	24	15	22	171	149	422
Lower Delaware	do	110	17	97	1	96	91	229
North	do	400	36	18	12	390	389	1,055
High Street	do	177	16	3	2	135	162	423
South	do	150	6	4	4	135	136	354
Middle	do	362	21	7	5	322	324	817
Chestnut	do	107	11	7	2	98	100	248
Walnut	do	105	5	2	1	94	83	241
Dock	do	880	102	14	10	688	690	1,946
All Houses &c in the City		3,509	352	183	62	3,016	2,924	8,028
Southwark		781	108	9	—	670	590	1,581
Northern Liberties		1,170	137	32	1	1,255	958	2,735

	Number of Houses	Empty Dwelling Houses	Stores		Males		Females Generally
			Empty	Occupied	Under 18 Years	Above 18 and Under 60	
All Houses &c in South^r & the Lib^s	1,951	245	41	1	1,925	1,548	4,316
All Houses &c in the City &c	5,460	597	224	63	4,941	4,472	12,344

On the original, three errors in addition were noted under the column "above 18 years," but they have been corrected in the above table. (Stevens, *Facsimiles*, no. 2085.)

Early historians of Philadelphia have usually accepted a version published in the *Pennsylvania Evening Post* of 14 September 1778. There are differences in the figures for virtually every statistic. (Scharf and Westcott, *History of Philadelphia,* 1:367.)

Most authorities seem to agree that the average household consisted of between 6 and 6.6 residents. In 1794, Davies declared there were 19 people in every three houses. One modern study believes there were 4 persons in the average household (Sam Bass Warner, Jr., *The Private City,* p. 17). Many uncertainties remain, but a study of the tax returns appear to support the figures of 6.3 or 6.4. Unquestionably many householders, especially widows and craftsmen, did not report every lodger, bonded servant, or apprentice, as it would increase their ratables.

Galloway's figures for 1777 seem reasonable and, when multiplied by 6.33 as an average for the number of persons in each dwelling, indicates an urban population of 24,440 and a suburban population of 13,900, or 38,340 in metropolitan Philadelphia. Galloway stated that over ten percent of the houses were vacant, caused by an exodus of Americans when the British army neared the city; however, the tax returns reveal that the norm was under two percent.

The British Army in America in 1777

Some uncertainty exists as to the exact size of the army Howe took to Philadelphia. If a return of this campaign was made, it no longer exists. Many estimates have been made, ranging from 13,000 to 18,000 rank and file, exclusive of officers and staff. In the Colonial Records Office in London is a "Precis of the 1777-1778 Campaign" (C.O. 5/253), a succinct narrative with marginal notations added at a later date. Benefiting from hindsight, some of these notes reflect an after-the-fact knowledge and should be used with caution. Of interest are several returns, included with the precis, for the army in 1777. They include effectives available for duty, sick, wounded, those on command or public employment (such as recruiting in England), and those who were prisoners of the Americans. The return of 20 March 1777 is a starting point to develop a reasonable approximation of the number taken by Howe on the transports.

British (all service branches effectives)	12,374	
(sick, wounded or on command)	3,563	
		15,937
Hessian (effectives)	6,859	
(sick and wounded)	2,346	
		9,205
Total return (excluding prisoners)		25,142

Recruits and reinforcements received
    May and June   <u>3,622</u>
                                           28,764

Provincials   <u>3,000</u>

Total British Army available July 1, 1777*   31,764

The garrison left with Clinton (return dated 7 July 1777) included 5,524 British and Hessian rank and file and 2,782 Provincials, or a garrison of 8,306. In addition, at Rhode Island he had a force of 2,631, or a total of 10,937 at the two posts. On paper this would leave 20,827 troops available to Howe. Of course, this figure is too high, as there was always a significant number of convalescent troops who were unable to accompany their regiments into the field.

Also included with the precis is another set of statistics comprising a group of rough worksheets that used the aforementioned figures as a base and claimed Howe took 19,500 rank and file.

Commissary Wier probably provides the most accurate guide to the size of the invasion force. On 5 September, shortly after landing at Head of Elk, he prepared a return of rations issued. Rations were given to 18,006 rank and file, exclusive of most officers. He also issued rations to 652 women and children. With the officers, this would bring the total close to 20,000. In a letter to John Robinson on 1 September, "He supposes 20,000 men have been victual'd on board the transports at 2/3 allowance . . ." (Daniel Wier, Commissary to the British Army in America, to John Robinson, Secretary to the Lords Commissioners, 1 September 1777, Dreer Collection, Historical Society of Pennsylvania.)

Howe prepared a return on 13 October, after the battles of Germantown and Brandywine, showing a total force of 20,478 rank and file and officers. This figure included 1,790 prisoners of war.

Although Howe had 3,000 Provincial troops available in New York, it is claimed he only took one Loyalist regiment, the Queen's Rangers, to Philadelphia. Wier recorded he issued rations to 328 rank and file of the Queen's Rangers, although Simcoe never claimed this number. Wier also indicates that other Provincial units were with the invasion force — the Second Battalion of the New Jersey Volunteers

---

*An insignificant number of casualties (killed and missing) had been sustained in New Jersey in the second quarter of 1777 which would slightly reduce this figure.

with 76 rank and file, Stuart's black company with 46, and Crow's black company with 10. It appears that Crow's company was recruited while on the march from Head of Elk to Philadelphia. They may have been the black men who boarded the fleet in the Chesapeake.

Notes

Abbreviations used in notes follow. For full citations, see Bibliography.

Amory   Thomas C. Amory, *The Military Services and Public Life of Major General John Sullivan.*

Andre   John Andre, *Major Andre's Journal: Operations of the British Army . . . June 1777 to November 1778.*

Bancroft   New York Public Library, Bancraft Papers.

Baurmeister   Carl Leopold Baurmeister, "Letters of Major Baurmeister during the Philadelphia Campaign, 1777-1778," *Pennsylvania Magazine of History and Biography* 59(1935), 60(1936).

BHP   New York Public Library, British Headquarters Papers.

Boudinot   Historical Society of Pennsylvania, Boudinot Papers.

Burnett   Edmund C. Burnett, ed., *Letters of Members of the Continental Congress.*

Bute-Stuart   Charles Stuart, *A Prime Minister and His Son.*

Carleton   Colonial Williamsburg, Research Department, Carleton Papers.

Clinton   University of Michigan, Clements Library, Clinton Papers.

C.O.	Public Record Office (London), British Headquarters Papers.
Coote	National Army Museum (Woolwich), Coote Papers, Orderly Books, North America.
CR	*Colonial Records of Pennsylvania,* vol. 11.
Dreer	Historical Society of Pennsylvania, Dreer Collection.
Drinker	Elizabeth Drinker, ''Extracts from the Journal of Mrs. Henry Drinker, from Sept. 25, 1777 to July 8, 1778,'' *Pennsylvania Magazine of History and Biography* 13(1889).
Evans	Charles Evans, *American Bibliography.*
Ewald	Johann Ewald, *A Diary of the American War.*
Fisher	Sarah Logan Fisher, ''A Diary of Trifling Occurrences, Philadelphia, 1776-1778,'' Nicholas B. Wainwright, ed., *Pennsylvania Magazine of History and Biography* 82(1958).
Force	Library of Congress, Peter Force Papers.
George-North	George III, *The Correspondence of King George the Third with Lord North from 1768 to 1783.*
Gratz	Historical Society of Pennsylvania, Gratz Collection.
Hale	W. Hale, *Some British Soldiers in America.*
Hamond Accounts	University of Virginia, Tracy McGregor
Hamond Autobiography	Library, Hamond Papers.
Hamond Letters	
Howe-Narrative	William Howe, *The Narrative of Lieut. Gen. Sir William Howe . . . Relative to His Conduct . . . in North America.*
Howe-Orders	William Howe, ''General Sir William Howe's Orders, 1777-1778,'' *Collections of the New York Historical Society for the Year 1883.*
Howe-Orders MSS	University of Michigan, Clements Library, Orderly Book of Sir William

Howe, 27 Jan. 1776-1 May 1778.

HSP   Historical Society of Pennsylvania

LCP   Library Company of Philadelphia

Miller   New York Historical Society, Reed Papers, Diary of John Miller.

Montresor   John Montresor, *The Montresor Journals.*

Morton   Robert Morton, "The Diary of Robert Morton . . . 1777," *Pennsylvania Magazine of History and Biography* 1(1877).

Newcastle   University of Nottingham, Department of Manuscripts, Newcastle Manuscripts.

PA   *Pennsylvania Archives.*

Pa Navy   John W. Jackson, *The Pennsylvania Navy, 1775-1781.*

Parker   Colonial Williamsburg, Research Department, Parker Family Papers.

Papers-Congress   National Archives, Papers of the Continental Congress.

Peebles   Scottish Record Office, General Register House (Edinburgh), Cunningham of Thornton Papers, Journal of Captain John Peebles.

Pemberton   Historical Society of Pennsylvania, Pemberton Papers.

PEP   *Pennsylvania Evening Post.*

PJ   *Pennsylvania Journal.*

PL   *Pennsylvania Ledger.*

PMHB   *Pennsylvania Magazine of History and Biography.*

PP   *Pennsylvania Packet.*

PR   John Almon and John Debrett, eds., *The Parliamentary Register; or History of the Proceedings and Debates of the House of Commons.*

PRO   Public Record Office (London).

Quaker   Haverford College, Quaker Collection.

Robertson   Archibald Robertson, *Archibald Robertson, Lt. General, Royal Engineers: His Diaries and Sketches in America, 1762-1780.*

RPG   *Royal Pennsylvania Gazette.*

Sackville-Germain   University of Michigan, Clements Library, Papers of Lord George Sackville Germain.

S & W Philadelphia   J. Thomas Scharf and Thompson Westcott, *History of Philadelphia, 1609-1884.*

Searle   Ambrose Serle, *The American Journal of Ambrose Serle, Secretary to Lord Howe.*

Seybolt   Robert Francis Seybolt, ''A Contemporary British Account of General Sir William Howe's Military Operations in 1777,'' *Proceedings of the American Antiquarian Society,* n.s. 40(1931).

Simcoe   J.G. Simcoe, *Simcoe's Military Journal.*

Stevens   B.F. Stevens, comp., *Facsimiles of Manuscripts in European Archives Relating to America, 1773-1783.*

Stuart Steven   National Library of Scotland, Stuart Steven Papers.

Sullivan   Historical Society of Pennsylvania, Sergeant Thomas Sullivan's Journal, 1775-78.

Ward   Christopher Ward, *The War of the Revolution.*

Itinerary-Washington   William S. Baker, *Itinerary of General Washington from June 15, 1775 to December 23, 1783.*

Washington Papers   Library of Congress, Washington Papers.

Writings-Washington   George Washington, *The Writings of George Washington from the Original Manuscript Sources, 1745-1799.*

Watson   John F. Watson, *Annals of Philadelphia and Pennsylvania in the Olden Time.*

Watson MSS   Historical Society of Pennsylvania-Library Company of Philadelphia, John Fanning Watson Manuscripts.

Wier   Historical Society of Pennsylvania, Dreer Collection, Wier-Robinson Correspondence.

Chapter I

1. Howe to Germain, 30 Nov. 1776 (Received 30 Dec.), *PR*, 11:361.
2. Serle, pp. 163-57, 190-94, passim; Serle to Lord Dartmouth, 25 Apr. 1777, Stevens, no. 2057.
3. Howe to Germain, 20 Dec. 1776 (Received 23 Feb. 1777), *PR*, 11:369-70.
4. Germain to Howe, 3 Mar. 1777 (Received 8 May), *PR*, 11:394-96; Carleton, vol. 4, no. 423.
5. George III to Lord North, 10 Jan. 1778, *George-North*, 2:117-18.
6. Hamond Autobiography; Hamond Account.
7. *Ibid.*

Chapter II

1. Papers — Congress, reel 66.
2. Congressional Resolution, 28 Aug. 1777, Quaker Collection; *CR*, 11:283-84.
3. *CR*, 11:286-89, passim. The twenty-two prisoners were James, Israel, and John Pemberton; Thomas, Samuel R., and Miers Fisher; Owen Jones, Jr.; Elijah Brown; Thomas Gilpin; Edward Pennington; Thomas Affleck; Thomas Pike; Henry Drinker; Samuel Pleasants; Thomas Wharton, Sr.; John Hunt; Rev. Thomas Coombe; Charles Jervis; William Smith; William Drewit Smith; Charles Eddy; and Phineas Bond. Coombe and Bond were released before the prisoners were transferred to Virginia. John Adams to Mrs. Adams, 8 Sept. 1777, Burnett, 2:486-87.
4. Morton, p. 6; Fisher, p. 449; Drinker, pp. 50-51.
5. Edmund Coty Burnett, *The Continental Congress*, pp. 246-47; Thomas Burke to the governor of North Carolina, 20 Sept. 1777, and Charles Carroll of Carrollton to George Washington, 22 Sept. 1777, Burnett, *Letters*, 2:498-99.
6. James Lovell to Joseph Trumbull, 23 Sept. 1777, Eliphalet Dyer to Joseph Trumbull, 28 Sept. 1777, and Henry Laurens to John Lewis Gervais, 18 Sept. 1777, Burnett, 2:500, 502-3; Adams, Diary, 2:263.
7. *PEP*, 23 Sept. 1777.
8. Drinker, p. 52; Morton, p. 7.
9. Drinker, p. 52.

10. Accounts of British and Hessian officers vary on the time of Cornwallis's departure from Germantown and his arrival in Philadelphia; times of departure range from 8:00 to 9:00 A.M., and his entrance into the city from 10:00 A.M. to noon.

11. Seybolt, p. 83; Montresor, p. 458; Peebles, 26 Sept. 1777, 21.492.4.

12. Bond and Story left the city with the British army in June 1778 and subsequently settled in England. Bond returned to Philadelphia in 1786 as the British consul general.

13. Fisher, p. 450; Jacob Mordecai, "Addenda to Watson's Annals of Philadelphia," *PMHB*, 98:162; Captain Jacob Coats Account of the British in Philadelphia, Watson MSS; Sir George Otto Trevelyan, *The American Revolution*, 3:236; *Rivington's New York Gazette*, 8 Nov. 1777.

14. Morton, pp. 7-8; Fisher, pp. 450-51.

15. James Allen, "Diary," *PMHB*, 9:291; Governor Thomas Wharton's Escape at the British Occupation of Philadelphia, essay read by Charles H. H. Esling, Gratz Collection.

16. Montresor, p. 458; Peebles, 21.492.4; Baurmeister to Jungkenn, [17(?)Oct. 1777] Baurmeister, p. 413; Deborah Logan, "Recollections of the Entry of the British into Philadelphia," Watson MSS.

17. Montresor, p. 458; Howe to Germain, 10 Oct. 1777, *PR*, 11:424-35 (433); Sullivan. Numerous entries in Sergeant Thomas Sullivan's Journal are precise duplications of paragraphs and passages from the official letters of Howe to Germain. It appears Sullivan supplemented his personal observations with these quotations on events he did not personally witness without citing their origin. How he obtained copies of Howe's correspondence can only be conjectured.

There is some question concerning the armament of the batteries. Cornwallis brought six medium twelve-pounders and four Royal howitzers with his column in addition to the normal grenadier battalion complement of light field pieces. Baurmeister claimed the heavier artillery was placed at the northern and southern extremities of the city, with none assigned to the British grenadiers guarding the line west of center city. Another source states two medium twelve-pounders, two 5½-inch howitzers, and four six-pounders of the grenadiers were erected in the bat-

teries; Clinton. The light six-pounders were a normal complement for a British grenadier battalion. The Southwark section of
the peninsula was considered vulnerable to the waspish attacks of
the State navy and Continental ships. To protect this area, the
heavy artillery pieces were moved into the lower batteries. Morton, p. 8; Baurmeister to Jungkenn [17(?) Oct. 1777] Baurmeister, p. 413; *S & W Philadelphia,* 1:352; *Pa Navy,* p. 123.

18. Commodore John Hazelwood had been given command of the
combined Continental and State fleets. Congress and
Washington were aware that the Continental ships would be ineffective operating through and around the chevaux-de-frise. On
the other hand, the shallow draft galleys of the State navy were
designed for this purpose. This fact combined with Hazelwood's
knowledge of the treacherous shoals and currents of the
Delaware made him the perfect choice for overall command.

19. Evidently, no court of inquiry examined Alexander's conduct, although after his escape he appears to have been deliberately
bypassed when he requested an assignment. "Instructions,
Hazelwood to Alexander," 27 Sept. 1777, *PA,* First Series, 5:637.

20. Howe to Germain, 10 Oct. 1777, *PR,* 11:424-35 (433);
Montresor, pp. 459-61; Seybolt, pp. 84-85; Morton, pp. 8-9;
Baurmeister to Jungkenn, [17(?) Oct. 1777] Baurmeister, pp.
413-14; Drinker, p. 53; Parker, 27 Sept. 1777; John Marshall,
The Life of George Washington, 2:320; *Pa Navy,* pp. 124-25; Andre,
p. 53.

21. Joseph Galloway's "account of the Number of Houses and Inhabitants" in Stevens, no. 2085 has a footnote indicating that in
the Lord Dartmouth manuscripts is a duplicate of Galloway's account with the note, "It is computed that about 10,000 Souls
quitted the Town upon the approach of the King's Troops."

22. Foraging and Commissary Papers, 358.8, Stewart Manuscripts,
Glassboro (N. J.) State College; Drinker, p. 53.

23. A demilune was a low earthwork in the form of a crescent. A
ravelin was somewhat similar to a demilune except it was shaped
like an inverted V. Fraises were pointed stakes projecting from
the face of an earthwork or curtain in a horizontal or inclined
position. An abatis was a line of trees or branches, sharpened at
the ends and pointed toward the enemy; it could be termed eighteenth-century barbed wire. The curtain was the plain part of the

290 *With the British Army in Philadelphia*

wall of a fixed fortification connecting bastions, redoubts, or similar defenses; while usually constructed of stone, the field curtain at Philadelphia was earthen.

24. Montresor, in his journal, recorded that 300 men reported on 3 October, but his "Notes and Memoranda" states 200. The latter seems the more likely figure, as the citizenry were reluctant to accept the menial employment of laborers.
25. Montresor, pp. 461-68, passim; Montresor, "Notes and Memoranda," p. 129.
26. Howe to Germain, 10 Oct. 1777, *PR*, 11:424-35 (433).
27. *Howe-Orders*, 1:505-7, passim.
28. *Ibid.*, pp. 506-7; Miller, 28 and 29 Sept. 1777; Morton, pp. 9-11, passim; Mary Pemberton to General Howe, 9 Sept. 1777, Early American Letters, Charles Patterson Van Pelt Library, University of Pennsylvania.
29. Account of Deborah Logan, Watson MSS.
30. Miller, 30 Sept. and 1 Oct. 1777; Andre, p. 54.
31. Some American accounts have claimed that Stirling moved his detachment from Wilmington to Chester. Samuel Smith to Washington, 2 Oct. 1777, and Alexander Spotswood Dandridge to Wayne, 1 Oct. 1777, Washington Papers, reel 44.
32. Howe to Germain, 10 Oct. 1777, *PR*, 11:424-35 (433); Baurmeister to Jungkenn, [17(?) Oct. 1777] Baurmeister, p. 414; *Howe-Orders*, 1:507; *Pa Navy*, pp. 88-89, 131-36.

Chapter III

1. Sometimes incorrectly referred to as Pennybackers, Pennybeckers, Pennibeckers, or Pennibakers.
2. Worthington Chauncy Ford, ed., *Defences of Philadelphia in 1777,* pp. 51-54.
3. During the Revolution, Germantown Road, now Germantown Avenue, was referred to as Skippack Road and, occasionally, Main Street.
4. With General Benjamin Lincoln ordered to join Gates at Saratoga, Wayne was assigned as acting commander of Lincoln's division. Under Wayne's command was his own 1st Pennsylvania Brigade and the 2nd Pennsylvania Brigade, commanded by Lieutenant Colonel William Butler (Colonel Lam-

bert Cadwalader was on parole). John B. Linn and William E. Egle, eds., *Pennsylvania in the War of the Revolution*, 1:294.

5. John Muhlenberg, "Orderly Book," *PMHB*, 35:63; Washington to the president of Congress, 5 Oct. 1777, *Writings-Washington*, 9:308-11.

6. Samuel Kriebel Brecht, ed., *The Genealogical Record of the Schwenkfelder Families*, 2:1441.

7. Sullivan to the President [Weare] of New Hampshire, 25 Oct. 1777, Amory, pp. 57-61; Washington to the president of Congress, 5 Oct. 1777, *Writings-Washington*, 9:308-11.

8. *Ibid.*

9. Modern route 73 at this point is still called Church Road. The Whitemarsh Church is Saint Thomas Episcopal Church.

10. Watson, 2:47. Most modern roads closely follow the path of the colonial roads, although sections of some, especially Skippack Road, have been relocated. However, the changes have not materially affected the total mileage traversed by each column. All locations except Smallwood's route to Church Lane are modern designations and can be followed. Luken's Mill is no longer standing, and modern streets have completely changed the area. Sullivan to the president [Weare] of New Hampshire, 25 Oct. 1777, Amory, pp. 57-61.

11. *Ibid.*

12. "General Orders," 3 Oct. 1777, *Writings-Washington*, 9:308; Andre, p. 57; Charles Cochrane to Andrew Steuart, 19 Oct. 1777, Stuart Steven, MS5375, f36v; Parker, 4 Oct. 1777.

13. Joseph Jackson, *Encyclopedia of Philadelphia*, 1:264. British and Hessian officers called the area below Mt. Airy Beggarstown; Jackson said it was Bebberstown, named for Matthias Bebber. Hazard, in preparing the third volume of Watson's *Annals of Philadelphia* makes the same statement (p. 461). Howe to Germain, 10 Oct. 1777, *PR*, 11:424-35 (433); "Distribution of the British and Foreign Corps, under the Command of his Excellency General Sir William Howe," 8 May 1777, *PR*, vol. 11; Andre, pp. 36-37.

14. Howe to Germain, 10 Oct. 1777, *PR*, 11:424-35 (433).

15. Andre, p. 54; Charles Cochrane to Andrew Steuart, 19 Oct. 1777, Stuart Steven, MS5375, f36v; Baurmeister to Jungkenn [17(?) Oct. 1777] Baurmeister, p. 415; Ewald.

16. *Ibid.*
17. Sullivan to the president [Weare] of New Hampshire, 25 Oct. 1777, Amory, pp. 57-61.
18. *Ibid.;* Howe to Germain, 10 Oct. 1777, *PR,* 11:424-35 (433); Alfred A. Lambdin, "Battle of Germantown," *PMHB,* 1:383; Parker, 4 Oct. 1777.
19. Sullivan to the president [Weare] of New Hampshire, 25 Oct. 1777, Amory, pp. 57-61. Writing three weeks after the battle, Sullivan made several comments that have led to a series of misinterpretations revolving around the employment of Wayne's division. He stated that because "our left wing, which had nearly four miles farther to march than the right, had not arrived. I was obliged to form General Wayne's division on the east of the road." Continuing, he said there was "no evidence being given of General Armstrong's arrival," forcing him to redeploy to the right, a regiment from Wayne's division and one from his division. Several constructions have been placed on these remarks; it has been assumed that Sullivan anticipated that Greene and Armstrong were to make a junction with his left and right. It appears that, not hearing firing on either flank (it was said that the fog muffled the sound of firing), Sullivan feared he might be faced by Howe with a superior force. If he was apprehensive of his situation, why did he continue his almost headlong pursuit of the fleeing light infantry which was obviously only of battalion strength? A more plausible explanation was that Sullivan had expected to hear that Greene and Armstrong were attacking the British on the left and far right in cooperation with his advance down the Germantown Road. To place any other interpretation on Sullivan's observations is to assume that Washington and Sullivan were ignorant of their own battle strategy. Washington did not believe Greene would encounter a British picket until he reached Luken's Mill. This would partially account for the four miles mentioned by Sullivan. Actually, Greene found a British force, of equal strength to that facing Sullivan, at Limekiln Pike and Abington Road, about two miles in advance of Luken's Mill. In the same letter, Sullivan observed that Greene had been given two-thirds of the Continental army for the purpose of attacking the British right and rear and pushing Howe back against the Schuylkill. Clearly this obviated any possible junction of the two columns. Otherwise, we must conclude that Sullivan was totally

unaware of his position or had no knowledge of the topography of the area. Sullivan to the president [Weare] of New Hampshire, 25 Oct. 1777, Amory, pp. 57-61; Lambdin, ''Battle of Germantown,'' *PMHB,* 1:378-79fn; ''General Orders,'' 3 Oct. 1777, *Writings-Washington,* 9:308.

20. Henry B. Dawson, *Battles of the United States by Sea and Land,* 1:328; Wayne to Mrs. Wayne, 6 Oct. 1777, Wayne Papers, HSP.

21. [Frederich Ernest von Munchhausen], ''The Battle of Germantown Described by a Hessian Officer,'' *PMHB,* 16:198.

22. Timothy Pickering to (?), 23 Aug. 1826; Sherman Day, *Historical Collections of the State of Pennsylvania,* pp. 492-94; North Callahan, *Henry Knox,* pp. 120-21. British and Hessian officers were equally puzzled by Washington's decision to waste time and men on Cliveden. As an example, Ewald comments on ''usually so-called 'Clever Washington' attacking the house instead of using a battalion to invest the house, and continuing his advance.'' Ewald.

23. Sullivan; Baurmeister to Jungkenn, [17(?) Oct. 1777] Baurmeister, p. 416; Howe to Germain, 10 Oct. 1777, *PR,* 11:424-35 (433); Lambdin, ''Battle of Germantown,'' *PMHB,* 1:382, 382fn. Lambdin cites Colonel E. Dayton's report in the *Proceedings of the New Jersey Historical Society,* 9:187.

24. This house is still standing at Upsal Street and Germantown Avenue.

25. Sullivan to the president [Weare] of New Hampshire, 25 Oct. 1777, Amory, pp. 57-61; Pickering to (?), 23 Aug. 1826, Day, *Historical Collections,* pp. 492-94.

26. Howe to Germain, 10 Oct. 1777, *PR,* 11:424-35 (433); ''Distribution of the British and Foreign Corps,'' 8 May 1777, *PR,* vol. 11; Andre, pp. 55-56; Sullivan; Baurmeister to Jungkenn, [17(?) Oct. 1777] Baurmeister, p. 416.

27. Marshall, *Life of George Washington,* 2:323-25.

28. Most contemporaries state Greene engaged the British from a half to three-quarters of an hour after Sullivan overran the pickets at Mount Airy. Washington claims three-quarters of an hour; Washington to the president of Congress, 5 Oct. 1777, *Writings-Washington,* 9:308-11. On the other hand, British accounts are somewhat nebulous; Andre says the attack by Greene began ''soon after'' the engagement at Mount Airy; Andre, p. 55. Howe is in agreement with Andre, saying the ''1st light infantry

and pickets . . . were engaged soon after the attack began upon the head of the village." Howe to Germain, 10 Oct. 1777, *PR*, 11:424-35 (433). Sergeant Sullivan said the engagement on the right started at five-thirty and lasted till eight o'clock; Sullivan. Sullivan's claim that the action continued for two and a half hours on the British right is more accurate for the entire battle. It is generally agreed that the two armies were engaged about two and a half hours or two hours and forty minutes. Sullivan, with the 49th Regiment, was an eyewitness on the right.

29. Sullivan; Howe to Germain, 10 Oct. 1777, *PR*, 9:424-35 (433); Andre, pp. 55-56; Sullivan; Lambdin, ''Battle of Germantown,'' pp. 383-86, passim; Douglas Freeman, *George Washington*, 4:512.

30. Watson said that Hessian huts at Germantown ''were constructed of the rails from fences, set up at an angle of 45°, resting on a crossbeam centre; over these were laid straw, and above the straw grass sod — they were close and warm.'' Watson, 2:55. No other American outfit penetrated this deep inside the British lines, except for small parties or individuals who became lost in the fog.

31. Charles Cochrane to Andrew Steuart, 19 Oct. 1777, Steven, MS5375, f36v. (Italics Cochrane's.)

32. Sullivan; Howe to Germain, 10 Oct. 1777, *PR*, 11:424-35 (433).

33. Howe to Germain, 10 Oct. 1777, *PR*, 11:424-35 (433); Sullivan; Andre, p. 56.

34. Sullivan to the president [Weare] of New Hampshire, 25 Oct. 1777, Amory, pp. 57-61.

35. [Munchhausen], ''Battle of Germantown,'' p. 197; Howe to Germain, 10 Oct. 1777, *PR*, 11:424-35 (433).

36. Morton, p. 13.

37. Armstrong mentions coming out—probably out of the heavily wooded area at the head of the upper gorge of Wissahickon Creek. Like Sullivan and Wayne, Armstrong appears to be guilty of overestimating distance. Mystery surrounds the timing of Washington's order; assuming an aide was dispatched to reach Armstrong about 9:00 A.M., he would have left the Billmeyer house no later than 8:30. At that time the outcome of the battle was evident, with Wayne in full retreat and Sullivan pulling back, although Washington may have been unaware of what had happened to Greene. Accepting this as a reasonable premise, it would have brought Armstrong onto the Bethlehem Road (over modern Wissahickon Avenue) in Flourtown. Where his en-

counter with the British took place cannot be ascertained. One explanation could be that Armstrong was confused about the time and that it occurred earlier than he reported. The engagement is not mentioned in any other contemporary account.

38. Watson, 2:50.
39. Parker, 4 Oct. 1777; Hale to his parents, 21 Oct. 1777, Hale, pp. 229-33.
40. Washington to the president of Congress, 5 Oct. 1777, *Writings-Washington*, 9:308-11; Sullivan to the president [Weare] of New Hampshire, 25 Oct. 1777, Amory, pp. 57-61; Brecht, ed., *Genealogical Record*, 2:1441; "Military Operations Near Philadelphia in the Campaign of 1777-78, Describing a Letter from Thomas Paine to Dr. Franklin, May 16, 1778," *PMHB*, 2:288-89.
41. Washington to the president of Congress, 5 Oct. 1777, *Writings-Washington*, 9:308-11.
42. Thomas Rodney to General Rodney, 10 Oct. 1777, Society Collection, HSP; Armstrong to Wharton, 8 Oct. 1777, *PA*, First Series, 5:655-57.
43. Kemble Journal, *Kemble Papers*, 1:137; Sullivan.
44. Montresor, p. 462.

Chapter IV

1. For the American viewpoint and a more detailed account of the actions along the Delaware, see *Pa Navy*, pp. 120-281, passim.
2. Montresor, "Notes and Memoranda," p. 137; Seybolt, p. 90.
3. *Howe-Narrative*, p. 29.
4. Montresor, p. 467; "Notes and Memoranda," p. 130.
5. Montresor, p. 461.
6. Hazelwood to Washington, 10 Oct. 1777, Washington Papers, reel 44. Bradford also mentions this episode; see Bradford to Wharton, 7 Oct. 1777, *PA*, First Series, 5:648-49.
7. Parker, 14 Oct. 1777; Log Books of the *Roebuck, Camilla*, and *Experiment*, Historical Research Section, Department of the Navy.
8. Orderly Book kept by a British Soldier, Oct.-Dec., 1777, RG93, item 24, National Archives; Montresor, pp. 463-68, passim; Joseph Galloway, *Letters to a Nobleman on the Conduct of the War in the Middle Colonies*, p. 78.
9. Robertson, p. 152; Montresor, pp. 464-65; Seybolt, p. 88; Bradford to Wharton, 11 Oct. 1777, *PA*, First Series, 5:663-64; Brad-

ford and Hazelwood to Washington, 11 Oct. 1777, Washington
Papers, reel 44.

10. Howe's return of 13 October 1777 indicates a total of 17,752 rank
and file on the regimental and battalion musters (12,745 British
and 5,007 Hessians), with 15,898 present and fit for duty; the remainder were prisoners of the Americans. Of the present and fit
for duty, 3,302 were listed as sick or wounded. British Headquarters Papers, C.O. 5/253.

11. Kemble Journal, Kemble Papers, 1:139, 142.

12. Montresor, p. 464; "Notes and Memoranda," pp. 129, 130;
"Captain Montresor and the Auditor's Office in London," Appendix VII, Montresor, pp. 534-42; Miller, 17 Oct. 1777; Howe
to Gordon and Crowder, 26 Oct. 1777, Carleton, 6:719.

13. Montresor, pp. 467-69, passim; Ewald.

14. Lord Howe to Stephens (Admiralty Office), 25 Oct. 1777, J.
Almon, *The Remembrancer or Impartial Repository of Public Events,*
5:428-31; Howe to Germain, 25 Oct. 1777 (Received 1 Dec.
1777), *PR,* 11:438-39; Montresor, p. 470.

15. Donop's column numbered about 2,100. (Regretfully in typing
the author's manuscript for the *Pennsylvania Navy,* this figure was
transposed as 1,200.) On 7 May 1777, the Hessian grenadier battalions and the infantry regiment numbered 1,792 rank and file
but on Wier's ration list of 5 September, it had increased to
1,822—possibly because of the arrival of new recruits from
Europe in June. According to Ewald, the jäger corps totaled
nearly 300. A patrol of twenty mounted jägers was left in
Philadelphia. Added to these figures would be the small detachment of British artillerists. The Hessian losses, since landing at
the Head of Elk, had been insignificant; however, if Ewald is correct, the jägers, alone, lost twenty-five or thirty men. Otherwise,
the musters of these elements closely represent the size of
Donop's column. "Distribution of the British and Foreign
Corps," *PR,* vol. 11; Wier, 5 Sept. 1777; Ewald.

16. Some Hessian accounts claim Donop was ordered to delay his attack on Fort Mercer until 23 October, when he could be supported by the fleet. At the same time a detachment of British
grenadiers was to stage a diversionary action by crossing from
Province Island and storming Fort Mifflin. Some credence may
be attached to this claim, inasmuch as the grenadiers were not
ready to board their attack craft until the twenty-third. They were

recalled after the destruction of the *Augusta* and the *Merlin,* the *Vigilant* not being able to come up the back channel because of gale-force winds. Ewald; Lord Howe to Stephens, 25 Oct. 1777, Almon, *Remembrancer,* 5:428-31; Montresor, p. 470; Seybolt, p. 89; Edward J. Lowell, *The Hessians and other German Auxiliaries of Great Britain in the Revolutionary War,* p. 206fn.

17. Ewald; Max von Eelking, *German Allied Troops,* p. 118.
18. Stuart to Lord Bute, 27 Oct. 1777, and Robertson to Lord Bute, 13 Nov. 1777, *Bute-Stuart,* pp. 116-17. The meeting between the lines of Stuart and Lieutenant-Colonel Jeremiah Olney (second in command of Greene's regiment) is found in every account of the battle and varies only in the detail of the conversation and the haughty demeanor of Stuart. *Howe-Narrative,* pp. 28-29.
19. A banquette was a platform built along the inside of the parapet for soldiers to stand on when firing.
20. If Ewald is correct and the officers were carried on guns and not on carriages, it would account for the many unsuccessful attempts to locate the guns in Timber Creek. It is known that Linsing commandeered wagons along the route to Haddonfield. Ewald.
21. Frank H. Stewart, *Notes on Old Gloucester County,* 3:67, 76.
22. Lowell, *Hessians . . . in the Revolutionary War,* p. 208fn; Baurmeister to Jungkenn, 26 Oct. 1777, Baurmeister, p. 35; Ward to Washington, 23 Oct. 1777, Samuel Hazard, *Register of Pennsylvania,* 3:181.
23. Howe to Germain, 22 Oct. 1777 (Received 1 Dec. 1777), *PR,* 11:436-37; Sackville-Germain, 6:95.
24. The major units in Lord Howe's command on the Delaware, in addition to his flagship *Eagle,* were:

Augusta	Captain Francis Reynolds	500 men	64 guns
Somerset	Captain George Curry	500 men	64 guns
Isis	Captain William Cornwallis	350 men	50 guns
Roebuck	Captain Andrew Hamond	280 men	44 guns
Pearl	Captain John Linzee	220 men	32 guns
Liverpool	Captain Henry Bellew	200 men	28 guns
Camilla	Captain Charles Phipps	160 men	28 guns
Merlin	Captain Samuel Reeve	125 men	18 guns
Zebra	Captain John Tollemache	125 men	14 guns
Cornwallis	Lieutenant Johnston	40 men	1 gun
Vigilant	Captain John Henry	150 men	16 guns
Fury	Lieutenant John Botham	—	3 guns

The *Cornwallis* was a galley constructed along lines similar to the Pennsylvania galleys. The *Vigilant* was a converted merchantman armed with sixteen twenty-four-pounders on the starboard side, while the *Fury* was a hulk, also used as a floating battery. Both the *Vigilant* and the *Fury* were ballasted with rock on their port sides. For more details see *Pa Navy*, pp. 446-47, note 70. The Sol Feinstone Collection of the American Philosophical Society has a roster of Lord Howe's command. Also see, Lord Howe to Stephens, 23 Nov. 1777, and Sir William Howe to Germain, 28 Nov. 1777 (Received 7 Jan. 1778), Almon, *Remembrancer,* 5:499-502. Hamond stated that the *Somerset* was a seventy-gun ship, but all lists of Lord Howe's command state that the *Somerset* was a sixty-four-gun ship.

25. Lord Howe to Stephens, 25 Oct. 1777, Almon, *Remembrancer,* 5:428-31; Log Books of the *Roebuck, Camilla, Eagle, Experiment, Solebay* and *Pearl,* Historical Research Section, Department of the Navy; Hamond Autobiography.

26. Log Books of the *Roebuck, Camilla,* and *Eagle,* Historical Research Section, Department of the Navy; Hamond Autobiography.

27. Miller, 23 Oct. 1777; "Extract of a Letter from Hugh Smyth, Esq., Postmaster," 1777, *PA,* First Series, 5:703-04; Statement of J. P. Norris, Watson MSS; "Paine letter to Franklin," *PMHB,* 2:291-92.

28. Howe to Germain, 25 Oct. 1777, *PA,* 11:438-39.

29. Montresor, pp. 470-74, passim; "Notes and Memoranda," pp. 133-34; Seybolt, pp. 90-91.

30. Montresor, pp. 470-74, passim.

31. Montresor, "Notes and Memoranda," p. 134.

32. Howe to Germain, 28 Nov. 1777, *PR,* 11:439-40; Montresor, p. 474.

33. In military nomenclature, a carcase, or carcass, is a hollow shell wrapped with an incendiary material used to set fire to wooden buildings and ships. The two thirty-two-pounders at the pest house battery are believed to have been removed from the *Somerset.*

34. Log Books *Roebuck* and *Camilla,* Historical Research Section, Department of the Navy; Hamond Autobiography.

35. Montresor, pp. 474-77, passim; Parker, 10-15 Oct.; Lord Howe to Stephens, 23 Nov. 1777, Almon, *Remembrancer,* 5:499-501; Log Books *Camilla, Roebuck,* and *Eagle,* Historical Research Section,

Department of the Navy; Seybolt, pp. 90-92, passim; Peebles, 21.492.4; Andre, pp. 62-64, passim.

36. Montresor, pp. 477-78; Parker, 17 Nov. 1777; Andre, p. 64; Ewald.

Chapter V

1. Howe-Orders MSS, 5-11 Oct. 1777, passim.
2. Ewald; Jehu Eyre's Orderly Book, Oct. 11, 1777, NYHS.
3. Charles Cochrane to Andrew Steuart, 19 Oct. 1777, Stuart Steven, MS5375, f38.
4. Walter Hart Blumenthal, *Women Camp Followers of the American Revolution*, pp. 21-54, passim; Wier, 5 Sept. 1777, 13 Dec. 1777; M. Antonia Lynch, *The Old District of Southward in the County of Philadelphia*, p. 114.
5. Howe-Orders MSS, 25 and 28 Sept., 1, 5, 7, 11-14, Oct. 1777.
6. *PL*, 10 and 15 Oct. 1777; *PEP*, 10 and 14 Oct. 1777. Almost all proclamations issued by the British occupation authorities were released as broadsides; most are listed in Evans.
7. Minutes of the Meetings of the Managers of the Pennsylvania Hospital, 29 Sept., 27 Oct., 11 and 26 Nov. 1777, 25 and 27 April, 25 May, 29 June, 25 July, 29 Aug., 26 Sept. 1778, APS.
8.   To Sir William Howe General & Commander in Chief of the Kings Forces in America &c.

The Memorial of the Managers of the Contributions to the Relief and Employment of the Poor in the City of Philadelphia

Respectfully Sheweth

That we have now not less than two hundred helpless and destitute poor under our care and Superintendance who have heretofore been supported by an equal Taxation laid on the inhabitants of the City and Suburbs; but from the late total abolition of all Civil Government these miserable objects of our humanity and Compassion, notwithstanding our utmost exertions in borrowing & begging Money for their relief are likely not only to Suffer all the miseries of the extreme distress but must soon perish thro' the want of the Necessaries of life as we have not more provisions than will keep them three Weeks, nor are we by any means in our power capable of procuring them Articles, there being no police established to which we can apply for that purpose—Under these distressing Circumstances we are induced to apply to the General for such relief for these unhappy People as his Wisdom & Goodness shall think most proper & expedient.

9. Treasurer's Accounts, 1766-80, Corporation of Contributors, Relief of the Poor; Minutes, 1776-78, Alms House Managers;

Minutes, 1774-82, Overseers of the Poor, Philadelphia City Archives.

10. Minutes, 1766-80, Alms House Managers Meetings (including "General State of the Acco^t of the Contributors for the Relief & Employment of the Poor . . . 12th May 1777 to 11th May 1778"). Other principal sources of revenue were "Goods Manufactured & Sold," L697 10s.; lots sold at the Old Almshouse location brought L591 5s., and L440 13s. was borrowed. Major expenses were: provisions, L1069 9s. 4½d.; firewood, L852 9s. 6d.; and manufacturers' wages, L333 4s. 1d. Until their financial position became precarious, the managers employed two weavers to assist in their textile operations.

11. Among the public buildings converted into British hospitals were the First and Second Presbyterian, Old Pine Street, and Scotch Presbyterian (Seceders) churches; Saint Michael's and Zion Lutheran churches; and the German Reformed, Moravian, and Saint Paul's Episcopal churches. Later, during the occupation period, some of these churches were turned into riding stables. The playhouse on South Street and at least one commercial establishment, a sugar refinery, were also used by the British surgeons. *S & W Philadelphia,* 1:359; Mordecai, "Addenda to Watson's Annals of Philadelphia," p. 149; Morton, pp. 15-16; *Writings-Washington,* 9:322, note 75.

12. Abstract of the State of the Forces under Sir William Howe, 13 Oct. 1777, C.O. 5/253. The British sick totalled 1,875 and the wounded 793, while 737 Hessians were sick and 57 were wounded. The small number of Hessian wounded is a further confirmation that few Hessian battalions had been committed to front line action at Brandywine or Germantown—the jägers excepted.

13. Deborah Logan to Alexander Garden, 26 Sept. 1822, *Collections of the Historical Society* [of Pennsylvania], 1:118-21; Letter of Deborah Logan, Watson MSS; David Forman to Washington, 7 Sept. [7 Oct.] 1777, Washington Papers, reel 44.

14. Martin I. J. Griffin, *Stephen Moylan,* p. 62; Robert B. Douglas, ed. and trans., *A French Volunteer of the War of Independence,* p. 47; Washington to Howe, 6 Oct. 1775, *Writings-Washington,* 9:315.

15. Rev. Edward Duffield Neill, "Rev. Jacob Duché," *PMHB,* 2:58-73, passim; Worthington Chauncey Ford, ed., *The Washington-Duché Letters,* pp. 5-37, passim; *Washington at Valley*

Forge, together with the Duché Correspondence, pp. 45-77, passim; Washington to Hopkinson, 21 Nov. 1777, *Writings-Washington,* 10:92-93; [Washington to ?], 16 Oct. 1777, Elizabeth Graeme Ferguson Correspondence; Gratz.

16. Pickering to McLane, 7 Nov. 1777 and 15 Nov. 1777, John Fitzgerald to McLane, 12 Nov. 1777, McLane Papers, NYHS; Miller, 20 and 22 Nov. 1777; Hay to Irvine, 14 Nov. 1777, Irvine Papers, vol. 1, HSP.

17. *PL,* 29 Oct. 1777.

18. Parke to J. Pemberton, 10 Nov. 1777, Pemberton, vol. 30; Clarke to Washington, 18 Nov. 1777, "Letters from Major John Clarke to George Washington," *Historical Society of Pennsylvania Bulletin,* no. 1; Morton, 1:19-20; Fisher, p. 455; Muhlenberg, *Journals,* 3:94,97; *Writings-Washington,* 9:323, note 75.

19. David Griffith to his wife, 13 Nov. 1777, Griffith Papers, Virginia Historical Society; Nathanael Green[e] to (?), 27 Oct. 1777, Bancroft, vol. 2; A Letter brought me by a Spy sent into the City of Philadel^d by order of General Washington (unsigned), 29 Nov. 1777, NYHS; Two unsigned Letters, 17 and 21 Nov. 1777, Washington Papers, reel 45; Morton, p. 19; Fisher, pp. 454, 455; Drinker, pp. 59, 60, 63, 66; Proud to his brother, 1 Dec. 1777, "Letters of Robert Proud," *PMHB,* 34:62; Hay to Irvine, 14 Nov. 1777, Irvine Papers, HSP; B. Rush to J. Searly, 19 Nov. 1777, Conarroe Collection, HSP; Letters of Deborah Logan and Captain Coates, Watson MSS; Ewald; Sir George Otto Trevelyan, *The American Revolution,* 3:278.

20. Minutes of the Monthly Meeting of Friends of Philadelphia, 26 Sept., 31 Oct., 28 Nov. 1777, and Philadelphia Yearly Meeting for Sufferings, Minutes 1775-1785, 20 Nov. 1777 (Monthly Meeting), Department of Records, Society of Friends; Mary Pemberton to Howe, 11 Nov. 1777, Pemberton, vol. 30.

21. Wier to Robinson, 25 Oct. and 29 Nov. 1777, Robinson to Wier, n.d. [Nov. 1777], Wier.

22. Serle, p. 265; Dansey to his mother, 16 Oct. 1777, Dansey Letters, Delaware Historical Society.

23. Phineas Pemberton to James Pemberton, 18 Nov. 1777, T. Parke to J. Pemberton, 10 Nov. 1777, Pemberton; Oswald Seidensticker, *Geschichte der Deutschen Gesellschaft bon Pennsylvanien,* p. 75; Harry W. Pfund, *A History of the German Society of Pennsylvania,* p. 7; Fisher, p. 454; Morton, p. 27; Evans. No. 15347

24. *Ibid.* No. 15337; *PL,* 26 Nov. and 3 Dec. 1777; *PEP,* 25 Nov. 1777.

25. Wier to Howe, 27 Nov. 1777, and Howe to Robinson, 30 Nov. 1777, Carleton.

26. Andrew Elliot to Howe, 27 Oct. 1777, Carleton, vol. 6; Peebles, 21 Nov. 1777; Meteorological Observations taken near Philadelphia, Jan. 1777 to 10 May 1778, APS; Evans, no. 15346.

27. The barracks were built in 1753 during the French and Indian War and occupied an entire square of ground; they were bounded by Green and Tammany streets on the north and south, and Third and Second on the west and east, with the main entrance on Third Street. Barracks were built around three sides of the site, with the officers' quarters in the middle facing Third Street. All were built of brick; the soldiers' barracks were two stories high and the officers' quarters three stories. They accommodated about 3,000 men. The area was known as Campingtown, later shortened to Camptown, although it was actually a part of Northern Liberties.

   The location of the barracks has created some misunderstanding as to the exact position of the defense line. Certain maps have mistakenly put them in the city block bounded by Race, Vine, Fourth, and Third streets, thus placing the redoubts on a general line with Callowhill Street. Accepting this premise would fix the barracks within the city limits. One contemporary map does place the barracks in the city, but extends the redoubts along the slight elevation suggested in this narrative. Watson, 1:415; English Lines Near Philadelphia, 1777, Maps and Plans of the Revolution, 1771-1775, HSP; Lewis Nicola, A Plan of the City and Environs of Philadelphia with works and encampments of His Majesty's Forces . . ., Douglas MacFarlan Papers, HSP; *S & W Philadelphia* (1:361) includes a copy of William Faden's map of 1 Jan. 1779 like MacFarlan's. Although less detailed, Nicola's map appears to be the most accurate.

28. *S & W Philadelphia,* 1:351. Westcott made a thorough study of all available records for the quarters of British military personnel. A current study of newspapers and manuscript sources has revealed the lodgings of a few junior officers. Of the important officers, Sir William Howe resided first at John Cadwalader's house on Second, below Spruce Street, and then moved to Market between Fifth and Sixth — later the residence of Washington when presi-

dent. Lord Howe was on the north side of Chestnut between Fourth and Fifth. Knyphausen took over the Cadwalader house vacated by Howe. Cornwallis lived at Peter Reeve's house on Second and, later, at Second and Spruce. Sir William Erskine resided in the house of Dr. Samuel Jackson, on Vine below Second Street. Franklin's house, in a court off Market between Third and Fourth, was occupied by Andre.

The main town guardhouse was located on Market between Front and Second. Wier's office was on Front Street, while his staff occupied Thomas Wharton, Sr.'s stores on Carpenters' Wharf (just north of Walnut Street). A contemporary description by one of Wier's commissaries states there were "two detached Buildings. The one on the North Side having Six Rooms on the Ground floor, with as many on the first [second] floor beside the same number of Garretts for Bread &c &c on the South Side I had four Rooms, which I turned into two Stores." Captain Benjamin C. Payne, deputy barrack master in charge at Philadelphia, had his office on Front near Chestnut, and Captain Edward Madden, the town major, was on Arch Street.

A List of the General and Staff Officers of the Several Regiments serving in North-America, Scottish Register's Office, G. D. 2/229; "Wharton's Storehouses occupied by the British Commissary Department, 1777-78," *PMHB*, 17:371; *Writings-Washington*, 9:323, note 75; unsigned letters dated 17 and 21 Nov. 1777, Washington Papers, reel 45; A Letter brought to me by a Spy sent into the City of Philadel^d by order of General Washington (unsigned), NYHS; Howe-Orders MSS, 28 Oct.-28 Nov. 1777, passim; Orderly Book Kept by a British Soldier, 2 Nov. 1777, Revolutionary War Records, RG 93, item 24, National Archives; Mordecai, "Addenda," p. 169; Minutes Meeting of Directors of Philadelphia Contributionship, 8 Nov. and 2 Dec. 1777.

29. Kitty Livingston to Mr. and Mrs. John Jay, 21 Nov. 1777, American Revolution Papers, vol. 2, Bancroft; Nathanael Green[e], 27 Oct. 1777, Military and Political Papers, vol. 2, Bancroft.
30. Morton, p. 23.
31. Proclamations against depredations, 7 Nov. 1777, Mackenzie Papers, Clements Library, University of Michigan; *PL*, 12, 19 and 26 Nov., 3 and 27 Dec. 1777, 21, 25 and 28 Feb. 1778; *PEP*,

8 Nov., 27 and 30 Dec. 1777, 3 and 6 Jan. 1778; Evans, No. 15329.

32. Howe-Orders MSS, 28 Oct.-28 Nov. 1777, passim; Orderly Book kept by a British Soldier, 31 Oct.-28 Nov. 1777, passim.

33. Memoranda of Fact: Deposition of William McIlhening, Watson MSS.

34. *PL*, 8, 15, 22, and 29 Oct., 5, 12, 19 and 26 Nov., 3 and 24 Dec. 1777; *PEP*, 14 Oct. 1777; Evans, No. 15327.

35. *PL*, 22 and 29 Oct., 5, 12 and 19 Nov. 1777; Mackenzie to Clifton, 7 Oct. 1777, Military and Political Papers, vol. 2, Bancroft; Howe to Mackenzie [Dec. 1777], BHP; *Howe-Narrative*, pp. 51-53; Martin I. Griffin, *Catholics and the American Revolution*, 2:172; Caleb Jones, *Orderly Book . . . June 18, 1778 to October 12, 1778*, pp. 6-7.

36. *PEP*, 11 Oct. 1777; *PL*, 10, 22 and 29 Oct., 5, 12, 19 and 26 Nov. 1777; Howe-Orders MSS, 29 Oct. 1777.

37. *PL*, 15 and 22 Oct., 10, 24 and 31 Dec. 1777; Evans, No. 15342 and No. 15345.

38. John Eyres Orderly Book, 13 and 24 Oct., 1 and 15 Nov. 1777, NYHS; American Orderly Books, 11 and 13 Nov. 1777, Revolutionary War Records, 853, reel 3, National Archives; T. Pickering to McLane, 17 Nov. 1777, McLane Papers, NYHS. Pickering advised McLane that only the major general of the day could grant a pass to enter Philadelphia. Wier distributed an attractive offer to farmers for cattle, sheep, and forage to be delivered at designated locations in the city to "be paid for in Gold and Silver." *PL*, 15 and 22 Oct. 1777; Evans, No. 15338.

39. Howe-Orders MSS, 15 Nov. 1777; Parker, 22 Nov. 1777, 11 Dec. 1777; Peebles, 25 Nov. 1777, 21.492.4; Ewald.

40. *PL*, 22 Oct., 3, 12, 19 and 26 Nov. 1777; *PEP*, 21 Oct. 1777.

41. William Cunningham served as provost of the British prison facilities in New York and Philadelphia. His name ranks in infamy for his abuse and harsh treatment of American prisoners.

42. Minutes, Society for the Relief of Poor and Distressed Masters of Ships, Their Widows and Children HSP, Philadelphia Masonic Temple, Minutes Royal Arch Lodge No. 3, 1767-1788; Norris Barratt and Julius F. Sachse, comp., *Freemasonry in Pennsylvania 1727-1907*, 1:290-94; Mahlon Addis, *200 Years of Ancient York Masonry in the Western World 1758-1958*, pp. 14-21, passim.

43. *PL*, 20 Dec. 1777; *S & W Philadelphia*, 3:2065. Scharf and

Westcott confirm a lodge at this location, but stated it was attended principally by enlisted men. The newspaper insertion contradicts this assumption, unless the brethren of lodges numbers 3 and 4 permitted the soldiers use of their lodge room.

44. *PEP,* 1 Nov. 1777.
45. *PL,* 18 Oct., 1, 8 and 17 Nov. 1777.
46. *PL,* 10 and 15 Oct., 3, 12, 19 and 26 Nov. 1777.
47. *PEP,* 29 Nov. 1777; *Poor Will's Almanack,* John Pemberton's copy, manuscript notation, 22 Nov. 1777, LCP; Miller, 23 Nov. 1777.
48. Miller, 22 and 23 Nov. 1777; Morton, p. 30; Deborah Logan's letter, Watson MSS; Drinker, p. 66; Joseph Reed to President Thomas Wharton, 30 Nov. 1777, William B. Reed, *Life and Correspondence of Joseph Reed,* pp. 340-41.
49. Peebles, 23, 24, 25 and 26 Nov. 1777, 21.492.4; Morton, pp. 31-32; Parker to Steuart, 23 and 24 Nov. 1777, Parker; Baurmeister to Jungkenn, 1 Dec. 1777, Baurmeister, pp. 38-39; Evans, No. 15348.
50. Parker to Steuart, 29 Nov. 1777, Parker; Peebles, 27 Nov. 1777; *List of General and Staff Officers . . . in North America,* Scottish Record Office, G.D. 2/229.
51. Howe to Germain, 30 Nov. 1777 (Received 7 Jan. 1778), *PR,* 11:442-43; Carleton, 7:113.

Chapter VI

1. Howe to Germain, 13 Dec. 1777 (Received 18 Jan. 1778), *PR,* 11:354-449 (448).
2. This hill was designated Militia Hill because the Pennsylvania militia was stationed there. It is now a part of Fort Washington State Park. The major gap through the American line separated Militia Hill from the extreme right of the Continental line. In 1777, as today, two roads—Skippack Pike and Bethlehem Road (Pike)—were located in the pass. The extreme left of the Continental brigades rested on Limekiln Pike, above Fitzwatertown. Beyond this position, extending for over a half mile to Susquehanna Road, was the Maryland militia, later to be joined by Morgan's riflemen. The intervening spaces between the militia wings and the Continental brigades were covered by the dragoons.
3. Howe-Orders MSS, 20 Nov. 1777; Orderly Book kept by a

British Soldier, 20 Nov. 1777, Revolutionary War Records, RG93, item 24, National Archives; Clark to Washington, 29 Nov. 1777, Washington Papers, reel 45; Sir James Murray to Mrs. Smyth, 29 Nov. 1777, Murray, *Letters from America 1773 to 1780 . . .* , pp. 49-51.

4. She is sometimes (incorrectly) referred to as Darrah or Darrach.

5. *PP,* 18 Feb. 1777. This house became 177 South Second Street and was called the Loxley House.

6. Mrs. Thomas Newton of Norfolk, Virginia, said, ''In my childhood the story was frequently related to me by the daughter [Ann] of Lydia Darragh.'' This would have happened in the 1830s. Mrs. Newton, the grandniece of Ann, was born in 1824. In 1827, Robert Walsh published a slightly different version which had been furnished him by unnamed friends of Mrs. Darragh. Watson obtained additional data from an elderly friend of Lydia. The latter two accounts add nothing of significance, but serve to verify the basic Darragh story.

7. Henry Darrach, *Lydia Darragh: One of the Heroines of the Revolution,* pp. 379-403, passim; Margaret D. Rex, ''The Story of Lydia Darrah,'' *Historical Sketches of the Historical Society of Montgomery County,* 1:90-93.

8. Clark to Washington, 1 Dec. 1777, ''Letters from Major John Clark, Jr., to General Washington during the occupation of Philadelphia,'' *Historical Society of Pennsylvania Bulletin,* no. 1, pp. 20-21; Craig to Washington, 2 and 3 Dec. 1777, McLane to Washington, 3 Dec. 1777, and Robert Smith to Washington, 2 Dec. 1777, Washington Papers, reel 45.

9. W.D.————to Washington, 4 Dec. 1777, Washington Papers, reel 45.

10. J.J. Boudinot, ed., *The Life and Public Services, Addresses, and Letters of Elias Boudinot,* 1:68-69. It has been suggested that Boudinot omitted names to protect his informants; however, as this incident was recorded in his reminiscences years after the war ended, secrecy was unnecessary.

11. Parker to Steuart, 4 Dec. 1777, Parker; Howe-Orders MSS, 4 Dec. 1777; Robertson, p. 158; Baurmeister to Jungkenn, 16 Dec. 1777, Baurmeister, p. 41.

12. Order of Battle [4-5 Dec. 1777], Washington to Congress, 10 Dec. 1777, *Washington-Writings,* 10:138-39. Fitzpatrick has ascribed the dates 4 and 5 December to the order of battle. Ac-

companying the instructions were two diagrams of "Line of Battle" prepared by Washington which suggest that diagram one was the order of battle before the arrival of Howe at Chestnut Hill. The text of this draft emphasizes the deployment of the dragoons and militia to protect the flanks. These instructions are incorporated in diagram two and were probably made when Washington had his first glimpse of the British position at Chestnut Hill.

13. Baurmeister to Jungkenn, 16 Dec. 1777, Baurmeister, p. 42; Howe-Orders MSS, 3 and 4 Dec. 1777.

14. *Ibid.* The hospitals remained crowded; however, there were about two thousand convalescents on duty with their respective units. It appears that the number of sick and wounded had remained constant during the first two months of the occupation. On 13 October, Howe reported 1,812 sick and 850 wounded in Philadelphia. While no separate return can be located for December, a return of the entire army (New York, Newport, and Philadelphia) for 14 December 1777 records 4,279 sick and wounded, not including Loyalist troops. Abstract of the State of the Forces under Sir William Howe, C.O. 5/253.

15. Meteorological observations taken near Philadelphia, Jan. 1777 to 10 May 1778, APS (believed kept by Phineas Pemberton at his country estate). Pemberton's notes have been used throughout the narrative for most meteorological statements.

16. Robertson, p. 158; Howe-Orders MSS, 3 and 4 Dec. 1777; Baurmeister to Jungkenn, 16 Dec. 1777, Baurmeister, p. 41. Ewald provides the most detailed account of the British army's march, although in some details at variance with other eyewitness versions. Cornwallis had two battalions of light infantry, British grenadiers, Hessian grenadiers, the 4th Brigade of British infantry, two squadrons of the 16th Dragoons, and the Hessian chasseurs. The vanguard carried two medium twelve-pounders and two howitzers — probably in addition to the battalion field pieces.

17. Baurmeister, pp. 41-42; Howe-Orders MSS, 3 and 4 Dec. 1777; Robertson, pp. 158-59. The main column included the 1st and 3rd Brigades of British infantry, two battalions of British guards, the Du Corps (Lieb) and Donop regiments, the 5th 7th, 26th, and 27th British infantry regiments, the 2nd Battalion of the 71st Regiment, one squadron of the 16th Dragoons, three squadrons

of the 17th Dragoons, and the mounted jägers. Hospital, rum, and empty wagons were with the train, and the Queen's Rangers were to cover their right flank. Four light twelve-pounders were carried by Knyphausen.

18. Robertson, p. 159; Andre, p. 67; E. Boudinot to (?), 9 Dec. 1777, John Armstrong to Thomas Wharton, 7 Dec. 1777, Reed Papers, NYHS; Miller, 5 Dec. 1777; Ewald; "Diary of Surgeon Albigence Waldo, of the Connecticut Line," *PMHB,* 21:303; Sullivan, 4 Dec. 1777; Howe to Germain, 13 Dec. 1777, *PR,* 11:354-449 (448); Baurmeister to Jungkenn, 16 Dec. 1777, Baurmeister, p. 42.

19. Howe to Germain, 13 Dec. 1777, *PR,* 11:354-449 (448); Robertson, p. 159; Parker to Steuart, 5 Dec. 1777, Parker; Andre, pp. 67-68.

20. Montresor, p. 480.

21. Sullivan, 5 Dec. 1777; Parker to Steuart, 5 Dec. 1777, Parker; Andre, p. 68. Andre seems confused in his dating of the activities of this expedition. Henry Dearborn, *Revolutionary War Journals of Henry Dearborn 1775-1783,* pp. 115-16; Robertson, p. 160; Reed to Wharton, 10 Dec. 1777, William B. Reed, *The Life and Correspondence of Joseph Reed,* 1:350; E. Boudinot to (?), 9 Dec. 1777, John Armstrong to Wharton, 7 Dec. 1777, Reed Papers, NYHS; William J. Buck, "The Battle of Edge Hill," *Historical Sketches, Historical Society, Montgomery County,* 2:216.

22. Howe to Germain, 13 Dec. 1777, *PR,* 11:354-449; Robertson, p. 160; Baurmeister to Jungkenn, 16 Dec. 1777, Baurmeister, pp. 42-43.

23. Dearborn, *Revolutionary War Journals,* p. 116; Waldo, "Diary," *PMHB,* 21:303.

24. Andre, pp. 68-69; Robertson, p. 160; Baurmeister to Jungkenn, 16 Dec. 1777, Baurmeister, pp. 43-44; Ewald; Simcoe, pp. 30-31; Buck, "The Battle of Edge Hill," pp. 214-33, passim. Buck details the many relics of these engagements found between the ridge at Edge Hill and the heights above Fitzwatertown. Howe to Germain, 13 Dec. 1777, *PR,* 11:354-449.

25. Howe to Germain, 13 Dec. 1777, *PR,* 11:354-449.

26. Morton, pp. 34-35; Miller, 8 Dec. 1777.

27. Robertson, p. 161.

28. Return of the Killed, Wounded and Missing in the different Skirmishes from 4th to 8th Dec. 1778, Sackville-Germain, vol. 6.

Chapter VII

1. *PEP,* 1 Apr. 1778; *RPG,* 3 Apr. 1778; Danske Dandridge, *American Prisoners of the Revolution,* pp. 33-47, passim; Binns, *Recollections of the Life of John Binns,* pp. 147-48; Charles E. Green, "An Infamous Brother," *California Freemason,* 16:132-33; Minutes, Royal Arch Lodge No. 3, 1767-88, Masonic Temple, Philadelphia; "Confession and last dying words of Capt. William Cunningham," The American Apollo, 1:68-69.
2. Etting Collection, HSP; *S & W Philadelphia,* 3:1827.
3. Samuel Howell to Howe, 16 Oct. 1777, HSP; Stephen Collins to Galloway, 23 May 1778, Thompson Papers, HSP.
4. Unsigned deposition taken before General Potter, 17 Nov. 1777, Washington Papers, reel 45; Clark to Washington, 17 and 24 Nov. 1777, *Historical Society of Pennsylvania Bulletin,* no. 1, pp. 10, 18-19; Watson, 2:300-1; Waldo, "Diary," *PMHB,* 21:309.
5. David Griffith to his wife, 13 Nov. 1777, Griffith Papers, Virginia Historical Society; Deposition taken before General Potter, 17 Nov. 1777, Cloyd and Dewees to Washington, 17 Nov. 1777, Washington Papers, reel 45; Clark to Washington, 17 Nov. 1777, *Historical Society of Pennsylvania Bulletin,* no. 1, p. 10; Deposition of Joseph Cloyd and William Dewees to Howe, 15 Nov. 1777, BHP; Pelatiah Webster to any officer of General Washington's Army, 19 Nov. 1777, Letters to Washington, box 559, p. 370; Force.
6. Charles Croxall to Washington, 20 Nov. 1777, Washington Papers; Fowles for Prisoners and other American officers confined to the State House to Sir William Howe, 17 Nov. 1777, BHP, no. 749; Matthews to J. Simon, 18 Nov. 1777, General Revolution Papers, Gratz; John Cordell to Daniel Clymer, 6 Jan. 1778, John Poulson to Clymer, 6 Jan. 1778, John Brewer to (?), 11 Jan. 1778, John LeFaver to Clymer, 29 Jan. 1778, Thomas Bradford Papers, vol. 1, HSP.
7. Summary of Elias Boudinot meeting with Hugh Ferguson, British Commissary of Prisoners and other officers, 1 Dec. 1777, Boudinot, vol. 1, p. 32; Ferguson to Boudinot, 2 Dec. 1777, English Military, vol. 1, Dreer; Howe to Washington, 26 Nov. 1777, BHP, no. 761.
8. Thomas Hartley to Atlee, 17 Dec. 1777, *Pennsylvania Miscellany,* vol. 10, Library of Congress; Joshua Loring's Long Account, 27

Aug. 1776-3 Sept. 1782, A.O. 1/bundle 494 no. 98, Audit Office Records, PRO.

9. "General Charles Grey Orderly Book, 23 Feb. 1778 to 30 May 1778," (?) May 1778, Rutgers University; Wayne Papers, HSP.

10. The adventures of Persifor Frazer can be traced in greater detail in the following sources: [Joseph S. Harris], *The Collateral Ancestry of Stephen Harris and Marianne Smith,* pp. 42-47, 113-23, passim; Persifor Frazer, *General Persifor Frazer: A Memoir Compiled Principally from His Own Papers,* pp. 161-81, 235-37, 403-4, passim. Lieutenant Colonel R.H. Harrison, aide to Washington, on 5 November requested Frazer to compile a list of American officers taken prisoner since Howe landed at Head of Elk. While this list, if compiled, is missing, Frazer did prepare a summary of the number of prisoners in each room at the new gaol, showing a total of 553. This was probably compiled soon after the date of Harrison's letter. Persifor Frazer, "Lieutenant Colonel Persifor Frazer, of Pennsylvania, did not Break his Parole," *PMHB,* 20:73-80; "Some Extracts from the Papers of General Persifor Frazer," *PMHB,* 31:129-32, passim.

11. Franklin to Boudinot, 28 May 1778, Thomas Bradford Papers, 1:42, 46, HSP; Franklin to Bradford, 15 June 1778.

12. McKinly to his wife, 11 Oct. 1777 to 14 Aug. 1778, McKinly Papers, Delaware Historical Society; Cloyd and Dewees to Howe, 15 Nov. 1777, BHP; Cloyd and Dewees to Washington, 17 Nov. 1777, Washington Papers, reel 45.

13. "Two rosters of Hessian soldiers employed by farmers," Richard Peters to Atlee, 14 Nov. 1777, Boudinot to Atlee, 24 Dec. 1777, Atlee to Peters, 14 May 1778, Force series 9; Deposition of Myer Hart, Boudinot, 1:104.

14. Frazer to Washington, 9 Oct. 1777, Washington Papers, reel 44; Washington to Frazer, 4 Nov. 1777, *Writings-Washington,* pp. 6-7.

15. Washington to Howe, 4 Nov. 1777, *Writings-Washington,* pp. 1-2; Boudinot to Washington, 13 Oct. 1777, BHP, no. 747.

16. Elias Boudinot, ed., *Journal of Historical Recollections of American Events during the Revolutionary War,* p. 56; Loring to Boudinot, 15 Nov. 1777, Gratz, Foreign Officers and Loyalists.

17. Howe to Washington, 6 Nov. 1777, Washington Papers, reel 45; Washington to Howe, 14 Nov. 1777, *Writings-Washington,* 10:64-66.

18. Howe to Washington, 24 Nov. 1777, Force.

19. Howe to Washington, 26 Nov. 1777, BHP, no. 761; Washington to the president of Congress, 23 Nov. 1777, Washington to Howe, 28 Nov. 1777, *Writings-Washington*, 10:97-100, 118-19.

20. Orderly Book Kept by a British Soldier, 17 Nov. 1777, National Archives, RG93, item 24.

21. Ferguson to Boudinot, 2 Dec. 1777, Dreer, English Military Papers, vol. 1; Summary of Meeting, 1 Dec. 1777, Boudinot, 1:32; H. Hugh Ferguson, "A General Return of Prisoners," 10 Jan. 1778, Force Series 7; Howe-Orders MSS, 14 Dec. 1777.

22. Joshua Loring's Long Account, 27 Aug. 1776-3Sept. 1782, A.O. 1/bundle 494 no. 98, Audit Office Records, PRO.

23. Nourse to Wharton, 22 Dec. 1777, *PA*, First Series, 6:127.

24. Boudinot to Ferguson, 10 Jan. 1778, Washington Papers, reel 46.

25. Howe to Washington, 19 Jan. 1778, Washington Papers, reel 46; Washington to Howe, 30 Jan. 1778, *Writings-Washington*, 10:408-09.

26. Washington to Howe, 10 Feb. 1778, *Writings-Washington*, pp. 444-45; Howe to Washington, 5 and 14 Feb. 1778, Washington Papers, reel 47; Howe to Washington, 21 Feb. 1778, BHP, no. 959.

27. Howe to Washington, 21 Feb. 1778, BHP, no. 959.

28. Declaration of Thomas Franklin, 16 Feb. 1778, BHP, no. 944.

29. Deposition of Joseph Simon, 3 Mar. 1778, and Deposition of Myers Hart, 19 Mar. 1778, Boudinot, 1:94-96, 104. Hart's statement closely parallels Simon's, but he added that prisoners were allowed to work for inhabitants at one dollar per day.

30. Joseph Simon to David Franks, 26 Mar. 1778, Pennsylvania Counties, HSP. The account was settled on 11 June. Simon furnished several hundred thousand provision rations, thousands of cords of wood and varying quantities of candles, vinegar, salt, tobacco, soap, shoes, brooms, pails, buckets, and 200 bundles of straw. He also provided the care of doctors and female nurses. His expenditures also list such macabre items as coffins and the service of grave diggers. The prisoners were in gaols at Lancaster, Lebanon, Hanover, Reading, York, Carlisle, Middletown in Pennsylvania, and Hagerstown, Frederick, and Sharpsburg in Maryland.

31. Boudinot to Atlee, 7 Jan. 1778, Force, series 9; Howe to Washington, 8 Jan. 1778, BHP, no. 850; Ferguson to Boudinot, 16 Jan. 1778, Foreign Officers, Gratz; Receipts for provisions,

cattle, etc., 1, 20, and 23 Apr. 1778, Bradford Papers, 1:26, 30, 34, HSP; Boudinot to Peters, 1 Jan. 1778, Papers-Congress, reel 91.

32. Clymer Manuscripts, p. 44, HSP; Boudinot to Bradford, 21 Jan. 1778, Franklin to Bradford, 24 Jan., 11 and 25 Apr., 7, 9, 12, 14, and 25 May, 5 and 15 June 1778, Robert Haughey to Ferguson, 12 Mar. 1778, Bradford Papers, 1:11-46, passim; HSP; Haughey to Boudinot, 3 Feb. 1778, Boudinot to Robertson, 15 Feb. 1778, Boudinot, 1:81, 84; Franklin to Boudinot, 24 Feb. 1778, Boudinot Papers, NYHS; Bradford to (?), 11 Feb. 1778, Washington Papers, reel 47; Peebles, 21.492-4.

33. Franklin to Boudinot, 24 Feb. 1778, Boudinot Papers, NYHS.

34. Only English guards were assigned to the gaol and prisoner hospitals; with the grenadiers they seemed to have drawn this assignment more than any other battalion. Because of the difficulties of communication, the Hessians were never ordered on city patrol or prison guard duty. General Orders of the Army in North America under General Howe, 3 Feb. 1778, Royal Artillery Library, Woolwich.

35. "General Orders . . . Howe," 1 and 3 Feb. 1778; Coote, 31 Jan. 1778, MS6912/14/38; Howe-Orders MSS, 31 Jan., 1 and 3 Feb. 1778.

36. Boudinot to Mrs. Ferguson, 24 Mar. 1778, Elizabeth Graeme Ferguson Correspondence, Gratz; Graeme Park is still standing and in excellent condition near Hatboro, Pennsylvania.

37. R. L. Hooper to Boudinot, 6 and 21 Feb. 1778, Boudinot, 1:83, 89.

38. Hooper to Boudinot, 23 Mar. 1778, Boudinot; Boudinot to Bradford, 13 Mar. 1778, Bradford Papers, 1:22; Atlee to Boudinot, 13 Mar. 1778, Boudinot Papers, NYHS; Deposition of Sgt. George Thompson, 63rd Regiment, 16 Feb. 1778, BHP, no. 945; Deposition of Thomas Wileman, 17th Dragoons, 18 Feb. 1778, BHP, no. 948; Gibson to Washington, 24 Mar. 1778, Washington Papers, reel 48; Peebles, 20 Apr. 1778, 21.492.4; Baurmeister to Jungkenn, 18 Apr. 1778, Baurmeister, p. 70.

39. Extract of a Report from Mr. Thomas Sandford, Quartermaster to the Brigade of Guards, Jan. 1778, Washington Papers, reel 47; Washington to the Board of War, 26 and 27 Jan. 1778, *Writings-Washington,* 10:351-52, 355-56.

40. Boudinot to Gates, 10 Mar. 1778, Papers-Congress, reel 91.
41. Howe to Washington, 10 Mar. 1778, Washington Papers, reel 47; Howe to Washington, 19 Mar. 1778, Washington Papers, reel 48; Howe to Washington, 2 and 15 Mar. 1778, BHP; Washington to Howe, 9, 12, and 22 Mar. 1778, *Writings-Washington,* 11:55, 70-71, 129-31.
42. Washington to Congress, 12 Mar. 1778, *Writings-Washington,* pp. 72-73.
43. Boudinot, ed., *The Life . . . of Elias Boudinot,* 1:75-77, passim; Laurens to Duane, 18 Apr. 1778, Burnett, 3:171-72.
44. Boudinot, ed., *The Life . . . of Elias Boudinot,* 1:75-82; ''Colonel Elias Boudinot's Notes on Two Conferences held by the American and British Commissioners to settle a General Cartel for the Exchange of Prisoners of War, 1778,'' *PMHB,* 24:291-305; Washington to Howe, 29 Mar. 1778, Washington to American Commissioners, 1 and 4 Apr. 1778, Washington to the president of Congress, 4 Apr. 1778, *Writings-Washington,* 11:173, 197-98, 212-13, 216-19; Howe to Washington, 2 Mar., and 2 Apr. 1778, Howe to Commissioners, 5 Mar. 1778, Memorandum, summary of issues to be considered, unsigned and undated, British Commissioners to Howe, 11 Apr. 1778, American Commissioners to the British representatives, 10 Apr. 1778, BHP; In Congress, 30 Mar. 1778, British Commissioners to American Commissioners, 1 Apr. 1778, Grayson to British Commissioners, 2 Apr. 1778, Howe to Washington, 3 Apr. 1778, American Commissioners to Washington, 4 Apr. 1778, Washington to Commissioners, 4 Apr. 1778, Commissioners to Washington, 11 Apr. 1778, Rough notes on proposed cartel, n.d., Congressional Resolve approving intent of cartel, 21 Apr. 1778, Washington Papers, reel 48; A draft of the ''Treaty and Convention,'' Apr. 1778, Boudinot; Almon *(Remembrancer,* 6:315-22) has a detailed summary with correspondence on the cartel; Howe to Commissioners, 5 Mar. 1778, Carleton.
45. Washington Papers, reel 49; *Writings-Washington,* 11:441.
46. Clinton to Washington, 3 June 1778, BHP, no. 1205.
47. *Journal of the American Congress* 1774-88, 11:366; Boudinot to his wife, 11 June 1778, Boudinot Collection, Princeton University Library; Agreement signed by Joshua Loring and Witnessed by John Beatty and Hugh Ferguson, British Commissary, 9 June

1778, 9 June 1778, Force, series 7; Washington to Clinton, 6 June 1778, *Writings-Washington,* 12:25; [A. Hamilton's] Declaration of Prisoners, [May 1778], *Writings-Washington,* 11:502-3.

48. Memorandum of an Agreement of Exchange of Prisoners made this Day [6 June 1778], Force, series 7. Boudinot had agreed to act as commissary until Beatty could assume full responsibility for the prisoners.

49. Boudinot to Hooper, 10 June 1778, Hooper to Boudinot, 13 June 1778, Boudinot, 2:27, 32.

50. Clinton's Orderly Book, 16 June 1778, Clements Library, University of Michigan; Conditions in city, unsigned, sent by P. Dickinson to Washington, Washington Papers, reel 49. Dickinson received the latter from General Maxwell on 1 June 1778, but it is more relevant to the evacuation.

51. Loring to Boudinot, 17 June 1778, Boudinot, ed., *The Life . . . of Elias Boudinot,* 1:133-34; Boudinot to Robertson, 17 June 1778, Force series 7.

52. Arnold to Bradford, 20 June 1778, Gratz; Franklin to Bradford, 4 Aug. 1778, Bradford Papers, 1:63, HSP; Beatty to Atlee, 30 June 1778, Force series 9.

53. [List of Prisoners at Philadelphia taken to Long Island, June 1778], [Prisoners on Long Island that were at Philadelphia, 25 Dec. 1779], [Estimate-partial-cost care of Prisoners in Philadelphia], Papers-Congress, reel 159; Proposition for exchange by General Phillips, 4 Nov. 1780, Phillips to American negotiators, 30 Nov. 1780, Papers-Congress, reel 184; BHP, nos. 2491, 2549, 2991, 2992, 3165; Washington to Clinton, 20 Nov. 1780, Washington to the president of Congress, 8 Dec. 1780, *Writings-Washington,* 20:375-76, 443-44; Washington to Abraham Skinner, 17 Feb. 1781, Washington to Board of War, 13 Apr. 1781, *Writings-Washington,* 21:236-37, 454-55; Washington to John Beatty, 23 Sept. 1779, Washington to the president of Congress, 10 July 1780, Worthington C. Ford, ed., *The Writings of George Washington,* 8:54-57, 338-41.

Chapter VIII

1. Between 1775 and 1790 there were six English-language newspapers in Philadelphia. Their publication was periodically inter-

rupted; the frequency of their issue varied from weekly to triweekly. During the occupation *Pennsylvania Gazette, Pennsylvania Journal,* and *Pennsylvania Packet* suspended operations in Philadelphia. The *Gazette* and *Packet,* after a short hiatus, resumed publication with slightly modified formats at York and Lancaster, respectively. The *Journal* discontinued publication until December 1778. In Philadelphia during the winter of 1777-78 the *Pennsylvania Evening Post* and *Pennsylvania Ledger* were joined by the *Royal Pennsylvania Gazette* for a brief period in March through May 1778. All were studied to establish the advertising mores of the Philadelphia business community between 1775 and 1790.

2. All issues of the *Pennsylvania Evening Post, Pennsylvania Ledger,* and *Royal Pennsylvania Gazette* were checked for the names and types of business people operating in the city during the occupation period. A significant number did not place advertisements in the newspapers; however, their names were found in noncommercial items, such as robberies, lost and found, property and slave sales, and personal notices. In addition, the voluminous collection of business correspondence and account books at HSP were consulted. Christopher Marshall, writing in Lancaster, recorded that 121 new stores were kept by Englishmen, Scotchmen, Irishmen and fellow Americans. There is no other substantiation for this number. Unfortunately Marshall's figures are secondhand and do not benefit from personal observation. Christopher Marshall, *Extracts from the Diary . . . during the American Revolution, 1774-81,* William Duane, ed., p. 169. Parker, a former Virginia merchant, recorded that several of the incoming merchants were from Virginia. Parker to Steuart, 15 Dec. 1777, Parker.

3. Fisher, p. 458. Mrs. Fisher had a tendency to mix her currency, but all prices except the one for butter are in pounds and shillings; Allen, "Diary," *PMHB,* 9:429; Morton, p. 35.

4. "Robert Proud to his brother William Proud, Anno 10, 1778," *PMHB,* 29:229-31.

5. *PEP,* 17 Jan. 1778 and 3 Feb. 1778.

6. *PL,* 26 Nov. and 10 Dec. 1777; Evans, nos. 15330, 15337, 15349.

7. Evans, no. 15333; *PEP,* 13 Dec. 1777.

8. *PL,* 21 Feb. 1778; *PEP,* 19 Feb. 1778; Almon, *Remembrancer,* 6:210-11.

9. *PEP,* 22 Jan. 1778; *PL,* 24 Jan. 1778.
10. *RPG,* 20 and 24 Mar. 1778. These advertisements and others of similar listings were found in all newspapers throughout the winter. Some merchants preferred one paper, but the majority used all three English-language and occasionally, Sower's German-language newspapers. Advertisements were usually inserted in two or more issues, although not necessarily consecutively. Artisans and craftsmen rarely advertised; however, an occasional notice is encountered. A carpenter named Kean offered a marquee for sale. *PL,* 1 Apr. 1778.
11. *RPG,* 28 Apr. 1778.
12. *Ibid.,* 13 Mar. and 28 Apr. 1778.
13. *RPG,* 21 Apr. 1778.
14. Coxe to Edward Goold, 1 Mar. 1778, Tench Coxe Papers, HSP.
15. Coxe to C. Barrell, 26 Jan. 1778, Coxe to Hamilton Young, 31 Jan. 1778, Coxe to Goold, 7 Feb. 1778, Coxe to James Thompson, 3 Mar. 1778, Coxe to Abraham C. Cuyler, 8 Mar. 1778, Goold to Coxe, 6 Dec. 1777, Tench Coxe Papers, HSP; Hamond to Philip Stephens, 23 Jan. 1778, Hamond Letters.
16. Coxe to James Meyrick, 24 Jan. 1778, Tench Coxe Papers, HSP.
17. Coxe to R. Wigran, 23 Mar. 1778, Tench Coxe Papers, HSP; Jacob E. Cooke, "Tench Coxe, Tory Merchant," *PMHB,* 96:62; Edward E. Curtis, *The British Army in the American Revolution,* pp. 100, 145-46. Before sailing from New York, Howe had ordered a suspension on all issuances of back rations to officers because they were selling them "to promiscuous people about Town." Peter Paumier to Clinton, 21 Jan. 1778, Clinton Papers.
18. Coxe to Isaac Lowe, 1 Apr. 1778, Tench Coxe Papers, HSP.
19. *PEP,* 20 Feb. 1778; *RPG,* 14 Apr., 15 and 19 May 1778; *PL,* 24 Jan., 14 and 18 Mar. 1778.
20. Coxe to Isaac Hartman, 26 Apr. 1778, Coxe to Tennant & Ross, Alexander Kennedy, and John Morris, 30 Apr. 1778, Tench Coxe Papers, HSP.
21. *PEP,* 10 Feb. 1778; E. Story, "An Account of Prohibited Goods Imported in Philadelphia, also what has been Sold, and what is to remain," 27 May 1778, Clinton.
22. *PL,* 4 Feb. 1778.
23. Coxe to Tennant & Ross, Alexander Kennedy & John Morris, 30 Apr. 1778, Tench Coxe Papers, HSP.

Chapter IX

1. Hamond to Captain Linzee, 1 Jan. 1778, Hamond to Lord Howe, 5 Feb. 1778, Hamond to Fowler, 7 Mar. 1778, Hamond Letters. The navy captains patronized several Philadelphia merchants. Hamond acknowledged drawing three bills of exchange (sterling) on Henry Fowler, naval officer at New York. They were given to Tench Coxe on 12 February for *L*67 10s.; to Samuel Inglis on 23 February for *L*183 3s. 7d.; and to Thomas Charles Williams on 6 March for *L*1,050.
2. Hamond to (?), 7 (?) Jan. 1778, Hamond to masters of ships, 9 Jan. 1778, Hamond Letters.
3. Hamond to Linzee, 1 Jan. 1778, Hamond to James Mason, 1 Jan. 1778, Hamond to Lord Howe, 5 Feb. 1778, Hamond Letters.
4. Hamond to Linzee, 10 Mar. 1778, Hamond to Wallace, 11 Feb. 1778, Hamond Letters.
5. *Pa Navy,* pp. 285-86.
6. Hamond to Captains and Commanders, 9 Jan. 1778, Hamond Letters.
7. Hamond to Lord Howe, 1 Feb. and 13 Mar. 1778, Hamond Letters.
8. Hamond to Captain Ferguson, 7 Apr. 1778, Hamond Letters; Howe to Pigot, 5 Feb. 1778, Clinton.
9. Howe to Clinton, 19 Jan. 1778, Clinton; Hamond to Commodore Hotham, 21 and 23 Jan., 7 Mar. 1778, Hamond Letters.
10. Wayne to Washington, 26 Dec. 1777, Wayne Papers, vol. 4, HSP; Hart to Lacey, 20 Jan. 1778, Lacey to Greene, 27 Apr. 1778, Lacey Papers, Dreer; Malcolm Orderly Book, 6 Mar. 1778, NYHS; Lacey to Council, 4 Mar., 13 Apr. 1778, NYHS; *PEP,* 20 Mar. 1778.
11. Depositions of Farmers, McLane Papers, NYHS; Letter Revolutionary Officer, Watson MSS; Ewald.
12. *Ibid.,* February 9, 1778; Washington to Walter Stewart, 22 Jan. 1778, Washington to Israel Angell, 1 Feb. 1778, General Orders, 4 Feb. 1778, *Writings-Washington,* pp. 336, 412, 420-21; James Murray to Steuart, 21 Dec. 1777, Stuart Steven, MS.5030.ff.168-9v.
13. Nicholas Collin, *The Journal and Biography of Nicholas Collin, 1746-1831,* Amandus Johnson, ed., pp. 244, 245, 246-49;

Gloucester County Indictments, Inquisitions and Fugitives, Revolutionary War Papers, Gloucester County Historical Society; Frank H. Stewart, *Salem County in the Revolution*, pp. 82-85.

14. Howe to Robinson, 13 Dec. 1777, Bancroft, vol. 2.

15. Howe to Galloway, 4 Dec. 1777, BHP, no. 782.

16. Galloway to Howe, 14 Dec. 1777, Galloway to [Howe], 20 Dec. 1777, Mackenzie to Galloway, 24 Mar. 1778, BHP nos. 805, 814, and 1047.

17. *PEP*, 7, 10, 15, 17, 21, and 24 Jan., 23 Mar. 1778; *PL*, 10 and 14 Jan., 18, 25, and 28 Mar., 4 and 8 Apr. 1778; Evans, no. 15817.

18. Evans, no. 15831; *PL*, 3 and 7 Jan. 1778, 25 Apr. 1778; Minutes, Philadelphia Contributionship . . . Loss by Fire, 22 Dec. 1777, 1 Jan., and 25 Mar. 1778.

19. *PEP*, 15 Jan., 12 Feb., 18 and 23 Mar. 1778; *PL*, 17, 21, and 24 Jan., 14 Feb., 25 and 28 Mar., 4 and 8 Apr. 1778; Evans, nos. 15822 and 15823.

20. Robertson, p. 161; Ewald; Miller, 11 Dec. 1777; Sullivan; *New Jersey Gazette*, 17 Dec. 1777; Howe-Orders MSS, 13 Dec. 1777; Parker to Steuart, 11 and 13 Dec. 1777, Parker; Andre, p. 71.

21. Montresor, p. 480; Robertson, pp. 162-63. Montresor declared the force exceeded 7,000, while Robertson said twenty-four battalions—a somewhat larger number of troops. Ewald.

22. Ewald; Potter to Washington, 22 and 23 Dec. 1777, Intelligence Report (unsigned), 22 Dec. 1777, Washington Papers, reel 46; Orders for a Move That was Intended Against Philadelphia by Way of Surprise [25 Dec. 1777], *Writings-Washington*, 10:202-5; Parker to Steuart, 22 and 23 Dec. 1777, Parker; *PEP*, 27 Dec. 1777; Andre, p. 73; Peebles, 22-30 Dec. 1777, passim, 21.492.4; Baurmeister to Jungkenn, 20 Jan. 1778, Baurmeister, pp. 48-49; Howe to Germain, 19 Jan. 1778 (received 14 Mar.), Howe to Germain, 19 Apr. 1778 (received 1 June), *PR*, 11:453-54, 464-65.

23. Robertson, p. 163; *Royal American Gazette*, 12 Feb. 1778.

24. Baurmeister to Jungkenn, 16 Dec. 1777, Baurmeister, p. 46; Howe-Orders MSS, 2 Jan. 1778.

25. Howe-Orders MSS, 27 Dec. 1777, 2, 13, and 18 Jan., 5 Feb. 1778; "Popps Journal," 31 Dec. 1777, *PMHB*, vol. 26; Evans, no. 15819; Peebles, 31 Dec. 1777, 21.492.4.

26. Howe-Orders MSS, 1 Jan. and 28 Feb. 1778; Ewald; General

State of Cash in the Military Chest to 1st Mar. 1778, Carleton, vol. 95; Howe-Orders MSS, 2 and 24 Jan. 1778.

27. Elizabeth Drinker to Henry Drinker, 26 Feb. 1778, Quaker; Drinker, pp. 73, 74, 76; Phebe [sic] Pemberton, 26 Mar. 1778, Pemberton.

28. Baurmeister to Jungkenn, 20 Jan. 1778, Baurmeister, p. 52; Doehla, Tagebuch, p. 57; Howe-Orders MSS, 18 and 25 Apr. 1778.

29. Howe-Orders MSS, 8 Feb. 1778; *PEP*, 20 Jan. and 4 Apr. 1778. Dr. Yeldall was one of the Loyalists employed by Galloway to disarm suspected Americans.

30. The cost of remodeling the State House was £197 19s. 6d. and included wages for the overseers, carpenters, and laborers over a thirty-six-day period. Lumber, nails and other materials were included. A copy of the invoice for these costs is in the archives of the Independence National Historic Park Library. Pattison to Lord Amherst, 23 Jan. 1778, Pattison to Lord Viscount Townshend, 22 Jan. 1778, Letter Book of Brig. General James Pattison from Philadelphia and New York 1777-78, MS7, pp. 30, 51, Royal Artillery Library, Woolwich.

31. Brigade Orders Royal Artillery, 28 Sept. 1777, 21 Feb. 1778, MS57 f.166-67, Royal Artillery Library, Woolwich.

32. Howe-Orders MSS, 22 Mar. 1778.

33. Journal of Lieutenant von Kraft, 15 June 1778, Collections of NYHS, 1882.

34. Pattison to Robert Mackenzie, 23 May 1778, MS7, p. 126, Royal Artillery Library, Woolwich; Vestry Minutes, Christ Church, 29 Jan., 1 Feb., and 17 July 1778; Account of House Rent Paid by Captain Payne Barrack Master of Philadelphia by order of the Commander in Chief [circa June, 1778], Clinton.

35. *PEP*, 1 Apr. 1778; *PL*, 1 Apr. 1778; Meteorological Observations taken near Philadelphia, Jan. 1777 to 10 May 1778, APS.

36. W. Knox to Howe, 12 Dec. 1777 (with an undated enclosure denoted as ''Intelligence''), Carleton, 7:800, 801.

37. Howe-Orders MSS, 31 Dec. 1777, 21 and 22 Jan., and 25 Feb. 1778; ''A Plan of the City and Environs of Philadelphia,'' *S & W Philadelphia*, vol. 1, facing page 361; Baurmeister to Jungkenn, 20 Jan. 1778, Baurmeister, pp. 49-50; Watson, 1:136.

38. Howe-Orders MSS, 7 and 8 Mar. 1778.

39. M. Morris, C. Blagden and I. Mervin North to Howe, 21 Mar. 1778, BHP, no. 1034.

40. Miss Amiel to Polly Richie, 8 Dec. 1778, Hildeburn, HSP; James Morton to J. Pemberton, 5 Dec. 1778, Hannah Lloyd to J. Pemberton, 29 Dec. 1778, Israel Pemberton to J. Pemberton, 30 May 1778, Pemberton, HSP; Edward Shippen, Jr., to Edward Shippen, 25 June 1778, Gratz; Henry Hill to Margaret Morris, Smith MSS, HSP-LCP.

41. Howe to Clinton, 19 Jan. 1778, Clinton.

42. Recruitment Posters for the *Vigilant, Stanley, Roebuck, Pearl, Philadelphia* (galley), *Liverpool,* and *Camilla* (Evans, nos. 15321, 15350, 15814, 15815, 15829, and 15830). Evans no. 15839 is a standard recruiting poster for the various galleys, with space for insertion of the galley and captain's name.

43. Sackville-Germain, 7:31, 46; *PEP,* 31 Jan. and 24 Feb. 1778; *PL,* 20 Dec. 1777, 28 Feb. 1778.

44. "Extracts from the Letter-Book of Captain Johann Heinrichs of the Hessian Jäger Corps, 1778-1780," Julius F. Sachse, trans., *PMHB,* vol. 22; *Letters of Brunswick and Hessian Officers during the American Revolution,* Wm. L. Stone, trans., p. 214; Murray to Bessie, 5 Mar. 1778, Murray, *Letters from America,* pp. 51-53; Serle, p. 265; Lieutenant W. Hale to his parents, 23 Mar. 1778, Hale, pp. 236-47; Gott save the King, signed J. R., Journal of von Jahr 1776-84, Clements Library, University of Michigan.

45. Frederick Wagner, *Submarine Fighter of the American Revolution,* pp. 84-89; *Pa Navy,* pp. 288-89.

46. Lacey to Washington, 18 Feb. and 11 Mar. 1778, Lacey Papers, Dreer.

47. Simcoe, pp. 33-34; Ewald; John Granger, Richard Swanwick, John Roberts, John Knight, Christopher Sower, Abraham Iredell, and Gideon Vernon admitted acting as guides; Loyalist Transcripts, vols. 49 and 50, NYPL. Present Montgomery County was a part of Philadelphia County in 1778.

48. The capture of the cattle occurred near the present town of Skippack. Robertson, p. 163; Peebles, 24 and 25 Feb., 2 Mar. 1778, 21.492.5; Wayne to Washington, 23, 25, and 26 Feb., 14 Mar. 1778, Barry to Washington, 26 Feb. 1778, Washington Papers, reel 47.

49. Hamond to Linzee, 10 Mar. 1778, Hamond to Phipps, 12 Mar. 1778, Hamond to Lord Howe, 13 Mar. 1778, Hamond Papers.

The *Roebuck* did not accompany the flotilla, but, as Hamond's flagship, remained at anchor off Chester.

50. Robertson, p. 164; Simcoe, p. 46; Peebles, 12 Mar. 1778, 21.492.5.
51. Robertson probably was along as an observer.
52. Robertson, pp. 164-66; Simcoe, p. 46. Robertson reported the flotilla with a man of war *(Pearl)* passed through the chevaux-de-frise and proceeded down stream on the fifteenth.
53. Space prohibits detailed narratives on the military activities in the no-man's-land around Philadelphia and in Pennsylvania, New Jersey, and Delaware. Bitterness and hatred frequently make an impartial evaluation difficult. Many fine studies by local historians are available, although unfortunately slightly biased. However, these three incorporate the main elements of the American version on Mawhood's expedition: Frank H. Stewart, *Salem County in the Revolution;* Joseph S. Sickler, *The History of Salem County New Jersey;* George B. Macaltioner, *150th Anniversary of the Skirmich at Quinton's Bridge and the Massacre at Hancock's Bridge.* The most detailed British account can be found in Simcoe. The Simcoe Papers at Colonial Williamsburg Research Department contain Mawhood's ultimatum and the American correspondence denouncing it. See also, Robertson, pp. 164-67; Ewald; Peebles, 12 and 30 Mar. 1778, 21.492.5. I am especially grateful to my friend, Dr. William C. Timmins of Woodstown, New Jersey, for his painstaking research into the local history of Salem County.
54. All newspapers carried numerous notices of runaway apprentices, slaves, and wives. For examples see: *PEP,* 9 Dec. 1777, 6 and 27 Jan., 9, 11, and 23 Mar., 15 Apr., 1, 8, and 11 May 1778; *PL,* 28 Mar. 1778; Drinker, p. 74; Ewald.
55. "Letter of Friends in Philadelphia to Friends in Ireland, soliciting aid during the Occupation of Philadelphia by the British," *PMHB,* 18:125-27; Letters which passed between the Meeting for Sufferings in London and the Meetings for Sufferings in Philadelphia, Royal Society of Medicine, London; Minutes of the Monthly Meetings of Friends of Philadelphia, 31 Oct., 28 Nov., 26 Dec. 1777; Jas. Woods to Dr. T. Park[e], 10 Feb. 1778, Robert Barclay to Parke, 16 Feb. 1778, Pemberton.
56. Vestry Minutes, Christ Church, 19 Jan. 1778.
57. *PP,* 7 Jan. 1778; *PG,* 21 Jan. and 10 June 1778.

58. *PEP,* 1 Jan. and 7 Feb. 1778; *PL,* 4 Feb. 1778.
59. Elias Boudinot to Elisha Boudinot, 6 Mar. 1778, "Letters of . . . the American Revolution," Dreer; *New Jersey Gazette,* 4 and 18 Feb. 1778; *PL,* 21 Feb. 1778; *PEP,* 6 July 1778; Kenneth Scott, *Counterfeiting in Colonial America,* pp. 253-63, passim.
60. Proclamation of Howe, 2 Mar. 1778, Carleton; Peebles, 24 Mar. 1778, 21.492.5

Chapter X

1. Frederick Bernays Wiener, *Civilians Under Military Justice,* p. 147; Coote, 19 Feb. 1778, MS6912/14/38; Howe-Orders MSS, 12 and 19 Feb. 1778.
2. Howe-Orders MSS, 20 and 29 Dec., 3 Jan. 1778; Coote, 22 Dec. 1777, 3 Jan. 1778, MS6912/14/38; General Orders, Howe, 22 Dec. 1777, MS58, Royal Artillery Library, Woolwich.
3. Coote, 22, 28, and 31 Dec. 1777, MS6912/14/38.
4. Coote, 18 Dec. 1777, 10 Jan. 1778; Drinker, pp. 71, 77; Howe-Orders MSS, 18 Dec. 1777, 10 Jan., 5 Feb. 1778.
5. Peebles, 4 Apr. 1778, 21.492.5; Howe-Orders MSS, 14 Dec. 1777 and 16 and 19 Mar. 1778; Coote, 14 Dec. 1777, MS6912/14/38.
6. Coote, 3, 11, and 15 Jan. 1778, 2 Mar. 1778, 6912/14/38-39; Peebles, 7-30 Jan., passim, 5 Feb., 9, 15, and 21 Apr. 1778, 21.492.4, 21.492.5; Evans, no. 15818; Howe-Orders MSS, 11, 15, 16, 24, and 29 Jan., 9 and 18 Feb. 1778.
7. Coote, 10 and 31 Jan. 1778, MS6912/14/38; *RPG,* 20 Mar. 1778; Drinker, pp. 71, 72.
8. Notice of robberies may be seen in virtually every issue of the *Pennsylvania Ledger, Pennsylvania Evening Post,* and *Royal Pennsylvania Gazette.*
9. Punishments inflicted for various crimes may be found throughout the Records of General Court Martials, 1777-78, PRO W.O. 71/85; Howe-Orders MSS, 1 Jan.-22 Apr. 1778, passim. Scattering references are noted in many regimental and corps orderly books.
10. Campbell was the *Fourier de la Cour* of the army. This officer was answerable to the commander in chief for his quarters and those of his staff.

11. Records of General Court Martials, 1777-78, pp. 305-65, 442-57, PRO W.O. 71/85; Coote, 30 Mar. 1778, MS6912/14/39; Peebles, 23 Feb., 10 and 23 Mar. 1778, 21.492.5; Murray to Bessie, 5 Mar. 1778, Murray, *Letters,* pp. 52-54; Howe-Orders MSS, 29 and 30 Mar. 1778.

12. *Ibid.,* Mar. 15, 1778; Records of General Court Martials, pp. 290-301, W.O. 71/85; Peebles, 23 Mar. 1778, 21.492.5; Howe to Germain, 23 Mar. 1778, BHP, no. 1043.

13. Brigade Orders, Royal Artillery, 9 Feb. 1778, f. 168-77, Royal Artillery Library, Woolwich; Howe-Orders MSS, 1 Feb. 1778.

14. Howe-Orders MSS, 4 Jan. 1778; Records of General Court Martials, pp. 137-41, W.O. 71/85; Howe to Germain, 19 Jan. 1778, Carleton.

15. Howe-Orders MSS, 4 Apr. 1778.

16. *Ibid.,* 11 Jan. 1778; Records of General Court Martials, pp. 203-12, W.O. 71/85.

17. Records of General Court Martials, pp. 154-55, 158, W.O. 71/85; Howe-Orders MSS, 26 Dec. 1777.

18. *RPG,* 20 Mar. 1778.

19. Howe-Orders MSS, 6 Jan. 1778.

Chapter XI

1. A. H. Quinn, *A History of the American Drama,* p. 16; Peebles, 21.492.4. There is a gap in Peeble's journal between 7 January and 30 January 1778. After he resumed his journal, he summarized the activities for the period omitted. For special studies on the British military theatre, see: Charles Durang, *History of the Philadelphia Stage 1749-1855,* Series I, chapters 10 and 12; Fred Lewis Pattie, "The British Theater in Philadelphia in 1778," *American Literature,* 6:381-88; Thomas Clark Pollock, *The Philadelphia Theatre in the Eighteenth Century,* pp. 34-37, 130-33; Winthrop Sargent, *The Life and Career of Major John Andre, Adjutant General of the British Army in America,* New Edition, William Abbatt, ed., pp. 170-75; Helen Roberts Yalof, *British Military Theatricals in Philadelphia During the Revolutionary War.*

2. *PL,* 24 and 31 Dec. 1777, 14 Jan. 1778; Evans, no. 15995; Pattie, "British Theater," p. 383.

3. All handbills and announcements in the newspapers indicated

where tickets could be obtained. *PL,* 26 Jan. 1778; Andre, p. 172.

4. Durang, *History of the Philadelphia Stage,* chapter 10; *PL,* 27 and 31 Dec. 1777, 3 Jan. 1778.

5. *PL,* 3, 7, and 17 Jan., 2 and 9 May 1778; Peebles, 19 May 1778, 21.492.5.

6. Pierre du Simitière, Commonplace Book-Notes, Force, Series 7E, box 42; Pollock, *Philadelphia Theater,* p. 132; *PL,* 14, 17, and 24 Jan., 4, 7, 14, and 28 Feb., 4, 7, and 21 Mar., 8, 11, 15, 18, 22, and 29 Apr. 2, 6, and 16 May 1778; *RPG,* 7 Apr. 1, 5, 15, and 19 May 1778; Evans, Nos. 25995-16001, 16003-16011.

7. A small manuscript book in the HSP identified as the Commonplace Book, 1775-80, was presented to the Society by Dr. I. T. Sharpless in 1868. Dr. Sharpless did not know the author, nor apparently who had owned the book before him. It reproduces a copy of the prologue, and an interpolated note attributes its authorship to Dr. Jonathan Odell and also mentions that it was delivered to the audience by Major Robert Crewe. It also states Crewe was the first director of the theatre. Sargent believed Andre was the author, but gives no authority. All that can be said of its authorship with certainty is that its style is reminiscent of the stilted works of Dr. Odell and the flamboyancy of Andre.

    There are two known versions of the prologue, the one mentioned above and another in contemporary newspapers. Pattie claimed Sargent's version differed radically from the one in the Commonplace Book, possibly because he disagreed with Sargent's contention about the author. Apparently Pattie was unaware that Sargent had used the rendition appearing in the *Royal American Gazette* of 26 February 1778. Regardless, the differences are minor. If either account is to be considered accurate, it would seem the contemporary published version would be accepted over an unknown, undated, and undocumented manuscript. Therefore, the account reproduced here is from the newspapers.

8. Blumenthal, *Women Camp Followers,* p. 36; Peebles, 9 Feb., 16 and 25 Mar., and 19 May 1778, 21.492.4 and 21.492.5.

9. Peebles, 19 May 1778, 21.492.5.

10. Pattie, ''British Theater in Philadelphia,'' p. 382; Pattie quoted from William Dunlap, *History of the American Theatre,* regarding the New York theatricals; Durang, *History of the Philadelphia Stage,* chapters 10 and 12.

11. Minutes, Meetings for Sufferings, 2, 7, 14, and 21 May 1778, Department of Records, Philadelphia Yearly Meeting.
12. Muhlenberg, *Journals,* 3:150.
13. *PL,* 29 Apr., 16 May 1778; *RPG,* 1, 5, 15, and 19 May 1778.

Chapter XII

1. Lieutenant Hale to his parents, 23 Mar. 1778, Hale, pp. 236-47.
2. Hamond Autobiography.
3. Throughout Peebles's journal from 1 January to the end of May 1778 are numerous entries on his dining habits. See 2 January 1778 for the reference to tavern dinner costs; Peebles, 21.492.4 and 21.492.5.
4. *Ibid.,* 15 Feb., 19 Mar., and 17 May 1778.
5. *Ibid.,* 5 Feb. and 21 Mar. 1778.
6. *Ibid.,* 5 and 19 Apr. 1778.
7. *Ibid.,* 5 Jan. 1778.
8. *Ibid.,* 7 and 8 May 1778.
9. *Ibid.,* 24 May 1778.
10. Howe-Orders MSS, 15 and 25 Jan. 1778; Coote, 18 Jan. 1778, MS6912/14/38; Peebles, Summary, 7 to 30 Jan. 1778, 21.492.4.
11. Peebles, 17 Feb., 23 Mar., and 1 May 1778, 21.492.4; Howe-Orders MSS, 18 Jan. 1778; Ewald; Blumenthal, *Women Camp Followers,* p. 36; Lieutenant Hale to his parents, 23 Mar. 1778, Hale, pp. 236-47.
12. Hale, pp. 236-47; Stedman, *American War,* 1:309; Ewald; Peebles, 5 May 1778, 21.492.5.
13. *PL,* 24 and 28 Jan., 18 and 21 Feb., 25 Apr., and 9 May 1778; *RPG,* 17, 24, and 31 Mar., 7, 14, 17, and 21 Apr. 1778; Howe-Orders MSS, 26 and 27 Jan. 1778.
14. Howe-Orders MSS, 7 May 1778; Ewald; Molly Pemberton to Israel Pemberton, 2 Feb. 1778, Pemberton; Miss Franks to Mrs. William Paca, 26 Feb. 1778, "A Letter of Miss Rebecca Franks, 1778," *PMHB,* 16:216-18.
15. *PL,* 24 Dec. 1777.
16. *Ibid.,* 21 Jan., 14 Feb., 7, 21 and 25 Mar., and 4, 11, 18, and 22 Apr. 1778; *PEP,* 20 Jan. and 12 Feb. 1778; Howe-Orders MSS, 12 Feb. 1778; Evans, no. 15992; Minutes, Directors of the LCP, vol. 2, LCP; "British Army Orderly Book of General Charles

Grey, 12 Mar. 1778," Rutgers University Library; *S & W Philadelphia*, 1:371.

17. *RPG*, 24 Mar. 1778; *PEP*, 17 Apr. 1778.
18. *RPG*, 7 and 24 Apr. 1778; Drinker, pp. 83, 84, 87-88.
19. Peebles, 8, 15, and 21 Feb., 9, 18, and 19 Mar., and 11 June 1778, 21.492.5.
20. *Ibid.*, 27 Apr. 1778; *RPG*, 20, 24, 27, and 31 Mar., 3 and 7 Apr. 1778; *S & W Philadelphia*, 1:371; Deposition of Jacob Coates, 5 Jan. 1826, Watson MSS; Mordecai, "Addenda to Watson's Annals," *PMHB*, 98:143; Journal of John C. P. von Kraft, 5 May 1778, Collections of NYHS, 1882.
21. Peebles, 25 Dec. 1777, 17 and 18 Mar. 1778, 21.492.4 and 21.492.5.
22. *Ibid.*, 23 Apr., 4 June 1778; Ewald, 4 May 1778.
23. Doehla, Tagebuch, 1 Jan. 1778, p. 62.
24. Peebles, 25 Mar. 1778, 21.492.5; Illustrations may be found in *RPG*, 13, 17, 27 Mar., 7 and 21 Apr., 1 and 22 May 1778; *PL*, 14 and 17 Jan. 1778; *PEP*, 10 Jan., 9, 13, 18, and 25 Mar., 23 May 1778.
25. Illustrations can be seen in *PL*, 5 Nov., 3 and 31 Dec. 1777, 7 and 24 Jan., 14 Feb., 4 and 28 Mar., 2 May 1778; *PEP*, 16 Dec. 1777, 3 and 30 Mar., 8 Apr. 1778.

Chapter XIII

1. George III to Lord North, 10 and 13 Jan. 1778, *George-North*, 2:117-20; George III to North, 10 Jan. 1778, *Correspondence of King George III*, Fortescue, ed., 4:9.
2. Germain to Clinton, 4 Feb. 1778, Clinton; George III to North, 3 Mar. 1778, *George-North*, 2:140-41.
3. George III to North, 17 Mar. 1778, *George-North*, 2:152-53; Germain to Clinton, 8 Mar. 1778, Sackville-Germain, 7:17; Germain to Clinton (Most Secret), 21 Mar. 1778, Secret Instructions from George III to Clinton, 21 Mar. 1778, American Revolution Military and Political, Miscellaneous Letters, Bancroft.
4. George III to North, 2 Feb. and 17 Mar. 1778, *George-North*, 2:129, 153-54; George III to North, 2 Feb. 1778, *Correspondence of King George III*, Fortescue, ed., 4:33; Germain to Clinton, 12 and 13 Apr. 1778, Clinton.

5. Some illustrations may be found in the *PEP,* 10 Apr. 1778; *RPG,* 7, 10, 21, and 28 Apr., 5 May 1778; Parker to Steuart, 8, 25 and 26 Apr. 1778, Parker; Montresor, pp. 484-87, passim; Baurmeister to Jungkenn, 10 May 1778, Baurmeister, pp. 169-71, passim; Peebles, 5, 7, 8, 15, 17, 21, and 26 Apr., 1 May 1778, 21.492.5.

6. Montresor, pp. 484, 488; Israel Shreve to Washington, 6 Apr., 3 May 1778, Washington Papers, reel 49.

7. Shreve to Washington, 4 May 1778, Moylan to Washington, 7 May 1778, Washington Papers, reel 49; Montresor, pp. 487-90, passim; Parker to Steuart, 28 Apr. 1778, Parker; Howe to Germain, 11 May 1777 [1778], *Gentlemen's Magazine,* June 1778, p. 281; Peebles, 3 and 7 May 1778, 21.492.5; Baurmeister to Jungkenn, 10 May 1778, Baurmeister, pp. 168-74. A conservative estimate of the wood used as fuel by troops, exclusive of that used by the inhabitants, to 30 April is twenty thousand cords.

8. Loyalist guides were used by all expeditions. The letter of Richard Swanwick to Howe illustrates the attitude and dedication of those desiring to serve as guides. Learning of Howe's departure, he requested the commander in chief intercede with Clinton and Lord Howe on his behalf, stating that he "would Wish to accompany any detachment of the Troops that may go against M^r. Washington's Incampment — because I know the Country & Inhabitants for many Miles thereabouts and Wish to be of service to the British Army — at same time it may be possible for me to recover my Unhappy Family." Swanwick to Howe, 14 May 1778, Clinton.

9. Depositions of F. Watts, Samuel Henry, William Stayner, Thos. Craven (or Creven), and Samuel Erwin, Washington Papers, reel 49; these were taken on 14 and 15 May 1778 and forwarded to Washington by Potter. Lacey to Council, 4 May 1778, Lacey to Washington, 2 May 1778, Lacey Papers, NYHS; Montresor, p. 484; Sullivan, 1 May 1778; Parker to Steuart, 1 May 1778, Parker; Peebles, 1 May 1778, 21.492.5; Baurmeister to Jungkenn, 10 May 1778, Baurmeister, p. 172; Simcoe, pp. 56-60; *PEP,* 1 May 1778; General W.W.H. Davis, "The Battle of Crooked Billet," *Papers of the Bucks County Historical Society,* 2:173-86.

10. Report of Major John Maitland, 11 May 1778, Report of John

Henry, 11 May 1778, Letter of Howe to Germain, 11 May 1778,
Lord Howe to Stephens, 10 May 1778, *Universal Magazine,* June
1778; *Pa Navy,* pp. 295-98.

11. Grant's column consisted of the 16th and 17th Dragoons, 1st and
2nd Battalions of light infantry, two battalions of British and two
of Hessian grenadiers, the British guards, three battalions of
British infantry, and Simcoe's Queen's Rangers acting as the
vanguard. These units represented the elite of the British army in
Philadelphia.

12. The composition of Howe's column is uncertain, although most
reports state he had a force ranging from five to seven thousand.
After excluding Grant's command and those left in the garrison,
the regular units remaining to accompany Howe would approxi-
mate six thousand.

13. Clinton; the Provincial units in the garrison and their rank and
file fit for duty, according to 20 May return, were:

Queen's American Rangers	342
2nd Battalion New Jersey Volunteers	136
Pennsylvania Loyalists	134
Maryland Loyalists	304
Roman Catholic Volunteers	166
Jersey Volunteers	129
	1,211
1st Philadelphia Light Dragoons	39
2nd Philadelphia Light Dragoons	48
One Troop Bucks County Light Dragoons	45
Total Provincials	1,343

14. Local tradition says the obese Grant stopped for refreshments at
the Broad Axe Tavern. This seems improbable, as the column
passed this point between 4:00 and 5:00 A.M.

15. Ewald, 19-21 May 1778; Peebles, 20 May 1778, 21.492.5;
Sullivan, 19-20 May 1778; Baurmeister to Jungkenn, 15 June
1778, Baurmeister, pp. 176-78; Simcoe, pp. 60-61; Montresor,
pp. 492-93; William J. Wilcox, "The Comic Opera that made a
General," *Pennsylvania History,* 13:265-73; Charlemagne Tower,
The Marquie de LaFayette, 1:328-37; C. Stedman, *The History . . . of
the American War,* 2:420-23; Irvin C. Williams, "Lafayette at
Barren Hill," *Sketches of the Montgomery County Historical Society,*
2:291-305; Levi Streeper, "Lafayette's Retreat from Barren Hill,"

Sketches of the Montgomery County Historical Society, 2:268-81; James K. Helms, "Lafayette's Escape from British at Barren Hill in Spring of 1778," *The Picket Post,* pp. 9-13; Hale to his parents, 15 June 1778, Hale, pp. 252-57.

16. *PL,* 9 May 1778; *RPG,* 19 May 1778.
17. Letters of Charles Blagden, 20 Apr. 1778, NYPL.
18. *PL,* 23 May 1778.
19. Montresor, pp. 486, 487, 491; Peebles, 24 Apr. 1778, 21.492.5.
20. Peebles, 8 May 1778, 21.492.5; *New Jersey Gazette,* 13 May 1778; Parker to Steuart, 6 May 1778, Parker.
21. Peebles, 7 and 28 Apr. 1778, 4 May 1778, 21.492.5.
22. *Ibid.,* 11 May 1778.
23. Clinton to the Governors and Garrison Commanders, 12 May 1778, BHP, no. 1167; Clinton to Newcastle, 23 May 1778, Newcastle MSS, University of Nottingham.
24. Peebles, 15 May 1778, 21.492.5; British Army Orderly Book, 14 May 1778, Rutgers University Library; Mackenzie Papers, 15 May 1778, Clements Library, University of Michigan.
25. *Ibid.,* Howe to [Germain], 18 May 1778, Clinton.
26. Daniel Coxe to Galloway, 17 Dec. 1777, "Letters to Joseph Galloway from Leading Tories in America," *Historical Magazine . . . Antiquities, History and Biography,* 5:357-59.
27. Lieutenant Hale to his parents, 20 Apr. 1778, Hale, pp. 249-50.
28. Thomas Stirling to his brother, 13-15 Apr. 1778, Abercairny Muniments, Sec. 1 no. 458 GD 24/1/458, Scottish Record Office.
29. *Ibid.;* Peebles, 24 May 1778, 21.492.5.
30. Hill to Clinton, 23 May 1778, Clinton.

Chapter XIV

1. Reports of the exact number of officers in the cadre vary between twenty-one and twenty-three; Andre mentions twenty-two. Morris Bishop ("You are Invited to a Mischianza," *American Heritage,* 25:71) states that twenty-two field officers put up 3,312 guineas. Baurmeister stated staff officers paid 3,312 guineas for the fete; Baurmeister to Jungkenn, 15 June 1778, Baurmeister, p. 180. The location of the establishment of Coffin and Anderson has puzzled historians; the only reference found was in the *Pennsylvania Evening Post* on 1 January 1778; their name appeared in the advertisement of Rundle & Robeson. Blumenthal *(Women Camp*

Followers of the Revolution, p. 36) mentions twenty-three staff officers expended 3,300 guineas. On the other hand, Peebles recorded that twenty-one or twenty-two officers, who each subscribed £140 sterling, were given four tickets to the fete to dispose of; Peebles, 18 May 1778, 21.492.5.

2. A manuscript note in the Commonplace Book (HSP) shows "Meschianza" derived from the Italian mescere, to mix and mischiare, to mingle.

3. Parker to Steuart, 6 and 17 May 1778, Parker; Peebles, 12, 16, and 17 May 1778, 21.492.5.The Wharton mansion had been the quarters during the winter of Sir Henry Calder, one of the managers.

4. Hamond Autobiography.

5. A good illustration of the invitation may be seen in *American Historical and Literary Curiosities,* collected and edited by J. Jay Smith and John F. Watson. It is noteworthy that Calder, on all copies of invitation seen, called the fete the Meschianza.

6. Several accounts of the Meschianza were written; however the most detailed were those versions written by Andre and an eyewitness account at the HSP. John Andre, "Particulars of the Mischianza," *Annual Register . . . for 1778,* pp. 264-70; "Major Andre's Story of the Mischianza, With a Preface by Sophie Howard Ward," *Century Magazine,* 48:684-91 (This account was written especially for Miss Peggy Chew on 2 June 1778.); Samuel Hazard, *Register of Pennsylvania,* 14:295-97; Sargent, *Life-John Andre,* pp. 183-201; Anne H. Wharton, *Genealogy of the Wharton Family,* pp. 112-21 (also in her *Through Colonial Doorways,* pp. 23-64); Bishop, "You are Invited to a Mischianza," pp. 70-75; Lynch, *The Old District of Southwark,* pp. 123-25; Carlisle, *Manuscripts of the Earl of Carlisle,* Fifteenth Report, Appendix VI, p. 346; Abbreviated accounts may be found in: *RPG,* 22 and 26 May 1778; *New York Gazette and Weekly Mercury,* 8 June 1778; *Rivington's Loyal Gazette,* 2 June 1778; *Gentlemen's Magazine,* July 1778, p. 330; Parker to Steuart, 18 May 1778, Parker; Peebles, 18 May 1778, 21.492.5; Account of the Meschianza, HSP (This account closely follows that appearing in the *PL,* 23 May 1778.); Baurmeister to Jungkenn, 15 June 1778, Baurmeister, pp. 179-80; Knight's wharf was the northernmost pier in the city, at the foot of Green Street.

7. It may be contended that this narrative is remiss in not including frequent references to Mrs. Loring. Except that she was Howe's

paramour (and the wife of Joshua Loring, commissary of prisoners), she was little different from any other officer's mistress in the city. Many officers had left wives in New York and had either brought their kept women with them (or sent for them), or acquired new ones in Philadelphia. Their importance is only significant if they were instrumental in diverting Howe or any officer from his duty. No documentary evidence, only hearsay, exists that indicates Mrs. Loring was anything more than Howe's mistress and a pleasant diversion.

8. There are minor variations between Andre's account and the one in the Commonplace Book concerning the inscriptions on the arches.

9. Some contemporary accounts describe the pavilions as tiered rows of seats, while others called them sofas.

10. Pierre Eugene du Simitière, Memoranda, Nov. 1778, Library of Congress.

11. The number of trumpeters is variously reported as two, three, and four. Andre stated there were four in his letter of 23 May, and then changed it to three in the account for Miss Chew on 2 June. Other eyewitness accounts mention two trumpeters with each herald.

12. In Andre's first account, Captain Cathcart's lady was Miss N. White, but in his version of 2 June Miss White was the lady of Lieutenant Underwood of the black knights. This switch was unquestionably prompted by the withdrawal from the fete of the Shippen sisters, on orders from their father. Andre had included the three sisters as present in his letter of 23 May, but omitted them from the June description. This omission confirmed the Shippen family tradition that the sisters had been forbidden from appearing garbed in such garish dress. The family tradition is presented in Lewis Burd Walker, ''The Life of Margaret Shippen,'' *PMHB*, Vols. 24, 25, 26; Edward Shippen, ''Two or Three Old Letters,'' *PMHB*, 23:184-95; Charles Henry Hart, ''Did Peggy Shippen and Her Sisters Attend the Mischianza?'' *PMHB*, 23:119-20, 412-13; Frederick D. Stone, ''Philadelphia Society One Hundred Years Ago,'' *PMHB*, 3:366-67. Judge Shippen ''was driven to distraction by the inordinate proclivities of his luxury-loving wife and daughters.'' *(Nancy Shippen, Her Journal Book, pp. 22-23.)*

13. Major John Andre's brother.

14. Although there are minor variations between the different Andre

accounts, they do not significantly alter the narrative of the Meschianza. In his first account, Andre said Hobart's shield was ''A Coat of Mail with his Arrow'' and his motto, ''Proof to all but Love.''

15. It is claimed all carpets, mirrors, and candelabra borrowed from the residents were returned without a blemish.
16. A Revolutionary Officer, Watson MSS.
17. Commonplace Book, 1775-80, HSP; Watson, 3:470-71; *S & W Philadelphia*, 1:379-81; Anne Wharton, *Through Colonial Doorways*, pp. 56-71; Burton A. Konkle, *Benjamin Chew*, p. 190.
18. Wharton, *Diplomatic Correspondence of the American Revolution*, Vol. I, pp. 307-9; Drinker, p. 103; [Israel Mauduit], *Strictures on the Philadelphia Mischianza or Triumph upon Leaving America Unconquered;* Serle, p. 294.
19. *PL*, 23 May 1778.

Chapter XV

1. Parker to Steuart, 26 May 1778, Parker; Serle, p. 295.
2. Serle, pp. 295-99, passim; Parker to Steuart, 26 May 1778, Parker.
3. Serle, p. 300.
4. *Ibid.,* pp. 302-3; Stevens, nos. 2095, 2096, 2097.
5. Serle, pp. 299-302, passim; Boudinot to his wife, 11 June 1778, Boudinot Collection, Princeton University Library.
6. Draft of a letter, possibly never sent, Clinton to Germain, 23 May 1778, Clinton (also in Stevens, no. 1084); Clinton to Germain, 5 June (finished on 13 June) 1778, Clinton (also in Carleton, no. 1213); Clinton to Newcastle, 16 June 1778, Clinton to Newcastle, 11 July 1778, 9/44NEC2,642 and 9/44NEC2,645, Newcastle.
7. Peebles, 24 May, 2 and 9 June 1778, 21.492.5; Parker to Steuart, [1] June 1778, Parker; Baurmeister to Jungkenn, 15 June 1778, Baurmeister, p. 176.
8. Baurmeister to Jungkenn, 15 June 1778, Baurmeister, p. 175; Peebles, 24 May 1778, 21.492.5; Pattison to Board of Ordnance, 22 May 1778, Pattison to Lord Viscount Townshend, 12 June 1778, Letter Book of General Pattison, MS7, Royal Artillery Library, Woolwich; Kraft, ''Journal,'' *Collections of the NYHS for 1882*, p. 37; P. Dickinson to Washington, 31 May 1778, Washington Papers, reel 49.

9. Miller, 3, 6, and 10 June 1778.

10. Henry Laurens to Heath, 20 June 1778, Heath Papers, Massachusetts Historical Society; General Orders, 1 June 1778, Washington to John Augustine Washington, 10 June 1778, Washington to the president of Congress, 18 June 1778, *Writings-Washington,* 12:4-5, 82-83.

11. Dickinson to Washington, 19 May 1778, W. Livingston to Washington, 17 May 1778, Washington Papers, reel 49.

12. Dickinson to Washington, 27 May 1778, *Ibid.;* Wm. Grand Letter, F. T. to Norgrave, 22 June 1778, NYHS; Parker to Steuart, 24 May 1778, Parker.

13. Handbill for a meeting of merchants and citizens, 25 May 1778, LCP; Evans, no. 15991.

14. Minutes of a conversation between Clinton, Lord Howe, and Galloway [May 1778], Clinton. The minutes are in Lord Rawdon's handwriting, except the last paragraph, which is in Clinton's hand. The final paragraph refers to Lord Howe's opinion.

15. Washington to Henry Laurens, 2 June 1778; John Laurens to Henry Laurens, 27 May 1778, Long Island Historical Society; Boudinot to his wife, 11 June 1778, Boudinot Collection, Princeton University Library; letter from ———, 27 [May] 1778, *Virginia Gazette,* 19 June 1778.

16. Samuel Huntington to General Jedediah Huntington, 5 June 1778, Bancroft, vol. 2.

17. Account of House Rent paid by Captain Payne Barrack Master of Philadelphia by order of the Commander in Chief, Clinton; Tavern Licenses and Petitions, Memorial to Sir Henry Clinton by divers Inhabitants (owners of Wharves & Stores) in the City of Philadelphia, HSP.

18. Ewald, 4 June 1778; Dickinson to Washington, 31 May 1778, Shreve to Maxwell, 1 June 1778, Washington Papers, reel 49; letter from ———, 27 [May 1778] *Virginia Gazette,* 19 June 1778.

19. *Ibid.;* Ewald, 4 June 1778.

20. Ewald; Boudinot to his wife, 11 June 1778, Boudinot Collection, Princeton University Library; Eden to Alexander Wedderburn, 18, 19, and 20 June 1778, Stevens, nos. 500, 501, 502.

21. "Conditions of Loyalists in New York, winter 1778-79," *The United States Magazine, a Repository of History, Politics, and Literature,* Henry Montgomery Brackenridge, ed., p. 90.

22. I. Shreve to Washington, 24 May 1778, Washington Papers, reel 49.

23. The role of the Peace Commission has received definitive treatment by many historians; a few suggested studies are: Weldon A. Brown, *Empire or Independence: A Study in the Failure of Reconciliation, 1774-1783,* pp. 244-92; Nathan R. Einhorn, "The Reception of the British Peace Offer of 1778," *Pennsylvania History,* 16:191-214; John F. Reed, "The British Peace Commission 1778," *Bulletin of the Historical Society of Montgomery County,* 17:5-73; William B. Reed, *Life and Correspondence of Joseph Reed,* 1:371-96. Scattered letters and papers relating to the Commission may be found in: Stevens, nos. 1107, 1109, 1115, 1120, and 1144; Precis of Military Operations 1777-78, C.O. 5/253; Papers-Congress, reel 97; Washington Papers, reels 49 and 50; Force, Series 9, box 24; Sackville-Germain; Clinton; Reed Papers, NYHS; American Revolution Military and Political, Miscellaneous Letters, vols. 1, 3, and 4, Bancroft.

24. Carlisle to Rev. Ekins, n.d., Eden to Alexander Wedderburn, 19 June 1778, Stevens, nos. 101, 501.

25. Wm. Eden, Minutes written on receiving news of the proposed Evacuation of Philadelphia, 5 June 1778, Stevens.

26. McLane to (?), 3 June 1778, American Officers in Revolution, Gratz; Intelligence sent from city to Maxwell, Washington Papers, reel 49; Maxwell sent the memo to Dickinson, who forwarded it to Washington on 3 June.

27. Maxwell to Dickinson, 14 June 1778, Dickinson to Washington, 15 June 1778, Washington Papers, reel 49; Ewald, 15 June 1778; Kraft, "Journal," *Collections-NYHS for 1882,* pp. 39-40.

28. Ration Returns 1777-78, Rations Lost by British Army upon evacuation, Clinton; An Account of Prohibited Goods supposed to remain in the City of Philadelphia this 5th day of June 1778, Sackville-Germain; Drinker, p. 104; Peebles, 30 May 1778, 21.492.5.

29. Lovell to Gates, 9 June 1778, Wentworth to John Langdon, 10 June 1778, Burnett, 3:285.

30. It is not possible to determine the exact date each corps or battalion passed over to New Jersey. The reports of contemporary diarists and orders are not in agreement. Andre, Montresor, Robertson, Baurmeister, Ewald, Sullivan, Peebles, Parker, and Mackenzie all disagree in some detail. There is no way to es-

tablish where each officer, except Mackenzie, was stationed during these hectic days. These differences are common throughout the war, especially between eyewitness and secondhand accounts. It is unimportant, but tends to support the confused conditions existing in the city during the last few days. Ewald, 16 and 17 June 1778; McLane to Washington, 16 June 1778, Dickinson to Washington, 14 June 1778, Washington Papers, reel 49; Kraft, "Journal," *Collections-NYHS for 1882,* p. 40; Mackenzie Orders, 8 and 16 June 1778, Clements Library, University of Michigan; Andre, p. 74; Baurmeister to Jungkenn, 15 June 1778, Baurmeister, p. 87; Montresor, pp. 498-99; Muhlenberg, *Journals,* 3:153.

31. Sullivan, 17 and 18 June 1778; Andre, p. 74.
32. Proclamation by Sir Henry Clinton-Philadelphia, 13 June 1778, BHP, no 1233.

Chapter XVI

1. *CR,* 11:483-85, 504, 505, 512-18, 587, 12:27, 496, 665, 710; Wilbur Siebert, *The Loyalists of Pennsylvania,* p. 58. Siebert made a study of the proscribed lists naming the 453 attainted traitors— 109 were from the city of Philadelphia, 76 from Philadelphia County, 77 from Bucks, 87 from Chester, 9 from York, 35 from Northampton, 4 from Bedford, with 3 from New Jersey, 1 each from Maryland and New York. For illustrations of the sale of Loyalist property, see *PP,* 6 and 8 Aug., 5 Sept., 6 Oct. 1778.
2. "Extracts from the Diplomatic Correspondence of Conrad Alexander Gerard, First Minister Plenipotentiary to the United States July 1778 to Oct. 1779," *Records of the American Catholic Historical Society,* 31:223.
3. Josiah Bartlett to John Langdon, 13 July 1778, Burnett, 3:328-29.
4. "Autobiographical Letters of Peter S. Duponceau," *PMHB,* 15:184; *Autobiography of Benjamin Rush,* p. 138; Richard Peters to Pickering, 26 June and 4 July 1778, Pickering Papers, Massachusetts Historical Society.
5. Nesbitt to Aleck (?), 4 July 1778, HSP. Other views of the filthy and desolate condition may be found in "Autobiographical Letters of Peter S. Duponceau," *PMHB,* vol. 15; Autobiographical Letters-Duponceau, Meng, ed., *American Catholic Historical Society,* vol. 45; Bartlett to Langdon, 13 July 1778, Bartlett to Wm. Whip-

ple, 20 July 1778, "Sessions of the Continental Congress held in the College of Philadelphia in July, 1778," *PMHB*, 22:114-15; Fisher, p. 464; Letter of Mrs. Eliza Farmer, 25 Oct. 1783, "Notes and Queries," *PMHB*, 40:364-65; Marshall, *Extracts from the Diary . . . During the Revolution*, p. 189; Gerard to Vergennes, 25 July 1778, *Records of the American Catholic Historical Society*, 42:36.

6. Josiah Bartlett to John Langdon, 13 July 1778, Henry Laurens to the president of South Carolina (Rawlins Lowndes), 15 June [1778], Burnett, 3:328-29, 332-33.

7. *PEP*, 18 July 1778.

8. George Bryan to the Pennsylvania Assembly, 18 Mar. 1779.

9. Marion V. Brewington, "Maritime Philadelphia, 1609-1837," *PMHB*, 43:107-8.

10. Richard Bache to Franklin, 14 July 1778, *Letters to Benjamin Franklin from His Family and Friends, 1751-1790*, pp. 77-80; Franklin's Ledger, 7 Nov. 1764 to July 1775, Dr. Franklin's Journal 1764-74, Benjamin Franklin Papers, APS; The Wilson Portrait of Franklin; "Earl Grey's Gift to the Nation," Charles Henry Hart, *PMHB*, 30:409; Edward M. Riley, "Franklin's Home," *Historic Philadelphia*, p. 156; Nicholas B. Wainwright, *Colonial Grandeur in Philadelphia*, p 65.

11. Illustrations of advertisements for lost property may be found through Feb. 1779. For examples see *PP*, 8, 14, 16, 21, and 28 July, 6, 22, and 27 Aug., 1, 3, 24, and 29 Sept., 10, 24, and 27 Oct., 7, 14, 26, and 28 Nov., 12, 17, 19, 22, and 31 Dec. 1778, 2 and 5 Jan., 6 and 13 Feb. 1779; *PEP*, 8 July, 1 Aug. 1778.

12. *PP*, 24 Oct. 1778.

13. *Ibid.*, 27 Aug. 1778.

14. *Ibid.*, 27 Oct. 1778; *PEP*, 8 July 1778.

15. Schlater to Howe, (?) Apr. 1778, Carleton; *PP*, 2 Jan. 1779.

16. This story was incorporated in a letter that appeared in the *Virginia Gazette*, 19 June 1778. It was headed "letter from ———, 27 May 1778." Pemberton's biographer makes no mention of this incident. Theodore Thayer, *Israel Pemberton*, pp. 232-33.

17. *PP*, 18 and 25 July, 1, 8, 18, and 25 Aug., 6 and 17 Oct., 1 and 19 Dec. 1778; *PEP*, 2, 4, 6, 18, and 30 July, 13 Aug., 7 and 11 Sept., 25 Nov. 1778, 22 Feb. 1779.

18. *PP*, 1 Dec. 1778.

19. *Ibid.*, 18 July 1778.

20. *Journals of the House of Representatives of the Commonwealth of Pennsylvania, 1776-1781,* 1:217, 18 Aug. 1778; An Act for Procuring an Estimate of the Damages, sustained by the Inhabitants of Pennsylvania, from the Troops and Adherents of the King of Great Britain during the Present War, *The Statues at Large of Pennsylvania from 1682-1801,* 10:530-33.

21. Records of Haverford Meeting, Wayne Papers, HSP; British Depredations, Revolutionary Miscellaneous, HSP; I. Shreve to wife, Polly, 28 Nov. 1777, Revolutionary Soldiers, vol. 4; Dreer; Jonathan Evans Account Book, Haverford College Library. Scattered references to the losses sustained by inhabitants on both sides of the political fence also are found in the Quaker and Roberts Collections at Haverford College.

22. Estimate of Damages Done by the British, 1777-78, HSP. (This schedule is reproduced in *PMHB,* 25:323-35, 544-59.)

23. List of Subscriptions to Repair Dilapidations Suffered by First Presbyterian Church of Philadelphia at the hands of the British during the Occupation of the City, 14 May 1779; Minutes of the Meetings of the Committee for Regulating Pews, 1774-78; Subscriptions and Contributions Received for Repairs and Paving 1779-83, Presbyterian Historical Society.

24. Estimate of the Cost of Repair for damage done to the Second Presbyterian Church by the British Army during its occupation of Philadelphia, 1778; Corporation Minutes and Resolutions, 1772-1916, Presbyterian Historical Society; Carl F. Haussman, "History of St. Michael's and Zion Congregations, Philadelphia, Pa.," Lutheran Seminary Library; Muhlenberg, *Journals,* 3:172; Robert G. Torbet, *A Social History of the Philadelphia Baptist Association: 1707-1940,* pp. 49-50.

25. *PP,* 10 Nov. 1778.

26. Winthrop Sargent, ed., *Loyalist Poetry of the Revolution,* p. 81; Barrow *(Life of Earl Howe,* p. 220) gives this epigram in slightly different form.

Bibliography

MANUSCRIPTS

England

PUBLIC RECORD OFFICE (LONDON)

Audit Office Records: Joshua Loring's Account. A.O. 1/bundle 494 no. 98.

British Headquarters Papers: Military Correspondence 1776-78. C.O. 5/93-95.
    Correspondence between the Colonial Secretary and the Secretary of War. C.O. 5/167-73.
    Precis of Correspondence on Military Campaign, 1777-78. C.O. 5/253.

Treasury Board Papers. Letters. T/1/573/66-67.

WAR OFFICE (LONDON)

Correspondence of Generals Howe and Clinton with the Secretary of War, 1776-80. WO 1/10.

Records of General Courts-Martial. W.O. 71/85.

NATIONAL ARMY MUSEUM (WOOLWICH)

Coote Papers. Orderly Books, North America. MS. 6912/14, 37-39.

ROYAL ARTILLERY LIBRARY, OLD ROYAL MILITARY ACADEMY (WOOLWICH)

Brigade Orders, Royal Artillery, 28 Sept. 1777-21 Feb. 1778 [Brigadier General James Pattison]. MS.57.

General Orders, Sept. 1777-Feb. 1778. MS.58.

Letter Book of James Pattison. MS.7.

UNIVERSITY OF NOTTINGHAM, DEPARTMENT OF MANUSCRIPTS

Mellish of Hodsock. MSS 172/111.
Newcastle Manuscripts. 2,337-2,385, bundle 2.

Scotland

SCOTTISH RECORD OFFICE, GENERAL REGISTER HOUSE (EDINBURGH)

Abercairny Muniments sec. 1 no. 458. Thomas Stirling to Sir
    William Stirling, 1760-97. GD 24/1/1458.
Cunningham of Thornton Papers, 1776-82. Journal of Captain John
    Peebles, 1776-82. 21.492.4-6 (1777-78).
————. List of General Staff Officers. GD 2/229.
————. Miscellaneous Accounts of Captain John Peebles. GD
    21/490.

NATIONAL LIBRARY OF SCOTLAND (EDINBURGH)

Steuart Papers. Charles Steuart. MS5030, ff. 168-169v, 191.
Stuart Steven Papers. MS5375, ff. 35-42.

United States

HISTORICAL SOCIETY OF PENNSYLVANIA (PHILADELPHIA)

Gratz Collection. Foreign Officers in the British Army in the Revolu-
    tion and American Loyalists.
————. Loyalist Poetry of the Revolution.
————. American Officers in the Revolution.
————. Generals in the American Revolution.
————. Governor Thomas Wharton's Escape at the British Occupa-
    tion of Philadelphia. Essay read by Charles H. H. Esling.
Thompson Collection. Papers of Henry Drinker, Thomas Pleasants,
    Joseph Galloway, and Abel James.
Miscellaneous Collection of the Historical Society.
————. Edward Carey Gardner Collection.
————. British Depredations, 1778-83.
————. Affidavits and Courts-Martial, 1777-1805.
————. Prisoners and Paroles, 1776-81.
————. Revolutionary Miscellaneous.
————. Miscellaneous Societies and Companies.
————. John Maxwell Nesbitt Letters.
Pemberton Papers.

————. Clifford Correspondence.

Incidents of the Revolution.

Thomas Bradford Papers.

David McNeely Stauffer Collection.

Colonel Elias Boudinot Papers.

Maps and Plans of the Revolution, 1777-78.

Commonplace Book, 1775-80.

Captain Francis Nichols. Revolutionary Journal, 1777-78.

The Meschianza. [Catalogue of books portrayed by the characters in the Meschianza.]

Dreer Collection. Daniel Wier, Commissary to the British Army in America. Correspondence [with John Robinson].

————. Letters of Soldiers, Surgeons, and Chaplains of the American Revolution.

————. English Military.

————. General John Lacey Papers (compiled by William Darlington).

————. Lacey Memoirs.

————. General Orders issued by Lacey, 1778, 1780, and 1781 (compiled by William Darlington).

Charles R. Hildeburn. Loyalist Ladies in Revolutionary Times.

Etting Collection. Officers of the British and American Armies.

————. Generals of the Revolution.

————. Revolutionary Papers.

Pennsylvania Counties, Lancaster County. Letters and Accounts of David Franks, Bernard Gratz, L. Andrew Levy, and Joseph Simon.

————. Provisioning British and American Prisoners and Soldiers.

Estimates of Damage Done by British, 1777-78.

Conarroe Autograph Collection.

English Lines Near Philadelphia, 1777. [Map by Lewis Nicola.]

Daniel C. Clymer Family Papers.

British Prisoners and Parole Papers.

Hessian, Waldeck, and British Prisoners, 1776-79.

Prisoners of War Letter Book and Ration Book, 1778-82.

James T. Mitchell Collection.

Sergeant Thomas Sullivan Journal, 1775-78.

John Hinrichs Diary, 1778-80 [in German].

Wharton Papers. Thomas Wharton Letter Book, 1773-84.

————. Charles Wharton Daybook, 1775-85.

Cadwalader Collection. General John Cadwalader Papers, 1742-86.

James Drinker Papers. Typescripts of letters between Henry Drinker and Elizabeth Drinker, 1777-78.

Thomas Nickleson Letter Book, 1772-93.

Irvine Papers. Letters of Colonel William Irvine.

Douglas McFarlan Papers. Maps and Views of Pennsylvania.

————. Campaign, 1777-78.

Joshua Francis Fisher Family Papers, 1755-1865.

Balch Collection. Swift and Willing Family Correspondence, 1743-82.

————. Balch Papers.

————. Correspondence of Thomas Willing.

General Anthony Wayne Papers.

Massachusetts Papers. Board of War Letters, 1777-80.

Tench Coxe Papers. Coxe, Furman & Coxe Letter Book, 1776-79.

————. Tench Coxe Letter Book, 1778.

HSP-Library Company of Philadelphia. Revolutionary War Papers.

————. Smith Manuscripts. Correspondence of Henry Hill.

————. John Fanning Watson Manuscripts.

UNIVERSITY OF VIRGINIA (CHARLOTTESVILLE), TRACY W. MCGREGOR LIBRARY

Hamond Papers (microfilm). Life of Sir Andrew Snape Hamond Bart, written merely for the Private Information of Family; as the Narrative will shew; being of little interest to the world at large [written circa 1815]. M1722.

————. Account of Andrew Snape Hamond's part in the American Revolution, 1775 through 1777 [written between 1783 and 1785].

————. Orders issued, 1 Jan. 1778-18 July 1779. M1723.

————. Letters sent 1 Jan. 1778-25 Apr. 1778. M1723.

UNIVERSITY OF MICHIGAN (ANN ARBOR), CLEMENTS LIBRARY

Orderly Book of Sir William Howe, 27 Jan. 1776-1 May 1778.

Journal of von Jahr 1776-84; Gott save the King, signed J. R.

Papers of Lord George Sackville-Germain.

Sir Henry Clinton Papers.

Mackenzie Papers.

Von Jungkenn Papers.

Orderly Book of Sir Henry Clinton, 24 May 1778-8 Nov. 1781.

DEPARTMENT OF THE NAVY (WASHINGTON, D.C.),
  HISTORICAL RESEARCH SECTION

Log Books of the *Camilla, Experiment, Eagle, Roebuck, Solebay,* and *Pearl* [originals in the Public Records Office, London].

GLOUCESTER COUNTY (NEW JERSEY) HISTORICAL SOCIETY

Revolutionary War Papers (Indictments, Inquisitions, Fugitives).

HAVERFORD COLLEGE (PENNSYLVANIA)

Quaker Collection.
Roberts Collection.
Journal of George Churchman 1777-80.
Diary of David Cooper, 1777-94.
Account Book of Jonathan Evans.
Memorandum, Transcripts of Pieces in Wartime and after the Revolution to 1788.

LIBRARY OF CONGRESS (WASHINGTON, D.C.)

Peter Force Papers. Pierre Eugene du Simitière. Memoranda, 1774-83; Commonplace Book; Notes on Publication. Series 7 E, box 42.
Loyalist Rhapsodies. Series 8 D, box 95.
Joseph Shippen Papers. Series 8 D, box 163.
Miscellaneous Manuscript Collection. Letters to and from Henry Strachey.
British Headquarters Papers.
Stephen Collins Papers.

NATIONAL ARCHIVES (WASHINGTON, D.C.)

Papers of George Washington (microfilm).
Papers of the Continental Congress (microfilm).
War Department Collection of Revolutionary War Records (manuscript and microfilm).

UNIVERSITY OF PENNSYLVANIA (PHILADELPHIA)

Charles Patterson Van Pelt Library. Early American Letters.
Secretary's Office. Minutes of the Trustees of the College, Academy, and Charitable Schools, 1768-91, Vol. 2.

MASONIC TEMPLE, PHILADELPHIA

Minutes Royal Arch Lodge No. 3, 1767-1788.

PHILADELPHIA YEARLY MEETING OF THE SOCIETY OF FRIENDS, DEPARTMENT OF RECORDS

Meetings for Sufferings. Minutes, 1775-1785.

PHILADELPHIA MONTHLY MEETING OF THE SOCIETY OF FRIENDS, DEPARTMENT OF RECORDS

Northern District Minutes, 1772-81.
Southern District Minutes, 1772-80.
Minutes of the Monthly Meetings Friends of Philadelphia, Commencing 26th Day of the 9th Month 1777 ending 12th Month 1778.

PHILADELPHIA CITY ARCHIVES

Corporation of Contributors, Relief of the Poor. Treasurer's Accounts, 1766-80. 35.1.
Alms House Managers Minutes, 1766-78. 35.3.
Constables Returns, South Part of Dock Ward, 1775; Middle Ward, 1775. 96.1.
County Tax Assessment Ledger, Philadelphia County, 1775. 1.10.
County Tax Assessment Ledger, Philadelphia County, 1774. 1.10.
Provincial Tax Duplicate, Philadelphia County, 1775. 1.10.
Constables Returns for City, 1775. 96.1.
Constables Returns for City, 1780. 96.1.
Overseers of the Poor. Minutes, 1774-82. 35.4.

PRINCETON UNIVERSITY LIBRARY

Elias Boudinot Collection.
Andre de Coppet Collection.

COLONIAL WILLIAMSBURG, RESEARCH DEPARTMENT (WILLIAMSBURG, VA.)

Parker Family Papers (microfilm) used with permission of the Liverpool City Libraries.
Simcoe Papers.
Carleton Papers (British Headquarter Papers).

DELAWARE HISTORICAL SOCIETY

Letters of Captain William Dansey, 1771-85.
Letters of John McKinly, 1777-78.

NEW YORK HISTORICAL SOCIETY

Miscellaneous Manuscripts. Letter of William Grand.
————. Unsigned Letter from Philadelphia, 29 Nov. 1777.
————. Correspondence of John Lacey.
————. Correspondence of Elias Boudinot.
Allen McLane Papers.
Orderly Book of Captain Jehu Eyre, 20 Sept.-18 Dec. 1777.
Walter Stewart Papers.
John Lamb Papers.
Joseph Reed Papers (includes diary of John Miller).
Orderly Book of Colonel William Malcolm's Regiment, 18-27 Nov.
    1777 and 2 Mar.-10 Oct. 1778.

NEW YORK PUBLIC LIBRARY

Bancroft Collection (typescript). Letters to Henry Strachey.
————. American Revolution, Military and Political [miscellaneous
    letters].
————. Balch Papers.
————. Abstracts of King George's letters to Lord North 1770-83.
————. Letters of Charles Blagden.
————. Chalmers Collection.
————. Loyalists Transcripts.
————. British Headquarters Papers in America (photostat).
————. American Loyalist, Royal Institute Transcripts.

CHRIST CHURCH, PHILADELPHIA

Vestry Minutes, 19 June 1761-10 Apr. 1784.

GLASSBORO (NEW JERSEY) STATE COLLEGE

Stewart Manuscripts.

RUTGERS UNIVERSITY

British Army Orderly Book [General Charles Grey] 23 Feb. 1778-30
    May 1778 (microfilm, original owned by Mr. Norman C. Witwer).

Sol Feinstone Collection.
Archives of the Pennsylvania Hospital (microfilm).
Meteorological Observations near Philadelphia, January 1777-10 May 1778 [Phineas Pemberton].
Records of the Carpenters Company.

Book of Minutes belonging to the Directors of the Library Company of Philadelphia. Vol. 2.

Minutes, Sept. 1777 to June 1778.

Revolutionary War Letters of William Van Horne to Colonel Joseph Hart.
Captain Nathaniel Vansandt Papers. Folio 11.
Samuel Hart Collection (Forfeited Estates, Philadelphia County). Folio 8.
General W. W. H. Davis Collection. Folios 100 and 169.
The Battle of Crooked Billet Papers. Folios 2, 3 and 5.
Elizabeth Graeme Ferguson Papers. Folio 2.
Society of Friends, Epistles and Testimonies 1755-1777 [8]. Folio 4.

First Presbyterian Church [Buttonwood]. List of Subscriptions to Repair Dilapidations Suffered by the First Presbyterian Church of Philadelphia at the hands of the British during their Occupation of the City, May 14, 1779.
————. Minutes of the Meetings of the Committee for Regulating Pews, 1774-86.
————. Subscriptions and Contributions Received for Repairs and Paving, 1779-83.
Second Presbyterian Church. Estimate of the cost of Repair for damage done to the Second Presbyterian Church by the British Army during its occupation in Philadelphia, 1778.
————. Corporation Minutes and Resolutions, 1772-1916.
————. Register and other Records 1744-1929. Communicants 1771-1801; Baptisms 1774-1833.

Third Presbyterian Church. Records 1768-1837. Baptisms, 1775-1810; Communicants, 1768-1839.
―――. Information Supplied Concerning Churches.
―――. Old Pine Street Church, built 1768, cradle of the American Revolution.

ASSOCIATE CHURCH OF NORTH AMERICA [SCOTS PRESBYTERIAN CHURCH]

William Marshall's register of births and baptisms in the Scots Presbyterian Church of Philadelphia 1767-1801.

MRS. WELSH STRAWBRIDGE, GRAEME PARK

Elizabeth Graeme Ferguson, Book of Memoranda and Poetry.

NEWSPAPERS

Continental Journal and Weekly Advertiser (Boston)
Der Wochentliche Philadelphische Staatsbote
Freeman's Journal (Philadelphia)
Maryland Gazette (Baltimore)
New Jersey Gazette (Burlington)
Pennsylvania Aurora, General Advertiser (Philadelphia)
Pennsylvania Evening Post (Philadelphia)
Pennsylvania Gazette (Philadelphia and York)
Pennsylvania Journal (Philadelphia)
Pennsylvania Ledger (Philadelphia)
Pennsylvania Mercury (Philadelphia)
Pennsylvania Packet (Philadelphia and Lancaster)
Rivington's New York Gazette
Royal American Gazette (New York)
Royal Pennsylvania Gazette (Philadelphia)
Virginia Gazette (Williamsburg)

BIBLIOGRAPHICAL WORKS AND GENERAL SOURCES

Adams, Randolph G. *The Headquarters Papers of the British Army in North America during the War of the American Revolution.* Ann Arbor, 1926.

Andrews, Charles M. *Guide to the Materials for American History, to 1783, in the Public Record Office of Great Britain.* 2 vols. Washington, 1914.

Brigham, Clarence S. *History and Bibliography of American Newspapers, 1690-1820.* 2 vols. Worcester, Mass., 1947.

Cappon, Lester J. and Duff, Stella F. *Virginia Gazette Index 1736-1780.* 2 vols. Williamsburg, 1950.

Clark, William Bell and Morgan, W. J., eds. *Naval Documents of the American Revolution.* 6 vols. Washington, D.C., 1964-.

Crick, B. R. and Alman, Miriam. *A Guide to Manuscripts Relating to America in Great Britain and Ireland.* London, 1961.

Daly, John. *Descriptive Inventory of the Archives of the City and County of Philadelphia.* Philadelphia, 1970.

Drake, Milton, comp. *Almanacs of the United States.* 2 vols. New York, 1962.

Evans, Charles. *American Bibliography.* 10 vols. Chicago, 1903-29.

Griffin, Grace Gardner. *A Guide to Manuscripts Relating to American History in British Depositories Reproduced for the U. S. Library of Congress.* Washington, D.C., 1946.

Guide to the Manuscript Collection of the Historical Society of Pennsylvania. 2nd ed. Philadelphia, 1949.

Matthews, William, comp. *American Diaries: An Annotated Bibliography of American Diaries Written Prior to the Year 1861.* Berkeley and Los Angeles, 1945.

Writings on Pennsylvania History. Edited by Arthur C. Bining, Robert L. Brunhouse, Norman B. Wilkinson. Harrisburg, 1948.

Preliminary Guide to the Research Materials of the Pennsylvania Historical and Museum Commission. Harrisburg, 1959.

Phillips, P. Lee. *A Descriptive List of Maps and Views of Philadelphia in the Library of Congress 1683-1865.* Philadelphia, 1926.

————. *A List of Maps of America in the Library of Congress.* Washington, D.C., 1901.

Report of the Committee on Pensions and Revolutionary Claims on the Petition of Sarah Deweas and others, for payment for property destroyed by the enemy in the Revolutionary war. Washington, D.C., 17 Jan. 1817.

War Department Collection of Revolutionary War Records. Compiled by Mabel E. Deutrich, revised by Howard H. Wehmann. National Archives, Washington, D.C., 1970.

PRINTED PRIMARY SOURCES: COLLECTIONS

Almon, John and Debrett, John, eds. *The Parliamentary Register; or History of the Proceedings and Debates of the House of Commons.* 62 vols. (especially vols. 11 and 12). London, 1775-96.

———. *The Remembrancer or Impartial Repository of Public Events.* 12 vols. London, 1775-83.

Archives of the State of New Jersey. 2nd ser. 5 vols. Trenton, 1901-17.

Burnett, Edmund C., ed. *Letters of Members of the Continental Congress.* 8 vols. Washington, D.C., 1921-36.

Colonial Records of Pennsylvania. Vol. 11. Harrisburg, 1852.

Delaware Archives. 3 vols. Wilmington, 1911-19.

Hazard, Samuel, ed. *Register of Pennsylvania.* 16 vols. Philadelphia, 1828-38.

Linn, John Blair and Egle, William H., eds. *Pennsylvania in the War of the Revolution: Battalions and Line 1775-1783.* 2 vols. Harrisburg, 1880.

Journal of the American Congress . . . from 1774 to 1788. 4 vols. Washington, D.C., 1823.

Journals of the Continental Congress 1774-89. Edited by W. C. Ford, Gaillard Hunt, John C. Fitzpatrick, and Roscoe R. Hill. 34 vols. Washington, D.C., 1904-37.

Journals of the House of Representatives of the Commonwealth of Pennsylvania. Vol. 1, 1776-81. Philadelphia, 1782.

Pennsylvania Archives. 1st ser., vols. 5, 6, 7, 9; 3rd ser., vols. 3, 14. 1853, 1896, 1897.

The Statutes at Large of Pennsylvania from 1682 to 1801. Compiled by James T. Mitchell and Henry Flanders. 16 vols. Harrisburg, 1896-1911.

Stevens, B. F., comp. *Facsimiles of Manuscripts in European Archives Relating to America, 1773-1783.* 25 vols. London, 1889-98.

UNPUBLISHED THESES

Davies, Elizabeth H. "Loyalism in Philadelphia during the American Revolution." Ph.D. dissertation, Bryn Mawr, 1952.

Haussmann, Carl F. "History of St. Michael's and Zion Congregation, Philadelphia, Pa." Mt. Airy, Lutheran Seminary (Philadelphia), 1949?.

Yalof, Helen Roberts. "British Military Theatricals in Philadelphia During the Revolutionary War." Ph.D. dissertation, New York University. Xerox by University Microfilm, Ann Arbor, 1972.

PUBLISHED LETTERS, DIARIES, AND JOURNALS

Adams, John. *Diary and Autobiography of John Adams.* Edited by L. H. Butterfield. 4 vols. Cambridge, 1961.

―――. *Familiar Letters of John Adams and His Wife Abigail Adams, during the Revolution.* Edited by Charles Francis Adams. New York, 1876.

Allen, James. "Diary of James Allen, Esq., of Philadelphia, Counsellor-at-Law, 1770-78." *Pennsylvania Magazine of History and Biography* 9 (1885-86).

Andre, John. *Major Andre's Journal: Operations of the British Army under General Sir William Howe and Sir Henry Clinton, June 1777 to November 1778.* Edited by William Abbatt. New York, 1930.

―――. "Major Andre's Story of the Mischianza." Preface by Sophie Howard Ward. *Century Magazine* N.S.25 (1894).

―――. "Particulars of the Mischianza, exhibited in America at the Departure of General Howe: Copy of a Letter from an Officer at Philadelphia to his Correspondent in London." *Annual Register, or a View of the History, Politics, and Literature for the Year 1778.* London, 1778. Also in *Gentlemen's Magazine and Historical Chronicle* (London) 48 (1778).

Bartlett, Josiah. "Letters of Josiah Bartlett: Sessions of the Continental Congress Held in the College of Philadelphia in July 1778." *Pennsylvania Magazine of History and Biography* 22 (1898).

Baurmeister, Carl Leopold, "Letters of Major Baurmeister during the Philadelphia Campaign, 1777-1778." Edited by Bernhard A. Uhlendorf and Edna Vosper. *Pennsylvania Magazine of History and Biography* 59 (1935), 60 (1936).

Binns, John. *Recollections of the Life of John Binns.* Philadelphia, 1854.

Bogart, John. *The John Bogart Letters 1776-1782.* New Brunswick, N.J., 1914.

Boudinot, Elias. "[Journal of] Colonel Elias Boudinot in New York City, February 1778." Contributed by Helen Jordan. *Pennsylvania Magazine of History and Biography* 24 (1900).

————. *Journal of Historical Recollections of American Events during the Revolutionary War.* Philadelphia, 1894.

————. "Colonel Elias Boudinot's Notes of Two Conferences Held by the American and British Commissioners to Settle a General Cartel for the Exchange of Prisoners of War, 1778." *Pennsylvania Magazine of History and Biography* 24 (1900).

Buettner, Johann Carl. *Narrative of Johann Carl Buettner in the American Revolution.* New York, n.d.

Carlisle, Frederick Howard. *The Manuscripts of the Earl of Carlisle Preserved at Castle Howard.* Historical Manuscripts Commission, 15th report, appendix 6. London, 1897.

Clark, John, Jr. "Letters from Major John Clark, Jr., to General Washington during the Occupation of Philadelphia by the British Army." *Bulletin of the Historical Society of Pennsylvania* 1 (1845-47).

Clinton, Sir Henry. *The American Rebellion: Sir Henry Clinton's Narrative of His Campaigns, 1775-1782, with an Appendix of Original Documents.* Edited by William B. Willcox. New Haven, 1954.

————. "General Sir Henry Clinton's Orders, 1778." *Collections of New York Historical Society for the Year 1883.* New York, 1884.

Coke, Daniel Parker. *The Royal Commission on the Losses and Services of American Loyalists, 1783 to 1785.* Edited by Hugh Edward Egerton. Oxford, 1915.

Collin, Nicholas. *The Journal and Biography of Nicholas Collin, 1746-1831.* Edited by Amandus Johnson. Philadelphia, 1936.

Cooper, Samuel, "Extracts from the Letters of Samuel Cooper, 1777-78." Contributed by John W. Jordan. *Pennsylvania Magazine of History and Biography* 10 (1886).

Cunningham, William. "The Life, confession and last dying words of Capt. William Cunningham, formerly British Provost Marshall in the city of New York, who was executed in London, the 10th of August, 1791." *American Apollo* 1 (1792).

David, Ebenezer. *A Rhode Island Chaplain in the Revolution: Letters of Ebenezer David to Nicholas Brown, 1775-1778.* Edited by Jeanette D. Black and William Green Roelker. Providence, R.I., 1949.

Dearborn, Henry. *Revolutionary War Journals of Henry Dearborn, 1775-1783.* Edited by Lloyd A. Brown and Howard H. Peckham. Chicago, 1939.

De Pontgibaud, Chevalier. *A French Volunteer of the War of Independence.* Translated and edited by Robert B. Douglas. 2nd ed. Paris, 1897.

Doehla, Tagebuch, (original in Archives of Ansbach, Bavaria), A partial translation in the *William and Mary Quarterly.* July, 1942.

Drinker, Elizabeth. *Extracts from the Journal of Elizabeth Drinker, from 1759 to 1807, A.D.* Edited by Henry D. Biddle. Philadelphia, 1889.

———. "Extracts from the Journal of Mrs. Henry Drinker, from Sept. 25, 1777 to July 8, 1778." *Pennsylvania Magazine of History and Biography* 13 (1889).

Duponceau, Peter S. "Autobiographical Letters of Peter S. Duponceau." *Pennsylvania Magazine of History and Biography* 40 (1916), 63 (1939).

Durant, John, ed. *New Materials for the History of the American Revolution* (translated from documents in the French Archives). New York, 1889.

Elliot, Hugh. *A Memoir of the Right Honourable Hugh Elliot.* [Letters of William and Mrs. Eden, Countess of Minto.] Edinburgh, 1868.

Ewald, Johann. *A Diary of the American War.* Edited by Joseph P. Tustin. New Haven, 1978.

Farmar, Eliza. "Letter of Mrs. Eliza Farmar, 1783." *Pennsylvania Magazine of History and Biography* 40 (1916).

Fisher, Sarah Logan. "A Diary of Trifling Occurrences, Philadelphia, 1776-1778." Edited by Nicholas B. Wainwright. *Pennsylvania Magazine of History and Biography* 82 (1958).

Ford, Worthington C., ed. *Defences of Philadelphia in 1777.* Brooklyn, New York 1897.

Franklin, Benjamin. *Letters to Benjamin Franklin from His Family and Friends, 1751-90.* Edited by William Duane. New York, 1859.

Franks, Rebecca. "A Letter of Miss Rebecca Franks, 1778." Contributed by Henry F. Thompson. *Pennsylvania Magazine of History and Biography* 16 (1892).

Frazer, Persifor. *General Persifor Frazer: A Memoir Compiled . . . by his Great-grandson Persifor Frazer. . . .* Philadelphia, 1907.

———. "Some Extracts from the Papers of General Persifor Frazer." *Pennsylvania Magazine of History and Biography* 31 (1907).

Galloway, Joseph. *The Examination of Joseph Galloway, Esq., by a Committee of the House of Commons.* Edited by Thomas Balch. Philadelphia, 1855.

———. *A Letter to the People of America, Lately printed at New York; now re-published by an American. With a Postscript by the Editor Addressed to Sir W—— H——* [Attributed to Galloway.] London, 1778.

———. "Joseph Galloway to Charles Jenkinson on the British Constitution." Edited by Julian P. Boyd. *Pennsylvania Magazine of History and Biography* 64 (1940).

———. "Joseph Galloway's Plans of Union for the British Empire, 1774-88." Edited by Julian P. Boyd. *Pennsylvania Magazine of History and Biography* 64 (1940).

———. *An Account of the Conduct of the War in the Middle Colonies.* London, 1780.

———. *A Letter to the Right Honourable Lord Viscount H———E on His Naval Conduct in the American War.* 2nd ed., corrected. London, 1781.

———. *Letters to a Nobleman on the Conduct of the War in the Middle Colonies.* 2nd ed. London, 1779.

———. *A Reply to the Observations to Lieut. Gen. Sir William Howe, on a pamphlet, entitled Letters to a Nobleman.* London, 1780.

———. "Letters to Joseph Galloway from Leading Tories in America." *Historical Magazine, and Notes and Queries concerning the Antiquities, History and Biography of America* 5 (1861).

George III. *The Correspondence of King George the Third from 1760 to December 1783.* Edited and arranged by John Fortescue. 5 vols. London, 1927-28.

———. *The Correspondence of King George the Third with Lord North from 1768 to 1783.* Edited by W. Bodham Donne. 2 vols. London, 1867.

Gerard, Conrad Alexander. "Philadelphia and the Revolution: French Diplomacy in the United States, 1778-79." [Letters of Conrad Alexander Gerard.] Translated by Jules A. Baisnee and John J. Meng. *Records of the American Catholic Historical Society of Philadelphia* 56-59. (1946-49).

———. "Extracts from the Diplomatic Correspondence of Conrad Alexander Gerard, First Minister Plenipotentiary to the United States, July 1778 to October 1779," Edited by Elizabeth S. Kite. *Records of the American Catholic Historical Society of Philadelphia* 31 (1920).

Hale, W. *Some British Soldiers in America.* [Letters of Lieutenant W. Hale to his parents.] Edited by W. H. Wilkin. London, 1914.

Heinrichs, Johann. "Extracts from the Letter Book of Captain Johann Heinrichs of the Hessian Jäger Corps, 1778-1780." Translated by Julius F. Sachse. *Pennsylvania Magazine of History and Biography* 22 (1898).

———. "The Hessians in Philadelphia: A German Officer's Impression of Our City (A Letter of Captain Johann Heinrichs taken from the Correspondence of Professor Schlözen of Gottingen)." Translated by Helen Bell. *Pennsylvania Magazine of History and Biography* 1 (1877).

Historical Anecdotes, Civil and Military: In a Series of Letters Written from America in the Years 1777-78 to Different Persons in England. London, 1779.

Howe, William. *Reflections on a Pamphlet Intitled "A Letter to the Right Honble Lord Vic^t H——E."* Edited with an Introduction by Gerald Saxon Brown. Ann Arbor, n.d.

———. "General Sir William Howe's Orders, 1777-1778." *Collections of the New York Historical Society for the Year 1883.* New York, 1884.

———. *The Narrative of Lieut. Gen. Sir William Howe in a Committee of the House of Commons, on the 29th of April, 1779, Relative to His Conduct during His Late Command of the King's Troops in North America.* 2nd ed. London, 1780.

Inman, George. "George Inman's Narrative of the American Revolution." *Pennsylvania Magazine of History and Biography* 7 (1883).

Jones, Caleb. *Orderly Book of the Maryland Loyalists Regiment June 18, 1778 to October 12, 1778.* Edited by Paul L. Ford. Brooklyn, 1891.

Kemble Papers. *Collections of the New York Historical Society for the years 1883-1884.* 2 vols. New York, 1884-85.

Kirkwood, Robert. *The Journal and Order Book of Captain Robert Kirkwood of the Delaware Regiment of the Continental Line.* Edited by Joseph Brown Turner. Port Washington, N. Y., 1970.

Kraft, John Charles Philip von. "Journal of Lieutenant John Charles Philip von Kraft, 1776-1784." *Collections of the New York Historical Society for the Year 1882.* New York, 1883.

Lacey, John. "Memoirs of Brigadier General John Lacey, of Pennsylvania." *Pennsylvania Magazine of History and Biography* 25 (1901), 26 (1902).

Laurens, John. *The Army Correspondence of Colonel John Laurens in the Years 1777-8.* With a memoir by William Gilmore Simms. New York, 1867.

"Letters of Two Distinguished Penna. Officers." *Pennsylvania Magazine of History and Biography* 35 (1911).

Logan, Deborah. "Letter of Deborah Logan to Major Alexander Garden." *Collections of the Historical Society of Pennsylvania.* Vol. 1. 1853.

McKinly, John. "Letters of Dr. John McKinly to His Wife while a Prisoner of War, 1777-78." Edited by Mary T. Evans. *Pennsylvania Magazine of History and Biography* 34 (1910).

McMichael, James. "Diary of Lieutenant James McMichael of the Pennsylvania Line." Edited by William P. McMichael. *Pennsylvania Magazine of History and Biography* 16 (1892).

Marshall, Christopher. *Extracts from the Diary of Christopher Marshall kept in Philadelphia and Lancaster during the Revolution, 1774-1781.* Edited by William Duane. Albany, 1877.

Marshall, William. *Memoirs of the Late Rev. William Marshall.* Philadelphia, 1806.

[Mauduit, Israel]. *Strictures on the Philadelphia Mischianza, or Triumph upon Leaving America Unconquered.* London, 1779.

Montresor, John. *The Montresor Journals.* Edited and annotated by G.D. Scull. *Collections of the New York Historical Society for the Year 1881.* New York, 1882.

Moore, Frank, ed. *The Diary of the Revolution.* 2 vols. New York, 1969.

Mordecai, Jacob. "Addenda to Watson's Annals of Philadelphia: Notes by Jacob Mordecai, 1836." Edited by Whitfield J. Bell, Jr. *Pennsylvania Magazine of History and Biography* (1974).

Morton, Robert. "The Diary of Robert Morton, Kept in Philadelphia While that City Was Occupied by the British Army in 1777." *Pennsylvania Magazine of History and Biography* 1 (1877).

Moylan, Stephen. "Selections from the Correspondence of Col. Stephen Moylan, of the Continental Cavalry." *Pennsylvania Magazine of History and Biography* 37 (1913).

Muhlenberg, Henry M. "Extracts from the Journal of Rev. Henry M. Muhlenberg D.D., for 1776 and 1777." Translated by Hiester H. Muhlenberg. *Collections of the Historical Society of Pennsylvania.* 1. 1853.

———. *The Journals of Henry Melchior Muhlenberg.* Translated by Theodore G. Tappet and John W. Doberstein. 3 vols. Philadelphia, 1942-1958.

———. *Notebook of a Colonial Clergyman.* [Condensed from the Journals of Henry Melchior Muhlenberg.] Translated and edited by Theodore G. Tappet and John W. Doberstein. Philadelphia, 1959.

Muhlenberg, John Peter Gabriel. "Orderly Book of General John Peter Gabriel Muhlenberg, Mar. 26-Dec. 20, 1777." *Pennsylvania Magazine of History and Biography* 33 (1909), 34 (1910), 35 (1911).

[Munchhausen, Frederick Ernest von]. "The Battle of Germantown described by a Hessian Officer." [Extract from the journal and report of Captain Frederick Ernest von Munchhausen.] *Pennsylvania Magazine of History and Biography* 16 (1892).

Murray, James. *Letters from America, 1773 to 1780, Being the Letters of a Scots Officer, Sir James Murray.* Edited by Eric Robson. Manchester, England, 1951.

Paine, Thomas. *Common Sense Together with the American Crisis 1776-1783.* New York, n.d.

————. "Letter of Thomas Paine to Dr. Franklin: Military Operations near Philadelphia in the Campaign of 1777-78." *Pennsylvania Magazine of History and Biography* 2 (1878).

Papers Relating to the American Loyalists. London, 1821.

Popp, Stephan. "Stephan Popp's Journal, 1777-1783." Edited by Joseph G. Rosengarten. *Pennsylvania Magazine of History and Biography* 26 (1902).

"Proceedings of a Board of General Officers of the British Army at New York, 1781." *Collections of the New York Historical Society for the Year 1916.* New York, 1916.

Proud, Robert. "Letter of Robert Proud, the Historian, 1778." *Pennsylvania Magazine of History and Biography* 29 (1905).

————. "Letters of Robert Proud." *Pennsylvania Magazine of History and Biography* 34 (1910).

Reed, William B., *Life and Correspondence of Joseph Reed.* 2 vols. Philadelphia, 1847.

Robertson, Archibald. *Archibald Robertson, Lt. General, Royal Engineers: His Diaries and Sketches in America, 1762-1780.* New York, 1930.

Rodney, Caesar. *Letters to and from Caesar Rodney 1756-1784.* Edited by George Herbert Ryden. Philadelphia, 1933.

Rush, Benjamin. *Letters of Benjamin Rush.* Edited by L. H. Butterfield, 2. Princeton, 1951.

Sargent, Winthrop, ed. *The Loyalist Poetry of the Revolution.* Philadelphia, 1857.

Serle, Ambrose. *The American Journal of Ambrose Serle, Secretary to Lord Howe.* Edited by Edward H. Tatum, Jr., San Marino, Calif., 1940.

Seybolt, Robert Francis. "A Contemporary British Account of General Sir William Howe's Military Operations in 1777." *Proceedings of the American Antiquarian Society* (Worcester, Mass.) N.s. 40 (1931).

Shippen, Nancy. *Nancy Shippen; Her Journal Book.* Compiled and edited by Ethel Armes. Philadelphia, 1935.

Simcoe, J. G. *Simcoe's Military Journal: A History of the Operations of a*

Partisan Corps, Called the Queen's Rangers, Commanded by Lieut. Col. J. G. Simcoe. New York, 1844.

Stansbury, Joseph and Odell, Jonathan. *The Loyal Verses of Joseph Stansbury and Dr. Jonathan Odell relating to the American Revolution.* Edited by Winthrop Sargent. Albany, 1860.

Stone, William L., trans. *Letters of Brunswick and Hessian Officers during the American Revolution.* Albany, 1891.

Stuart, Charles. *A Prime Minister and His Son, from the Correspondence of the 3rd Earl of Bute and of Lt. General the Hon. Sir Charles Stuart, K.B.* Edited by E. Stuart-Wortley. New York, 1925.

Sullivan, John. *Letters and Papers of Major General John Sullivan.* Edited by Otis G. Hammond. 3 vols. Concord, N.H., 1930-39.

Waldo, Albigence. "Diary of Surgeon Albigence Waldo of the Connecticut Line." *Pennsylvania Magazine of History and Biography* 21 (1897).

Washington, George. *The Washington-Duché Letters.* Introductory note by Worthington Chauncey Ford. Brooklyn, New York 1890.

———. *Orderly Book of General George Washington Kept at Valley Forge, 18 May-11 June 1778.* Boston, 1898.

———. *Revolutionary Orders of General Washington Issued during the Years 1778, 1780, 1781, and 1782.* Selected from MSS of John Whitney. Edited by Henry Whitney. New York, 1844.

———. *Basic Writings of George Washington.* Edited by Saxe Commins. New York, 1948.

———. *The Writings of George Washington from the Original Manuscript Sources, 1745-1799.* Edited by John C. Fitzpatrick. 39 vols. Washington, 1931-44.

———. *The Writings of George Washington.* Edited by Worthington C. Ford. 14 vols. New York, 1889-93.

White, William. *The Life and Letters of Bishop William White.* Edited by Walter Herbert Stowe. New York, 1937.

Willing, Thomas. *Letters and Papers of Thomas Willing.* Edited by Thomas Willing Balch. Philadelphia, 1922.

Wister, Sally. *Sally Wister's Journal.* Edited by Albert Cook Myers. Philadelphia, 1902.

[Witherspoon, John]. *The Humble Confession, Declaration, Recantation, and Apology of Benjamin Towne, Printer, Printer in Philadelphia.* Philadelphia, 1783.

PUBLICATIONS AND PERIODICALS OF LEARNED SOCIETIES

Alexander, John K. "The Philadelphia Numbers Game: An Analysis of Philadelphia's Eighteenth Century Population." *Pennsylvania Magazine of History and Biography* 98 (1974).

"Assessment of Damages Done by the British Troops During the Occupation of Philadelphia, 1777-1778." *Pennsylvania Magazine of History and Biography* 25 (1901).

Baldwin, Ernest H. "Joseph Galloway, the Loyalist Politician." *Pennsylvania Magazine of History and Biography* 26 (1902).

Barnsley, Edward R. "Snapshots of Revolutionary Newtown." *Papers of the Bucks County Historical Society.* 8. 1940.

Brewington, Marion V. "Maritime Philadelphia, 1609-1837," *Pennsylvania Magazine of History and Biography* 63 (1939).

Brown, Ralph Adams. *"The Pennsylvania Ledger:* Tory News Sheet." *Pennsylvania History* 9 (1942).

Buck, William J. "The Battle of Edge Hill." *Historical Sketches of the Historical Society of Montgomery County.* 2. 1900.

———. "The History of Moreland from its first purchase and settlement to the present time." *Collections of the Historical Society of Pennsylvania.* 1. 1853.

Coleman, John M. "Joseph Galloway and the British Occupation of Philadelphia." *Pennsylvania History* 30 (1963).

Cooke, Jacob E. "Tench Coxe, Tory Merchant." *Pennsylvania Magazine of History and Biography* 96 (1972).

Darrach, Henry. "Lydia Darragh, of the Revolution." *Pennsylvania Magazine of History and Biography* 33 (1899).

Davis, W. W. H. "The Battle of the Crooked Billet." *Papers of the Bucks County Historical Society.* 2. 1909.

———. "General John Lacey: Our Quaker General." *Papers of the Bucks County Historical Society.* 3. 1909.

Duffield, Edward Neill. "Rev. Jacob Duche, the First Chaplain of Congress." *Pennsylvania Magazine of History and Biography* 2 (1878).

Dye, William S. "Pennsylvania versus the Theatre." *Pennsylvania Magazine of History and Biography* 55 (1931).

Einhorn, Nathan R. "The Reception of the British Peace Offer of 1778." *Pennsylvania History* 16 (1949).

Ferling, John E. "Joseph Galloway: A Reassessment of the Motivations of a Pennsylvania Loyalist." *Pennsylvania History* 39 (1972).

————. "Joseph Galloway's Military Advice: A Loyalist's View of the Revolution." *Pennsylvania Magazine of History and Biography* 98 (1974).

Fisher, Darlene Emmett. "Social Life in Philadelphia during the British Occupation." *Pennsylvania History* 37 (1970).

Ford, Worthington C. "British and American Prisoners of War, 1778." *Pennsylvania Magazine of History and Biography* 17 (1893).

Frazer, Persifor. "Lieutenant Colonel Persifor Frazer of Pennsylvania Did Not Break his Parole." *Pennsylvania Magazine of History and Biography* 18 (1894).

Godfrey, Carlos E. "Muster Rolls of Three Troops of Loyalist Light Dragoons Raised in Pennsylvania 1777-1778." *Pennsylvania Magazine of History and Biography* 34 (1910).

Green, Charles E. "An Infamous Brother." *California Freemason* 16 (1969).

Hancock, Harold. "The Kent County Loyalists." *Delaware History* 6 (1954-55).

————. "The New Castle County Loyalists." *Delaware History* 4 (1950-51).

Hart, Charles Henry. "Did Peggy Shippen (Mrs. Arnold) and Her Sisters attend the Meschianza?" *Pennsylvania Magazine of History and Biography* 23 (1899).

Jeffreys, C. P. B. "The Provincial and Revolutionary History of St. Peters Church, Philadelphia, 1753-1783." *Pennsylvania Magazine of History and Biography* 48 (1924).

Kurjack, Dennis C. "St. Joseph's and St. Mary's Churches." In *Historic Philadelphia*. Philadelphia, 1953.

Lambdin, Alfred C. "Battle of Germantown." *Pennsylvania Magazine of History and Biography* 1 (1877).

Macaltioner, George V. "The Coming of the British Army into Salem County during the American Revolution." In *150ᵗʰ Anniversary of the Skirmish at Quinton's Bridge and the Massacre at Hancock's Bridge*. 1928.

Mackie, Rev. Alexander. "The Presbyterian Churches of Old Philadelphia." In *Historic Philadelphia*. Philadelphia, 1953.

Meng, John J. "Philadelphia Welcomes America's First Foreign Representative." *Records of the American Catholic Historical Society of Philadelphia* 45 (1934).

Metzger, Charles H. S. J. "Catholics in the Period of the American

Revolution." *Records of the American Catholic Historical Society of Philadelphia* 59 (1948).

Mishoff, Willard O. "Business in Philadelphia during the British Occupation." *Pennsylvania Magazine of History and Biography* 61 (1937).

"Notes on Revolutionary Philadelphia," *The Historical Magazine and Notes and Queries concerning the Antiquities, History and Biography of America.* N.s. 3 (1862), 6 (1866), 10 (1868).

Oaks, Robert F. "Philadelphians in Exile: The Problem of Loyalty during the American Revolution." *Pennsylvania Magazine of History and Biography* 96 (1972).

Pattee, Fred Lewis. "The British Theater in Philadelphia in 1778." *American Literature* 6 (1935).

Pennington, Edgar Legare. "The Anglican Clergy of Pennsylvania in the American Revolution." *Pennsylvania Magazine of History and Biography* 63 (1939).

Rawle, William Brooke. "Plundering by the British Army during the American Revolution." *Pennsylvania Magazine of History and Biography* 25 (1901).

Reed, John F. "The British Peace Commission 1778." *Bulletin of the Historical Society of Montgomery County* 17 (1969-70).

Rex, Margaret D. "The Story of Lydia Darrah." *Historical Sketches of the Historical Society of Montgomery County* 1 (1895).

Richardson, W. H. "Montgomery County in the Campaign of 1777-78." *Historical Sketches of the Historical Society of Montgomery County.* Vol. 7. 1935.

Roach, Hannah B. "The Pennsylvania Militia in 1777." *Pennsylvania Genealogical Magazine* 23 (1964).

Shea, John G. "Catholic Churches in American History." *American Catholic Quarterly Review* 1 (1876).

Shippen, Edward. "Two or Three Old Letters." *Pennsylvania Magazine of History and Biography* 23 (1899).

Shoemaker, Robert W. "Christ Church, St. Peter's and St. Paul's." In *Historic Philadelphia.* Philadelphia, 1953.

Siebert, Wilbur H. "The Dispersion of the American Tories." *Mississippi Valley Historical Review* 1 (1914).

Smyth, Samuel G. "Revolutionary Events about Newtown." *Papers of the Bucks County Historical Society.* Vol. 3. 1909.

Stone, Frederick D. "Philadelphia Society One Hundred Years Ago or the Reign of Continental Money." *Pennsylvania Magazine of History and Biography* 3 (1879).

Streeper, Levi. "Lafayette's Retreat from Barren Hill." *Historical Sketches of the Historical Society of Montgomery County.* Vol. 2. 1900.

Thompson, Louis Ely. "An Introduction to the Loyalists of Bucks County and Some Queries Concerning Them." *Papers of the Bucks County Historical Society.* Vol. 2. 1937.

Vaux, George. "Incidents at the Time of the American Revolution Connected with Some Members of the Society of Friends." *Journal of the Friends Historical Society* 6 (1909).

Williams, Irvin C. "Lafayette at Barren Hill." *Historical Sketches of the Historical Society of Montgomery County.* Vol. 2. 1900.

SECONDARY SOURCES: BOOKS AND PAMPHLETS

Addis, Mahlon. *200 Years of Ancient York Masonry in the Western World, 1758-1958.* Philadelphia, n.d.

Amory, Thomas C. *The Military Services and Public Life of Major General John Sullivan, of the American Revolutionary Army.* Port Washington, N. Y., 1968.

Anderson, Troyer Steele. *The Command of the Howe Brothers during the American Revolution.* New York, 1936.

Baker, William S. *Itinerary of General Washington from June 15, 1775 to December 23, 1783.* Lambertville, N. J., 1970.

Barratt, Norris S. and Julius F. Sachse. *Freemasonry in Pennsylvania 1727-1907 As Shown by the Records of Lodge No. 2 F. and A. M. of Philadelphia.* 3 vols. Philadelphia, 1907-9.

Blumenthal, Walter Hart. *Women Camp Followers of the American Revolution.* Philadelphia, 1952.

Boudinot, J. J., ed. *The Life, Public Services, Addresses, and Letters of Elias Boudinot.* 2 vols. New York, 1896.

Boyd, George A. *Elias Boudinot, Patriot and Statesman.* Princeton, 1952.

Brown, Wallace. *The Good Americans: the Loyalists in the American Revolution.* New York, 1969.

———. *The King's Friends.* Providence, R. I., 1965.

Burnett, Edmund Coty. *The Continental Congress.* New York, 1941.

Campbell, William B. *Old Towns and Districts of Philadelphia.* Philadelphia, 1942.

Carrington, Henry B. *Battles of the American Revolution 1775-1781.* New York, 1888.

Curtis, Edward E. *The British Army in the American Revolution.* Yorkshire, England, 1972.

Dandridge, Danske. *American Prisoners of the Revolution.* Charlottesville, Va., 1911.

Darrach, Henry. *Lydia Darragh: One of the Heroines of the Revolution.* Philadelphia, 1916.

Davies, Benjamin. *Some Account of the City of Philadelphia.* Philadelphia, 1794.

Day, Sherman. *Historical Collection of the State of Pennsylvania.* Philadelphia, 1843.

Dorr, Benjamin. *A Historical Account of Christ Church, Philadelphia, from Its Foundation A.D. 1695, to A.D. 1841, and of St. Peter's and St. James's.* New York, 1841.

Durang, Charles. *History of the Philadelphia Stage 1749-1855.* 2 vols. (Partly taken from the Papers of John Durang and run serially in the *Sunday Dispatch* around 1860-70.

Eardley-Wilmot, John. *Historical View of the Commission for Enquiring into the Losses, Services, and Claims, of the American Loyalists. . . .* London, 1815.

Edgar, W. J. B. *Historical Sketch of the First United Presbyterian Church of Philadelphia.* Philadelphia, 1902.

Eelking, Max von. *The German Allied Troops in the North American War of Independence 1776-1783.* Translated by J. G. Rosengarten. Baltimore, 1969.

Fisher, Sydney George. *Pennsylvania Colony and Commonwealth.* Philadelphia, 1908.

Fortescue, J. W. *A History of the British Army.* 13 vols. London, 1911-35.

Freeman, Douglas S. *George Washington.* 7 vols. New York, 1948-57.

Gibbons, Hughes O. *A History of Old Pine Street.* Philadelphia, 1905.

Gilpin, Thomas. *Exiles in Virginia: with Observations on the Conduct of the Society of Friends during the Revolutionary War.* Philadelphia, 1848.

Greene, Francis V. *The Revolutionary War and the Military Policy of the United States.* Port Washington, N. Y., 1967.

Griffin, Martin I. J. *Catholics and the American Revolution.* 3 vols. Philadelphia, 1911.

———. *Stephen Moylan.* Philadelphia, 1909.

Gruber, Ira D. *The Howe Brothers and the American Revolution.* New York, 1972.

Hancock, Harold B. *The Delaware Loyalists.* Wilmington, 1940.

[Harris, Joseph S.]. *The Collateral Ancestry of Stephen Harris and Marianne Smith.* Philadelphia, 1908.

Hastings, Everett. *The Life and Works of Francis Hopkinson.* Chicago, 1926.

Historical Sketches of the Catholic Churches and Institutions of Philadelphia. Philadelphia, 1895.

Jackson, John W. *The Pennsylvania Navy, 1775-1781.* New Brunswick, N. J., 1974.

Jones, Rufus M. *The Quakers in the American Colonies.* New York, 1966.

Jones, Thomas. *History of New York during the Revolutionary War and of the Leading Events in the Other Colonies of that Period.* Edited by Floyd de Lancey. 2 vols. New York, 1879.

Konkle, Burton A. *Benjamin Chew, 1722-1810.* Philadelphia, 1932.

————. *Thomas Willing and the First American Financial System.* Philadelphia, 1937.

Lawrence, Charles, comp. *History of the Philadelphia Almshouses and Hospitals.* Philadelphia, 1905.

Lecky, William E. H. *The American Revolution 1763-1783.* Arranged and edited by James A. Woodburn. New York, 1922.

Lossing, Benson J. *Pictorial Field Book of the American Revolution.* 2 vols. New York, 1860.

Lowell, Edward J. *The Hessians and the Other German Auxiliaries of Great Britain in the Revolutionary War.* New York, 1884.

Lutnick, Solomon. *The American Revolution and the British Press 1775-1783.* Columbia, Missouri, 1967.

Lynch, M. Antonia. *The Old District of Southwark in the County of Philadelphia.* Philadelphia, 1909.

Marshall, John. *The Life of George Washington.* 5 vols. Citizens Guild ed. Fredericksburg, Va., 1926.

Nelson, William H. *The American Tory.* Oxford, 1961.

Norton, Mary Beth. *The British-Americans: The Loyalist Exiles in England 1774-1789.* Boston, 1972.

Oberholtzer, Ellis Paxson. *Philadelphia: A History of the City and its People.* 4 vols. Philadelphia, n.d.

Packard, Francis R. *Some Account of the Pennsylvania Hospital from its First Rise to the Beginning of the Year 1938.* Philadelphia, 1957.

Partridge, Bellamy. *Sir Billy Howe.* London, 1932.

Pollock, Thomas C. *The Philadelphia Theatre in the Eighteenth Century.* Philadelphia, 1933.

Records of the Presbyterian Church in the United States, 1706-1788. Philadelphia, 1841.

Reed, John F. *Campaign to Valley Forge, July 1, 1777-December 19, 1777.* Philadelphia, 1965.

[Reed, William B.] *The Life of Esther de Berdt, Afterwards Esther Reed of Pennsylvania.* Philadelphia, 1853.

Robson, Eric. *The American Revolution in Its Political and Military Aspects 1763-1783.* New York, 1972.

Rosenbach, Hyman P. *The Jews in Philadelphia Prior to 1800.* Philadelphia, 1883.

Sabine, Lorenzo. *Biographical Sketches of Loyalists of the American Revolution.* 2 vols. Boston, 1864.

Sargent, Winthrop. *The Life and Career of Major John Andre, Adjutant General of the British Army in America.* New ed. Edited by William Abbatt. New York, 1902.

Scharf, J. Thomas and Westcott, Thompson. *History of Philadelphia, 1609-1884.* 3 vols. Philadelphia, 1884.

Scott, Kenneth. *Counterfeiting in Colonial America.* New York, 1957.

Sharpless, Isaac. *A Quaker Experiment in Government.* 2 vols. Philadelphia, 1902.

Shepherd, William R. *History of Proprietary Government in Pennsylvania.* New York, 1896.

Sickler, Joseph S. *The History of Salem County New Jersey.* Salem, 1937.

Siebert, Wilbur H. *The Loyalists of Pennsylvania.* Columbus, 1905.

Smith, J. Jay and Watson, John F., comps. and eds. *American Historical and Literary Curiosities.* 2 vols. Philadelphia, 1847.

Smith, Paul H. *Loyalists and Redcoats.* Chapel Hill, 1964.

Souder, Caspar. *History of Chestnut Street.* Philadelphia, 1860. (Originally serialized in the *Philadelphia Sunday Dispatch,* 18 Apr. 1858 to 9 Oct. 1859.

Stedman, C. *The History of the Origin, Progress, and Termination of the American War.* 2 vols. London, 1794.

Stewart, Frank H. *Foraging for Valley Forge by General Anthony Wayne in Salem and Gloucester Counties, New Jersey.* Woodbury, N. J., 1929.

———. *Salem County in the Revolution.* Salem, N. J., 1932.

Tees, Francis H. *The Ancient Landmark of American Methodism or Historic Old St. George's.* Philadelphia, 1941.

Thayer, Theodore. *Israel Pemberton, King of the Quakers.* Philadelphia, 1943.

Torbet, Robert G. *A Social History of the Philadelphia Baptist Association.* Philadelphia, 1944.

Tower, Charlemagne. *The Marquis de La Fayette in the American Revolution.* 2 vols. Philadelphia, 1895, 1901.

Trevelyan, Sir George Otto. *The American Revolution.* 6 vols. London, 1909-14.

Tyler, Moses Coit. *The Literary History of the American Revolution, 1763-83.* 2 vols. New York, 1897.

Van Doren, Carl. *Benjamin Franklin.* New York, 1938.

———. *Secret History of the American Revolution.* New York, 1951.

Van Tyne, Claude H. *The Loyalists in the American Revolution.* New York, 1902.

Vaughn, Alden T., ed. *Chronicles of the American Revolution.* New York, 1965. Originally compiled by Hezekiah Niles.

Wainwright, Nicholas B. *Colonial Grandeur in Philadelphia: the House and Furniture of General John Cadwalader.* Philadelphia, 1964.

Wagner, Frederick. *Submarine Fighter of the American Revolution: The Story of David Bushnell.* New York, 1963.

Ward, Christopher. *The War of the Revolution.* Edited by John R. Alden. 2 vols. New York, 1952.

Warner, Sam Bass. *The Private City: Philadelphia in Three Periods of Its Growth.* Philadelphia, 1968.

Washington at Valley Forge together With the Duché Correspondence. Philadelphia, 1858.

Watson, John F. *Annals of Philadelphia and Pennsylvania in the Olden Time.* Enlarged, with many revisions and additions by Willis P. Hazard. 3 vols. Philadelphia, 1884.

Westcott, Thompson. *The Historic Mansions and Buildings of Philadelphia with Some Notice of Their Owners and Occupants.* Rev. ed. Philadelphia, 1895.

Wharton, Anne H. *Genealogy of the Wharton Family of Philadelphia, 1664-1880.* Philadelphia, 1880.

———. *Through Colonial Doorways.* Philadelphia, 1893.

Wickwire, Franklin and Mary. *Cornwallis The American Adventure.* Boston, 1970.

Wolf, II, Edwin and Whiteman, Maxwell. *The History of the Jews of Philadelphia.* Philadelphia, 1957.

Young, Eleanor. *Forgotten Patriot: Robert Morris.* New York, 1950.

Index